REVEALED IN EPHESIANS

THE MYSTERY OF WHO I AM IN CHRIST

BRIANA NEI

WESTBOW
PRESS®
A DIVISION OF THOMAS NELSON
& ZONDERVAN

WestBow Press books may be ordered through booksellers or by contacting:

WestBow Press
A Division of Thomas Nelson & Zondervan
1663 Liberty Drive
Bloomington, IN 47403
www.westbowpress.com
1 (866) 928-1240

ISBN: 978-1-9736-4775-1 (sc)
ISBN: 978-1-9736-4773-7 (e)

Print information available on the last page.

WestBow Press rev. date: 01/23/2019

TABLE OF CONTENTS

WEEK SIX

WEEK SEVEN

WEEK EIGHT

WEEK NINE

WEEK TEN

WEEK ELEVEN

WEEK TWELVE

ACKNOWLEDGMENT

Much like when a baby is conceived—you may not even know it, and when you do become aware of its growing, you won't know the gender for a while, and even when you discover if it's a boy or a girl, you still don't know the personality of the child or what he or she will like or dislike, or what passions will drive the little one—so was this book in its conception. I want to begin by acknowledging the hand of God and his loving, gentle leading and revelation as he unfolded his plan to me slowly and methodically, at a pace I could handle. Father God, you have changed my life with this journey! Thank you! Also, much love to my mother, Jeanne Dean, who came alongside me from the very beginning, spending hours every week editing and eventually designing the book's look. Mom, you are an inspiration in the way that you serve and love the people of God and your children with great joy and a servant's heart. I am so blessed to be your daughter! To my father, Mike Dean, you taught me to serve the Lord and to love truth. You provided an example of courage and resiliency in ministry through decades of my life. You listened to me read my manuscript and offered challenging insight that would send me back to study, to make sure I presented a complete and balanced understanding of scripture. I love you so much!

And when our first little Bible study group began digging into my rough draft, it was Barb Genda who emphatically and excitedly encouraged me to publish my little manuscript. (Since then it's become a big manuscript.) And all along the way, the women in the pilot group—Barb, Jaime, Denise, Holly, Sue, Joyce, Sharon, Jen and others near and far—cheered me on, using their own gifts in the body of Christ to birth a new and growing women's ministry and kept me focused on what God was directing me to do. And thank you to all the eyes that rested on this book and gave editorial feedback and encouragement! Alisha, Barb, Marlisa, Dedire and my brother Seth! Thank you for the time and the courage to help me be a better writer. And to the people of Emmaus Church, the elders and their families, thank you for your support and encouragement along the way!

And then, when we hit a number of family medical crises in the middle of the final stretch of editing the book, the Lord renewed a friendship from years gone by and through the tireless expert eyes and heart of DuAnne Thrush, my book found a new editor who was able to take the rough content and challenge me to take it to the next level. DuAnne, thank you for your love for the Word of God and your desire to see women understand everything they have in Christ. You spent months, days and hours helping to perfect the clarity of this manuscript! Your reward will be great in heaven!

And last but certainly not least, thank you to my husband Caleb for always generously encouraging me to be the person God has called me to be. Thank you for all the loads of laundry you did and for understanding when I would need to work on my laptop in the car on road trips. We make a great team! I love you! And to my beautiful children, Ariel, Ellis and Isaac, thank you for sharing me with those I minister to. That is a sacrifice the Lord will reward you for. Thank you for growing in Christ alongside of your parents. Thank you for giving us grace when we aren't perfect and for being willing for me to publish stories about your walk with the Lord. I love you more than life itself.

The Mystery Of Who I Am In Christ

by
Briana Nei

INTRODUCTION

To the woman picking up this book looking for truth to nourish her soul, strengthen her resolve, encourage her heart and, perhaps, lighten her step, I wrote this Bible study for you. Writing this book was an unexpected journey, taken to equip women to gain confidence in their own personal Bible study. What this study turned out to be was my own personal revelation and strengthening, as God's Word soaked into every pore of my spirit for the past year. When you approach the Bible, what do you expect to find? You may come to find knowledge, or encouragement, or to know God better. But, what you will really find—as you lose yourself in knowing Jesus—is that in seeking him you will discover who you truly are, and who God created you to be. The following account is a conversation you may relate to, even in a small way. It reveals a common theme of mystery running through the lives of women all over the world today who are all longing to find the purpose of their own stories, and to know who they really are.

Sitting on the sidelines in sunglasses and camping chairs, Mary and Kathi watched their boys running up and down the field, practicing in the intense, noonday sun. The first day of football camp, this summer ritual—so familiar to them both, brought back memories and nostalgia. Most of the time talk was small, covering weekly schedules and family vacation stories. On this day, it took an unexpected and unusual turn.

"I am feeling so weird lately," Mary offered as both women trained their eyes on the athletes sweating out their best efforts on the practice field in the hot August sun. "I feel off. I feel like something is wrong and I just can't put my finger on it."

"Are you anxious? Do you feel stressed about something going on in your life right now?" Kathi questioned. She remembered a few minutes earlier that Mary had been listing all the big, expensive family events she would be juggling over the next couple of weeks.

"Yeah. Definitely. I mean, who am I? I pour myself out for everyone every day. I take my kids everywhere. I clean the house, then I go to work. When I get home, it is destroyed again. I'm tired. I am not sure I have ever known who I am. Maybe it's because I always give to everyone else that I have never discovered who I really am." Mary continued to open up raw stories of days gone by, personal disappointments from childhood up to the present. Her candor even surprised herself. Why was she sharing so openly with Kathi? But, the words continued to leak out, even as she wished she could pull them back. Why couldn't she stop this sudden and vulnerable full disclosure of her soul?

Mary had always struggled to survive, as adult after adult in her life let her down. In her younger years, she travelled so many secret and dangerous paths looking to numb the pain in her heart. Now she was the grown-up, pouring into others, trying to be the mother she never had, but with nothing left to give. This raw moment of soul baring is rarely seen in such a setting where people work to make the best impressions. But, Mary couldn't take it anymore. The dam was breaking. Everything she had bottled up inside came flooding out, as she gave voice to a thousand thoughts and feelings.

Compassion rose up in Kathi, accompanied by some relief. It was so nice to have a real conversation, instead of the normal small talk and smiles that hide the reality and pain of motherhood on the sidelines of a football field. There was not an ounce of judgment in her heart for Mary. None of the uncomfortable blank stares or haughty looks that Mary feared ever crossed Kathi's mind or face. "Mary, you are a mother. You are a wife. You are great at your job. These are all legitimate identities from God. You pour out into others all the time, because that is what a mom and a wife does. We are the life-bearers. We carry our children and they drain our emotional and spiritual bank accounts. I think it is a great honor to be a mother. It is completely normal to feel poured out and empty, though. Many of us women struggle with this."

"Really?" Surprise and clarity rose up inside Mary. Just the assurance without judgment from Kathi filled Mary with some relief. "Well, it actually feels better to know that other people feel this way, too. I thought it was just me."

Kathi gently ventured a little deeper. Normally she wouldn't dare explore this emotional territory with an acquaintance, but Mary was wearing her heart on her sleeve and Kathi saw an open door to encourage her. "What was your childhood like? Did you ever feel loved and filled up by your parents? Sometimes emotional bankruptcy from childhood can leave us feeling like we have nothing to give our own children."

Mary continued to be vulnerable with Kathi, even though she barely knew her. She felt an unusual peace during this soul-baring, and for a moment leaned into that assurance. Without flinching she said, "I think I am struggling because no one ever poured into me. I walked a rocky road growing up. I barely knew my own mother. But, I did give my life to Jesus five years ago. I try my best to be a good person and to do what is right. I really do." She hesitated. "I guess I have trouble trusting God, even though I know I'm supposed to, because every adult in my life has let me down. No one has ever been there for me. I know I am supposed to trust God, but there is always something inside that holds me back."

"God is not like your earthly Father." Kathi encouraged her. "Your earthly father is flawed and he sinned against you. He damaged your heart. God is the opposite of this. He never leaves you or forsakes you. There is so much more for you in Christ. There is so much freedom, so much love, so much power. God really wants to bless you with it all. You can find your true identity in him."

Kathi assured Mary that every woman struggles with self-doubt and identity questions at some point. "I know you believe in Jesus, but do you know that in Christ we have more than the future hope of heaven? We have identity in God's family right now. Your place in God's family is not just about playing the part of being a good little girl, Mary. It's about belonging to God. If you focus on 'doing' all the time, and never let God into the deep, inner part of your soul to heal you, all your 'doing' will leave you feeling empty. Failure is inevitable. That is why we need Jesus. Jesus doesn't reject you in your failure or sin, but he came to forgive and to heal what was broken—your broken relationship with the Father."

Mary settled into deep thought, with an occasional break in the silence to cheer on her son. Then she share, "I really have been in a low place. I need to get back on track. I haven't really thought about God this way. I mostly just try to do my best. I never feel like I am enough. I am just very tired. This was very helpful. I'm glad to know I am not alone." After a quick hug, both women picked up their chairs and walked toward their cars as football camp wrapped up for the day.

Many of us women walk through life like Mary. We are poured out and empty, trying to get things right and wondering when it will be our turn to feel fulfilled. Many marriages fall apart when this tension and feeling of disillusionment cannot be resolved in a woman's heart. Then, the vicious cycle starts over with the broken children. "Who am I? Where do I belong? What is my purpose? When will I feel loved?" Many times a woman believes there is something she is missing out on. "Is there something I can do just for me? I love to run. I love to write. I love to sing and make music." While life is meant to be enjoyed and hobbies are wonderful outlets which are fulfilling and meaningful, they will never take away the ache that stems from a heart in crisis or confusion over personal identity.

Confusion like this is from the devil. In Genesis 3, the devil's first lie to the first woman, who was perfect in every way, was to tell her God was holding something back from her. Was she missing something? The liar told Eve that God was lying to her. He painted a false picture where God did not want her to find everything there was to be had in life. The temptation to believe that God did not have her best in mind led Eve into the first act of rebellion against God, and plunged the world into darkness. The relationship was truly compromised. Unlike Eve, we need to trust what God says, so we are not deceived by our adversary, the devil. When we hear the enemy's tempting words, we need to run to God and ask him what the truth is. His words are life that bring us strength and give us hope for living. In his Son Jesus, we find rest and we find our true identity and calling. His words help us resist the devil's lies.

The purpose of the following pages in this book is to encourage you, the reader, and to teach you how to search the scriptures to find everything the Lord has for you, including your identity, your purpose and your calling. Don't just survive when you can thrive! You thrive when you are encouraged, supported, and spiritually nourished. You should not be living off of spiritual left-overs. We need the fresh spiritual nutrition that comes directly from God's Word.

BIBLE GUILT

Our home has at least 100 Bibles in it—a gift Bible from a pregnancy, Bibles left behind by youth group teens, personal Bibles for each family member, extra Bibles from graduation gifts, a huge family Bible with a white cover, seemingly needed for recording our genealogy, and Bibles from every version imaginable, even translations I don't particularly care for, yet I can't think of what to do with them. Isn't it sacrilegious to get rid of a Bible? Through the years, we have purchased Bibles for our growing children, hoping that the cool cover theme or "relevant devos" inside would help them "get into the Word more." So many Bibles. The real question is, why are they so dusty? Why so many Bibles and so little use?

I have perpetual Bible Guilt. This is a condition I've coined, and whose symptoms I define as, "The painful feeling I have when I see a Bible lying there and I realize I haven't taken time to read it." The more places I look in my home throughout the day, the more Bible Guilt I have. Bibles peeking out from under beds. Bibles unread on shelves. Oops, that Bible fell behind my teen's bed when he fell asleep with it half a year ago. I get so busy that it is hard to find time to read. But then there is social media. I find lots of time for that. Then there is more guilt.

OVERCOMING PERFECTIONISTIC GUILT

Guilt leads to negative feelings associated with reading the Bible. However, I shouldn't reject reading the Bible because of these negative feelings. I should reject the feelings of inadequacy associated with the guilt. I think that I have some sort of idealism concerning reading God's Word. It is holy and sacred. It needs extra-special time in order to be read … time to focus … time to reflect and pray … time to digest and understand.

All my idealism and perfectionism keep me from taking in my daily nourishment from God's Word because I do not have time to prepare it perfectly. This is very similar to any other task I face as a woman. What about the garden that needs weeding or the baking that I have been wanting to do with the kids? There never seems to be a perfect time, so the time passes by and all those things I want to do never get done.

There is one thing that I have a hard time getting through the day without doing, though. That is eating! Eating is so very important to me because I have a biological clock that tells me that it is time to eat. All the time. Even though ball practice, my work commute, driving the kids around, appointments, and many other motherly "shenanigans" make finding time to prepare a perfect meal impossible, I can always find time to eat. If it is just a wrap, a quick salad or a snack, (maybe even junk food, if I am honest) I am always putting something in my mouth! If it is not a really nutritious meal, I will sigh and say to myself, "Next time I need to make sure I take time to make something healthier to eat!"

God's Word is nutrition for us. In John 6:35 Jesus said, "I am the Bread of Life." Surely we need to know that just like physical food, and even more than physical food, we need and crave the Word of God! We just can not always pinpoint what we are craving. When Jesus was being tempted by Satan in the wilderness,

> Jesus answered, 'It is written: "Man shall not live on bread alone, but on every word that comes from the mouth of God."'
> — Matthew 4:4

If Jesus said we need the Word even more than bread, then we definitely do!

Have you ever had a mouthful of dry chicken? Just chewing up dry chicken feels like burning a thousand calories in a great jaw workout. It takes forever, and it is not at all enjoyable the way eating is truly meant to be. If you have a bad experience with a food, it is very likely you are not going back to that food, even if everyone says it is good for you, and even if you know your body needs it. Not going back. Nope. I know people who will not eat chicken because memories of eating it while growing up tell them it will be super dry and tough. You need a whole lot of mayo or sauce on a sandwich that is made with a dry chicken breast.

Many people feel that reading the Bible is as enjoyable as chewing on a tough dry piece of chicken. Believe me, ladies, this is a very serious issue that many people face. In my time speaking with women about God's Word, I've heard the same attitude. One conversation stands out: "I know that I should want to read the Bible, but I have such a hard time reading it on my own. If I have a good Bible study book, I feel like I can understand it, but if I pick it up myself, it just seems so dry. I'm not sure if it is my personality or the way my brain works."

God's Word was never meant to be approached intellectually alone. Doing this will make God's Word as tasteless as dry chicken. We can understand it in a limited way with our minds, but spiritual truths are discerned spiritually. We absolutely need the Holy Spirit to teach us and speak to us through God's Word. Through this study, we are going to learn from Ephesians what the Apostle Paul teaches us, and we are going to learn how to pray to help God's Word come alive to us—to be our spiritual nourishment and to find our identity in Christ! We absolutely need the Holy Spirit to teach us and speak to us through God's Word, to make it tender and tasty to our souls. When our souls are fed, we will begin to feel the satisfaction that comes from the fullness of our relationship with Christ.

Let's think back on Mary, struggling with the dilemma of having a relationship with Christ, but not finding full satisfaction from it. She, like many other Christian women, knows how to be good, and how to do the right things, but her inner life feels anemic and starved. She longs for purpose and direction. Only a life that is led by the Spirit of God will have this revelation and fulfillment. When we read God's Word, we must always go to it prayerfully—rather than dutifully—with our spiritual eyes open to what the Spirit is saying to us. Let's look at a passage from 1 Corinthians that reveals to us what this relationship with God looks like, when we approach the scriptures spiritually. God has prepared so much for us! He wants to nourish and bless us deeply and freely, in our inner beings. He blesses us from the inside out. When we understand our position and authority in Christ, through his Word, we will be encouraged in our faith and in our prayers. Our families will see the change. Our relationships will see the change. Our hearts will feel the change. This is all by his Spirit's work in our lives.

1 Corinthians 2:9-12

[9] However, as it is written:

'What no eye has seen,
    what no ear has heard,
and what no human mind has conceived' –
    the things God has prepared for those who love him –

[10] these are the things God has revealed to us by his Spirit.

The Spirit searches all things, even the deep things of God. [11] For who knows a person's thoughts except their own spirit within them? In the same way no one knows the thoughts of God except the Spirit of God. [12] What we have received is not the spirit of the world, but the Spirit who is from God, so that we may understand what God has freely given us.

THE BIBLE VS GMOS

How does this Word food work? In Luke 8:11, Jesus describes the Word as a seed—true raw food eating. You do not get more pure and organic than studying straight from the Bible. Also, God says of his Word, in Isaiah 55:11 NKJV, "It will not return to me empty." We have all heard about bio-available food. The Word of God is spirit-available! It is ready to be absorbed by your inner "person" as soon as you take it in. So, whether you have time for your perfect quiet time or just a short snack, God will nourish you with His Word. Throw that perfection out the window! You were made for God's Word. It is your literal sustenance. Just pick it up and start fueling your spirit!

The goal of this study is to help you become more comfortable in reading the straight up non-GMO Bible.

That's right! Most women know what GMOs are and refuse to buy food that contains them. What are GMOs? Genetically Modified Organisms. A large corporation decides to modify the wheat, corn or other food to be able to produce it in large quantities and to make it look better in order to make more money. Strawberries in the grocery store are now much larger than the ones our grandparents remember eating. The massive chicken breasts we buy in the meat department make one wonder if that bird on steroids looked like Dwayne "The Rock" Johnson.

Now, stick with me here.

While Christian books are very popular with Christian women, and book studies abound, I assert that if you are trying to survive spiritually from what another author has put out there without also being in the Word of God, you are very likely surviving on spiritual GMOs, and not knowing it. Spiritual GMOs can do everything, from under-nourishing you—the powerful faith-building parts are taken out—to withholding important nourishing truth from you—not telling you about spiritually toxic things you need to eliminate from your life by the power of Christ. They sugar coat sin so that it looks acceptable. It is easy to sell books about God when you do not want to talk about sin. Some even introduce destructive and twisted heresies that could completely derail someone's faith! WOW!

This is NOT a petition to stop doing book studies. This is one woman to another asking you to take a chance to learn to become comfortable feeding yourself and your family straight from the Word of God.

If you have been taking in good spiritual nutrition, you will definitely know when you pick up a book that is a GMO. You spirit will reject the lies, in much the same way a well-fed body reacts strongly to foods that it should not be eating. Also, just like food preparation, the more we learn to cook or bake, the more comfortable we are doing it. The more we study God's Word, with others or alone, the more comfortable we will be doing it.

You do not have to be perfect. God's Word is perfect. It is powerful to work in your life just when you need it. Simply trust that God has got you. No fear! His Word is there to fill you up with His love and His truth and to give you power to overcome your greatest fears, girlfriend!

Jesus said,

> Behold, I stand at the door, and knock: if any man hear my voice, and open the door, I will come in to him, and will sup with him, and he with me. — Revelation 3:20 KJV

Jesus is calling out to you to open the door. He wants to eat with you. Let's invite him in and dine on his Word together!

PRAYER FROM SCRIPTURE

HOW & WHY TO PRAY

Today, as we begin Ephesians Chapter 1, the apostle Paul gives us his very own prayer for the Ephesians, which we can learn and pray for ourselves and our loved ones! I love this prayer, in particular, because it is asking God to help us learn and understand his truth, by the power of his Holy Spirit. This is our memory verse prayer for the first few weeks of this study. Memorizing it and learning to pray it in faith will greatly increase our ability to understand God's Word. Praying it with our families will equip them to pray with power and to receive revelation from the Lord, too!

MEMORY VERSE

[17] I keep asking that the God of our Lord Jesus Christ, the glorious Father, may give you the Spirit of wisdom and revelation, so that you may know him better. [18] I pray that the eyes of your heart may be enlightened in order that you may know the hope to which he has called you, the riches of his glorious inheritance in his holy people, [19] and his incomparably great power for us who believe. That power is the same as the mighty strength [20] he exerted when he raised Christ from the dead and seated him at his right hand in the heavenly realms, [21] far above all rule and authority, power and dominion, and every name that is invoked, not only in the present age but also in the one to come. [22] And God placed all things under his feet and appointed him to be head over everything for the church, [23] which is his body, the fullness of him who fills everything in every way. — Ephesians 1:17-23

This prayer is a really long, complex paragraph! It can be hard to read. Let's break it down to help ourselves understand what Paul the apostle is praying and why. Doing this can help our own prayer lives. Is this a one-time prayer? No! Paul specifically says he prays this prayer *continually.*

Many people pray over a grocery list of people and concerns, from healing for people who are sick, to protection for loved ones, to comfort for those who are grieving. How is Paul's approach different from just praying for a specific need someone may have?

Paul is praying that the Ephesians will know and understand God himself, and who believers are in Christ, by inviting the Father to fill them with the Spirit of wisdom and revelation. He is also praying for their faith in the resurrection power of Jesus. The same power that raised Jesus from the dead fills every believer! When we pray and invite the Holy Spirit to enlighten our eyes to know the hope to which we are called, it changes the way we read our Bibles. We can read with hope! This intimate interaction with the Holy Spirit makes all the difference between reading the Bible in a chore-like manner or academic way and reading it as an interaction with the King of kings and the Lord of lords.

> **TODAY'S BIBLE STUDY TOOL**
>
> **Prayer.** Pray for the Holy Spirit's wisdom and revelation as you read God's Word. Every time!

Paul's prayer for the Ephesians is for them to have hope from the Holy Spirit to see the glorious calling and inheritance they have in Christ. Our hope is in Christ and in his power to save us and work in our lives. People filled with the knowledge and understanding of God's work in their lives will have faith to trust the Lord to answer those long grocery lists of prayer requests. Whether your prayer is for a child in college, a conflict in a marriage, a financial need, or a future spouse, knowing who you are talking to and his great power, ability, and desire to meet your needs, will increase your faith in the Lord to intervene in the situation. This spiritual revelation and ability to trust God comes from the Holy Spirit.

PRAYER

Take a minute right now. Pray this prayer for yourself! Instead of praying the word "you," insert your own name or say "me" or "mine." For example,

"I, _____, ask you, the God of MY Lord Jesus Christ, the glorious Father, that you may give me, _____, the Spirit of wisdom and revelation, so that I, _____, may know you better. I pray that ..."

Continue this example of praying scripture through all of the memory verse from Ephesians 1:17-23.

Ladies, you have to pray for yourself before you can pray for anyone else! Why? It's like being in an airplane. In case of an emergency, flight attendants always teach you to first put the oxygen mask on yourself, so you can then help your children or friends around you. This is exactly the same concept! You need Christ to enlighten you and strengthen your faith. As you know him more, through every hardship and situation you may face, you will gain confidence in his ability to work in the lives of the people you are praying for. Read Romans 5 for more information about this topic.

Why is it so easy to pray for other people and not for ourselves? Well, perhaps, it comes from the nurturing nature of a woman. This is a God-given ability to put aside our own needs and take on the needs of a child, spouse, or friend.

We are created to propagate the human race. We birth life out of our bodies. When I was a new mom, one of my mother's lifelong friends called to wish me well on our new arrival. She asked me how nursing was going with my little Ariel. This woman was a leader in a women's nursing support network. I related to her that we had overcome the initial difficult phase and that Ariel was nursing like a champ. "How are you eating?" she asked. "Um, I'm eating okay, I guess." I looked at the box of Oreo cookies on the table that I had tapped for my breakfast. I felt a twinge of guilt thinking that my daughter was not getting the nutrition she needed, because I was not eating correctly. To be honest, I did not really know what healthy eating meant. Back in the 90's, I was most concerned with watching my fat and calorie intake to lose weight after my delivery. I did not quite know how to answer her friendly and caring question because I didn't know how a new mom was supposed to be eating, anyway.

After a brief pause, I was surprised at her response. I expected her to chide me for depriving my daughter. I only found the opposite. "Briana, be sure to take care of yourself. God designed a mother's milk to feed the baby everything the baby needs. If you aren't eating well, your body will take the calcium and protein from your own bones and muscles to make the milk." I was kind of shocked and set back by her kind and insightful answer. I had no idea that was happening!

As I slowly learned about nutrition, I started to discover that I was eliminating all fats from my diet to stay "skinny." I did not know I needed healthy Omega fatty acids for healthy joints and skin. I was 25 but starting to feel like I had arthritis. Every time I walked up and down stairs my knees hurt and even had a creaking sound. In the morning, my hands were stiff like I was old. I was nursing my baby and achieving my goal of being skinny, but I was not properly nourishing my own body. The fat my baby needed was coming from my joints and I was aging prematurely. I started adding good fish oil supplements and vitamins to my diet, along with healthy fats and fruits and vegetables. My knees stopped squeaking, my hands stopped aching, and I felt so much better!

As women, whether we are mothers or not, we have a desire to give to and help others. I knew a young college student who would spend hours online chatting with other girls she did not know in person, trying to help them with their emotional issues, but this girl would rarely pray for herself or take care of herself physically, emotionally, or spiritually. The devil had deceived her into thinking that it was selfish to do these things, or even that she did not deserve to do anything nice for herself. That is what the devil does. He takes truth and good tendencies and twists them into lies and deception. We absolutely must learn to feed ourselves first, seek God ourselves, and handle God's Word ourselves, so we can have an overflow to give to those in our lives who need us the most. Remember, here is a true saying: "For everyone born of God overcomes the world. This is the victory that overcomes the world, even our faith. Who is it that overcomes the world? Only the one who believes that Jesus is the Son of God." – 1 John 5:4-5

FAITH is our victory to overcome. It is our ability to trust in Jesus and his ability, power and desire to help us to overcome. So, Lord, please increase MY faith. That is my starting point before I pray for others. This is why we are memorizing this prayer.

You may copy the memory verse (Ephesians 1:17-23) located at the beginning of this lesson to put on your fridge, the mirror in your bathroom, or another prime location for memorizing it daily. Now that you are doing this, you can also help your children to learn it. This will spiritually nurture your whole family as you do this together. If you are single or married without children, find a prayer partner to share in this memorization work. This will encourage you both. You can also pray it for each other!

DIGGING DEEPER

This is super easy. We have already prayed for God to enlighten us while we read.

- Set your timer for 10 minutes.
- Read through all of Ephesians Chapter 1.
- Write down everything that Ephesians Chapter 1 teaches you about God.

In the margins of this page or on another piece of paper, list all the attributes of God that you can find. If you are artistic, doodle away! Have fun illustrating who Christ is, according to Ephesians Chapter 1.

BRINGING IT HOME

Begin to teach your children to

- ask the Father to fill them with the Holy Spirit in wisdom and revelation.
- ask God to open the eyes of their hearts so they can truly see Jesus for who he is.
- know they can understand God's Word by the power of his Spirit. Make it a habit that you add these into your daily bedtime and meal prayers!

FROM SAUL TO PAUL
SALVATION & TRANSFORMATION

No matter where you are from, or what your past may be, Jesus Christ loves you. He calls you to do a 180-degree life change. This is a transformation done by the Spirit of the living God. Today, learn the old identity and lifestyle of the author of Ephesians. If God can call Saul and give him a new identity, imagine what he will do for you!

MEMORY VERSE

[17] I keep asking that the God of our Lord Jesus Christ, the glorious Father, may give you the Spirit of wisdom and revelation, so that you may know him better. [18] I pray that the eyes of your heart may be enlightened in order that you may know the hope to which he has called you, the riches of his glorious inheritance in his holy people, [19] and his incomparably great power for us who believe. That power is the same as the mighty strength [20] he exerted when he raised Christ from the dead and seated him at his right hand in the heavenly realms, [21] far above all rule and authority, power and dominion, and every name that is invoked, not only in the present age but also in the one to come. [22] And God placed all things under his feet and appointed him to be head over everything for the church, [23] which is his body, the fullness of him who fills everything in every way. — Ephesians 1:17-23

PRAYER

Let's start our time with the Lord by praying Paul's prayer for ourselves and our family. Be sure to change the pronouns and personalize it! Today we are praying it a bit differently.

Example:

Lord, it says in Ephesians that all things are under your feet. I praise you that (insert problem or person you are praying for) is under your feet. That means you have all the power over that situation. I claim that promise for this situation in Jesus' name! Thank you that the working of your mighty strength that raised Jesus from the dead lives in me, as I have repented of my sin and trust in him. I pray that power will manifest in me today and that I will grasp who you are in me, as you fill me in every way!

This is just an example. The more you pray and meditate on this scripture passage, the more you will be filled with the awesome faith that will touch the throne of heaven, by God's power and grace.

READING

Re-read Ephesians Chapter 1 today. Look back over your list of the attributes of God. Is it exhaustive? Did anything new pop out at you today? Pray as you read. Ask God questions!

AUTHOR BACKGROUND

Yesterday, we began a faith-building exercise by skipping ahead to Ephesians 1:17-23 and learning to pray Paul's prayer for deepening and strengthening our relationship with Jesus by inviting the Holy Spirit to fill us as we read. Today, let's look at some very basic things about the author.

> **TODAY'S BIBLE STUDY TOOL**
>
> **Author Background**. Learn what you can about the person who is writing the text.

When I read a book, I want to know if the author is really an authority on the subject. Can I trust the person writing this health book? Is this financial author actually helping people get out of debt? Is this new trendy book a conspiracy theory, or is it truthful? So, today, let's learn about the author of Ephesians and why he knows what he is talking about when it comes to Jesus.

The letter to the Ephesians is written by the apostle Paul. Apostle is more than a title. It is a spiritual position of authority in Christ. Paul was called by Jesus when he was an enemy of God and he walked out of darkness into the light. His name was even changed when he found Christ! His given name was Saul of Tarsus. "Of Tarsus" is added, because in ancient times people were frequently named by the place of their birth or their father's first name. For example, Jesus was called Jesus of Nazareth, because he grew up in Nazareth. Saul's new name became Paul the apostle. He went from being known by his past and his origins to his identity in Christ Jesus. Before he came to Christ, Saul was a very powerful, young religious leader in the Sanhedrin, which was kind of like the Jewish Congress of the time. He was climbing the ladder quickly for his age. He was zealous—a mover and a shaker. The Sanhedrin had political and spiritual authority over Israel. In this way, it was different from our Congress, which does not have spiritual authority over us.

CROSS-REFERENCE

For today's study, let's engage in a tiny, but powerful Bible study tool called cross-referencing. It's just like it sounds. Cross-referencing is strategically jumping somewhere else in the Bible to better understand what we are reading, in this case, Ephesians. This will help us to have more of the full counsel of the Word of God.

> **TODAY'S BIBLE STUDY TOOL**
>
> **Cross Reference**. Use a Bible concordance or search your Bible app to find other passages in scripture on the same subject.

Cross-referencing is not hard. It is kind of like learning to pair side dishes of healthy carbs and vegetables with a main dish of protein in order to get a balanced meal. Different passages of scripture help to give us a complete look at who God is and what he is speaking to us through his Word.

The Word of God is not a random collection of stories. It is, from beginning to end, the account of our relationship with the Lord and his long-term plan to redeem us because of his great love for us.

Now we are going to read a part of the apostle Paul's story from THE BIBLE! Remember, non-GMO here!

FROM SAUL TO PAUL
Salvation and Transformation

Turn in your Bible to read Acts 6:1–8:3. This first part of Saul's story covers two chapters and may take you about 10 minutes to read. You may be surprised to not find his name in this part of the story until the end, but his role and the fact that he was a participant in this major event are huge parts of his testimony, as well as the story of the early church.

Get your highlighter. Look for the word "apostle" to highlight. Also, look for "the twelve," which is a reference to the eleven apostles that Christ appointed to lead his church, plus the one who was chosen after Judas Iscariot, one of the original twelve, died. Prepare yourself—Saul is not a good guy in this story! He was not an apostle, yet. This is a great picture of the grace and power of God to change anyone.

I'm giving you some questions to review before you start your Bible reading. These will help you hunt down and discover kernels of truth in this passage. You don't have to write in the answers if you don't have time. This is just to stimulate your thinking. If you have time, and want to dig deeper, go ahead—write in the answers!

CHALLENGE LEVELS

Level 1. If you are short on time or want an easier level, you only need to read Acts 8:1-3 and answer the questions under that section.

Level 2. If you want to dig deeper and see the bigger picture, be sure to read Acts 6:1—8:3 and answer the questions under all the sections.

QUESTIONS TO THINK ABOUT WHILE READING ACTS CHAPTER 6

1. What was Stephen's role in the church? What did they do when they presented Stephen and why?

2. What was the result of the apostles appointing the seven men? (verse 5)

3. Why did opposition rise up against Stephen?

4. Where did Stephen get his wisdom for the confrontation?

QUESTIONS FOR ACTS CHAPTER 7

1. What kind of picture of God's faithfulness does Stephen paint in his account of Israel's history?

2. Why did the truthful and striking ending of Stephen's sermon create such rage in the men who were listening?

3. Who was the witness to this event who watched the coats of the men who murdered Stephen?

4. In what frame of mind did Stephen die? What were his last words?

QUESTIONS FOR ACTS CHAPTER 8:1-3

If you're short on time, look at this passage only. It sums up what type of person Saul was before he was changed by Jesus.

5. Saul did not kill Stephen, but what did he do after Stephen's death? What does this passage teach you about the nature of God? List as many things as you can think of.

6. What does this passage teach you about the nature of people? Go for it! Dig deep.

7. How did Stephen experience the power of God in the middle of persecution?

8. If you could ask God any questions about this passage, what would they be? Go ahead and ask! God is not afraid of your questions.

WRITTEN PRAYER

If God can change Saul-the-Murderer to Paul-the-Apostle, who wrote Ephesians and most of the New Testament, how can he change you today? Jesus, transform me! Write your prayer.

BRINGING IT HOME

If you are reading Ephesians with your children at night, do they know who the author is? Tell them you are going to read the story about the author. Read the story of Stephen (Acts 6:1-8:3) to your children.

Here are some things to talk about:

- Who are the good guys?
- Who are the bad guys?
- What do you think God thinks about Saul and Stephen?
- Guess who the author of Ephesians is (from this story)?
- Do you think the apostle Paul is an expert to talk about the power of God to change someone?
- Talk to them about the mercy and love of God to transform a person.
- Are you excited to read the rest of the story?

I AM CHOSEN BY GOD!

MEMORY VERSE

[17] I keep asking that the God of our Lord Jesus Christ, the glorious Father, may give you the Spirit of wisdom and revelation, so that you may know him better. [18] I pray that the eyes of your heart may be enlightened in order that you may know the hope to which he has called you, the riches of his glorious inheritance in his holy people, [19] and his incomparably great power for us who believe. That power is the same as the mighty strength [20] he exerted when he raised Christ from the dead and seated him at his right hand in the heavenly realms, [21] far above all rule and authority, power and dominion, and every name that is invoked, not only in the present age but also in the one to come. [22] And God placed all things under his feet and appointed him to be head over everything for the church, [23] which is his body, the fullness of him who fills everything in every way. — Ephesians 1:17-23

PRAYER

Pray our memory verse prayer, Ephesians 1:17-23, in a personalized way. If a certain part jumps out at you as you are praying, don't feel locked in. You may expound as the Holy Spirit leads. I have spent time just "vamping" on one part, like "I want to know you! Open my eyes. Open the eyes of my heart. I need your hope, Lord. I need to see the hope in Christ. Please let me understand my inheritance in you!" Remember that your prayer should be centered on inviting the Holy Spirit to teach you, fill you, open your eyes and interact with you as you read. That is why we use Paul's prayer!

Ephesians Chapter 1 begins with the apostle Paul's clear, very personalized and impassioned case for God's sovereignty in our lives. Here is the definition I found on merriamwebster.com:

sovereign, *noun* | sov·er·eign | \ ˈsä-v(ə-)rən, -vərn *also* ˈsə- \

1   a : one possessing or held to possess supreme political power or sovereignty
     b : one that exercises supreme authority within a limited sphere
     c : an acknowledged leader : ARBITER

After all, Paul himself, as we learned on Day 2, was VERY undeserving of Christ's forgiveness. We have not read the rest of his story, but his own personal conversion story is one where God literally reached down and changed the course of his life. Paul's redemption is an absolute picture of undeserved grace and God's active sovereign role in our salvation. Sovereignty is power and authority over a kingdom. Since most of the western world functions in a democratic way, the idea of a kingdom and a sovereign reigning over that kingdom is very foreign to us. A king can have mercy over whom he decides to have mercy without explaining why. In this case, God looked in Saul's heart and saw a man who was passionately trying to serve God, the best way he knew how. He was very zealous for the things of God. He truly believed that the people following the way of Jesus were heretics leading Israel astray, and needed to be eliminated. We will use a Bible study tool called cross referencing to read more about the grace God gave to Saul.

CROSS REFERENCE

1 Timothy 1:12-17

[12] I thank Christ Jesus our Lord, who has given me strength, that he considered me trustworthy, appointing me to his service. [13] Even though I was once a blasphemer and a persecutor and a violent man, I was shown mercy because I acted in ignorance and unbelief. [14] The grace of our Lord was poured out on me abundantly, along with the faith and love that are in Christ Jesus.

[15] Here is a trustworthy saying that deserves full acceptance: Christ Jesus came into the world to save sinners – of whom I am the worst. [16] But for that very reason I was shown mercy so that in me, the worst of sinners, Christ Jesus might display his immense patience as an example for those who would believe in him and receive eternal life. [17] Now to the King eternal, immortal, invisible, the only God, be honour and glory for ever and ever. Amen.

God's sovereignty in our lives is not like a puppet master who manipulates, but like a king who has the authority and power to rule and to judge. In the United States, our governing power is divided up between three branches of government. However, in the kingdom of heaven, God contains all of these powers in himself. He is lawgiver, judge, and executor or enforcer. He gives out power and authority to governments on earth and he gives us authority in our own lives. Saul was using his own personal authority in ignorance to persecute and kill Christians, and the Lord intervened. God, in his sovereignty, opened Saul's spiritual eyes. He took away his ignorance and showed him Jesus clearly and definitively. When we turn to Christ, we respond to his call. He calls us out of darkness and brings us into the light. Saul responded to the light in faith and saw his life take a turn he never imagined. Let's look at the light he was brought into in Ephesians Chapter 1. This is the same light-filled life we are all called to in Christ.

As you read Ephesians Chapter 1, verses 1-10, underline all the ACTIVE VERBS in the passage, where God acts on our behalf. Can you find all of these words and mark them in the passage below?

WORD SEARCH

Underline, in Ephesians 1:1-10 below, the following active verbs expressing God acting on our behalf.

blessed · chose · predestined · given · lavished · made known · purposed

Ephesians 1:1-10

[1] Paul, an apostle of Christ Jesus by the will of God,

To God's holy people in Ephesus, the faithful in Christ Jesus:

[2] Grace and peace to you from God our Father and the Lord Jesus Christ.

[3] Praise be to the God and Father of our Lord Jesus Christ, who has blessed us in the heavenly realms with every spiritual blessing in Christ. [4] For he chose us in him before the creation of the world to be holy and blameless in his sight. In love [5] he predestined us for adoption to sonship through Jesus Christ, in accordance with his pleasure and will – [6] to the praise of his glorious grace, which he has freely given us in the One he loves. [7] In him we have redemption through his blood, the forgiveness of sins, in accordance with the riches of God's grace [8] that he lavished on us. With all wisdom and understanding, [9] he made known to us the mystery of his will according to his good pleasure, which he purposed in Christ, [10] to be put into effect when the times reach their fulfilment – to bring unity to all things in heaven and on earth under Christ.

In verses 11–14, Paul changes the subject of the sentences from God our Father to the redeemed believers, you and me! He starts laying down the beautiful new identities we have in Christ, because of what God has done to, through and for us in Jesus.

> **TODAY'S BIBLE STUDY TOOL**
>
> **Word Search.** When studying the Bible, be looking for recurring words which reveal a theme.

Circle, in the scripture passage below, the following descriptors of you and me, because of Christ. Then, underline what we perform as believers in Jesus.

chosen · predestined · first to put our hope in Christ · for the praise of his glory · included in Christ

heard the message of truth · believed · marked in him with a seal · God's possession

Ephesians 1:11-14

In him we were also chosen, having been predestined according to the plan of him who works out everything in conformity with the purpose of his will, in order that we, who were the first to put our hope in Christ, might be for the praise of his glory. And you were also included in Christ when you heard the message of truth, the gospel of your salvation. When you believed, you were marked in him with a seal, the promised Holy Spirit, who is a deposit guaranteeing our inheritance until the redemption of those who are God's possession—to the praise of his glory.

Now, if you have repented of your sin and put your faith in Christ, Sister, all these things describe YOU! Are you marking up your Bible yet?!!! Because we need this truth to be in our hearts and minds. Are you feeling insecure in your spiritual life and walk? That is because you are focusing on your weaknesses and your failures. Remember, we need to put our minds and hearts on Christ and on what our heavenly Father has done for us. This should spark true prayer, true faith and true worship!

READING

Take time to re-read Ephesians 1:1-10. This time, praise the Lord out loud for EACH thing he has done for you!

- Thank you, Father God, that you have blessed me in the heavenly realms with every spiritual blessing in Christ! I am blessed, in spiritual places I can't even see, because of Jesus!

- Thank you, my God and Father, for choosing me! You chose me! You called me! At the beginning of Creation, you knew my name. You knew when I would be born. You knew that Jesus would die for my sins and you had a plan to make me blameless and pure and holy in your sight.

- Thank you that you love me! Your predestined plan for all believers is that we would live in the covenant of adoption with you. I was fatherless and you called me your own. It is your pleasure AND your will that I be grafted into the family of God, my true family!

- Thank you for freely giving me grace in Jesus. You love Jesus and you gave him for my redemption. You have brought me into your family, a family marked by grace.

- I praise you, Lord, that you valued me by spilling your own blood for the forgiveness of my sin. My sin is great and messy and you have done the undeserved dirty work.

- I worship you, oh Lord! You have lavished me with your grace. There is so much beauty in this, I cannot comprehend it!

- Thank you, oh Lord, for revealing the great mysteries of your plan in Christ to me!

I am chosen! I am predestined! I have hope in Christ! I am included, not excluded! My ears are open to hear the Word of Truth! I have believed in you and you have sealed me with your Holy Spirit! I praise your name! Soak it in, ladies!

BRINGING IT HOME

Read through the short passage (Ephesians 1:1-17) with your child.

- Ask them to help you find the words that describe a believer in Jesus.

- Teach them how significant it is that we are all these things in Christ

WHY STUDY GOD'S WORD?

PRAYER

When we pray before meals, we thank God for our food and ask him to bless it to our bodies. How much more should we thank God for his Word and ask him to allow our spirits to receive it and be blessed by it? When we read the Word of God, we are not just reading a text written by human hands or minds; it is so much more. Invite the Spirit of wisdom and revelation to fill you, so you may understand God's truth today! Use the apostle Paul's prayer as a spring board. Spend time on our memory verse/prayer passage today!

MEMORY VERSE

[17] I keep asking that the God of our Lord Jesus Christ, the glorious Father, may give you the Spirit of wisdom and revelation, so that you may know him better. [18] I pray that the eyes of your heart may be enlightened in order that you may know the hope to which he has called you, the riches of his glorious inheritance in his holy people, [19] and his incomparably great power for us who believe. That power is the same as the mighty strength [20] he exerted when he raised Christ from the dead and seated him at his right hand in the heavenly realms, [21] far above all rule and authority, power and dominion, and every name that is invoked, not only in the present age but also in the one to come. [22] And God placed all things under his feet and appointed him to be head over everything for the church, [23] which is his body, the fullness of him who fills everything in every way. — Ephesians 1:17-23

KNOW THE POWER OF THE WORD OF GOD
What Does the Bible Say About Itself?

John 1:1-2 — In the beginning was the Word, and the Word was with God, and the Word was God. He was with God in the beginning. — *Jesus = The Word of God.*

Matthew 4:4 — Jesus answered, 'It is written: "Man shall not live on bread alone, but on every word that comes from the mouth of God."' — *God's Word is more important than physical food.*

Mark 4:1-20 — [1] Again Jesus began to teach by the lake. The crowd that gathered round him was so large that he got into a boat and sat in it out on the lake, while all the people were along the shore at the water's edge. [2] He taught them many things by parables, and in his teaching said: [3] 'Listen! A farmer went out to sow his seed. [4] As he was scattering the seed, some fell along the path, and the birds came and ate it up. [5] Some fell on rocky places, where it did not have much soil. It sprang up quickly, because the soil was shallow. [6] But when the sun came up, the plants were scorched, and they withered because they had no root. [7] Other seed fell among thorns, which grew up and choked the plants, so that they did not bear grain. [8] Still other seed fell on good soil. It came up, grew and produced a crop, some multiplying thirty, some sixty, some a hundred times.'

[9] Then Jesus said, 'Whoever has ears to hear, let them hear.'

[10] When he was alone, the Twelve and the others around him asked him about the parables. [11] He told them, 'The secret of the kingdom of God has been given to you. But to those on the outside everything is said in parables [12] so that,

> '"they may be ever seeing but never perceiving,
> and ever hearing but never understanding;
> otherwise they might turn and be forgiven!"'

[13] Then Jesus said to them, 'Don't you understand this parable? How then will you understand any parable? [14] The farmer sows the word. [15] Some people are like seed along the path, where the word is sown. As soon as they hear it, Satan comes and takes away the word that was sown in them. [16] Others, like seed sown on rocky places, hear the word and at once receive it with joy. [17] But since they have no root, they last only a short time. When trouble or persecution comes because of the word, they quickly fall away. [18] Still others, like seed sown among thorns, hear the word; [19] but the worries of this life, the deceitfulness of wealth and the desires for other things come in and choke the word, making it unfruitful. [20] Others, like seed sown on good soil, hear the word, accept it, and produce a crop – some thirty, some sixty, some a hundred times what was sown.' — *God's Word has the life-giving power and properties of a seed. When it comes into your spirit, through your ears by hearing or your eyes by reading, it takes spiritual root. Outside influences can choke out the influence of God's Word by affecting our faith.*

Mark 13:31 — Heaven and earth will pass away, but my words will never pass away. — *God's Word is eternal.*

John 6:63 — The Spirit gives life; the flesh counts for nothing. The words I have spoken to you – they are full of the Spirit and life. *When we read or hear the Bible, we are exposed to the power and life of the Spirit. The scripture is more than just words. They are infused with God's life.*

John 15:6-8 — If you do not remain in me, you are like a branch that is thrown away and withers; such branches are picked up, thrown into the fire and burned. If you remain in me and my words remain in you, ask whatever you wish, and it will be done for you. This is to my Father's glory, that you bear much fruit, showing yourselves to be my disciples. — *Remaining in God's Word — by obedience through the Spirit — will bring good fruit into your life and God will answer your prayers. Not remaining in the Word will cause you to spiritually wither up in your inner being. Your walk with God will be worthless to you and to God, because you will be cutting yourself off from the vine and the nourishment of Christ. Stay in the Word and walk with Jesus!*

Romans 10:17 — Consequently, faith comes from hearing the message, and the message is heard through the word about Christ. — *Our faith is built up through our hearing of the Word.*

Ephesians 5:25-27 — Husbands, love your wives, just as Christ loved the church and gave himself up for her to make her holy, cleansing her by the washing with water through the word, and to present her to himself as a radiant church, without stain or wrinkle or any other blemish, but holy and blameless. — *Christ cleanses us with his Word! We are made holy as his Word does its work in us.*

Hebrews 4:12-13 — For the Word of God is alive and active. Sharper than any double-edged sword, it penetrates even to dividing soul and spirit, joints and marrow; it judges the thoughts and attitudes of the heart. Nothing in all creation is hidden from God's sight. Everything is uncovered and laid bare before the eyes of him to whom we must give account. — *God's Word is a weapon. This passage speaks for itself!*

When we approach the Bible, we are approaching Jesus! When we read it, we are feeding on the spiritual seed of God. When we believe it, we obey it and the truth sets us free. When we obey God, we show him love and his power works in our lives and transforms us.

However, this work is a spiritual work, done by God in us! We cannot do it in our flesh. We are transformed by the Spirit and the power of the Word. So, as simply as I can state it —

- Pray before reading the Word.
- Pray while you are reading the Word.
- Ask God questions.
- Ask his Spirit to teach you spiritual truths.

This is why we pray the powerful prayer of the apostle Paul before reading the Word, or any time for that matter.

WORSHIP TIMEOUT

Think of your favorite worship song and sing it!

Do you ever struggle during worship to REALLY connect with the gravity of the message of the words in the song? I certainly do! Here's why —

God gave us the gift of salvation through Christ. Jesus did all the hard work. He laid down his life willingly through a brutal crucifixion. When we sing songs in church, sometimes we have trouble grasping the reality of what God did for us. We can't wrap our heads around it. Occasionally, I feel like I am going through the motions with my hands up in worship and the words coming out. In those moments, I know that I truly am not grasping the impact of what Christ did for me. How about you? Do you ever experience that?

Does it mean we are hypocrites if we have trouble wrapping our heads around the truth we confess? No way! That is why the apostle Paul prays this prayer for the Ephesians! It is a prayer that their head knowledge of God will be transformed by the move of the Spirit of wisdom and revelation. You CAN experience and know the power of Christ in a deep way, but it has to be of the Spirit. No emotionalism or stoicism can replace the move of the Spirit of God. Get busy with this prayer! More revelation, Jesus! More wisdom! Open my heart to know Christ and all that he is in me!

CLOSING PRAYER

Spend time in prayer. Take the Lord your deepest needs, and any and all emotional confusion. He will give you a breakthrough of clarity and the ability to see what you haven't been able to see before. This is found in Christ.

Dear God,

Center my prayer life on knowing Christ. Center my walk on you, trusting that you will take care of all of my needs, according to your riches in glory.

Amen

Pray Ephesians 1:17-23 again, paraphrased for personal prayer. Repetition for memorization!

MEMORY VERSE

[17] I keep asking that the God of our Lord Jesus Christ, the glorious Father, may give you the Spirit of wisdom and revelation, so that you may know him better. [18] I pray that the eyes of your heart may be enlightened in order that you may know the hope to which he has called you, the riches of his glorious inheritance in his holy people, [19] and his incomparably great power for us who believe. That power is the same as the mighty strength [20] he exerted when he raised Christ from the dead

and seated him at his right hand in the heavenly realms, [21] far above all rule and authority, power and dominion, and every name that is invoked, not only in the present age but also in the one to come. [22] And God placed all things under his feet and appointed him to be head over everything for the church, [23] which is his body, the fullness of him who fills everything in every way. — Ephesians 1:17-23

BRINGING IT HOME

Have you read to your children right out of the Bible? Try doing this every night before bed. Get the Word into them! (They won't always want to. That's OKAY! Kids also don't always want to take a bath or go to bed, but it's good for them.)

Start with the parable of the sower. Discuss with them the power of the Word of God to bring life into a person's heart. Discuss the different soils. How do they react differently to the Word?

THE POWER OF ADOPTION

God knows you personally and he has a plan! If you've noticed in our study so far of the first chapter of Ephesians, there are several themes and words that you can find throughout the message. What do you think they are? Can you remember without looking? If not, take a minute to re-read the passage we are becoming more familiar with this week. When Paul penned the letter to the church in Ephesus, he was writing what the Holy Spirit was speaking through him for this group of people. It is not just a bunch of euphemisms strung together. He was delivering a well-placed and timely message. We can still learn from their lessons today!

PRAYER

Start your study today with prayer from Ephesians 1:17-23.

MEMORY VERSE

[17] I keep asking that the God of our Lord Jesus Christ, the glorious Father, may give you the Spirit of wisdom and revelation, so that you may know him better. [18] I pray that the eyes of your heart may be enlightened in order that you may know the hope to which he has called you, the riches of his glorious inheritance in his holy people, [19] and his incomparably great power for us who believe. That power is the same as the mighty strength [20] he exerted when he raised Christ from the dead and seated him at his right hand in the heavenly realms, [21] far above all rule and authority, power and dominion, and every name that is invoked, not only in the present age but also in the one to come. [22] And God placed all things under his feet and appointed him to be head over everything for the church, [23] which is his body, the fullness of him who fills everything in every way. — Ephesians 1:17-23

READING

Read Ephesians 1:3-10. In Chapter 1, we see the theme of God knowing us ahead of time, from the creation of the world. This means that you are not an accident. God thought of you at creation and at the cross, when Christ was being sacrificed. In fact, Romans 6 says we died with Christ through baptism and were raised again with him at his resurrection. We were with him then and he is with us now. He is one and the same!

One of Jesus' titles in the Greek is Alpha and Omega, the beginning and the end. He is not a person from the past, but he was in the past. He is not just a futuristic person we will see at our death when we go to heaven. He is here right now! He is alive and well, bringing about his will on earth. He is with you at work. He is with you in your marriage. He is with you in school, in a race, in a plane, in your car, or in your room where you are sitting depressed, in the middle of your struggles.

What we see demonstrated in Ephesians Chapter 1 are two qualities of God that are hard to comprehend.

- He is our God and Father, creator in the heavenly realms. He is mysterious and his will is above our human ability to understand. This is why we need the Spirit of wisdom and revelation!

- He is also our personal Savior. He has a personal plan for you! He is making known to YOU the mystery of his will in Christ. He saw you and predestined you to be personally adopted into the family of God.

Ephesians 1:4-6 says,

> For he chose us in him before the creation of the world to be holy and blameless in his sight. In love he predestined us for adoption to sonship through Jesus Christ, in accordance with his pleasure and will – to the praise of his glorious grace, which he has freely given us in the One he loves. – Ephesians 1:4-6

These are very personal words. God not only chose YOU personally, but also called you by his Spirit. He designed and ordained your purpose as a believer. Our purpose is to be holy and blameless in his sight (v 4). As the church, we aren't saved for our own purposes and to live our own lives. We are saved to live for Christ. We are saved and set apart to be a testimony of God's love. It's not just the pastor's job to shine Jesus or know Jesus. It becomes a part of our nature, when we are adopted into his family.

I know families who have adopted children. This is a precious process. The emotional journey of adopting is not something I have personally experienced, but have watched close friends walk through. It seems that the day a match is made in the adoption process, the heavens are opened and the angels are singing! The day I got the call from my friend, who got the news that they were matched with two sweet boys from Ethiopia, after waiting for what seemed like years, was truly just the same as getting a call from a friend in labor that she was on her way to the hospital. Imagine how God must feel, as he chooses us and calls us! Imagine how he feels on the day we respond to his call!

In an international adoption, there is paperwork to be done and a visit to the country. There are shots for the family, and passports, and more paperwork, and more waiting. Even when the child comes home, and after both governments recognize the legal name change and the child is safe in his new home, there are many more obstacles to overcome. The adoptive parent is full of joy, and the hard work is just beginning. The adopted child can have a number of challenges, including failure to bond. Even though he is chosen, even though he is legally a child, the adopted child may struggle emotionally to grasp the reality that he belongs. There are ways to pray and to love a child that will help him to bond and begin to thrive in his new environment. The scriptures say that everything we need for life and godliness we have in Christ Jesus. This means EVERYTHING! Everything we need emotionally, everything we need to overcome our pasts, everything we need to understand the love of God we have in Jesus.

Paul is writing to the Ephesians and praying that they will grasp the fullness of the reality in which they are now living. They are recipients of a great love and a part of an eternal mystery. This love involves sacrifice, grace, hope and power.

ACTION POINT

Is there a part of you that struggles to emotionally connect with Father God? Do you, as an adopted child of the King of kings and Lord of lords, have a hard time believing in your heart the reality that you belong? The things that can keep an adopted child from bonding are the traumas, the rejection, the fear, the lack of emotional intimacy in infancy and early childhood, and even the spiritual bondages that have become part of his or her emotional and spiritual makeup. Are there things in your life that make it difficult to bond to the Father? Take time in prayer to ask God to help you with this. Jesus came to reveal the Father to us. Jesus loves his Father and his ultimate goal is to introduce us to our Father and our new place in the family.

Turn in your Bible to read John 14:5-21. Read the account of when Philip asked Jesus to show them the Father. Jesus promises that we will not be left alone as orphans.

How amazing is this? Why are we afraid of the Father? Our plan of salvation through Christ was his plan. It was his idea. Jesus submitted to his Father's will to save us. We need to switch our paradigm on this, in order to enjoy every good thing we have in the family of God. Ask him to hold you close and give you the Spirit of wisdom and revelation to comprehend his love. If you are struggling to connect with him, ask the Father to give you spiritual eyes to see his love, and to knock down the emotional and spiritual walls that are in the way of you comprehending this love.

A REAL-LIFE ADOPTION STORY

My close friend and her husband, parents to three natural children of their own, felt God calling them to adopt from Ethiopia. I was witness to this unfolding event in their lives, from the beginning of God's tug on their hearts, through the endless paperwork, interviews, and countless months of waiting, to the receiving of that long-awaited telephone call. They adopted two very young brothers and have lovingly knit them into their family. Below is a poem that my friend wrote to the youngest when he grew old enough to ask her questions about his adoption. Break out the tissues for this one!

TELL ME ABOUT WHEN I WAS A BABY IN ETHIOPIA ...

To: Isaiah
By: Marlisa Eyre

Mommy, tell me about when I was a baby in Ethiopia.

Oh, sweet love, when you were a tiny, tiny baby, you grew and grew and grew in Enat's belly, safe and sound, safe and sound.

In Enat's belly, Jesus whispered to you, "You are My beloved child. I will never leave you." When Enat carried you on her back and held you in her arms, and nursed you close and warm, Jesus was whispering to your heart how much He loves you, precious boy.

Tell me about when I was a baby in your heart, Mommy.

Oh, sweet love, when you were just a tiny baby, Jesus whispered to my heart that you would need a Mommy. And I waited and waited and waited for you. My heart grew big and big and BIG with love for you as I waited across the world for you.

Tell me about when I was a baby in your arms, Mommy.

Oh, sweet love, when you were finally a baby in my arms, I cried and cried with happy tears. I rocked you and sang to you and danced in circles around and around and around with you! Jesus whispered to my heart His love for you as I became your mommy.

Tell me about when I grew in your backpack, Mommy.

Oh, sweet love, when you were a baby in my backpack, you felt afraid for a while. You felt afraid that Mommy would leave. And so, I tucked you in close to my heart. I sang to you, I rubbed your back, and I kissed your soft cheeks and I prayed that Jesus would heal the broken places in your heart. When you were in my backpack, Jesus whispered to you, "I love you, My precious boy. I will never, ever, ever, ever leave you."

Tell me about how you love your little boy, Mommy!

Oh, sweet love, how I love my little boy! I love you because you are a treasure. I love your fingers and tiny toes and your soft brown skin. I love the way your eyes smile with joy! Long before I met you, Jesus whispered to my heart that you are His, a masterpiece created by God. Sweet love, I am so glad I get to be your mommy and I am so glad you are my little boy.

LET DOWN YOUR GUARD

I use this illustration from real life so that you might understand in some small way, what it means to God when we receive his Son as our savior. God has longed for us to come to him. He has a beautiful new life planned for us with him, made possible by his Son Jesus Christ. He will never leave us, nor forsake us.

Use the prayer below as a template. Give God the pain and fear that may be blocking you, in your deepest emotions, from experiencing the reality of your position in Christ.

Father in heaven,

I am struggling to understand your love and want to feel that you are my daddy. Show me if there is anything in the way of understanding your love for me. Please, fill me with your love, and drive out a spirit of fear, in Jesus' name. I thank you for your Holy Spirit, who gives me love, power and a sound mind. I claim the truth that in Christ I have all of these things.

TODAY'S BIBLE STUDY TOOL

Let Down Your Guard. Open your heart to God's truth. Sometimes our hearts are guarded by pain, preconceived ideas, and thinking patterns. By faith, allow the Spirit of God to renew your mind, heart, soul and spirit.

You are my Abba, my daddy. I am your daughter. I belong to you. Teach me of your love by your Spirit of wisdom and revelation. Open up my eyes to the inheritance I have in Christ. Right now, I give you the things in my life and the events that are full of pain that make it difficult for me to emotionally connect with the truth of my adoption in Christ. (Take time to list the things that come to mind.) I forgive those people who have hurt me, abandoned me, rejected me, and given me reason to feel unloved, in the name of Jesus. I forgive them and ask you to replace the spinning thoughts with the sound mind that comes in Christ.

In Jesus' name I pray, Amen.

SCRIPTURES TO HELP

2 Timothy 1:7 – For the Spirit God gave us does not make us timid, but gives us power, love and self-discipline.

1 John 4:18 – There is no fear in love. But perfect love drives out fear, because fear has to do with punishment. The one who fears is not made perfect in love.

Romans 8:15 – The Spirit you received does not make you slaves, so that you live in fear again; rather, the Spirit you received brought about your adoption to sonship. And by him we cry, 'Abba, Father.' (Abba means Daddy in Hebrew)

BRINGING IT HOME

How are you fostering the love of Christ in your home and/or relationships? Is your home full of anger and judgment or love, respect, and forgiveness?

One of the best ways to learn how to teach your children or those around you about the Lord is to ask God to help you. Ask him to help you create an atmosphere in your home and life that reflects his love and grace. Relationships are so important, child of God.

Dig into the Word of God and find his heart, not just knowledge. When you find his heart, by the power of his Spirit, ask the same Spirit that raised Christ Jesus from the dead to teach you how to be the parent you need to be, to be the spouse you need to be, and to be the daughter of God he created you to be.

Now, women, don't feel guilty! I can already see you crying or making a list of everything you've done wrong. Remember, we are purchased by the blood of Jesus, not by our perfection or works. Give Jesus your brokenness and the sin in your life, and he will give you newness.

Extend the security, love and grace you have received to your family, friends and co-workers today.

SEALED WITH THE HOLY SPIRIT
PART 1

Congratulations! You made it through our first week of studying God's Word! Many people assert that it takes 21 days to break a habit. We are breaking the habit of not studying God's Word. On days when I feel confused or I am needing direction, I will oftentimes find myself in prayer asking the Lord for help and clarity. Most every time, he says to me, "You need to get back in the Word. You need to be solid in it so this confusion will have no room for tripping you up." Thus, our prayer starts this study every day!

PRAYER

Begin your study today with our memory verse prayer from Ephesians 1:17-23.

MEMORY VERSE

[17] I keep asking that the God of our Lord Jesus Christ, the glorious Father, may give you the Spirit of wisdom and revelation, so that you may know him better. [18] I pray that the eyes of your heart may be enlightened in order that you may know the hope to which he has called you, the riches of his glorious inheritance in his holy people, [19] and his incomparably great power for us who believe. That power is the same as the mighty strength [20] he exerted when he raised Christ from the dead and seated him at his right hand in the heavenly realms, [21] far above all rule and authority, power and dominion, and every name that is invoked, not only in the present age but also in the one to come. [22] And God placed all things under his feet and appointed him to be head over everything for the church, [23] which is his body, the fullness of him who fills everything in every way. — Ephesians 1:17-23

READING

Ephesians 1:11-14

[11] In him we were also chosen, having been predestined according to the plan of him who works out everything in conformity with the purpose of his will, [12] in order that we, who were the first to put our hope in Christ, might be for the praise of his glory. [13] And you also were included in Christ when you heard the message of truth, the gospel of your salvation. When you believed, you were marked in him with a seal, the promised Holy Spirit, [14] who is a deposit guaranteeing our inheritance until the redemption of those who are God's possession – to the praise of his glory.

9. Once we believed, what did God give us to mark us, showing we belong to him?

10. What is the Holy Spirit described as in this passage?

11. What do you think it means when it refers to our redemption as a future event? "... a deposit guaranteeing our inheritance until the redemption of those who are God's possession ..." — Ephesians 1:14

This passage teaches that we belong to Christ while we live in this world. It doesn't always feel or look like we are redeemed. While you and I have a testimony of what the Lord has delivered us from, we are STILL waiting for the final redemption! We may feel overwhelmed with the darkness that we are surrounded by, sometimes even in our own Christian homes. This is because we are still in our fleshly bodies, we have a sin nature, and the world is full of sin.

However, the passage doesn't focus on our negative situation. The focus is the spiritual reality we live with in Christ. *We have the Holy Spirit, the Spirit of Christ himself, living inside of us as a deposit, a guarantee of what we are promised for eternity with God.* What does all this mean? Following is a narrative of my brother and me discussing the implications of being sealed.

TRUE STORY!

While snacking on some Veggie Straws with my brother, Seth, we discussed this passage and what it means for the Holy Spirit to be the SEAL that God the Father marks us with.

Me: This is a deposit, right? Is it a deposit like a down payment towards a vehicle? God is paying the debt for our sin, but we get to keep the car while he makes the payment. Eventually, we own the car in full. Hmmm?

Seth: It says inheritance. The seal is for a promised inheritance. So, I think it's confusing to use the car illustration.

Me: True. That's true! But, here it also says that the seal is a deposit awaiting our redemption. I think I will look up what a seal meant in biblical times, when it had to do with financial situations.

Seth: Sooooo, what it's really like is this—you have a mortgage on a house that you can't pay. The bank is coming in to foreclose. You are in debt beyond belief and you have no way out. God comes in and says, "Not only am I going to pay off your debt you can't pay, I am going to pay for it with my Son's life. Then I am going to make you my child and give you an inheritance."

Me: Yeah. That sounds way better. That's actually unbelievable. Hey! Look here what I found online ...

ONLINE BIBLE STUDY & ENCYCLOPEDIA

This is what the *Baker's Evangelical Dictionary of Biblical Theology* at biblestudytools.com says:

SEAL

A seal, in biblical times as today, is used to guarantee security or indicate ownership. Ancient seals were often made of wax, embedded with the personalized imprint of their guarantor. The Roman authorities used such a seal to secure Jesus' tomb (Matt 27:66). A signet ring was also called a seal. It was

> **TODAY'S BIBLE STUDY TOOL**
>
> **Online Bible Dictionary/Encyclopedia.** A Bible dictionary is a great tool you can use to help you understand the cultural significance of something in the Bible you may not have a frame of reference for in our society! With the internet, it is easier than ever to find good Bible dictionaries and encyclopedias and look up what you are studying.

valued among Israel's booty (Num 31:50). The significance of the act of sealing is dependent on the importance of the one doing the sealing. This is why Jezebel falsely authenticated letters she wrote in Ahab's name by affixing them with his seal (1 Kings 21:8).

Me: So, since it says the significance of the act is dependent on the one doing the sealing, the fact that God himself seals us with his Holy Spirit shows there is no greater authority or guarantor to follow through with the promised inheritance!

Seth: That's true.

Me: And the purpose of the Holy Spirit in our lives, as believers in Jesus, is ultimately not just giving us power, or leading us into truth, but he is a deposit on our future inheritance, our greatest reward, which is God himself.

This true account shows how I processed a question about scripture by discussing it with my brother, who is a well-studied man of God, and by using some Bible study tools. This was the beginning of my understanding of what it means to be sealed with the Holy Spirit, who is a deposit of our inheritance.

When you prepare to study a book of the Bible, there are some very easy steps you should take that you can teach your children to do, too. I am having my children take the following steps this summer, as they each study a book of the Bible they've chosen. They journal in a physical journal and send me their work through Google Docs when they get into researching passages that jump out at them.

These are basic steps that anyone can do to study a book or section of scripture!

- Pray for the Holy Spirit to give you wisdom and revelation. A famous early 20th century preacher and authority on prayer Leonard Ravenhill said he would study the Bible on his knees in prayer. God wants to reveal himself to you through his Word! Proverbs 25:2 says, "It is the glory of God to conceal a matter; to search out a matter is the glory of kings." The writer of Proverbs says kings (and queens like the Queen of Sheba!) find glory in searching out the deep truths of God.

- Read through the entire book or section for content and the big picture. Keep praying for revelation!

- On your second time reading the book or section of scripture, make an outline of it. Keep praying for revelation!

- On your third time through, read chapter by chapter and ask questions! Keep praying for revelation! Keep a journal handy when you are studying the Bible. Examine each chapter with a figurative magnifying glass. Write down all the questions you may have. Asking God questions is a healthy way to approach scripture. It's not a sign of a lack of faith. Curiosity is one of the ways that we learn and grow. The great people of faith like King David, Hannah, and Moses learned to trust God by asking him questions.

- Go back and research the questions more deeply by using Bible study tools I'll be teaching you and discussing more difficult questions with others who also study the Bible deeply.

- Write in your journal what you are learning from the Holy Spirit's wisdom and revelation.

During this study, we will follow these steps as I did in my personal study of Ephesians which took one year from beginning to end as I also wrote this book study. I took a magnifying glass to specific questions and words, as the Holy Spirit directed me. There are so many more words and passages that I could have examined, but the Holy Spirit led me to specific topics he wanted me to discover and write about. As God revealed his truth to me during my study of Ephesians, I wrote this book so you, the reader, could discover it as if we were studying together.

Let's return to my original question that was sparked by my curiosity about what Paul means when he says the Ephesians were sealed with the Holy Spirit. We will see what I learned about what it means for the Holy Spirit to be the SEAL that God the Father marks us with. After my discussion with Seth and using some Bible study tools, God revealed to me this truth. Let's look at Ephesians 1:13b-14:

When you believed, you were marked in him with a seal, the promised Holy Spirit, who is a deposit guaranteeing our inheritance until the redemption of those who are God's possession – to the praise of his glory. – Ephesians 1:13b-14

Our redemption makes us God's possession. Imagine something seemingly silly in comparison. If you redeem frequent flyer miles, you get to enjoy a flight you earned. In the same way, God has earned the right to enjoy a relationship with you! You belong to him. Verse

14 says that your inheritance will happen in a future setting upon the redemption of those who are God's possession. Jesus will return at the end of the age and all of those who have been purchased by his blood will enjoy a relationship with God in person in heaven.

Let's jump forward to Revelation 21:1-7. Open your Bible to get a glimpse of what God says about this beautiful moment in time, when we receive our inheritance! This is truly breathtaking.

Hallelujah! God shows his heart for us! His ultimate goal from the beginning of time has been to live in a pure relationship with the people he loves. Aren't you excited that the old order of things is passing away and the new is coming?! Can you imagine a place where every tear is wiped away and there will be no more death, mourning, crying or pain? It seems like a dream—almost too difficult to wrap our heads or hearts around. That is why we have been given the Holy Spirit as a deposit. We have a foreshadowing of this relationship here on earth. We experience him, as he lives inside of us, and manifests his wisdom, revelation, hope and love to us. His power brings miracles and his presence brings peace and healing. This gives us a taste of heaven. Once we get to heaven, God himself will be our reward and our full inheritance will be received. From the beginning of God's relationships with people, the relationship has always been the goal. God has his sights set on us, and we need to have our sights set on God. Do you understand that the greatest reward and experience you can have is God himself? In Genesis 15:1, God tells Abram—later to be named Abraham—that God is his very great reward. "After this, the word of the Lord came to Abram in a vision: 'Do not be afraid, Abram. I am your shield, your very great reward.'"

To understand the Holy Spirit's role in our lives, as we await our inheritance, let's cross reference to a pillar of New Testament teaching on the Holy Spirit, 1 Corinthians 12:31b—13:13. Here we can see what it says about heaven, being sealed with the Spirit, and God's love for us. When you think of putting a deposit down, it is usually such a small percentage of what will be paid in the future, isn't it? A deposit is a claim to ownership. God's deposit of his Holy Spirit shows he owns us! When we get to heaven, we will see with our eyes what Christ has fully done for us on the cross. Right now, through the deposit of his Spirit, we have just a small taste of the presence of God. In heaven, our reward will be received in person—our complete inheritance! We will bask in the presence of God, uninhibited by our fallen bodies and world!

This next powerful passage describes what it looks like to live with the deposit and seal of the Holy Spirit. Chapter 12 of 1 Corinthians describes the spiritual gifts we need to empower us to live for the Lord. If you have time today, check it out. Chapter 13 shows us the most excellent way to walk in these gifts; we always need to use them with love. A gift is the mark or seal of God's power on a believer's life. Love is a seal of his character being built in a believer. 1 Corinthians 13 says that love, one of the fruits of the Spirit, is greater than all power the Spirit may give you or any sacrifice you may make for God. Love does not negate the need for the gifts and the power of God; it just supersedes them. Our need for God to change our hearts is more important than the need for God to change our situation. If you want proof that 'God is in the house' of someone's life, you will see this clearly by the presence of the gifts and the fruit of the Spirit. Jesus says, "Make a tree good and its fruit will be good, or make a tree bad and its fruit will be bad, for a tree is recognised by its fruit." – Matthew 12:33

When we get to heaven, the fruit will remain, but we will no longer need these gifts—our deposit will be fulfilled and we will receive the complete inheritance in the presence of God!

1 Corinthians 12:31 b - 13:13

And yet I will show you the most excellent way.

[1] If I speak in the tongues of men or of angels, but do not have love, I am only a resounding gong or a clanging cymbal. [2] If I have the gift of prophecy and can fathom all mysteries and all knowledge, and if I have a faith that can move mountains, but do not have love, I am nothing. [3] If I give all I possess to the poor and give over my body to hardship that I may boast, but do not have love, I gain nothing.

[4] Love is patient, love is kind. It does not envy, it does not boast, it is not proud. [5] It does not dishonour others, it is not self-seeking, it is not easily angered, it keeps no record of wrongs. [6] Love does not delight in evil but rejoices with the truth. [7] It always protects, always trusts, always hopes, always perseveres.

[8] Love never fails. But where there are prophecies, they will cease; where there are tongues, they will be stilled; where there is knowledge, it will pass away. [9] For we know in part and we prophesy in part, [10] but when completeness comes, what is in part disappears. [11] When I was a child, I talked like a child, I thought like a child, I reasoned like a child. When

I became a man, I put the ways of childhood behind me. ¹²For now we see only a reflection as in a mirror; then we shall see face to face. Now I know in part; then I shall know fully, even as I am fully known.

¹³And now these three remain: faith, hope and love. But the greatest of these is love.

ASK QUESTIONS

What are some things God's Spirit does when he seals us? Ephesians 1:17 says his wisdom and revelation leads us into truth. Verse 18 says he comforts us with the hope of our promised inheritance in Christ. Verse 19 says he anoints us with the same power that raised Jesus from the dead. However, even though we know the truth of God through the leading of his Spirit, the faithful nature of God through manifesting the hope of the Spirit, and the power of God through walking in spiritual gifts, all of these experiences are only like seeing a picture of someone or looking in a mirror, compared to how we will experience God in heaven. We only know God two-dimensionally here on earth—through this deposit of his Spirit. In heaven we will walk with him and talk with him face to face. Yes, we can know God in amazing, deep, and powerful ways through his Spirit here, but it is simply a glimpse of how we will experience him in heaven! We were created for a relationship with him! Remember the verse about Abraham:

> **TODAY'S BIBLE STUDY TOOL**
>
> **Ask Questions. Lots of Questions.** Asking questions is one way that a little child learns about their world. Approach your discovery of the Word as a little child, asking questions as you read. Why? Where? When? Who?

I am your very great reward! — Genesis 15:1

Read back over 1 Corinthians 12:31b-13:13. It says the supernatural gifts of the Spirit, like speaking in tongues and prophecy, will cease and be stilled at some point. At what point does that happen? The clue is found in the last part of the chapter. Remember that we need to read the Bible in context. "For now we see only a reflection as in a mirror; then we shall see face to face." – 1 Corinthians 13:12

When will we be perfect? When will we see face to face? When will our deposit be realized? When we all get to heaven! God will not stop giving supernatural gifts to his believers, until they get to heaven. When we are in heaven, we will have no need for the gifts to help our fallen bodies overcome the flesh and know God. We will see him face to face. We will experience him in a way we cannot possibly comprehend right now. In this world, even the most profound experiences with God are childish compared with the perfect spiritual reality that we long for now—the spiritual reality we will enter into in heaven, when our faith will be our sight.

1 Corinthians 13:11 compares our present reality with God to being a child. Does this mean that the gifts are childish? By no means! Only relatively speaking are gifts childish—when we compare our present mortal life in God with our future, eternal life in heaven.

Are you experiencing the fullness of the Spirit on this earth? God has given you a deposit as a promise of what is to come! If you want to learn more about spiritual gifts, read 1 Corinthians Chapter 12. The last verse in the chapter says, "Now eagerly desire the greater gifts. And yet I will show you the most excellent way." Paul says to eagerly desire the greater gifts, but then teaches us in 1 Corinthians 13 how to walk in the gifts in complete love. Let's desire more of God's presence, power and character in our lives! Ask for it today!

BRINGING IT HOME

Do you ever sit and discuss difficult passages aloud with other believers? Is there a complicated or tricky turn of words that you are struggling with? Is there a concept or truth you are trying to understand?

Try mulling over the questions with your husband, friends, or even children. If it's someone you are discipling, explain to them that it's okay to ask questions. God is not afraid of our questions. Searching the scriptures should not just be for pastors and priests. The Word of God is for every believer.

Pray, as Paul did in Ephesians, for God to fill you with his Spirit continually. Ask the Lord to help you to enjoy his presence and the deposit of his Holy Spirit in your life. Ask him for more gifts and to fill your heart with real love for him and for others.

SEALED WITH THE HOLY SPIRIT
PART 2

MEMORY VERSE

[17] I keep asking that the God of our Lord Jesus Christ, the glorious Father, may give you the Spirit of wisdom and revelation, so that you may know him better. [18] I pray that the eyes of your heart may be enlightened in order that you may know the hope to which he has called you, the riches of his glorious inheritance in his holy people, [19] and his incomparably great power for us who believe. That power is the same as the mighty strength [20] he exerted when he raised Christ from the dead and seated him at his right hand in the heavenly realms, [21] far above all rule and authority, power and dominion, and every name that is invoked, not only in the present age but also in the one to come. [22] And God placed all things under his feet and appointed him to be head over everything for the church, [23] which is his body, the fullness of him who fills everything in every way. — Ephesians 1:17-23

PRAYER

Let's start off today's study with our prayer, focusing on the incomparably great power of Christ that is ours through faith. Our prayer for today is adapted from Ephesians 1:18-21.

Father,

In Jesus' name, I pray that the eyes of my heart may be enlightened in order that I may know the hope to which you have called me, the riches of your glorious inheritance in your holy people, and your incomparably great power for ME—I BELIEVE! That power is the same as the mighty strength, which YOU exerted when you raised Christ from the dead and seated him at your right hand in the heavenly realms, far above all rule and authority, power and dominion, and every name that is invoked, not only in the present age but also in the one to come. I am seated with Christ! I thank you that your power is in me. I thank you that more power is in me through Christ than I can comprehend. But, my prayer today is that I will comprehend the power of God.

Amen.

We learned yesterday that the Holy Spirit is the SEAL of the PROMISED INHERITANCE. When we study God's Word in depth, sometimes going over the same passage for a week can get stale unless we realize we are looking for treasure in God's Word. God wants to reveal to us the treasures that are ours in Christ today! When we study, which is different from just reading for content, we are looking for words that repeat and themes. We are asking God to open his Word to us while we read. When we think of the Holy Spirit being a seal of our inheritance, do we see that theme reappear later in this chapter?

READING

Read through the rest of the first chapter of Ephesians and see if you can find a recurring word and/or theme that has to do with the Holy Spirit. GO!

Did you find it? Check verse 17. That's right! It's a part of our memory verse passage! Now see the connection?

THE HOLY SPIRIT

The SPIRIT, who earlier in verses 13 and 14 was referred to as the SEAL and DEPOSIT guaranteeing our inheritance, is referred to as the Spirit of WISDOM and REVELATION—the way to know Christ better. Also, this Spirit—the Holy Spirit—in verse 18 is enlightening our hearts to know what?

- the HOPE to which we were called

- the RICHES of his glorious INHERITANCE in his holy people (that's you and me!)

- the incomparably GREAT POWER for us who believe

I keep asking that the God of our Lord Jesus Christ, the glorious Father, may give you the Spirit of wisdom and revelation, so that you may know him better. I pray that the eyes of your heart may be enlightened in order that you may know the hope to which he has called you, the riches of his glorious inheritance in his holy people — Ephesians 1:17-18

> **TODAY'S BIBLE STUDY TOOL**
>
> **The Holy Spirit.** Jesus explained the role of the Holy Spirit in a believer's life:
>
> But when he, the Spirit of truth, comes, he will guide you into all the truth. He will not speak on his own; he will speak only what he hears, and he will tell you what is yet to come. – John 16:13

So, through persistent prayer, (keep asking!) the Holy Spirit will give me hope, as he teaches me about who God is and the incomparably great power God has for me in Christ!

12. So, what have we learned about the Holy Spirit's role?

13. What is my role, according to the passage?

14. According to the passage of scripture, what does Paul do daily to increase the Ephesians' understanding of Christ?

This triangle diagram is to help you visualize who you are without the Holy Spirit (top), who the Holy Spirit is (middle) and who you are when the Holy Spirit fills your life (bottom).

Now, let's dig into Christ's incomparably great power for us who believe! What do verses 19 and 20 say about it?

> … and his incomparably great power for us who believe. That power is the same as the mighty strength he exerted when he raised Christ from the dead and seated him at his right hand in the heavenly realms — Ephesians 1:19-20

CROSS REFERENCE

Let's cross reference! I wanted to find out more about the power that raised Jesus from the dead. So, I quickly did a word study in my Bible app. I searched for the phrase "raised Jesus." What did I find? What can you find?

Acts 4:10 – Then know this, you and all the people of Israel: it is by the name of Jesus Christ of Nazareth, whom you crucified but whom God raised from the dead, that this man stands before you healed. (The resurrection power of Jesus heals the crippled.)

Acts 13:32 – 'We tell you the good news: what God promised our ancestors he has fulfilled for us, their children, by raising up Jesus. (God's good news and the promises to generations are fulfilled by the resurrection of Jesus. Our children—even our unborn children—have hope, because of the resurrection!)

Romans 8:9-11 – You, however, are not in the realm of the flesh but are in the realm of the Spirit, if indeed the Spirit of God lives in you. And if anyone does not have the Spirit of Christ, they do not belong to Christ. But if Christ is in you, then even though your body is subject to death because of sin, the Spirit gives life because of righteousness. And if the Spirit of him who raised Jesus from the dead is living in you, he who raised Christ from the dead will also give life to your mortal bodies because of his Spirit who lives in you. (The Spirit raised Christ from the dead. The Spirit lives in you. The Spirit + You = LIFE and RESURRECTION!)

POWERHOUSE WORD STUDY CHALLENGE

We are only scratching the surface on the Holy Spirit. If you want to dig in more and be blessed, do this challenge. For an extra blessing, call an accountability partner and discuss these passages together!

TODAY'S BIBLE STUDY TOOL	Look in the concordance in your Bible, on the Bible app on your phone, or use your computer to search for a good Bible study site like biblegateway.com. Once there, look up the key word "Spirit" in the program. Use your Bible to read the passages where Holy Spirit or Spirit (with a capital "S") are mentioned in the New Testament. If you don't have a device or a concordance handy, here are some verses to look up:
Word Study. Dig deeper into the meaning of a word by seeing what other scriptures have to say about it.	

Matt 3:11	Luke 11:11-13	John 20:21-23	Acts 7:51	Romans 14:17
Matt 28:19	John 14:15-18	Acts 1:8	Acts 8:14-17	1 Cor 6:19
Mark 13:11	John 14:26	Acts 2	Acts 19:1-7	1 Cor 12:3
Luke 3:22	John 15:26	Acts 4:23-32	Romans 5:5	Eph 4:30

BRINGING IT HOME

How do you talk to your children or others around you about the role of the Holy Spirit? When they hear Spirit do they think "spirit" or emotionalism or do they think third person of the Trinity? Do you teach your children about the Holy Spirit at all? It should be as frequent as asking them if they brushed their teeth before bed. We want our children to seek the Spirit of God, even before going to Google or trying to figure things out on their own. Create an atmosphere in the home where it's "normal" to speak of the Spirit of God and to understand the Spirit of God.

Do you find yourself speaking negative and faithless words when the going gets tough, or do you teach others to pray for wisdom, revelation, and power?

Do you need the power of the resurrection of Jesus Christ to raise your attitude from the dead today?

QUESTIONING

PRAYER

As believers, prayer is a time to seek the face of God. It is not merely a religious activity to get points with the Lord. Prayer is a time to hear what the Lord wants to tell you, but also it is a time when you can ask him questions. Specifically, the Lord reveals himself to us through his Word, so as you combine asking the Holy Spirit for revelation and spiritual understanding while reading God's Word, you will have exponential results! Do not try to just pray for revelation without studying God's Word. A believer needs both prayer and the Word to properly hear from the Lord. This is where we can take him questions about what he is saying in his Word and know that he will teach us by his Spirit. The Holy Spirit leads us into all truth. There may even be things the Lord wants to teach you that you do not know to ask for. This is why we pray for revelation and wisdom by the power of the Holy Spirit. "Lord, teach me to pray. Fill me with your Spirit. Give me revelation so that I can know your will and know you better. Open your Word to me, Lord." Ephesians 1:17 says that the goal of receiving revelation from the Father is to know him better. According to HELPS™ Word-studies, this word "knowledge" in the Greek is epígnōsis. It means,

"'knowledge gained through first-hand relationship' – properly, 'contact-knowledge' that is appropriate ('apt, fitting') to first-hand, experiential knowing. This is defined by the individual context.'"

So, as we seek the Lord in prayer, while studying Ephesians, and when we ask for revelation by his Spirit, we can expect to experience God himself. We can expect that the Lord will give us insight, hope, direction and wisdom to know how to pray and to understand his nature and character better through his Word. The more we know the character of God, the more we grow in our faith. So, let us start with this attitude of seeking God for revelation in his Word today.

Today's prayer is adapted from Ephesians 1:17-21.

Father,

Thank you for teaching me about your son Jesus through your Word. Today, give me the Spirit of wisdom and revelation, so that I can know Jesus better! Open the eyes of my heart, in order that I may know the hope to which you have called me. As I study your Word, speak to me. Direct me by your Spirit. Take away my fear of your Word, and remove everything blocking me from studying your Word on a regular basis. Forgive me for years of neglecting your Word and hearing from you. Forgive me for putting other idols before you and prioritizing less important things in my schedule while not putting my time with you in a place of importance. Give me a hunger for your Word, and direct me as I ask questions about what I read today. Fill me with hope in the riches of your glorious inheritance for your holy people and your incomparably great power for me! This is the same power that raised Christ from the dead. Raise me up today to overcome the flesh that wants to hold me back from the victory of Christ and from the faith that will grow, as I read your Word. Fill me with your Spirit, your power, and your gifting.

In Jesus' name, Amen.

Spend time worshiping the Lord today!

Here is a short verse to add to our memorization. Take time to copy it down and put it up somewhere in your home where you can focus on it and memorize it. Put it on your bathroom mirror, tape it above your kitchen sink, or maybe somewhere at your workplace.

MEMORY VERSE

[8] For it is by grace you have been saved, through faith – and this is not from yourselves, it is the gift of God – [9] not by works, so that no one can boast. [10] For we are God's handiwork, created in Christ Jesus to do good works, which God prepared in advance for us to do. — Ephesians 2:8-10

READING

Grab your Bible and prayerfully read Ephesians Chapter 2. Make sure to use a pen to underline recurring words or even write notes in the margins.

ASK QUESTIONS

Little questions. Easy questions. Hard questions. Short questions. Long questions!

This week, we will be focusing on asking our own questions about the scripture we are reading! In the margin beside a verse, please write any and all questions you may have about it. Make it a goal to ask God as many as you can.

Sometimes, it's easy to just read on auto-pilot in order to say we have read our Bible for the day. But, by the power of the Spirit, feel free to ask questions! There are 22 verses in this chapter. Can you write down 22 questions? One for each verse? Yes? No? Maybe so?

In the blank space below, write down any questions that come to your mind as you are reading Ephesians Chapter 2. The point in doing this is to have a conversation with God about what he is saying here. Make no assumptions. Allow the Holy Spirit to lead you. We are going to dig into one of my own personal questions from this activity later this week, to learn how to find answers!

KEY WORD SEARCH

Now that you have your questions written down, use the chart below to write the words you see more than once. Be sure to count any pronouns that refer to your word, too. It is not necessary to look for articles and conjunctions (a, the, and, to, with, etc.).

Only use Ephesians 2:1-10 for this activity. I put an example below. To make it easier, write the word down and then put a tally mark for each time you see it.

Word	#	Word	#
transgressions			

After discovering the high-frequency words, do you see a theme throughout this passage? Take time to pray about this.

Jesus,

I see that there are certain words jumping out at me when I read this passage. Please give me wisdom to see what you want me to see in it. Speak to me by your Spirit.

Amen.

TODAY'S BIBLE STUDY TOOL

Key Word Search. Repeated words or phrases are clues as to what the author is trying to convey. They are KEY to the text.

When we set aside our assumptions and approach the Word with open hearts and minds, asking God questions as we read, the Lord gives insight, fresh perspective and spiritual wisdom. The idea of fresh perspective takes me back to Scrabble nights with my family members over the holidays. Sometimes, after staring at the board for 5 minutes, I need someone to turn the board around, so I can see it from a different angle. When looking at the puzzle from a different angle, I have a big "ah-ha" moment and see where I can fit my collection of odd consonant letters into the crossword for 40 points. In the same way, when God turns our paradigm on its head, our new spiritual perspective — or revelation — changes everything.

I don't know about you, but when I used to read Ephesians 2, sometimes my eyes glazed over a bit. This is Christianity 101, after all, and when we read in our flesh, a familiarity can set in. But, when I started to ask God for revelation, his Spirit gently directed me to notice how Paul lists transgression and sin as two different words in Ephesians 2:1. That seems a bit redundant, unless they actually mean two different things. Also, the phrase "dead in transgression" is in the text twice within a couple of sentences. So, we know that this phrase is important for us to understand. We need to ask for revelation from God on this and do some research!

So, I used my Bible Hub app and looked up the Greek meaning for transgression. My eyes were opened to a spiritual truth! The word transgression in the Greek is paráptōma. The first part of the word para means beside. So, according to the Helps Word Studies, paráptōma means to fall away after being close-beside, i.e. a lapse (deviation) from the truth; an error, "slip up"; wrong doing that can be (relatively) unconscious, "non-deliberate." This is not a picture of someone who is malicious. Transgression refers to a state of being in spiritual death without even knowing it.

A great example of trangression happened this week with our oldest son (who suggested this story be used when I read this to him — thanks, Ellis!) He is a very "in the moment" kind of guy — a hard worker and very busy with sports, school, friends and his job. But if he is with someone, he is always present and focused on having fun! However, this wonderful character attribute of being "present" also makes it difficult for him to "change mental gears" and think about things he is not focused on at the moment. Over the past few days, his father and I have asked him to do simple things and he just plain forgets. As he was running out the door the other day to go to a friend's house, I told him to take the trash outside. He walked right past the bags in his excitement to get out the door with his friend. Finally, this morning, I called him to ask him to check a special short video message I sent to him. He forgot because he was getting ready for school when I called from my commute. When I picked him up from ball practice after school, we had a talk about it. I was a bit frustrated, but not angry. I knew he could sense my frustration.

He kept saying, "Mom, I really don't mean it. I just literally forget."

I persisted, "I think if it's something you really cared about, you would do it. You never forget to take your basketball gear to school for games."

"Actually, Mom, I have forgotten before. It's not that I don't care. I just get side-tracked."

I told him that I understood, but something had to change. "It's borderline sin to continue to not obey us over and over again, because you get side-tracked. You need to obey right away, as soon as we give you the job, so you won't forget." I continued in my mom lecture, trying to use a grace-filled tone. "God gives you parents for a reason. When you learn to obey us right away, you learn to obey God when you hear his voice. When you practice ignoring us, it's easy to learn to also ignore God when he speaks."

"I understand, Mom. I'll try to obey right away next time."

He's a good kid. Really great! But, still, as a good kid, he commits transgressions — just like I do. He is doing wrong without realizing it. His humility was the key in this conversation. He was willing to admit he was wrong, to apologize and to promise to make the change. But, if he had been defensive and acted like I was crazy for talking to him about his need to change, that would have taken the conversation to a whole new level, if you know what I mean.

Many people approach our Father God in a defensive posture. Instead of admitting their need, and accepting the grace that comes from his lavish love through the death of his perfect son Jesus, they insist that nothing is wrong and they are doing just fine. If you are a parent, you can imagine how that feels to God.

Now let's look at the word sin. How is the meaning for sin different than transgression? The word for sin is hamartía, according to Helps Word studies. It means "no-share ("no part of"); loss (forfeiture) because of not hitting the target; sin (missing the mark)." In this case, the word sin comes from an ancient archery term for missing the target. If you are missing the target, you at least are trying to hit it, right? So, people who sin, may try to hit perfection, but they fall short and they are aware of it (different than transgression).

Let's take Adam and Eve as examples of these two different ways to fall short of God's glory. When Eve, who was perfect in every way, was tempted by the devil, she was deceived by what she thought was good. She wasn't weakened by a fallen nature. She was spiritually alive. Her intention was not to disobey God, but to do what was best and to understand God's intentions. Even so, she still transgressed God's law, with the serpent twisting God's truth to bring about her spiritual death. He appealed to her emotions, her curiosity and her desire for knowledge and doing what was right and acceptable. In this way, she transgressed without realizing what was actually happening. Adam, on the other hand, knew exactly what he was doing. 1 Timothy 2:13 says, "Adam was not deceived, but the woman being deceived, fell into transgression." Adam forfeited his spiritual life with God, in order to follow Eve. He fell short of perfection and knew it. Romans 5:1-21 actually says that sin entered the world through Adam, not Eve. What was Adam's sin? He knew God's standard and intentionally decided to take another path, which he thought was better. So, he was aiming for what he thought was the best, but missed the target altogether.

This is an important concept to remember, as we go forward in the study. No matter how much people want to be positive, do what is right, and feel good, the sinful nature prevents them from living a perfect life of righteousness that God requires of us. We all commit both transgression and sin and fall short of the glory of God. For example, in a basketball game, even if a player hustles and has a great shot, no matter how good he is, if he still misses a basket, he won't get the points.

However, most people see themselves as working towards good, peace and the betterment of the world, resisting the idea that they are living in transgression and sin — words that would imply otherwise. But in reality, because the wages or payment for sin (including transgression) is death (see Romans 6:23), even those who are trying to do good need an intervention — an atonement — on their behalf. We like to justify our motives, intentions and actions, but in reality the only justification for our sin is faith in Jesus' death to take our punishment for sin and Jesus' resurrection to raise us up from spiritual death to spiritual life.

Have you ever experienced resistance to the gospel when sharing Jesus with someone? They may say, "I'm not a bad person!" Even if you were full of love, did they quickly put up the defenses when you invited them to church or even mentioned Jesus? One of the most important people in my life said this to me and mocked me, when I lovingly told her about Jesus. Why do people get offended and push back at the word sin? Is it personal pride? Perhaps they need to understand the grace, love, mercy and forgiveness of God, no matter what they have done.

Ephesians 2:1-2 says, "….As for you, you were dead in your transgressions and sins, in which you used to live when you followed the ways of this world and of the ruler of the kingdom of the air, the spirit who is now at work in those who are disobedient." The Greek word for "live" in verse 2 is peripateó, which means to walk around, in a complete circuit, or going full circle.

This describes the state of the world right now. Everyone is running in circles, like a hamster on a wheel, trying to live their best life now, but falling short, no matter how much success they appear to gain in the natural realm. Many are aware of the emptiness of the pursuit, as they run the race, wondering "Have I seen this part of the path before? I feel like I have passed this tree a thousand times. When am I going to feel like all my efforts are paying off? When will I find inner peace?" What is the answer to this futility, according to Ephesians 2:4-5? God's rich mercy in Christ! "But because of his great love for us, God, who is rich in mercy, made us alive with Christ even when we were dead in transgressions – it is by grace you have been saved."

WHAT ABOUT OTHER SPIRITUAL EXPERIENCES?

All this seeking for spiritual truth, personal growth and fulfillment leads many down deceptive spiritual paths. Honestly, I have listened to those who testify to the inner fear, deep pain and emptiness that they sought to escape without Jesus Christ by following New Age teaching. In their seemingly peace-filled experiences, they found power and enough supernatural bread crumbs to continue following the trail of promise in eastern religion and the occult.

They weren't submitted to Christ's forgiveness and were spiritually dead, so where do they and others without Christ get all that energy to do great things like philanthropy for the poor of the world, or have spiritual experiences in the New Age and other religions? (See how we ask questions, when we read the Bible?!) Let's look back at our passage for the answer. We can see it in the phrase "…when you followed the ways of this world and of the ruler of the kingdom of the air, the spirit who is now at work in those who are disobedient." When people follow the ways of the world, they are under the authority of the devil, the ruler of the kingdom of the air and so they have a type of power. It actually says that this spirit is now at work in those who are disobedient.

The original language for disobedience refers to willful unbelief. The breakdown of the word in the Greek actually means to be unpersuaded. God's Spirit brings conviction of truth. To reject his Spirit is to harden your heart in unbelief. Those who do this may or may not be in the occult or false religion. They may just be walking their own path, idolizing self, deciding that there has to be another way other than submitting to Christ. A person who persists in walking in his or her own way, rejecting the call and voice of the Lord to repent, is also working under the influence of the enemy, according to this passage.

The word "work" in the Greek — the same word where we get the word energy — is energéō and means, according to Helps Word Study, to "energize, working in a situation which brings it from one stage (point) to the next, like an electrical current energizing a wire, bringing it to a shining light bulb." So, someone may be having actual supernatural experiences, but the power is not good or from God. It is from our enemy, Satan.

Ultimately, any path that does not lead to God through faith in Christ and does not resolve the issue of our sin and spiritual death cannot lead to heaven or bring spiritual life. It may bring a spiritual experience, or a feeling of enlightenment, because the devil works in those who are not a part of God's kingdom to keep them in deception. 2 Corinthians 11:13-15 says that Satan masquerades as an angel of light. So, their experience gives them false hope, leading them away from the true hope that comes through the sacrifice of Jesus Christ, who takes away sin.

But, to those who humble themselves and stop resisting the call of the Spirit of God, hope is on the horizon! Praise be to God, justice and mercy meet at the cross. 2 Corinthians 5:20-21 (NKJV) says, "Now then, we are ambassadors for Christ, as though God were pleading through us: we implore *you* on Christ's behalf, be reconciled to God. For He made Him who knew no sin *to be* sin for us, that we might become the righteousness of God in Him." We are called to bring this hope to those living under the enemy's deception.

The beautiful, joyous news is that Jesus took on our sin and gave us his righteousness! He takes our pain, fear, failings, curses, and missteps and trades us for his healing, confidence, successes, blessings and hope. And this is just the beginning of our hope! As we learned in the last two days of study, we are filled with the true energy from God — his Holy Spirit who seals us — not a false spirit or the spirit of this age. We know we are God's children, by the Spirit he gives us.

BRINGING IT HOME

Do a word search with your children, or with a friend. Have them help you look for patterns and themes in scripture.

Spend time asking your spouse, child, or friend what questions they have about the passage. See if they can help you really think deeply about it.

OPENED EYES

PRAYER

In our search to discover who we are in Christ, we need to have spiritual eyes to see. Start with prayer! Ask the Lord to speak to your heart. Take time to pray these things for your friends, family, and those who are far from Christ.

Father,

In Jesus' name, fill me with the Spirit of wisdom and revelation that I may know you better. Reveal yourself to me in your Word. Open the eyes of my heart to know the hope of my calling in you and to understand my glorious inheritance in your holy people. Help me to know you in a personal and intimate way, not just to know facts and stories about you. I pray that you will transform my life with your power, through your Spirit. Lord, if I am closed to you in any way, show me so I can repent. Bring people into my life who know you in a deep way through your Spirit, and who can pray for me and join me in this journey of drawing close to you, Lord.

In Jesus' name, Amen!

MEMORY VERSE

[8] For it is by grace you have been saved, through faith – and this is not from yourselves, it is the gift of God – [9] not by works, so that no one can boast. [10] For we are God's handiwork, created in Christ Jesus to do good works, which God prepared in advance for us to do. — Ephesians 2:8-10

Take time to meditate on the truth in our new memory verse. Write it down, if that helps you memorize it. Say it aloud. Meditate on the meaning of the passage, to help yourself understand it better.

Let's look back at what you did yesterday. What word seemed to jump out at you more than any other word? Did you find the phrase that is repeated twice in the first 10 verses, once in verse 5 and once in verse 8? That phrase has a word in it that is found three times in the first verses of Ephesians 2. Go back and look. Write the word below.

Now, use your Bible dictionary to look up the meaning of this word and write it down in the space above.

CROSS REFERENCE

The apostle Paul had a great affinity for understanding this topic of grace and expressing it in all his letters. He experienced the true grace of God at his conversion. Let's have a cross reference day and read about the conversion experience of the apostle Paul.

Here we have the story of Saul being transformed to Paul. Saul, the persecutor, became Paul, the persecuted. Saul was on a mission, which he thought was from God. He believed he was acting in a way to advance the work of God, by snuffing out the people who followed what he called a cult or "The Way." All of his "works," all of the "good" he tried to do for God, did not make him right with God. It could not. He was opposing the true work of the Lord. However, when Jesus appeared to him on the road to Damascus, he was knocked on the ground and taught the difference between physical sight and spiritual sight. It was at this time that the invisible heavenly realms were opened to Saul and he truly saw who Jesus was.

AUTHOR BACKGROUND

Open your Bible and read Acts 9:1-31 to understand what God did to change the heart of the murderous Christ-hater Saul into the sacrificial Christ-lover Apostle Paul. Mark anything in the scriptures that refers to Saul's sight or eyes. Star anything that refers to his transformation after encountering and seeing Christ.

SEEING WITH SPIRITUAL EYES

Let's make some connections between Paul's story and Ephesians! Look at our first memory verse, Ephesians 1:17-23, located in Week One, Day 1. What is it that the apostle Paul is teaching us to pray every day? What are we asking God to do for us?

> **TODAY'S BIBLE STUDY TOOL**
>
> **Seeing with Spiritual Eyes.** Remember Paul's prayer for the Ephesians? "I pray that the eyes of your heart may be enlightened." This is a powerful prayer and that is why we are praying it daily for ourselves.

PRAYER

Holy Spirit, give me eyes to see and ears to hear what you are saying to me, in Jesus' name!

HERE IS PAUL'S CONNECTION

When Saul (Paul) met Christ, his religious reality, all that he performed as an act of valor for God, all that his physical eyes were set on, and everything by which he measured himself grew dim and dark. Jesus, who had already ascended to heaven in his physical resurrected body, appeared before him and spoke to him. Somehow, in that moment, NOT BECAUSE OF ANYTHING THAT SAUL HAD DONE, Saul heard and saw God for the first time in his life!!! He was gripped with fear and had questions, I am sure. But what did Jesus do? Jesus blinded Saul. He took away his physical sight to teach him to see and hear spiritually. Jesus taught Saul that there is an entire heavenly realm that he had been unaware of. Was Jesus punishing him? Not at all! Jesus was answering the prayers of the saints of God who were huddled in prayer in Damascus and all over the territory. Jesus brought Saul to salvation through the pure power of GRACE.

What happened next? Saul spent the next three days in darkness, praying, repenting, and waiting on the Lord, in a similar way to what the disciples did in the upper room. He sought the Lord on a spiritual level, with complete humility and openness. When Ananias came to lay hands on him, Saul was confronted with a man who was probably at the top of his list to capture and take back to Jerusalem. Here was a man that he intended to dominate, mock, and "teach a lesson." Instead, Ananias delivered Saul a word of knowledge through the Holy Spirit's wisdom and taught him a lesson about the power of God to open a man's spiritual and physical eyes.

In this way, Saul was introduced to the power of Christ in the heavenly realms. He found that knowing Christ and having a brief glimpse of him on the road of his salvation was just the beginning of an unsearchable road of spiritual riches. It was a foretaste. God rescued Saul, who didn't deserve it, and transformed him in an instant by his Spirit. This is the power of the Gospel.

What about his companions? There were other men on a mission to arrest Christians with him. Saul realized something incredible about them. Their eyes were not opened. They did NOT see Jesus. They just heard the sound of his voice. They had been granted power to hear, but not to see. Jesus was beginning to teach this new believer, even from his conversion, that it is by the Spirit of God that we can see Christ for who he is, in all his glory. Otherwise, we may miss him altogether and just hear some words. Were those men converted? It would be difficult to imagine otherwise. I guess we won't know till heaven.

MY QUESTIONS FOR YOU TODAY ARE:

15. When you pray for God to open the eyes of your heart, do you really expect him to give you spiritual wisdom and spiritual sight?

16. Are you carrying a heavy load of trying to obtain your salvation in this physical realm?

17. Even if you know all the answers in your head, where is your faith?

18. Are you trying to understand Jesus and his words with your mind and not with your spirit, nor with the help of the Spirit of wisdom and understanding?

PRAYER

Take time to pray and ask God to forgive you for trying to have a spiritual relationship with him in a fleshly way (a way that you can physically understand or see or hear or figure out). Ask him to open your eyes to see him clearly. Ask the Lord to help you see that your salvation is by faith in Christ alone. Ask him to fill you with his Spirit, the way he filled Saul when Ananias laid hands on him. Ask for the scales on your eyes to be removed, so you can see God's plan for you afresh!

BRINGING IT HOME

What is your testimony of grace? When did God remove the scales from your eyes? Share it with a friend today. Be sure to not just go to the safe zone—people who believe. Remember, the world needs to know your story!

GRACE & WORKS

PRAYER

Start your study today with our memory verse prayer from Ephesians 1:17-23.

Glorious Father,

In Jesus' name, fill my heart and mind with your Spirit of wisdom and revelation that I may know you deeply today. I want to have spiritual eyes to see spiritual truths and to know the hope to which I have been called! I want to understand your grace and my response to it.

In Jesus' name, Amen!

Now take time to meditate on the truth in our new memory verse for this week.

MEMORY VERSE

[8] For it is by grace you have been saved, through faith – and this is not from yourselves, it is the gift of God – [9] not by works, so that no one can boast. [10] For we are God's handiwork, created in Christ Jesus to do good works, which God prepared in advance for us to do. — Ephesians 2:8-10

READING

Open your Bible and read Ephesians 2:1-9.

SAVED BY GRACE TO DO GOOD WORKS

Have you ever been in a situation where you saw cliques that kept people out? Have you ever tried to break into a clique and been frustrated? Over the fourteen years I served as a youth leader, I noticed the good and bad things about cliques. Cliques seem to be groups of friends that are very close and have a lot of history together. People in a group have things in common and they experience life together. This is not a bad thing. Being bonded in a tight friend group is an amazing experience, unless you are on the outside looking in. Those on the outside feel alone and rejected, not quite sure of how to "break in" with the people who seem to be having fun. Belonging is always the goal.

In Christianity, there seem to be many theological cliques. You've got the Calvinists, the Arminians, the Reformed theologians, and the Pentecostals or Charismatics. The problem is that many people who are Christians spend more time in the church trying to fit into one of these groups instead of trying to understand what the scriptures say. Christians will argue with each other over whether the Christian life is about grace or works, predestination or free will, when all of these things are in the Bible. But, if you follow a man or woman instead of just studying the Word of God yourself, you may find yourself in the right "clique" but leaving out some of the truth of God that is very important for understanding God and knowing him.

Our memory verse for the past three days, Ephesians 2:8-10, shows us the word "works" twice. One is in a negative phrase and one is in a positive phrase. Ephesians 2:8-9 speaks about our salvation. The saving work of Jesus Christ to rescue our souls from hell is by _____ through _____.

19. According to our memory verse, is there a place for works in a believer's life?

20. What is the purpose of works, and where does our ability to do works come from?

21. What is not the purpose of works?

When Paul found Christ, by grace through faith, his boasting ended. He was a very proud and boastful man before his conversion and his pride was based on what he did for God. However, when he came to Christ, he found himself just as focused, if not more than before, on doing good works for God—not to earn his salvation, but because the power of the Spirit helped him to obey Christ and walk in the Spirit, not in the flesh, living for God instead of for himself.

In American culture, Christians many times put faith in Christ, but hear the gospel shared with sayings like, "Prayer doesn't make you a Christian," or "Going to church doesn't make you a Christian," or "Giving doesn't make you a Christian," or "Doing good things doesn't make you a Christian." They say that Christians don't need to pray or go to church or give or do good things. Are these statements true? Yes or no? Please use Ephesians to test these statements, not your mind.

According to Ephesians 2:8-9, the answer is YES, BUT. Our ability to be saved from sin has nothing to do with our works, our ability to obey God's law, or our ability to be good. This truth, in verses 8 and 9, needs balanced with the truth in the second part of the passage. The first truth is only half of the story of redemption.

Yes, we are saved by grace through faith, but that doesn't mean we are saved to live for ourselves. We are saved from living for ourselves. The oppressed who have lived in guilt and perfectionism now know that there is no need for guilt or perfectionism. Perfectionism is a form of fear. We live in freedom through Christ and his Spirit. We are destined to live for God. We put no confidence in the flesh or our abilities, which is WHY we pray, WHY we go to church, WHY we read our Bibles, WHY we give money to help others instead of hoarding it for ourselves, and WHY we do good works.

It is by the Spirit and the will of God that the believer in Jesus can be transformed by his grace into a humble person who has no illusion that their own good deeds will get them to heaven, but will humbly offer every part of their life and their good works as a sacrifice of praise and an offering to the Lord, who prepared these things in advance for them to do.

CROSS REFERENCE

Spend time jumping over to James. Read James Chapter 2. Pray for the Holy Spirit to give you wisdom and revelation to understand what he is saying in these two different parts of the New Testament. Don't be afraid of these two passages that may seem to disagree at first. Pray for insight. They actually agree! Write down some notes about how each of these passages support each other.

BRINGING IT HOME

How do you explain salvation to someone? When was the last time you shared the gospel? When was the last time you shared the gospel with your children or discussed the truth of salvation in detail with them? Are you sharing the full gospel, so they know they are saved by grace and that God now has a job for them to do by the power of his Spirit?

Today's challenge is to ask God to give you an opportunity to share with a friend or family member God's great grace AND his great commissioning for those who believe in him!

CHOOSING TO WALK IN VICTORY

PRAYER

Before you get started in your study today, pray Paul's prayer for greater revelation from the Holy Spirit. Remember that you need eyes opened by the Holy Spirit to understand God's Word.

Glorious Father,

Fill me with the Spirit of wisdom and revelation that I may know you better. Enlighten the eyes of my heart that I may know the hope to which I am called.

In Jesus' name, Amen.

Take time to ask God to teach you how the truth we are learning applies to situations you are struggling with in life right now.

MEMORY VERSE

[8] For it is by grace you have been saved, through faith – and this is not from yourselves, it is the gift of God – [9] not by works, so that no one can boast. [10] For we are God's handiwork, created in Christ Jesus to do good works, which God prepared in advance for us to do. — Ephesians 2:8-10

This week we are learning about our position in Christ, what that means, and how God the Father has given him authority over everything in heaven and earth. Today we will answer the hard questions like, "Why is there still pain and suffering in our lives?" and, "Why does it seem we can't get victory even when we are seated with Christ in the heavenly realms?"

We'll look in Chapter 2 for some answers. But first, let's look for contrasts (opposites) in this passage between the kingdom of the enemy and the kingdom of God.

Ephesians 2:1-10

[1] As for you, you were dead in your transgressions and sins, [2] in which you used to live when you followed the ways of this world and of the ruler of the kingdom of the air, the spirit who is now at work in those who are disobedient. [3] All of us also lived among them at one time, gratifying the cravings of our flesh and following its desires and thoughts. Like the rest, we were by nature deserving of wrath. [4] But because of his great love for us, God, who is rich in mercy, [5] made us alive with Christ even when we were dead in transgressions – it is by grace you have been saved. [6] And God raised us up with Christ and seated us with him in the heavenly realms in Christ Jesus, [7] in order that in the coming ages he might show the

incomparable riches of his grace, expressed in his kindness to us in Christ Jesus. [8] For it is by grace you have been saved, through faith – and this is not from yourselves, it is the gift of God – [9] not by works, so that no one can boast. [10] For we are God's handiwork, created in Christ Jesus to do good works, which God prepared in advance for us to do.

CONTRASTS/OPPOSITES

At the beginning of Chapter 2, Paul contrasts the condition of the Ephesians before Christ with their condition after Christ. We can see the opposing kingdoms. Let's make two columns, one for the kingdom of the enemy and one for the kingdom of God. Using scripture verses from Ephesians 2:1-10, find a contrasting statement for each of the scripture points listed below. Note: There may not be an exact match for each of the statements.

KINGDOM of the ENEMY		KINGDOM of GOD
Dead in transgression and sin	vs	Example: Alive with Christ (verse 5)
Followed the ways of this world and of the ruler of the kingdom of the air	vs	_____
Gratifying the cravings of our flesh and following its desires and thoughts	vs	_____
Deserving of wrath	vs	_____
Disobedient	vs	_____

BEFORE AND AFTER

> **TODAY'S BIBLE STUDY TOOL**
>
> **Contrasts.** Look for contrasts (opposites) in the passage of scripture. The author will use this tool to help paint a more vivid picture for the reader.

More contrasts! Before salvation we lived to reap death. Notice something interesting? Chapter 2:1 says, "… you were dead in your transgressions and sins, …" but the conclusion of the statement is found in verse 2. It says, "… in which you used to live ..." So, we were DEAD in our LIVING. We were spiritually dead because we were not raised with Christ, but we were alive in the world in our mortal bodies. This is another contrast! It is possible for a person to be spiritually dead WHILE physically living. This is because SIN = DEATH. When I was a youth leader, once I was teaching in an outreach situation. Students were asking lots of questions and this topic of spiritual death came up. One non-Christian girl was offended that the Bible says she is spiritually dead, because she felt very alive. A believer who was sitting beside her, wanting her to not feel bad, said, "Whoa, whoa. No one is saying that people who don't believe in Jesus are spiritually dead."

"Actually," I said, "The Bible really says that when Adam and Eve sinned, they died spiritually and they were separated from God. The whole human race came under the curse of death. But, that doesn't mean your soul, mind and emotions are dead. You feel very alive, because your person is alive. Have you considered that there is something inside of you that may need to come alive, but you don't know it, because you haven't experienced it yet? But, here's the good news. Jesus died to take the punishment for your sin and my sin upon himself. When you trust in Christ, your spirit will come alive and the Holy Spirit will come to live inside of you."

It is sad that the majority of people have not experienced the resurrection power of Jesus Christ and a relationship with God. We are called as believers to bring the life of Christ to others, not to appease emotions. How can someone know they need Jesus, if they never are made aware of what they are missing?

Romans 10:14-15

How, then, can they call on the one they have not believed in? And how can they believe in the one of whom they have not heard? And how can they hear without someone preaching to them? And how can anyone preach unless they are sent? As it is written: 'How beautiful are the feet of those who bring good news!'

Before we knew Christ, we were not elevated to the heavenly realms, nor were we rescued. Outside of Christ, what has authority over a person?

List the things that had authority over you before you came to Christ.

If we are rescued and alive in Christ, why do we still struggle after we come to Christ? Because the authority of sin is still something we can live under when we OBEY IT! We also are under the influence of other people who sin against us. We need the grace of God to deal with the hurts and stress that come from being sinned against.

Look back at verse 2:

> … followed the ways of this world and of the ruler of the kingdom of the air, the spirit who is now at work in those who are disobedient.

CROSS REFERENCE

Let's find a cross reference for this! The opposite of disobey is obey. Romans 6:16 says,

> … you are slaves of the one you obey – whether you are slaves to sin, which leads to death, or to obedience, which leads to righteousness.

Turn in your Bible to read all of Romans 6, so that you can have a deeper understanding of overcoming our slavery to sin.

As I was reading this through several times, the Holy Spirit grabbed hold of me with verses 13 and 14.

> Do not offer any part of yourself to sin as an instrument of wickedness, but rather offer yourselves to God as those who have been brought from death to life; and offer every part of yourself to him as an instrument of righteousness. For sin shall no longer be your master, because you are not under the law, but under grace. – Romans 6:13-14

Do not offer yourself. Do not offer yourself. It rings loud and clear. We have a choice, when we are in Christ, to choose which master we want to obey. Whenever we offer ourselves to a master in authority over us, that master has control over us. If your marriage or another relationship is piled up with years of unforgiveness and bitterness, that unforgiveness and bitterness will control you. They will become your master, until you cannot obey Christ's truth about love and forgiveness, because you are controlled by another master, the master of unforgiveness and bitterness. No matter how much you say you love Jesus with your mouth, your actions show who your master really is. OUCH. OUCHIE. OUCH.

I went for a walk after writing this. God brought this verse to my mind,

> Whoever claims to love God yet hates a brother or sister is a liar. For whoever does not love their brother and sister, whom they have seen, cannot love God, whom they have not seen. – 1 John 4:20

In your relationships, is God your master? Are you offering every part of yourself to him as an instrument of righteousness? Let's get practical here. One way you may struggle in your relationships involves how you want to be in control. If you live your life trying to control everything because you don't like surprises, and everything has to be in order, and the only way you can be happy is if you know that your schedule is in order for the day and that everyone will be doing what they are supposed to be doing, how are you able to walk in faith? "Faith is the substance of things hoped for and the evidence of things not seen." (Hebrews 11:1 KJV) Fear and anxiety may be gripping your life so that you can't be kind to someone who messes up your plan. Fear and control may be your master, instead of Christ.

Is rebellion your master? When you know your spouse has a need, do you recoil from helping him, just because he asks you for help? Is lying your master? Do you stretch the truth or exaggerate to keep people happy?

Fill in the blank with what is pressing on you. Pray this aloud.

I will not offer myself to _____ in Jesus' name!

Which master will you submit to? Even if you FEEL powerless, remember that you have the Holy Spirit with whom you have been sealed. You ARE NOT powerless!

In Romans 6, we see an appeal by Paul. He says count yourselves dead to sin and alive to God in Christ Jesus. We live in this world. The world has physical authority over us. Sin can have authority over us, if we obey it. Other people's sins against us can enslave us if we choose to walk in resentment. We become a slave to whomever we submit. The good news is that in Christ, we are elevated to the heavenly realms where Jesus has authority over every power and dominion. This includes, but is not limited to, the power that any sin, fear, or addiction may have over us!

Remember that this is not a call to live a life full of guilt. We are free in Christ. But, the freedom is not just freedom from guilt; it is freedom and power to overcome whatever we are wrestling with in our lives. This victory is won as we remember Paul's prayer for the Ephesians. Remember, there is hope:

I pray that the eyes of your heart may be enlightened in order that you may know the hope to which he has called you ...
— Ephesians 1:18

So, how do we pray about a sin or condition we may be stuck in? We need to dethrone its power and the authority that WE HAVE GIVEN IT, through prayer and the power of the Holy Spirit.

PRAYER FOR VICTORY OVER SIN

Pray for Jesus to teach you more about how to be victorious by walking in faith. The gospel is power! Jesus, give me power to live in hope.

Ask the Lord to bring to your mind something in your life that has power over you because you have given it authority. Here is a prayer of repentance for victory in Christ.

Father,

I struggle with _____. I know that I have given my heart over to this sin/weakness. It controls me, Father, because I have walked in it for so long. In the name of Jesus, please forgive me for this sin of _____. I renounce _____ in my life and declare that this stronghold has no power over me, because I belong to Jesus Christ, and I am raised to life with him and seated with him in the heavenly realms. I am forgiven.

God, forgive me for loving my sin. Help me to hate it, and teach me, by your Spirit, to put to death the deeds of the flesh. I pray for your Spirit to anoint me to walk by faith. Jesus is my master and I will serve him. Fill me with your Holy Spirit and power to walk in the Spirit and not in slavery to these things that have bound me.

You are the Chain Breaker, Jesus. You have power and life, and that life dwells in me. I praise you for your victory in my life, and I command the devil to leave me, in Jesus' name. Satan, your authority and power over me in this area are broken, and all authority I gave to you by following your temptations is broken off by the power of the name of Jesus Christ, my Lord! Be gone, in Jesus' name! Father God, fill me (and my marriage, relationships, family, home, etc.) with your Holy Spirit. May I walk in your power and freedom.

In Jesus' name, Amen!

BRINGING IT HOME

Do you truly believe that God can work in your family? Are you an example of the power of God's mercy and grace to them? Do they understand that through Christ they can be victorious over sin, too?

Spend time praying for your family. Ask the Lord how you can teach them to obey Christ without having a house of rules that are impossible to keep. Ask the Lord how to encourage obedience, in light of Christ's love, in an atmosphere of grace.

SEATED IN THE HEAVENLY REALMS

PRAYER

Let's start our study off by asking the Holy Spirit to fill our hearts and minds with spiritual understanding so we can see, hear and know Christ!

Remembering what God did in the apostle Paul's life and his conversion, and what he has done in your life, recite our memory verse for the week.

MEMORY VERSE

[8] For it is by grace you have been saved, through faith – and this is not from yourselves, it is the gift of God – [9] not by works, so that no one can boast. [10] For we are God's handiwork, created in Christ Jesus to do good works, which God prepared in advance for us to do. — Ephesians 2:8-10

READING

Ephesians 2:1-10

[1] As for you, you were dead in your transgressions and sins, [2] in which you used to live when you followed the ways of this world and of the ruler of the kingdom of the air, the spirit who is now at work in those who are disobedient. [3] All of us also lived among them at one time, gratifying the cravings of our flesh and following its desires and thoughts. Like the rest, we were by nature deserving of wrath. [4] But because of his great love for us, God, who is rich in mercy, [5] made us alive with Christ even when we were dead in transgressions – it is by grace you have been saved. [6] And God raised us up with Christ and seated us with him in the heavenly realms in Christ Jesus, [7] in order that in the coming ages he might show the incomparable riches of his grace, expressed in his kindness to us in Christ Jesus. [8] For it is by grace you have been saved, through faith – and this is not from yourselves, it is the gift of God – [9] not by works, so that no one can boast. [10] For we are God's handiwork, created in Christ Jesus to do good works, which God prepared in advance for us to do.

ASK QUESTIONS

Remember that we took time to ask God questions and write them down about this passage? Time to unpack this! Again, when we study the Word, we need to be led by the Holy Spirit! As I read over this passage again and again, and after reading the first chapter of Ephesians, I noticed that the phrase "heavenly realms" was a recurring theme. I felt a bit stuck on this. It sounds so lovely, doesn't it? Is it just a spiritual or religious phrase? I wanted to learn more about this. I will walk you through how I discovered more about it in the Word of God. If you have a burning question, hopefully this will teach you how to search for the answer, too.

WORD STUDY
Heavenly Realms

Hmmm. Verse 6 says, "And God raised us up with Christ and has seated us with him in the heavenly realms." So I prayed, "Lord, what is the significance of this? Why does Paul seem to repeat this phrase through the first two chapters? Where else is this phrase in the Bible so I can understand it better in context?"

> **TODAY'S BIBLE STUDY TOOL**
>
> **Word Study.** Dig deeper into the meaning of a word or phrase by seeing what other scriptures have to say about it.

So, the Holy Spirit led me to do a word study and find where else this phrase appears in the Bible. I did a quick search on my Bible app and this is what I found and screen shot from my phone! Ephesians is the ONLY book in the Bible that features this phrase. I double-checked.

Now, this handy dandy screen shot reveals an interesting bird's-eye view of Paul's development of this spiritual truth in his letter. Let's break it down. Each of these points matches a verse that references "heavenly realms" in Ephesians.

22. Paul's first assertion is that we are blessed in the heavenly realms with spiritual blessings in Christ. (Eph 1:3)

23. Paul reveals that Christ is currently seated in the heavenly realms. This seems to refer to heaven. The angels told his disciples he ascended into heaven in Acts 2. (Eph 1:20)

24. We were raised up with Christ at his resurrection and seated with him in the heavenly realms in Christ Jesus. This asserts that our current spiritual position is in the heavenly realms with Christ. Obviously, we are not there physically, so this seems to imply that there is something that happens spiritually that we cannot physically discern with our senses. (Eph. 2:6)

25. Somewhere in the heavenly realms there are rulers and authorities, other than God and Christ, who need to understand God's manifold wisdom. God intends that WE the church be the example of his wisdom to these rulers. Could this be talking about angels? Thinking of the passage, "Even angels long to look into these things," (1 Peter 3:12) or could it also be referring to demons and the devil? If so, this changes the idea that the phrase "heavenly realms" is just speaking of where God's throne is in heaven. It is much more complex. (Eph 3:10)

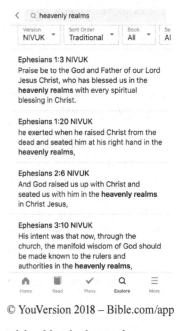

© YouVersion 2018 – Bible.com/app

26. The final passage that refers to the heavenly realms is Ephesians 6:12. This verse refers to a spiritual battle that we have—we are seated in the heavenly realms with Christ—against powers of this dark world and spiritual forces of evil. Clearly, the phrase "heavenly realms" is referring to a spiritual realm that is above and beyond the physical realm we live in. We have ascertained that Christ is currently in the heavenly realms and we are seated there with him, spiritually. We are blessed in the heavenly realms and we are an example to spiritual beings there. However, this scripture says that we battle evil powers and authority in the heavenly realms. This means it is an actual place and not literary imagery. Paul seems to be making an appeal through the book of Ephesians for his audience—which includes us now—to understand not only how our relationship with Jesus works, but also how incredibly powerful and wealthy we are in Christ in the spiritual realm, beyond what we can see with our physical eyes. Our faith is in Christ and his victory over our sin, death and the devil. Our secure position is in his lap and by grace! (Eph. 6:12)

HOW MANY HEAVENLY REALMS?

The word "realms" is plural, so we can assume that there is more than one realm in the heavens. In 2 Corinthians 12:2 Paul relates a story about a man who has an incredible experience where he is taken up to the third heaven. He says, "I know a man in Christ who fourteen years ago was caught up to the third heaven. Whether it was in the body or out of the body I do not know—God knows." So, here we see that Paul refers to a place called the third heaven. Revelation 12:7-12 gives the account of when the devil was thrown out of heaven, but we are told in Ephesians that we battle against him in the heavenly realms. So, the battle with the enemy happens in the realms beneath the third heaven. Perhaps these are the physical realms, such as the universe or the physical sky. This last sentence is just a possibility I am offering for thinking over. Let's look this up by doing a word study on heavenly realms!

GREEK WORD STUDY

Finally, let's use one more Bible study tool to get the meaning of the original Greek phrase "heavenly realms"—a Greek Lexicon. This is a search I did on Google. It suggests this website: biblehub.com. Go ahead! Look it up!

Here are some helpful directions:

Step 1 – After you open the app, click on the Bible icon.

Step 2 - In the search bar, type in the verse with the word you are studying. For our purposes today, type in Ephesians 6:12.

Step 3 - When the single verse comes up, you should see a list of the verse in many different versions. You can enjoy reading the different translations at this point, before going to the next step. If you want to read the verse in context, click on the version you are looking at. If you want to skip that step and get straight to the Greek, go to Step 4. *(If you are viewing the entire chapter, to isolate the verse you are wanting to look up, click on the verse number on your screen. That is a link to see the verse by itself, so you can open up the Greek or Hebrew chart.)*

Step 4 - Click on the initials GRK to find the Greek chart that graphs the verse. If your phone app isn't showing the GRK or HEB, you may click on INT for interlinear. This will also help you access a chart. *(If you are looking up an Old Testament verse, it will offer you the HEB abbreviation.)*

Step 5 - When the chart opens, the verse reads from top to bottom. Find the word you are looking for. There is a hyperlinked number in the far-left column. This is the Strong's Concordance "reference" number for the Greek word.

Step 6 - When you click on the Greek reference number—it's like the Dewey decimal system for Greek—it will open up the definition, and give you access to all the concordance information on that word. *(As the website updates, this information may change.)*

In the Thayer's Greek Lexicon, we see that the heavenly realms described in Ephesians 6:12 are the lower heavens, or the heavens of the clouds. This means that the devil's power is not in heaven—as we imagine heaven—where God's throne is encircled with cherubim and where our loved ones, in Christ, who have gone before us now live, but in a lower heavenly realm—a spiritual area above us, but not the highest heavens. The devil and this area of the heavenlies is also referred to in Ephesians 2:1-3 where he is called the ruler of the kingdom of the air.

> As for you, you were dead in your transgressions and sins, in which you used to live when you followed the ways of this world and of the ruler of the kingdom of the air, the spirit who is now at work in those who are disobedient. All of us also lived among them at one time, gratifying the cravings of our flesh and following its desires and thoughts. Like the rest, we were by nature deserving of wrath. – Ephesians 2:1-3

The word "kingdom" in verse 2 actually means authority in the Greek. This is the LIMITED authority the devil has over the earth. In the same verse, the apostle Paul describes Satan as the ruler over that kingdom (or authority) of the air. So many times when evil things happen including, but not limited to, tragedy, sickness, natural disaster, government corruption and other human distress, our tendency is to ask why God would allow such a thing or even DO such a thing. Our human response to pain and distress shows a very limited understanding of the state of the world we live in and the concept

Thayer's Greek Lexicon
STRONGS NT 2032: ἐπουράνιος

ἐπουράνιος, ἐπουράνιον (οὐρανός), properly, existing in or above heaven, heavenly;

1. **existing in heaven**: ὁ πατὴρ ἐπουράνιος, i. e. God, Matthew 18:35 Rec. (Θεοί, Θεός, Homer, Odyssey 17, 484; Iliad 6, 131, etc.; 3Macc. 6:28 3Macc. 7:6); οἱ ἐπουράνιοι the heavenly beings, the inhabitants of heaven, (Lucian, dial. deor. 4, 3; of the gods, in Theocritus, 25, 5): of angels, in opposition to ἐπιγειοι and καταχθονιοι, Philippians 2:10; Ignat. ad Trall. 9 [ET], (cf. Polycarp, ad Philipp. 2 [ET]); σώματα, the bodies of the stars (which the apostle, according to the universal ancient conception, seems to have regarded as animate (cf. Lightfoot on Colossians, p. 376; Gfrorer, Philo etc. 2te Aufl., p. 349f; Siegfried, Philo von Alex., p. 306; yet cf. Meyer ed. Heinrici, at the passage), cf. Job 38:7; Enoch 18:14ff) and of the angels, 1 Corinthians 15:40; ἡ βασιλεία ἡ ἐπουράνιος (on which see p. 97), 2 Timothy 4:18; substantially the same as ἡ πατρίς ἡ ἐπουράνιος Hebrews 11:16 and Ἰερουσαλήμ ἐπουρανίω, Hebrews 12:22; κλῆσις, a calling made (by God) in heaven, Hebrews 3:1 (others would include a reference to its end as well as to its origin; cf. Lunem. at the passage), cf. Philippians 3:14 (Lightfoot cites Philo, plant. Noe § 6) The neut. τὰ ἐπουράνια denotes (cf. Winers Grammar, § 34, 2)

a. the things that take place in heaven, i. e. the purposes of God to grant salvation to men through the death of Christ: John 3:12 (see ἐπίγειος).

b. the heavenly regions, i. e. heaven itself, the abode of God and angels: Ephesians 1:3, 20 (where Lachmann text οὐρανοῖς); Ephesians 2:6; Ephesians 3:10; the lower heavens, or the heaven of the clouds, Ephesians 6:12 (cf. B. D. American edition, under the word).

c. the heavenly temple or sanctuary: Hebrews 8:5; Hebrews 9:23.

2. **of heavenly origin and nature**: 1 Corinthians 15:48f (opposite to χοϊκός); ἡ δωρεά ἡ ἐπουράνιος. Hebrews 6:4.

of authority. There is so much that the devil is responsible for that gets blamed on God. Is this to say that God is not sovereign? No, but in God's sovereignty, when he created Lucifer and the other angelic beings, they were given power and authority that are eternal—which is why the devil and his angels or any other eternal soul separated from God will spend eternity in hell. God will hold Lucifer accountable for misused power and authority. When the devil rebelled and took a third of the heavenly hosts with him, he was still an angelic being—just a fallen one. He was thrown out of the highest heavens and is now using his power to battle against God from his lower position. This is how he came to deceive Adam and Eve and every other person who has fallen into his lies and destruction. This is why he is, as it says in Ephesians 2:2, "the spirit at work in those who are disobedient."

We, however, are no longer under his authority, unless we put ourselves under it through unconfessed, unrepented sin. Ephesians 4:25-27 says that by sinning in our anger, and letting the sun go down on our anger, we can give the devil a foothold. A believer in Jesus or an unbeliever can also give him or herself up to the devil's power through participating in the occult. (Later in our study we will read in Acts 19 about how the unbelieving Ephesians had done this and how they had a decision to make when they became believers.) Remember, we are under the authority of the one whom we obey. That is one of the reasons Paul spends so much time encouraging the Ephesians not to live like they used to live when they were truly under the power of the devil. We now are seated above the devil with Christ in heavenly realms. The Spirit we are to submit to is the Holy Spirit with whom we are sealed for the day of redemption! In fact, Ephesians 3:10 says that we are an example to the devil and other spiritual beings that God is in control and that he is here to bring unity to all people in heaven and on earth! Ephesians 1:7-10 tells us about God's mystery unfolding in Christ:

> In him we have redemption through his blood, the forgiveness of sins, in accordance with the riches of God's grace that he lavished on us. With all wisdom and understanding, he made known to us the mystery of his will according to his good pleasure, which he purposed in Christ, to be put into effect when the times reach their fulfilment – to bring unity to all things in heaven and on earth under Christ. – Ephesians 1:7-10

We are God's calling card to show the devil that his kingdom and authority are limited and that Jesus is here to destroy them and establish an eternal, unshakable kingdom in the hearts of believers! The devil is defeated by the cross of Jesus. Jesus is now seated:

> … far above all rule and authority, power and dominion, and every name that is invoked, not only in the present age but also in the one to come. And God placed all things under his feet and appointed him to be head over everything for the church, which is his body, the fullness of him who fills everything in every way. – Ephesians 1:21-23

Jesus is our head. We are in him, seated in heavenly realms. God has so many good things for us to do in Christ. We were created in Christ Jesus to do good works, which God prepared in advance for us to do. Let's not live in defeat! Live in the power of Christ in the heavenly realms.

Ladies, the more we dig into Ephesians, the more we see that Paul isn't randomly writing long run-on sentences to a group of toga-wearing believers. There is a theme. Did Paul intend this himself or is the Holy Spirit weaving this together in a way that Paul couldn't possibly plan out in advance?

What is really incredible to me in this day's passage is all that this implies. When God started to open this truth about the heavenly realms to me, I was simply overwhelmed! How many times am I so consumed by the things of this world, even the real and pressing things, that I do not realize that I am missing the true reality in Christ?

There is an old saying that goes, "They are too heavenly minded for earthly good." I am not sure I know anyone that fits this description. I believe there are more believers who are too earthly minded for any heavenly good.

BRINGING IT HOME

We are more than the day-to-day. We are more than car-pool, dinner-making, boss-pleasing, diaper-changing, friend-finding, fault-forgiving, husband-loving women.

Everything we do on earth touches heaven and everything in Christ is available to us to touch our lives. Shucks, we are seated in heaven. I just can't wrap my brain around this.

Guess our homework should be to pray for wisdom and understanding! Spend time on your knees today asking God to help you grasp the power of your position in Christ and all that this means for you today.

THE OPPOSITE OF DEFEAT IS VICTORY
BATTLE IN THE HEAVENLY REALMS

PRAYER

God,

I keep coming before you every day asking for greater revelation of your Son Jesus Christ. Glorious Father, give me the Spirit of wisdom and revelation, so that I may know you better. Open the eyes of my heart—insert family and friends here, too—that I may be enlightened and know the hope to which you have called me, the riches of your glorious inheritance in the saints and your incomparably great power for us who believe. That power is like the working of your mighty strength, which you exerted in Christ when you raised him from the dead and seated him at your right hand in the heavenly realms, far above all rule and authority, power and dominion and every title that can be given not only in the present age but also in the one to come. Thank you, God, that you placed all things under the feet of Jesus and appointed him to be head over everything for the church, which is his body, the fullness of him who fills everything in every way.

In Jesus' name, AMEN!

MEMORY VERSE

[8] For it is by grace you have been saved, through faith – and this is not from yourselves, it is the gift of God – [9] not by works, so that no one can boast. [10] For we are God's handiwork, created in Christ Jesus to do good works, which God prepared in advance for us to do. — Ephesians 2:8-10

FINDING OPPOSITES

Today, we are going to study the complete opposites we find in Ephesians Chapters 1 and 2. Let's start with Paul's prayer—he says that Jesus is seated in the heavenly realms in a position. Where is that position? Go back and find the verse and write it here.

Okay. It says FAR ABOVE, so, we have to assume the opposite of above is what? Below, right? Jesus is above what? Let's list the positions here that are BELOW Christ's authority. Beside each item, use your Bible Hub app or go to biblehub.com to look up Ephesians 1:21-23.

- After you open the app, click on the Bible icon.

- Enter the verse(s) in the search bar.

- Click on the initials GRK to find the Greek definitions. Click on the hyperlinked Strong's Concordance number for each word you want to study. Since we are in the New Testament we will be looking up the original Greek. If we were in the Old Testament we would be looking up the original in Hebrew.

- Write the information you find beside the following listed words.

- After you find the Greek information, write down examples of this in real life or spiritually.

FAR ABOVE

all rule: Example: The Greek for "rule" means highest position of power – kings or magistrates

all authority: _____

all power: _____

all dominion: _____

every title: _____

the Church: _____

So, our first opposites are the words "above" and "below." This is important, because when it comes to authority, whoever is above has the final say in a situation. I want you to think about a situation that you feel powerless in, maybe a marriage, school, a job, finances, fear, health, a child, an addiction, thoughts, dreams that haunt you, disappointment, or anything else. When you are seated in Christ, you are seated OPPOSITE of powerlessness! You are seated in power ABOVE the things that SEEM to have authority or dominion in your life. These are opposing forces. They are opposites.

Does anything have authority in our lives besides Christ? Let's read this again and think REALLY hard. Can you think of anything, good or bad, that has authority in your life? Scripture says,

> Far above all rule and authority, power and dominion and every title that can be given in the present age and in the one to come. – Ephesians 1:21

So, do other things have authority outside of Christ? Yes. Yes, they do. And THAT is why you struggle! Christ's authority and power is ABOVE all other authority. So, you may battle against fear, nightmares, financial turmoil, a situation with a child, anger, your past. All these things have authority over you. Persecuted Christians are oppressed by godless governments that have authority over them. The EXCITING truth is this—there is an Opposing Power that is OVER the "lower" authority or power or lordship in your life!

The diagram displays in picture form what we have been studying in Ephesians about the heavenly realms. There are things that are over us in the natural realm and in the spiritual realm. However, we are spiritually seated in Christ, so ultimately Christ is over all of the other authorities in our lives. Over the next several weeks, our study will dig in deeper

ABOVE ALL POWERS

SPHERE 3

The heavenly realms where Jesus is enthroned victorious above all rulers, authorities, sin, dominion and power! We are seated here spiritually and this is where we live by faith in Christ and find victory. Faith is the victory that overcomes the world!

God the Father. Jesus. Angels. The saints of God who have gone before us. We are here spiritually in Christ.

SPHERE 2

The heavenly realms where the prince of the power of the air has authority. We battle against him through Christ alone. Jesus has overcome him. Sometimes, he will harass us and exert authority over us, because of things that happen in the flesh, such as unforgiveness. We are not subject to him if we are living in the realm of Christ and submitting to God. Paul talks about giving Satan a foothold. This is the realm where we struggle against him.

The prince of the power of the air. Demons. Angels of God battle against the enemy in this realm.

SPHERE 1

We live in this world in the "tents" of our bodies or "flesh." We live under governmental and relational authority in this world, but still, Christ's authority is above all of this. It says in Romans 6:16 that we are slaves to the one we obey, whether slaves to sin, which leads to death, or to obedience, which leads to righteousness.

Us. Sin. Life. Death. Sickness. Family Authority. Work. Finances. Government.

BELOW
where we feel the battle

to see the nuts and bolts of how this reality affects our lives and the sin we can't overcome, marriage struggles, harassment from the devil, and trials in the greater world.

THE OPPOSITE OF DEFEAT IS VICTORY

Looking at the diagram, you can see that we are living in the physical realm in our bodies, but our spiritual reality is in Christ.

> Since, then, you have been raised with Christ, set your hearts on things above, where Christ is, seated at the right hand of God. Set your minds on things above, not on earthly things. For you died, and your life is now hidden with Christ in God. When Christ, who is your life, appears, then you also will appear with him in glory. – Colossians 3:1-4

We are tucked safely in Christ and Christ is seated at the right hand of God. Nothing can shake that position, so don't let the enemy of your soul lie to you.

Following is an example of a persecuted believer who truly experienced the brainwashing power of the lies of the enemy in prison. There was no sugar coating to hide that the brainwashing was taking place, but it was still effective. Our enemy the devil will consistently use people or institutions in authority over us to influence us and try to discourage us. On a side note—imagine how much more the enemy can influence us through music, the media and entertainment industry. We also can submit ourselves unknowingly to deceptive suggestions, when we watch movies or read blogs without any discretion. We can find ourselves participants in our own faith crisis. That is why I seek God about what movies my family watches and pray for protection and discernment when I am reading articles and books. Now back to the story!

Ravi Zacharias, famous Bible apologist and founder of RZIM, has shared the testimony of his friend Hien Pham in many of his talks. He also shared his story in the book Walking from East to West: God in the Shadows, 2006. It is a perfect example of how our lives are seated with God in heavenly realms, over every other power and authority. We may be in a battle for our minds and very lives, but we cannot forget who is in control. Ravi was ministering to the U.S. troops in Vietnam during the war. He befriended Hien Pham, an energetic, young Christian. Hien worked as a translator with the American forces, and was of immense help both to them and to the missionaries. Hien and Ravi traveled the length of the country and became very close friends before Ravi returned home. He never knew what happened to his old friend after he left. But, seventeen years later, Ravi received a telephone call. "Brother Ravi?" the man asked. Immediately, he recognized Hien's voice. Hein recounted his harrowing story of being captured by the Viet Cong after the fall of Vietnam to the communists. He was thrown into prison and treated as an American spy, being forced to endure terrible living conditions and intense brainwashing. His captors took away his Bible and forbade him to speak in English. This is the account from Ravi's book:

> "There is no such thing as God," came the refrain from his captors, day after hellish day.

> The day finally came when Hien wondered, "Maybe they are right. Maybe there is no such thing as God." As he thought back to some of my sermons and the shared blessings we had enjoyed, he wondered if perhaps I had been deluded too. That night he went to bed muttering to himself, "I'm through with God. When I wake up in the morning, no more God, no more prayer."

> The new day dawned and the commanding officer of the prison barked out the assignments for the day. Hien was to clean the latrines. He cringed when he heard it. It was the ultimate form of indignity for the prisoners … Hien spent the entire day in those inhospitable surroundings.

> His final task was to empty the trash cans which were filled with soiled toilet paper. All day long he labored with reminders to himself—"No God today." But as his work was coming to an end, something in the last trash can happened to catch his eye. It was a piece of paper with printed type. As Hien grew closer, he saw it was in English. … He looked around to make sure nobody was watching. (Then) He hastily rinsed off the filth and tucked the paper into his pocket.

> That night, after everyone had fallen asleep, he carefully took out his flashlight and removed the still damp paper from his pocket. In the upper right-hand corner of the page were the words "Romans 8."

The Bible.

Hien, in a state of shock, began reading.

"And we know that in all things God works for the good of those who love him, who have been called according to his purpose ... Who shall separate us from the love of Christ?"

Hien began crying. Of all the scripture verses he had known, these were the ones he needed to hear, and now they had come back to him. "Lord," he realized, "you would not let me out of your reach even for one day.'"

As it were, there was an official in the camp who was using a Bible as toilet paper. So Hien asked the commander if he could clean the latrines regularly. Each day he picked up a portion of scripture, cleaned it off, and added it to his collection of nightly reading.

This soul-stirring story of Hein Pham reveals to us the unstoppable power of God in a believer's life. Hein was not only seated in prison in Vietnam, he was seated with Christ in heavenly realms! In the physical realm, he was under the authority, lies, and oppression of a communist commander who arrogantly was using the Word of God as toilet paper. The commander was forcing Christians in prison to listen to Marx and daily anti-Christian readings and discouraging them with horrible tasks. I am sure the enemy thought his oppressive battle plan was working. But, remember that God is not mocked. God turned this commanding officer's profane use of scripture as toilet paper into a weapon to deliver his son Hein Pham out of the darkness of depression. The Word of God will not return to him void. When we look at our situation with physical eyes, we may be disappointed and even lose faith. We need to continue to ask for the Spirit of wisdom and revelation to see Jesus revealed and to know the hope to which we have been called!

BRINGING IT HOME

Ask God to reveal Christ to you through his Holy Spirit. This should be a daily task. Only through the Spirit of God can we have spiritual eyes to see what we cannot see with our physical eyes—our position in heavenly realms.

THE STORY OF THE EPHESIANS

PRAYER

Before we start our reading, take time to pray our memory verse from Week One.

[17] I keep asking that the God of our Lord Jesus Christ, the glorious Father, may give you the Spirit of wisdom and revelation, so that you may know him better. [18] I pray that the eyes of your heart may be enlightened in order that you may know the hope to which he has called you, the riches of his glorious inheritance in his holy people, [19] and his incomparably great power for us who believe. That power is the same as the mighty strength [20] he exerted when he raised Christ from the dead and seated him at his right hand in the heavenly realms, [21] far above all rule and authority, power and dominion, and every name that is invoked, not only in the present age but also in the one to come. [22] And God placed all things under his feet and appointed him to be head over everything for the church, [23] which is his body, the fullness of him who fills everything in every way. — Ephesians 1:17-23

Now check to see how you are doing with this memory verse from Week Two. Can you quote it from memory yet?

MEMORY VERSE

[8] For it is by grace you have been saved, through faith – and this is not from yourselves, it is the gift of God – [9] not by works, so that no one can boast. [10] For we are God's handiwork, created in Christ Jesus to do good works, which God prepared in advance for us to do. — Ephesians 2:8-10

READING

Who were the Ephesians? Today, since Paul is talking to the Ephesians about their past, let's read about them in Acts Chapter 19. Please go to your Bible and enjoy this lively reading. I promise it won't disappoint! Get ready to read about people getting baptized in the Holy Spirit and cured with handkerchief prayers, a demonized man beating up seven men, sorcery scrolls being burnt, and riots breaking out! Wow, oh Wow! What a chapter and what a CRAZY experience Paul had in Ephesus!

HISTORICAL BACKGROUND

Once you have read Acts Chapter 19, you might want to read more about Ephesus on wikipedia.com or in a Bible encyclopedia to learn the historical background of the city. Then continue on with the lesson.

> **TODAY'S BIBLE STUDY TOOL**
>
> **Historical Background.** A layman could look up Ephesus on Wikipedia.com or an online Bible encyclopedia. These are tools anyone can use.

PAUL MEETS THE EPHESIANS

Acts Chapter 19 puts meat on the bones of our understanding of Paul's experience with the Ephesians. Can you see their humanity as you read their conversion stories and peek into their persecution and personal deliverances? Let's get started in discussing what happens at the beginning of Paul's first interaction with the people who will become part of the Ephesus church. When Paul meets the twelve Ephesian men along the road, what does he ask them? He doesn't assume that these friendly men who seem to love God actually have a saving faith in Christ. He knows that if they are truly believers, they will have the Holy Spirit. They show no sign of knowing about the Holy Spirit, so he asks more questions. If you didn't read it, you definitely want to open up your Bible and read! Notice how Paul doesn't just assume that they know Jesus. Paul's mission is to genuinely sow the seeds of the kingdom. He is trying to see how to best minister to the people he meets on the road by digging in and asking them questions. He finds out that they had been baptized by John the Baptist, himself! This demonstrates they were sorry for their sins. John the Baptist was the way maker that paved the way for these men to know Christ. But, Paul wanted them to know the salvation of Jesus Christ and the POWER of the Holy Spirit. Why? Because faith in Christ is the only way for them to have a real relationship with God.

How many times do you assume things about people you meet or know? Making assumptions about others is a big relationship mistake! We don't know the hearts of other people and we should never make judgments without asking Spirit-led questions. Do you assume they know God because they are nice people, go to church, and do good things? They may appear to be Christians; they may even mention praying for others. But, you never know! Many men and women in our culture "know about" God and "pray to the man upstairs." They may even be genuinely sorry for their sins, like these men on the road. Do you know their testimonies? Are you intentional like Paul to dig deeper to learn how to minister to someone, or do you stay in the "safe zone"? The safe zone for you may be the danger zone for your friends! If they are not saved by Jesus Christ, and you never dig deeper in a loving way to have real-life discussions with them, they may be under the false assumption that they are going to heaven, when they are not.

Go back and re-read Acts 19:1-7, so we can look at Paul's first conversation with men from Ephesus more in-depth.

When I was in my early twenties and leading a small youth group, a young Russian girl began attending, when invited by a friend. She had difficulty with English and being a new immigrant to the country, she was excited to make some friends at youth group. One day, when I was particularly exhausted after a late youth meeting, I learned that she needed a ride home. I intended to drop her off and quickly leave. However, the lovely mother came outside and eagerly invited me in for tea. I inwardly sighed, tired from my long day, ventured up the steps and through the front door. We stayed in the living room, politely discussing life. I kept feeling a weight inside that I really needed to ask some questions to find out where the mother was spiritually. Reluctantly, knowing this would extend my stay, I probed in. With the young girl translating, I discovered that the woman was very religious. She excitedly jumped up and found a picture of a patron saint that she prayed to regularly. She was so sweet and eager that I sought the Lord in prayer. "How do I bridge this gap? How do I tell her about Jesus?" God immediately showed me to use what she had in her hands.

"Oh. The saints of God are so blessed!" I told her. She nodded in agreement and excitement, as her daughter translated. "They knew God so very well. They had an understanding of his son Jesus that was so special. If they were alive today, do you know what I think they would want to tell you?" Her eyes were full of wonder, as she sat on the edge of her couch in the dimly lit living room. "They would want you to know how to come be with them in heaven and how to have a relationship with Jesus, the way they did. See, each of the true saints understood that our sin separates us from God. Our sin makes us a foreigner to God. But, his son Jesus died on the cross for our sin to remove what is keeping us from becoming a citizen of heaven." We talked about how she was a natural born citizen of Russia living in the United States. "God wants you to become a citizen of heaven through his son Jesus Christ. Praying to other saints did not make the saints of God holy or right with God. Trusting in Jesus Christ did. They are there in heaven right now, because of Jesus. They would want you to know Christ the way they did." This darling woman, with tears in her eyes, became a citizen of heaven that night. She moved from the realm of being religious to someone who had a relationship with God through Jesus Christ. I was able to give them a Russian Bible that my husband had acquired in Russia when he went on a mission trip there as a teen.

In the same way, Paul is very intentional and deliberate when he leads these men to Christ. He uses their connection to John the Baptist to bridge the gap to Jesus, instead of telling them that their baptism under John didn't count—it counted for repentance, but now they need redemption—he gave them a positive direction. "John told the people to believe on Jesus!" What are the other two things he does with them? We already discussed that he makes sure that they know about the Holy Spirit. But, he also asks if they have been baptized into Christ. Let me stop here and throw this out there. There are many men and women in evangelical circles with misconceptions about baptism. I have encountered many different statements on what people think it is and it isn't. An encounter would go something like this:

"When did you get baptized?"

"Oh, I haven't been baptized, yet. I am just not sure I am ready."

"Hmmmm. Let me explain baptism to you a little bit. It's not something you have to be ready for; it's a command of Christ."

Person in a bit of a defensive posture, "Well, I just feel uncomfortable in front of people and I don't think God would want me to be uncomfortable. I have to be ready."

Me, "I get what you're saying. I really do. I think a lot of people are given this idea that baptism is about how they feel. You can't be any more ready than you are at the moment of salvation. Christians are commanded to get baptized and you can't be any more of a Christian than you are at your first moment of faith. We are saved by grace through faith, not by works so no one can boast that she or he is more ready or more of a Christian than someone else. Also, just think of how Jesus hung on a cross of shame for you in public. The least we can do for our Savior is show our obedience with a public confession of faith. The Christian life is not about how comfortable we feel following Christ. Jesus said, 'Take up your cross and follow me.'"

Baptism is simply an act of obedience to Christ and a public confession of faith. Baptism has nothing to do with feelings. It has everything to do with truth and obedience.

- Truth. Jesus commanded that the apostles baptize the disciples they led to Christ. It is a command from the one with all authority in heaven and on earth. In Matthew 28:19-20 he says, "All authority in heaven and earth has been given to me. Therefore, go and make disciples of all nations, baptizing them in the name of the Father and of the Son and of the Holy Spirit and teaching them to obey all I have commanded you."

- Truth. In John 14:15 Jesus said, "If you love me, keep my commandments."

- Truth. In Romans 6:3-4 Paul says, "Or don't you know that all of us who were baptised into Christ Jesus were baptised into his death? We were therefore buried with him through baptism into death in order that, just as Christ was raised from the dead through the glory of the Father, we too may live a new life." Again, baptism is not a sign of super maturity. It's not something only really serious Christians do. It is through baptism that we are buried and resurrected with Christ. It is a faithful, pivotal moment for a believer who is being baptized into Christ.

- Truth. Baptism is not a party. It can be a party. But, it's not about who is there watching or how formal or informal the ceremony is. It is not about the traditions surrounding the event. It's about obedience to Christ and a heart of faith that is confessing Christ to the world. It is not about feelings. It's about faith and truth and position in Christ!

SEALED WITH THE HOLY SPIRIT?!

Now, remember that Paul teaches the Ephesians to walk in the power of the Spirit, which they were sealed with. This may be the very story he is referencing in his letter to the Ephesians. He may have thought back to when he met them on the road and dug deeper, only to find out they were completely unfamiliar with the Holy Spirit. He may remember how he placed his hands on them to receive the Holy Spirit and how they prophesied and spoke in tongues. This "deposit" would remind them in the future, when things got a bit rocky and they were doubting their faith, that yes, indeed, they were filled with the power of God.

QUESTIONS TO ANSWER

27. Did everything seem to be easy for Paul in Ephesus?

28. We see power being demonstrated, but we also see difficulty. What kind of assumptions have you made about the power of God and suffering? Do you think suffering is a sign of weakness or a lack of the blessing of God?

29. Have you prayed, like the Ephesians, to receive the Holy Spirit into your life? Have you prayed and been baptized in the name of Jesus?

30. Are you sharing the gospel with others, by asking them intentional questions that are led by the Holy Spirit?

31. Are you boldly proclaiming the truth of Christ, even in the midst of persecution?

LAYING ON OF HANDS

At the time of conversion, Paul immediately instructs the Ephesian men on how to receive the Holy Spirit. Why did Paul lay hands on them to receive the Holy Spirit? What does that mean? Remember Paul's story of his conversion? What did God instruct Ananias to do?

HISTORICAL BACKGROUND

In the Old Testament, the priests would lay their hands on a person to transfer the sin of the person to the animal being sacrificed in order to cover his sin. The husband was the spiritual priest of the family, who would take the sacrifice to the priest. It was a sign and a spiritual act of transference. Remember that things happen in the spiritual or heavenly realms that we cannot see with our physical eyes. We may or may not understand this spiritual principle, but in the New Testament, we see commands for the laying on of hands for the baptism of the Holy Spirit. We also see it in the commissioning of those in spiritual offices. Paul told Timothy to fan into flame the gift he received when Paul laid his hands on Timothy. We read in James that if someone is sick, they should call the elders of the church to come lay hands upon them, confess their sin and the prayer of faith would heal the sick person.

We don't see a detailed explanation in scripture of why God has us lay hands on people, but we see the precedent and we see the principle played out throughout the Old and New Testaments. Paul also warns the leaders of a church not to be too hasty to lay hands on a person to ordain him as an elder. He didn't want to see someone put into authority too quickly when he was not ready. I am elaborating on this a bit more here, because I think it is an under-taught subject in the body of Christ today. I am assuming that most people think of the laying on of hands as a way to show camaraderie and emotional support. However, we need to understand that it is a very spiritual command of God to, by faith, activate spiritual power and authority. It is not to be taken lightly, but it is also something we should not be afraid of. Dig deeper! If you would like to study this further, here are some references for the laying on of hands.

- Numbers 8:12; 27:18
- Leviticus 3:2,8; 4:15; 16:21
- Luke 4:40
- 1 Timothy 4:14; 5:22
- 2 Timothy 1:6
- Hebrews 6:2

BRINGING IT HOME

Do you assume things about where your children or friends are with God?

Do you ask them spiritual questions and engage them when there are teachable moments? Deuteronomy says to instruct our children in the Lord when we rise up and when we walk along the road.

Have you been baptized into Jesus?

GOD'S REAL INGREDIENTS, OR SUBSTITUTIONS?

PRAYER

Father God,

I ask in the name of Jesus that you would fill me with the Spirit of wisdom and revelation as I study your Word today. Give me spiritual eyes to see. Enlighten the eyes of my heart to know the hope to which I am called in Jesus Christ and the riches of my glorious inheritance in him.

Amen.

Spend time memorizing your Bible verse!

MEMORY VERSE

[8] For it is by grace you have been saved, through faith – and this is not from yourselves, it is the gift of God – [9] not by works, so that no one can boast. [10] For we are God's handiwork, created in Christ Jesus to do good works, which God prepared in advance for us to do. — Ephesians 2:8-10

READING

Today, read Acts Chapter 19 again. We will spend more time studying the backstory of the Ephesus church today.

HISTORICAL BACKGROUND
Sorcery and the Bible

There is a great fascination with sorcery and witchcraft in the world today. Even in school book fairs, students can find books on how to cast spells. Parents believe that this is all fantasy and fairy tale, but what does Acts Chapter 19 tell us about sorcery?

Let's read a portion of the storyline:

Acts 19:11-20

[11] God did extraordinary miracles through Paul, [12] so that even handkerchiefs and aprons that had touched him were taken to those who were ill, and their illnesses were cured and the evil spirits left them.

[13] Some Jews who went around driving out evil spirits tried to invoke the name of the Lord Jesus over those who were demon-possessed. They would say, 'In the name of the Jesus whom Paul preaches, I command you to come out.' [14] Seven sons of Sceva, a Jewish chief priest, were doing this. [15] One day the evil spirit answered them, 'Jesus I know, and Paul I know about, but who are you?' [16] Then the man who had the evil spirit jumped on them and overpowered them all. He gave them such a beating that they ran out of the house naked and bleeding.

[17] When this became known to the Jews and Greeks living in Ephesus, they were all seized with fear, and the name of the Lord Jesus was held in high honour. [18] Many of those who believed now came and openly confessed what they had done. [19] A number who had practised sorcery brought their scrolls together and burned them publicly. When they calculated the value of the scrolls, the total came to fifty thousand drachmas. [20] In this way the word of the Lord spread widely and grew in power.

Paul's whirlwind tour through Ephesus begins with laying hands on twelve men to receive the seal of the Holy Spirit with power. Shortly thereafter he performs extraordinary miracles. This makes me chuckle, because I think, "Wow, there are your average, every-day, garden-variety miracles; then there are your 'extraordinary' miracles. If Paul couldn't make it to the other side of town that day, but someone was dying, he would just pray over a handkerchief and the person it was taken to would be healed!" Notice what it says happened to those who were ill? Can you write down the two things here?

> **TODAY'S BIBLE STUDY TOOL**
>
> **Historical Background.** You can research the historical use of a word. This is also called cross-referencing. It will help you understand what the author knew about that word when he chose to use it in his writing.

If you wrote down that they were cured, you are correct. If you wrote down that evil spirits left sick people, you are also correct! That is a very big truth to notice. There are other places in the scriptures where Jesus healed people by casting evil spirits out of them. In some cases he would cast spirits out to heal people; in other passages he would speak to them to be healed. In all cases, he was doing what his Father in heaven told him to do. That is why it's important to be open to the leading and the voice of the Holy Spirit. A shocking truth discovered in this passage is that some sickness can be caused by the devil. So, as believers we need to keep this in mind when praying for the sick. I was recently healed of a debilitating hip pain that I suffered under for years. I know how to do spiritual warfare, but had never prayed for my hip using spiritual warfare. I was led by God, after hearing a teaching on warfare prayer, to pray against tormenting spirits that were attacking my hip. It may seem a bit sensationalistic, but after years of exercising, going to the doctor, getting physical therapy and taking pain pills, it was very real to me when God delivered me by kicking out the devil, and I praise Jesus for his faithfulness! I am so thankful for my salvation in Christ and his deliverance.

I was so dumbfounded when my healing happened so quickly when God led me to command a spirit of pain to leave my hip in Jesus' name. I couldn't believe it! Honestly, I became discouraged later when I shared the story of healing with many believers who doubted my story with questions like, "Did you change your activities?" or "Maybe your hip was out of place and it just went back?" I had honestly been to the doctor so many times and had my hips put back in place more times than I can count. It would only provide temporary help for a day. This deliverance was permanent and immediate. There are times—especially when I am doing something for the Lord—that the pain will start to creep back. I rebuke it in Jesus' name and it leaves again. The raised eyebrows and incredulous statements began to weaken my confidence that God had performed a miracle and deliverance. However, one day, God brought me encouragement.

After hearing my story at one of our Revealed Ministries conferences, a woman later told me her testimony:

"I was in two serious car accidents when I was younger. I had very serious back injuries from those. Then, my back broke in childbirth with my son. I was so incapacitated. It would often go out of place and leave me on the floor in excruciating pain when I was home alone with my three boys and my husband was at work. I couldn't do anything, including volunteer at church and in ministry like I used to. The pain was affecting my marriage. I prayed. I fasted. I prayed for healing. I was getting physical therapy. I went to a doctor and was waiting to be scheduled for back surgery when I came to the Revealed Conference. After the conference, I was praying about what I learned during the sessions and God led me to pray against a spirit of pain in my back. I commanded a spirit of pain to leave in Jesus' name and I was instantly healed. I don't need surgery anymore! I am now able to exercise and am getting physical therapy to strengthen the muscles that were weakened by all those years of inactivity. I am now able to be what I need to be for my family. I even went on a long hike and then a date with my husband in the same day without any pain. Every so often, I will feel it start to hurt again and I just remind the devil that I told him to leave in Jesus' name and he is not welcome back."

I have to tell you, this really encouraged me. I know that this story may sound a bit out there, but the Bible has many examples of taking authority over the enemy as Jesus did and as the Holy Spirit led believers to do in specific situations. Here is Acts 19 it clearly says, "God did extraordinary miracles through Paul, so that even handkerchiefs and aprons that had touched him were taken to those who were ill, and their illnesses were cured and the evil spirits left them." These testimonies are not meant to make you believe every sickness or injury is from evil spirits, but to show you that what was true in Paul's time, is still true today. When God reveals to us that the enemy is causing a sickness, we can have victory over the enemy and be healed. In fact, remember that scripture calls these types of healings extraordinary miracles. You may or may not need an extraordinary miracle. You may just need to stop sleeping in your recliner to help stop your back pain. Through prayer, God will reveal to you if your specific difficulty needs this type of spiritual warfare.

Remember, Paul wasn't obsessed with the devil. Paul was teaching people about Jesus and miracles followed him. Our focus should always be Jesus. We should not shy away from knowing the truth about spiritual warfare and we should not obsess about the devil. Our hearts should be fixed on Christ and our salvation. If God gives you a testimony, don't be afraid to give Jesus glory!

Similarly, in the city of Ephesus, these life-changing healings and deliverances from Satan's power caught the attention of some curious people who were wanting in on the action. The seven sons of Sceva, a Jewish priest, decided to try out the name of Jesus on a demonized man. There is no indication that the men were believers. In fact, they most likely were the obstinate Jews who opposed Paul in the synagogue and were "in competition" with him, so to speak. They had no idea that it's not just the name of Jesus that the devil must obey, but that the devil is only required to obey those who are walking in faith in the authority of Christ and are actually seated with Christ in heavenly realms. What did the demon say to the seven men?

This whole scene seems a bit crazy, but somehow, the idea of seven naked, bleeding men running from the house of a demonized man helped all the believers in Ephesus get really serious about their faith. I would imagine, and maybe you would too, that such a sensationalistic event would make people embarrassed about their faith and perhaps some would disown those crazy people who believe in evil spirits.

Can you see the social media threads now?

"I think that people now-a-days are really out of control with their religious beliefs."

"It's believers like this that give the name of Jesus a bad reputation."

"Thankfully, my church isn't like that. We are very traditional. Anyone who wants a nice calm church that is a relaxing experience can come on Sunday at 11 a.m."

"These guys just don't understand spiritual warfare."

Right. Those social media posts are a very American response. Most American believers seem to want to distance themselves from very biblical truths that may seem a bit crazy to the outside world. Mind you, this same world is absolutely obsessed with witchcraft movies and books, but shun teachings from scripture on related topics. However, when this happened in Ephesus, there was a rather supernatural effect. The reality of the spiritual realm and the power of Christ was now clear to the people. The Holy Spirit came over people in Ephesus and what happened?

Acts 19:17-20

When this became known to the Jews and Greeks living in Ephesus, they were all seized with fear, and the name of the Lord Jesus was held in high honour. Many of those who believed now came and openly confessed what they had done. A number who had practised sorcery brought their scrolls together and burned them publicly. When they calculated the value of the scrolls, the total came to fifty thousand drachmas. In this way the word of the Lord spread widely and grew in power.

- The Jews AND Greeks—people from all walks of life were seized with holy fear of God.

- Suddenly the name of Jesus was held in honor.

- Believers who were in hiding openly confessed their new-found faith in Christ.

- A number of people who practiced sorcery brought all their sorcery scrolls together and burned all of their occult related items PUBLICLY. According to the way Luke (the author of Acts) wrote this passage, it seems that these people in verse 19 are believers. Verse 18 says, "Many of those who believed now came and openly confessed what they had done." A number—of those who came forward to confess—who had practiced sorcery, participated in this scroll-burning. When you have participated in Satan's kingdom through witchcraft or the occult, a time of confession is the first step to freedom. Don't just try to stop. Confess your sin and burn your occult related items. Make a clear stand for Christ.

So, first of all, notice how the bold ministry of the gospel and the supernatural manifestation of the Lord's power—and the devil's power, quite frankly—bring people who have been secretly fearful and playing in the devil's playground to boldly repent. Secondly, when true repentance happens, people rid their lives of the hidden things they have been holding back from the Lord. In this case, it was books of sorcery. What do the books represent? A life that had depended on the mystical ways of the occult to find power. Those sorcery items also cost a lot of money. How much did they cost altogether? 50,000 Drachmas. These were silver coins, each worth about one day's wages. This means it was worth a LOT more than 50,000 dollars in our own monetary system. How did I find this out? When you look up passages on biblegateway.com, there will be little letters in the text with parentheses around them that are hyperlinked to more background information. These new believers were willing to throw 50,000 days-worth of work into the fire because it was dishonoring to Christ and exalted the devil. They knew that they were playing with fire. This really makes one think!

The power of the devil is very real, but it is so insignificant compared to the power of God. The Ephesian believers dabbled in sorcery to try to find power in their lives. However, men and women who were steeped in superstition and demonic power, who saw it as a part of their daily life, who turned to magic for power, found Jesus Christ and the real power of the cross, because of a demonstration of the Spirit's power. They were now willing to cut ties with their former way of life, not just "add Jesus" to their pantheon of beliefs.

When you turned to Christ, what did you give up in response to his gift of salvation? Did the love of Christ compel you to rid yourself of the evil things in the world that you loved? Is the value of knowing Jesus worth throwing away the things of the world? Do you have any occult items, superstitions, habits, books or entertainment in your home that Jesus would want you to get rid of? Would you give up anything for him, no matter what the cost? If you do have items like this in your home that you are holding onto, you need to burn them. One of my team members was working with a believer who had been involved in occult activity before she gave her life fully to the Lord. It had given her a sense of control in the middle of a very broken life—until she turned to Christ and realized how Satan was really controlling her through it. She had gotten rid of all of her occult books, except one she was having a hard time parting with. My friend encouraged her to burn the book, just like the Ephesians did. Finally, the woman tried and she couldn't. It wouldn't burn! My friend gladly took the book and burnt it for her. The devil wants to hold onto any ground in your life that gives him authority. Do not give the books or other items away to others. You don't want anyone else to come under bondage to evil. Do not keep them or sell them or give them away. Remember how the Ephesians didn't covet the monetary value of their sorcery scrolls more than freedom in Christ. The love of money is the root of all evil. Burn them in Jesus' name and don't be afraid! When you stand in Christ, the devil is under your feet. Romans 19:20 says, "And the God of peace will soon crush Satan underneath your feet."

WORD STUDY
Witchcraft and Sorcery

Let's do a search for other passages in scripture about witchcraft and sorcery. Go ahead and search for these words on your Bible app. This is what I found!

> For rebellion is like the sin of divination (witchcraft), and arrogance like the evil of idolatry. Because you have rejected the word of the Lord, he has rejected you as king. — 1 Samuel 15:23

When you enter the land the Lord your God is giving you, do not learn to imitate the detestable ways of the nations there. Let no one be found among you who sacrifices their son or daughter in the fire, who practises divination or sorcery, interprets omens, engages in witchcraft, or casts spells, or who is a medium or spiritist or who consults the dead. — Deuteronomy 18:9-11

COMPROMISE
A Form of Godliness but Denying its Power

2 Timothy 3:1-5

But mark this: There will be terrible times in the last days. People will be lovers of themselves, lovers of money, boastful, proud, abusive, disobedient to their parents, ungrateful, unholy, without love, unforgiving, slanderous, without self-control, brutal, not lovers of the good, treacherous, rash, conceited, lovers of pleasure rather than lovers of God — having a form of godliness but denying its power. Have nothing to do with such people.

Have we traded the power of God for religion and the appearance of godliness in the church in America? Did the gospel lose its appeal when the church stopped walking in the power of God to change a life—to heal and deliver? Why try to just get someone to change their belief system with reason alone, when you have the power of the manifest Holy Spirit which you were sealed with to demonstrate the reality of the beliefs you are sharing?

1 Corinthians 2:1-5

And so it was with me, brothers and sisters. When I came to you, I did not come with eloquence or human wisdom as I proclaimed to you the testimony about God. For I resolved to know nothing while I was with you except Jesus Christ and him crucified. I came to you in weakness with great fear and trembling. My message and my preaching were not with wise and persuasive words, but with a demonstration of the Spirit's power, so that your faith might not rest on human wisdom, but on God's power.

Lots of religions have good teachings that sound appealing or occult powers that give the practitioners some idea that they are tapping into something real. Pharaoh's magicians mimicked most of Moses's miracles, until a certain point when they acknowledged that Moses was working by the "finger of God." (See Exodus 7 and 8) The ability for witches and other occult practitioners to perform miraculous signs is rooted in demonic power. Satan is performing budget miracles for people, having only a temporary fix, with bondage in this life and eternal separation from God in hell in the afterlife as the fine print at the bottom of the contract. In view of the reality that many people are turning to the occult for answers, how can the church continue to share Jesus in a way that is powerless and ineffective, void of the authority of Christ and the life-changing power of the Holy Spirit? Does your life and your faith manifest the life-changing power of the gospel in a way that will make non-believers thirsty for more? Remember that it is the Spirit's work in you, not your own talent or ability! Will those who have found power in Satan's kingdom taste and see that the Lord is good by the demonstration of the Spirit's power in your life? It is possible! You may not be the best at speaking in public, and you may not have all the most eloquent words, but you, my sister in Christ, have the power of God through the Holy Spirit.

BRINGING IT HOME
Prayer for Renouncing the Occult

The Ephesians took a stand for Christ and broke off all ties with their sorcery. If you have dabbled in these things, whether for fun or seriously, before or after salvation, it is important to "renounce" or turn your back on them and ask God for forgiveness. You need to battle in the name of Jesus.

The prayer may go something like this:

Father,

In Jesus' name, please forgive me for using a Ouija board or tarot cards, reading my horoscope, having palm readings, or dabbling in witchcraft—even for fun. Thank you for the forgiveness of the cross through Jesus Christ.

I break off all ties to the demonic realm that I was connected to, in the name of Jesus. I am in Christ, I am not a slave to the devil, in Jesus' name. I break off any and all curses and connections to darkness, and command Satan and all evil spirits to leave me and my family and never come back, in Jesus' name. Devil, you are vanquished by the blood of the Lamb and I am forgiven!

Father God, fill me and my family with your Holy Spirit. Fill me with your power. Anoint me to be free from my past and allow me to walk by faith in Jesus Christ for the rest of my life. Protect my family by the power of the blood of Jesus.

In Jesus' name, I pray, Amen.

WHAT CAN GOD DO FOR A CULTURE IN CRISIS?

Today's study focuses on what my role is, as a believer, in the culture and society I live in. How does this look to the Lord? Since I am seated in heavenly realms with Christ, how should that impact the society I live in?

PRAYER

Take time to pray using Paul's prayer for the Ephesians. Review your memory verse from Week One. By this time, hopefully, both scripture passages are becoming more and more familiar!

[17] I keep asking that the God of our Lord Jesus Christ, the glorious Father, may give you the Spirit of wisdom and revelation, so that you may know him better. [18] I pray that the eyes of your heart may be enlightened in order that you may know the hope to which he has called you, the riches of his glorious inheritance in his holy people, [19] and his incomparably great power for us who believe. That power is the same as the mighty strength [20] he exerted when he raised Christ from the dead and seated him at his right hand in the heavenly realms, [21] far above all rule and authority, power and dominion, and every name that is invoked, not only in the present age but also in the one to come. [22] And God placed all things under his feet and appointed him to be head over everything for the church, [23] which is his body, the fullness of him who fills everything in every way. — Ephesians 1:17-23

MEMORY VERSE

[8] For it is by grace you have been saved, through faith – and this is not from yourselves, it is the gift of God – [9] not by works, so that no one can boast. [10] For we are God's handiwork, created in Christ Jesus to do good works, which God prepared in advance for us to do. — Ephesians 2:8-10

READING

Open your Bible and read Acts Chapter 19. Pay attention to the progression of events. We will be creating a timeline for this chapter today.

HISTORICAL BACKGROUND
Christ's Power Over Satan, Sickness and a Crazy Mob?

Ephesus was a city with ancient history, even at the time of Paul's visit. Its roots in paganism reached down deep for generations. Sorcery wasn't the only deeply seated worship or practice that civilians were entrenched in. When studying an ancient city or culture, you can use the popular Wikipedia, which is open to editing by anyone at any time, or a more reliable Bible encyclopedia online to learn more. For the city of Ephesus, Wikipedia says,

> "Ephesus was an ancient Greek city on the coast of Ionia, 3 kilometers southwest of present-day Selcuk in Turkey. It was built in the 10th century BC." *(This means that it was about 1000 years old when Jesus and Paul were on the earth. It was a hub for commerce and "flourished" under the Roman Empire.)* "The city was famed for the nearby Temple of Artemis (completed around 550 BC), one of the seven wonders of the Ancient World. Among many other monumental buildings are Library of Celsus and a theater that held up to 25,000 people."

So, we find that the account of the mob in the book of Acts is not only geographically true, but it involved a mob that may have included thousands of people in the theater. Paul's escape from this mob is truly supernatural! In the end of Acts Chapter 19, when we read about the riot, we can see how God protects the believers even by using the powers of the government, through the city clerk. This is an example of how Christ is above all other authority and God is in control.

Greek and Roman pantheon worship—the worship of a group of gods and goddesses—and idolatry was firmly established in Ephesus for over 500 years. And where there is a demand for idols, be sure to find a business! There were business people, like Demetrius the silversmith, making good money off of the idol making trade. These businessmen felt threatened in their livelihood because the gospel of Christ—through Paul's ministry—was reaching so far into the Roman Empire. No wonder he started the riot! People were turning away from the worship of idols. The bottom line was at risk. The status quo of the pagan society was being challenged by the good news of Jesus Christ. This gospel calls people to turn from mute idols and false religion to the God who created the universe and his son Jesus. As Paul and other believers shared Christ, the prince of the power of the air began to lose his grip on the Roman Empire. It says in Isaiah that the government will be upon the shoulders of the Messiah. Jesus is over all authorities and the sharing of the gospel began to manifest his power over Ephesus as person after person turned to salvation.

CREATING A TIMELINE

After reading Acts Chapter 19, fill in the following time line to show how Paul and the Ephesian believers saw the power and authority of Christ exerted over rulers and authorities in the world. How did it play out? Show the back and forth spiritual battle that took place in Acts 19. From beginning to end, we see a cause and effect, or a tug of war, as the devil and the established spiritual forces fight to keep the gospel of Jesus Christ from overtaking the society of Ephesus and ultimately, the Roman Empire. I've started you out with three events. Add events as needed.

PAUL
Paul entered the synagogue and spoke boldly there for three months, arguing persuasively about the kingdom of God. (vs 8)

JEWS & GREEKS
But some of them became obstinate; they refused to believe and publicly maligned the Way. (vs 9)

PAUL
So Paul left them. He took the disciples with him and had discussions daily in the lecture hall of Tyrannus. This went on for two years, so that all the Jews and Greeks who lived in the province of Asia heard the Word of the Lord. (vs 10)

What did you come up with? Do you see the spiritual battle between the believers and the devil? What we see in Acts 19 is not only a battle for the hearts and minds of individuals, but for the culture of the Ephesians. Culture involves money, influence, and power. Remember that Jesus Christ is seated in heavenly realms above all other powers. However, the devil, in Ephesians Chapter 2, is referred to as the ruler of the kingdom of the air. When the devil tempts Jesus in Matthew 4, we see an example of this spiritual conflict.

Matthew 4:8-11

Again, the devil took him to a very high mountain and showed him all the kingdoms of the world and their splendour. 'All this I will give you,' he said, 'if you will bow down and worship me.'

Jesus said to him, 'Away from me, Satan! For it is written: "Worship the Lord your God, and serve him only."'

Then the devil left him, and angels came and attended him.

In this scripture, you can see the devil does have authority in this world. Jesus doesn't laugh and say, "No way, devil, I'm the son of God; these cultures belong to me. You're a liar." Instead, Jesus uses the Word of God to say that he will not sin by worshipping the devil to achieve the temporary power and fame that the kingdoms of the world offer.

Does the devil's ability to decide to whom he would give ownership of the world's kingdoms indicate that he is more powerful than Jesus? No way! It means that Jesus, fully God, humbled himself to also become a human to whom the devil could offer ownership of all the world's kingdoms. Jesus had another goal in mind, other than temporary fame and power. It means that Jesus was living a sinless life by rejecting that temptation with God's Word, so he could accomplish his goal of being the perfect sacrifice and obtain salvation for mankind.

What happens when individuals give their lives to Christ? Their lives change, and they share Jesus with others. The more people that this happens to, the more the devil slowly loses his power over societies. He loses his strongholds and Christ wins the battle for that person, family, community, and eventually nation! This is what happened in the great revivals of the past.

What does Demetrius say in Acts 19:25?

There is danger not only that our trade will lose its good name, but also that the temple of the great goddess Artemis will be discredited; and the goddess herself, who is worshipped throughout the province of Asia and the world, will be robbed of her divine majesty.' – Acts 19:25

When the people stop worshipping idols, the DEVIL loses his power over them and over the society! He certainly throws a fit, doesn't he? The riot is a climax of the battle, which ends very anti-climactically, with the Holy Spirit speaking through a little city clerk who tells everyone to go home and handle it legally. Christ has authority over governments!

We currently are seeing a battle in our own culture. Many Christians are deceived into thinking that, as believers, we have no right to expect our culture to follow Christ. Clearly, we are not reading our Bibles! It is the natural way, or rather the supernatural way that things go when people start sharing their faith in the power of God. Our personal faith and personal relationship with God is not meant to be a private relationship with God; it is meant to be shared personally with those around us. When we do this, and we are full of the Holy Spirit, the devil will begin to lose his power over our neighborhoods, cities, counties, and our nation. Person by person, God wins the battle.

We are in a spiritual battle, and when one contender decides to retreat from the battle, the other side wins. Some western nations live in more comfort, because their laws were founded in Christian morality that allows for freedom of religion and protection of individual rights. We have a responsibility, as believers, for this great opportunity, to use our religious freedom and to care for it as stewards of the Lord's earth. Naturally, when believers in Jesus pray for their communities and nation, and walk in righteousness, the powers will shift in the heavenly realms, and we will see the difference on earth. However, if we live a life of compromise and try to just blend in without sharing Christ, we lose our influence and impact on the world.

During the Great Awakening, a historic revival in America in the 1700s, bars shut down because no one went to get drunk anymore. Even the bar owners got saved and changed their occupation. In one report, a police station had to start a men's quartet because the police officers had so little to do since so many people had repented and turned to Christ. What are you expecting God to do in your culture?

BRINGING IT HOME

Examine your heart before God concerning how you look at Christ and culture. Do you pull back from influencing and engaging others, thus creating a vacuum for the darkness to fill? Or, are you prayerfully seeking God on how he wants you to engage your nation and world with the gospel?

Ask God if there are any lies the devil has convinced you to believe concerning how you, as a believer, should interact with those around you.

RECONCILIATION
PART 1

OIL & WATER?

Over the next several days, we will be doing a series on "Reconciliation of Relationships" based on Ephesians 2. Get excited, because there is so much truth in these passages about God's power to bring people together! Relationships are such a vital part of who we are as women. On a grand scale, the Lord has made a way so that no one who trusts in his Son can be left out of his family. Racial lines cannot divide us and social barriers cannot keep us apart, when we are walking with the Lord. What we are about to dive into is packed with truth that is spiritually discerned, so let's go before our Father in heaven and seek his face to understand what his truth is concerning the scripture passages during this week.

PRAYER

Father,

In the name of Jesus, give me the Spirit of wisdom and revelation, so that I may know you better. I pray that the eyes of my heart may be enlightened in order that I may know the HOPE to which you have called me, the riches of your glorious inheritance in the saints, and your incomparably great power for us who believe. Resurrect the relationships in my life that are in dysfunction, oh Lord. The same Spirit and power that raised Jesus from the dead lives in me and I am seated in heavenly realms with Christ. Work your mighty wonders in the lives of those around me in my family, in my home, at work, in my church and all my relationships. Fill me with a knowledge of your HOPE!

In Jesus' name, Amen!

NEW MEMORY VERSE

Our new memory verse introduces the powerful concept that Christ came to destroy hostility. This scripture reveals to us his ultimate purpose to bring together people who were separated by the law of God. Jesus didn't come to destroy the law. God's Word cannot be changed and stands forever. But, by keeping all of God's law and never sinning, Jesus fulfilled the righteous requirements of the law. Not only did he fulfill the law, he was able to stand in our place to take the punishment for the sin of every person who ever broke the law of God, knowingly or unknowingly. In this way, through his crucifixion, he set aside the law and replaced it with a higher and greater law of peace, reconciliation and forgiveness. Every person, through faith in Christ, can become a part of the family of God. It is important to remember that every division caused by the fall and by sin is overcome through the death and resurrection of Jesus. The major reconciliation situation we will learn about today is the division that kept all Gentiles—or non-Jews—from salvation in the kingdom of heaven.

MEMORY VERSE

[14] For he himself is our peace, who has made the two groups one and has destroyed the barrier, the dividing wall of hostility, [15] by setting aside in his flesh the law with its commands and regulations. His purpose was to create in himself one new humanity out of the two, thus making peace, [16] and in one body to reconcile both of them to God through the cross, by which he put to death their hostility. — Ephesians 2:14–16

READING

Open your Bible and read Ephesians 2.

HISTORY LESSON

Take time to think of a relationship you are in that is very taxing and difficult. Imagine for a minute that there is a possibility for that relationship to be not only healed, but also restored to a level of friendship or intimacy that it never had before. We are digging in this week to restoration. But, first, before we can talk about restoration, I need to give you the back story on what God did to restore the people in Ephesus.

The second half of Ephesians 2 shines a spotlight into a tricky relationship situation in the Ephesus Church and all of humanity, for that matter. This relationship conflict was an issue not unlike what we see today in our society. Two people groups were at odds. The tension was racial and ethnic. A group of people were enslaved and taken from their homeland hundreds of years earlier and at the time of our story they were trying to find peace with those around them while maintaining their cultural identity. We are not talking about the current social issues in American culture, but about a story that played out prophetically thousands of years ago in the Roman Empire. If we can spiritually see into this miracle of grace and redemption from brokenness, we can surely know that anything is possible for us in our day, our culture and our families. It's easy to read the Bible with our eyes glazed over as we read about cities and names of people groups. Let's take the time to learn about the real people behind these "faceless facts." King Solomon said in Ecclesiastes, "There is nothing new under the sun." The human race may have made incredible advancements over thousands of years, but the hearts of men and women still experience the emotion of life the same way. Ask the Holy Spirit to give you eyes to see and ears to hear what God is saying about redemption and reconciliation in these passages.

The conflict is woven into Acts 19, when Paul takes the gospel to the Jewish people who lived in Ephesus. Two thousand years ago, people were not well-travelled like they are now. A person would live his or her entire life in a little village and never leave. Ephesus was part of the Roman Empire. It was a Greek territory that was not part of the nation of Israel. The presence of Jews there was not because Jewish people got tired of living in Israel and decided to spread their wings and start a new community up north. They were there because of judgment and oppression. The Jews who lived in this city were descendants of the Jews who were taken captive between 744-720 BC when the Assyrians attacked and destroyed the Northern Kingdom of Israel. This is referred to as the diaspora.

> **di·as·po·ra**
> *noun*
>
> the dispersion of the Jews beyond Israel.
>
> o   Jews living outside Israel.
> o   The dispersion of any people from their original homeland.

God used the empire of Assyria to bring judgment on Israel after hundreds of years of turning their back on the Lord to worship false idols. They engaged in prostitution worship and they burned the babies born to their illicit relationships in the molten arms of the idol of Molech. The children of Israel didn't turn their backs on God overnight. It happened over hundreds of years and got progressively worse as they married people from other cultural belief systems and adopted their forms of worship. Prophet after prophet warned the people to repent and turn back, but eventually the judgment came.

During the siege, families were torn apart. The mother was taken away and shipped across the world to be married to another. The father was killed. Children were taken as slaves. (Daniel is an example of this, but he was taken from the Southern Kingdom of Judah by Babylon.) The Assyrians brutally and methodically attempted to destroy the identity of the nations they conquered to assure the complete domination of the new land. But, here we see in Acts 19, possibly almost 700 years later, displaced Jewish communities are still holding onto their roots and awaiting their Messiah, the Deliverer, to bring them back to Israel. The Assyrians could not snuff out the people of God. Remember this, dear sister, when the devil tries to break up your family. God's people can overcome. They are destined to. It's in their spiritual DNA. Don't give up hope!

We learned in our last lesson, God does not just deal with individuals, but he also deals specifically with nations. The nation of Israel is the nation of God's chosen people, who were descendants of Abraham, Isaac and Jacob (or Israel). God chose this nation to follow him and to teach them his ways, and to bring Jesus the Messiah, the Savior, into the world. Israel was chosen by the grace of God. Even in the Old Testament we see the power of God to call a people, because of his power and might, not because of their greatness. They were chosen to shine his light to the nations and to make his power known, but they turned their backs on the Lord.

This is how the ancestors of the Ephesian Jews came to live in Ephesus. Notice that they still managed to keep together and to form their own religious centers in the middle of the pagan culture. When Paul went there, in Acts 19, he preached to the Jews first. His job was to let the people of God in Ephesus know that the Messiah had come and accomplished his mission, and to entreat them to trust in Jesus Christ as their Savior. However, they did not all believe that Jesus was the promised Messiah.

> Paul entered the synagogue and spoke boldly there for three months, arguing persuasively about the kingdom of God. But some of them became obstinate; they refused to believe and publicly maligned the Way. So Paul left them. He took the disciples with him, and had discussion daily in the lecture hall of Tyrannus. This went on for two years, so that all the Jews and Greeks who lived in the province of Asia heard the word of the Lord. – Acts 19:8-10

Here we see a distinction between Jews and Greeks, otherwise known as Gentiles. They were at odds. Some of the Jews believed in Jesus, and some did not. Some of the Greeks believed. It says that all who lived in Asia heard the word of the Lord! Why? Because:

- Paul preached boldly in the Jewish synagogue for three months.

- When he encountered strong resistance from some of the obstinate Jews—don't be surprised or discouraged by opposition—he left and had daily discussions with Gentiles in the public arena for two years.

What tenacity for the gospel! He reached out to both people groups on a daily basis, engaging them with the good news of Jesus with his bold words in discussion form. He didn't throw big events to draw a crowd. He went to where the crowds already were meeting. He didn't try to be cool or attractive. He was faithful to reach out to both groups on a daily basis. Daily. How many of us do this daily sharing of the gospel by discussing Jesus with others? What were the results of Paul meeting both people groups on their own turf and in ways they could understand? In two years, all of Asia heard the Word of the Lord! Incredible! Between these two people groups, what obstacles was Paul dealing with?

The Jews had the Ten Commandments and the law. They had the prophets and their prophecies. They experienced God and worshiped him in concrete ways, specified by the Creator, who rescued them out of Egypt. The Gentiles did not know the revealed creator God. They worshiped idols that were made by human minds and human hands, and relied on sorcery. They were cut off from God. We read about this in the second half of Ephesians 2. God takes two groups of people at odds and makes them one in Christ! Using this passage from Ephesians 2:11-22, chart the similarities and/or differences between the Jews and the Gentiles (non-Jews/Greeks).

Ephesians 2:11-22

[11] Therefore, remember that formerly you who are Gentiles by birth and called 'uncircumcised' by those who call themselves 'the circumcision' (which is done in the body by human hands) — [12] remember that at that time you were separate from Christ, excluded from citizenship in Israel and foreigners to the covenants of the promise, without hope and without God in the world. [13] But now in Christ Jesus you who once were far away have been brought near by the blood of Christ.

[14] **For he himself is our peace, who has made the two groups one and has destroyed the barrier, the dividing wall of hostility,** [15] by setting aside in his flesh the law with its commands and regulations. His purpose was to create in himself one new humanity out of the two, thus making peace, [16] and in one body to reconcile both of them to God through the

cross, by which he put to death their hostility. [17] He came and preached peace to you who were far away and peace to those who were near. [18] For through him we both have access to the Father by one Spirit.

[19] Consequently, you are no longer foreigners and strangers, but fellow citizens with God's people and also members of his household, [20] built on the foundation of the apostles and prophets, with Christ Jesus himself as the chief cornerstone. [21] In him the whole building is joined together and rises to become a holy temple in the Lord. [22] And in him you too are being built together to become a dwelling in which God lives by his Spirit.

CONTRAST & COMPARISON
One in Christ

In the following diagram, list what you discover about the Jews and Gentiles before Christ. You will see some differences and some similarities. The triangle represents the oneness we have in Christ. List in it the similarities both groups have after they accept Christ as Savior.

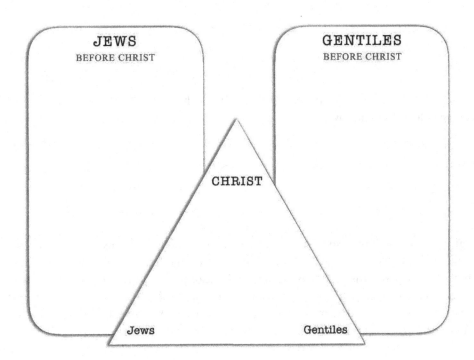

BRINGING IT HOME

The Bible says that in Christ there is no longer a distinction between Jew or Greek. In Christ, all are one. How does this line up with your paradigm of what the role of the Jews is?

Some people try to become Jewish after they come to Christ, hoping that it will bring them closer to God. While the Jews are still God's chosen people, and they have many promises and prophecies of God that apply to them which are still being fulfilled, we do not need to become Jewish or act Jewish to be "more" united with Christ. Christ levels the playing field. Many people underestimate the power and significance of the death and resurrection of Jesus. Do not allow the enemy to diminish the person or work of Jesus in your eyes.

RECONCILIATION
PART 2

TEARING DOWN THE DIVIDING WALLS

Today, we will see how God transformed us from beggars to children at his table. He destroys all barriers between him and his children. Nothing can separate us from his love!

PRAYER

Father,

In Jesus' name, give me the Spirit of wisdom and revelation to understand the truths in your Word, so I can know you better. Enlighten the eyes of my heart so that I may have hope. I need hope. I am called to hope. There are relationships in my life that are broken. I know in Christ that division and hostility can be torn down and peace can prevail. I can't imagine how this can happen. I have no idea how it will happen, but in the name of Jesus, open my eyes to see the truth in your Word. Teach me how to apply your truth to my unique situation. I am called to hope. I have hope that the same power that raised Jesus from the dead lives inside of me by the Holy Spirit.

Amen.

Review our new memory verse:

MEMORY VERSE

[14] For he himself is our peace, who has made the two groups one and has destroyed the barrier, the dividing wall of hostility, [15] by setting aside in his flesh the law with its commands and regulations. His purpose was to create in himself one new humanity out of the two, thus making peace, [16] and in one body to reconcile both of them to God through the cross, by which he put to death their hostility. — Ephesians 2:14–16

KEY WORD SEARCH

In the following passage from Ephesians 2, what are some repeated words and/or phrases? Using your highlighter, highlight them.

Ephesians 2:11-22

[11] Therefore, remember that formerly you who are Gentiles by birth and called 'uncircumcised' by those who call themselves 'the circumcision' (which is done in the body by human hands) — [12] remember that at that time you were separate from Christ, excluded from citizenship in Israel and foreigners to the covenants of the promise, without hope and without God in the world. [13] But now in Christ Jesus you who once were far away have been brought near by the blood of Christ.

[14] For he himself is our peace, who has made the two groups one and has destroyed the barrier, the dividing wall of hostility, [15] by setting aside in his flesh the law with its commands and regulations. His purpose was to create in himself one new humanity out of the two, thus making peace, [16] and in one body to reconcile both of them to God through the cross, by which he put to death their hostility. [17] He came and preached peace to you who were far away and peace to those who were near. [18] For through him we both have access to the Father by one Spirit.

[19] Consequently, you are no longer foreigners and strangers, but fellow citizens with God's people and also members of his household, [20] built on the foundation of the apostles and prophets, with Christ Jesus himself as the chief cornerstone. [21] In him the whole building is joined together and rises to become a holy temple in the Lord. [22] And in him you too are being built together to become a dwelling in which God lives by his Spirit.

> **TODAY'S BIBLE STUDY TOOL**
>
> **Key Word Search.** Repeated words or phrases are clues as to what the author is trying to convey. They are KEY to the text.

Write any repeated words and/or phrases below. Put a tally mark after it for each time it occurs.

_____   _____
_____   _____
_____   _____
_____   _____
_____   _____
_____   _____

OUTLINING SCRIPTURE

If you had to make a brief outline of Ephesians 2:11-22, what would it look like? Create one in the space below.

> **TODAY'S BIBLE STUDY TOOL**
>
> **Outlining Scripture.** This helps you see the main point(s) the author is trying to convey to his readers. It also gives you a synopsis of the passage and helps you to understand and remember it.

If I had to summarize the three paragraphs, they would be titled:

32. Covenants

33. Hostility and Peace

34. New Unity in Christ

The first paragraph deals with covenants that exclude the Gentiles. Have you ever felt excluded from a group? In this case, before the resurrection of Christ, the Gentiles were excluded from a relationship with God. By the authority of God's law, they were outsiders. There was no easy way for Gentiles to become insiders on their own merit, without becoming circumcised and following the Jewish law. Gentiles needed to go to great lengths; otherwise the law of God prevented them from entering in. They had little hope, except through a long and complicated conversion that involved many rituals, including circumcision. It may be hard to understand, but the plight of the Gentile before Christ came, died and rose again was the absolute most hopeless case in the history of mankind. It was very difficult for peoples of nations other than Israel to be reconciled. They were doomed to life without God and an eternity separated from God, unless they were circumcised and followed the law. But now, through faith, they can become insiders and be reconciled with God through Jesus Christ! To understand better, let's look at a story that is very difficult to understand without this context. In this story, the Canaanite woman is a Gentile, and not a Jew.

THE FAITH OF A CANAANITE WOMAN

Matthew 15:21-28

[21] Leaving that place, Jesus withdrew to the region of Tyre and Sidon. [22] A Canaanite woman from that vicinity came to him, crying out, 'Lord, Son of David, have mercy on me! My daughter is demon-possessed and suffering terribly.'

[23] Jesus did not answer a word. So his disciples came to him and urged him, 'Send her away, for she keeps crying out after us.'

[24] He answered, 'I was sent only to the lost sheep of Israel.'

[25] The woman came and knelt before him. 'Lord, help me!' she said.

[26] He replied, 'It is not right to take the children's bread and toss it to the dogs.'

[27] 'Yes it is, Lord,' she said. 'Even the dogs eat the crumbs that fall from their master's table.'

[28] Then Jesus said to her, 'Woman, you have great faith! Your request is granted.' And her daughter was healed at that moment.

At first glance, this story has some upsetting elements. Why would Jesus say the woman and her daughter were dogs?! What is he trying to say? In order to understand the desperation of this situation and why Jesus responded this way, we need to understand the division between Jews and Gentiles. When we can see the gravity of the separation, we will truly comprehend the reconciliation power of God in Jesus. Let's read Ephesians 2:11-22 again to gain understanding. The word "hostility" is used several times. In your own words, write what Paul said concerning this issue.

We are used to living in the age of grace. We take it for granted. At this point in history, Jesus was unable to go against his mission to take the gospel to the Jews first. God the Father made the nation of Israel a promise and he couldn't break it. The Messiah was their Messiah. In order for God to be just and perfect, he could not offer hope to the Gentiles until the Jews had ample opportunity to accept or reject Christ. They had to reject him and crucify him before the Gentiles could receive salvation. A Gentile was not even a child of God, spiritually speaking. Jesus, in this moment with the Canaanite woman, was there to fulfill prophecy and to obey his Father in heaven. That is why Jesus refers to her, in this situation, as a dog. I used to get really upset and confused about this before I owned a dog. Now I never could imagine loving an animal as much as our doggie Bella. I regularly "accidentally" drop a little piece of bacon or other meat on the floor while preparing dinner for my family. Other family members shamelessly feed her begging habit. She is so content to sit with the most perfect, lady-like posture and beautiful big brown eyes, without barking or growling or acting annoyed, and wait for her next treasure to fall from the table or counter top. When that little nibble falls down, she doesn't say, "How disgusting that you only give me such a tiny crumb! I'm better than that and you don't deserve me!" Each crumb emboldens her sweet face even more. Her ears even perk up in anticipation that this is the real deal. While my main dish may be prepared for my husband and children, there is no lack for the beautiful, reddish brown Rhodesian Ridgeback mix under my table. She is loved and she loves us so—especially for each and every crumb! That is all this Canaanite woman needed. She didn't need the full blessing, just yet. She just needed a crumb, because just a crumb from the master's table can move mountains and heal a demonized child. A word from the Father brought forth the earth, the sun, moon and stars. His breath in Adam's nostrils filled the human race with a divine spark and one drop of the Savior's blood can cleanse all the atrocities from every war that ever was fought on earthly soil.

Now get your head wrapped around this, and maybe ask the Holy Spirit for insight. Because, this was our state BEFORE the resurrection. The power of the crumb was enough to heal a child. But now, every Jew and Gentile—including us in the twenty-first century—who trusts in Christ is sealed with the Holy Spirit and lavished and blessed with all the blessings of a child of the living God. There is more than enough to go around at God's table for whatever your hungry heart needs. We have the full banquet, not the leftovers. Father God is a better papa than the best father of the year! All the children, the natural born and the adopted children—Jews and Gentiles, are reconciled with God through Christ.

If, through Jesus Christ, the people of the world, who are completely and hopelessly separated from God, can find peace and hope, how much more can any other relationship find hope through the same reconciling power of Jesus Christ?

But, what was it that caused the division? Our memory verse for this week explains this when it says the hostility was caused by "the law with its commands and regulations."

Ephesians 2:14-16

For he himself is our peace, who has made the two groups one and has destroyed the barrier, the dividing wall of hostility, by setting aside in his flesh the law with its commands and regulations. His purpose was to create in himself one new humanity out of the two, thus making peace, and in one body to reconcile both of them to God through the cross, by which he put to death their hostility.

Before Jesus died and rose again, in order for a Gentile man and his family to be unified with God, he had to be willing to be sealed by circumcision, which was the covenant of God for the Jews through Abraham. This was a huge and painful sacrifice. Circumcision identified who was in God's inner circle and who was out. As women, this topic may make us a bit uncomfortable, but let's do a cross reference to see how this applies to us, our families, and our relationships today. If you have extra time today, read about when God instituted his covenant relationship with Abraham through circumcision in Genesis 15.

CROSS REFERENCE
Circumcision

Look up "circumcision" on your Bible app.

I sorted through a LOT of verses to try to find one that is simple to understand.

A person is not a Jew who is one only outwardly, nor is circumcision merely outward and physical. No, a person is a Jew who is one inwardly; and circumcision is circumcision of the heart, by the Spirit, not by the written code. Such a person's praise is not from other people, but from God. – Romans 2:28-29

Now, the important thing to know is that God gave circumcision to Abraham and the Jews as a covenant that defined his relationship with his people. If you were a man—and family of that man—and you were circumcised, you were in. If you weren't circumcised, you were out. It reminded them who they belonged to. But, all of God's covenants ALWAYS had a deeper lesson behind them.

I once heard Pastor Dennis Miller, author of the Grow in His Word Series, teach on this with all the details on the significance of circumcision from a perspective that only a man can. He said, "Why only a physical seal for the men? In scripture, men are the spiritual priests of their families. If the man was sealed, the whole family was considered sealed. Through that part of the man's body comes the seed for the next generation. That was to be holy. He was aware of it every day—in his relationship with his wife and even when he went to the bathroom. The covenant of circumcision says that God wants all of you, not just the outward religious activity. He wants your heart and all the private and personal areas of your life. Your purity belongs to God. Your children belong to God. There are no secrets before God."

But now, through Christ, this work is a work of the Spirit. It says in Ephesians that not only do we no longer need this outward physical seal to define our relationship with God, but also that now the seal we each have that defines our relationship with God is what? Do you remember?

And you also were included in Christ when you heard the message of truth, the gospel of your salvation. When you believed, you were marked in him with a seal, the promised Holy Spirit, who is a deposit guaranteeing our inheritance until the redemption of those who are God's possession – to the praise of his glory. – Ephesians 1:13-14

God can see into our hearts and he lives in us by the Holy Spirit. So, both Jew and Gentile can belong to Christ through faith. The work of the Spirit seals us individually, but also together. Our sealing Holy Spirit brings about the reconciling work of God in our lives and people will begin to see with their eyes the inner life-giving work of salvation.

Remember our verse?

For it is by grace you have been saved, through faith — and this is not from yourselves, it is the gift of God — not by works, so that no one can boast. – Ephesians 2:8-9

Through Christ, God fulfilled the righteous requirements of the law in us. What does that mean? Jesus lived a perfect life. He was blameless. He never broke God's law in letter or in spirit. Because of this, he was able to take the punishment of death for all of our infractions of the law. In the death of his physical body, he legally took away the power of our death. We have nothing but faith to stand on to justify ourselves. Because of Christ, everyone far away and near to Christ has the same access. Faith. There is nothing of any significance that distinguishes us from one another. Nothing separates us from the love of Christ and nothing can separate us from each other, except the things we let get in the way.

BRINGING IT HOME

Are there things that you use to measure yourself against other believers as to what makes you better than them?

What are the implications for the truth that in Christ there is neither Jew nor Gentile? There is no race in God's eyes, except the human race. What does this mean for racial reconciliation?

Have you realized your spiritual power as a child of God, seated at his table?

RECONCILIATION
PART 3

CHRIST DESTROYS HOSTILITY WITH GRACE

PRAYER

Today is our last day for this prayer before we start a new prayer that the apostle Paul teaches the Ephesians. Let's pray it straight up the way he wrote it—for us to be filled with and led by the Holy Spirit today! Spend time asking the Lord to remove the barriers between you and those in your life you are at odds with. The same power that abolished the wall of hostility between the Jews and Gentiles, and between mankind and God, is in you through Christ Jesus.

[17] I keep asking that the God of our Lord Jesus Christ, the glorious Father, may give you the Spirit of wisdom and revelation, so that you may know him better. [18] I pray that the eyes of your heart may be enlightened in order that you may know the hope to which he has called you, the riches of his glorious inheritance in his holy people, [19] and his incomparably great power for us who believe. That power is the same as the mighty strength [20] he exerted when he raised Christ from the dead and seated him at his right hand in the heavenly realms, [21] far above all rule and authority, power and dominion, and every name that is invoked, not only in the present age but also in the one to come. [22] And God placed all things under his feet and appointed him to be head over everything for the church, [23] which is his body, the fullness of him who fills everything in every way. — Ephesians 1:17-23

Spend time meditating on our memory verse.

MEMORY VERSE

[14] For he himself is our peace, who has made the two groups one and has destroyed the barrier, the dividing wall of hostility, [15] by setting aside in his flesh the law with its commands and regulations. His purpose was to create in himself one new humanity out of the two, thus making peace, [16] and in one body to reconcile both of them to God through the cross, by which he put to death their hostility. — Ephesians 2:14–16

ABOLISHING HOSTILITY
The Ministry of Reconciliation

This is a tough pill to swallow, but the reality of this world is that people are in one of two places. They are either friends with God and part of his family, or they are enemies of God due to the sin in their lives and their rejection of his grace through Jesus Christ. The only difference between the two groups is God's grace through faith. We have already learned in our memory verse that it is by the good grace of God that we are saved. Here is where we drop all of our illusions of our own goodness apart from him. We are created by him. He knew us from the foundations of the earth. The true love of God is our example when we see that God loves his enemies. Without Christ, we are God's enemies. In sin, we are in rebellion against him and, apart from Christ, the punishment is unpaid. It isn't pretty.

Remember how the apostle Paul was set on destroying the beloved children of God? BUT GOD, by his great mercy and grace removed Paul from his path of destruction and set his feet on a path of being a slave to Christ. Fear of being judged or being rejected causes many people to brush past the part of the gospel that reminds us that we are sinners and calls us to examine our hearts and repent. But, ignoring our need and our own sin makes the GOOD NEWS seem like FAKE NEWS. It tells the news—gospel means good news—from one side, our side. Our side of the story tends to make us look good. We justify our actions and imagine that God loves our effort to please him so much that he will overlook our sin. Many women are trying so hard to be perfect that they cannot see that this effort is a hopeless cause that brings frustration to themselves and everyone else around them. Looking at Jesus and imagining that what you are doing for him is what makes you worthy of him is not good news. That, my friend, is fake news. Many people give Jesus a nod, but still want to believe that their personal religious acts are of some worth to God. Here is the little secret, ladies. Our good deeds, relatively speaking—compared to God's righteousness—are the same as menstrual rags. That's right. Check this out. Yuck, anyone?

> All of us have become like one who is unclean,
>   and all our righteous acts are like filthy rags;
> we all shrivel up like a leaf,
>   and like the wind our sins sweep us away. – Isaiah 64:6

WORD STUDY

I had heard this before when I was younger, that the Hebrew rendering of the word "filthy" in Isaiah 64:6 actually means menstrual rags. Since I am writing a book, of course I don't want to rely on someone else's word, I want to go straight to God's Word! I became a word detective and did my research on my Bible Hub app! If you are studying an Old Testament passage, you want to look up the Hebrew word; if you are studying a New Testament passage, you want to look up the Greek word. Look at the screenshot on my phone. Remember, you TOO can be a word detective. The implication is that the good works we do for God are continually being dirtied. Is there a nice image in your mind now?

I need to tell you something good, though! God knows everything. He knows every intention of your heart and still loves you. He is not a fair-weather friend who is here today and gone tomorrow. He loves you in spite of your weaknesses and failures. This is true, warm, beautiful, inviting love. This is the type of love we can drink in like a hot cup of coffee on a chilly morning. We can hide nothing from him, yet while we were still sinners, Christ died for us.

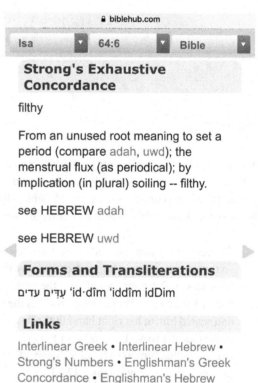

BE ENCOURAGED

Romans 5:6-11

[6] You see, at just the right time, when we were still powerless, Christ died for the ungodly. [7] Very rarely will anyone die for a righteous person, though for a good person someone might possibly dare to die. [8] But God demonstrates his own love for us in this: while we were still sinners, Christ died for us.

[9] Since we have now been justified by his blood, how much more shall we be saved from God's wrath through him! [10] For if, while we were God's enemies, we were reconciled to him through the death of his Son, how much more, having been

reconciled, shall we be saved through his life! [11] Not only is this so, but we also boast in God through our Lord Jesus Christ, through whom we have now received reconciliation.

Let's talk about how this grace of God towards us gives us the ministry of reconciliation. It's all about perspective. We have received grace in our sin, so now we are called to be grace-bearers. Others need to know about the love and grace of Jesus in the middle of our mess. So, God will turn your mess into the message that Jesus is in the business of forgiveness. The first reconciliation we bring is the gospel—the actual life-giving gospel. No one can be saved without it! We speak it. We use words the same way that Paul did when having discussions with the Ephesians who did not know Christ. The second reconciliation is our own living out of the gospel, where we give grace and mercy to others, even when it's undeserved!

What does this look like? It's easy to hold a grudge or a "hit list" against someone else when we are exalting our own behavior and our own intentions, giving ourselves the benefit of the doubt, while giving another person a cold shoulder. When we remember that God loved us in our sin and that even our own best intentions are contaminated with hidden pride, deception and unfaithfulness like a menstrual rag, we should be able to honestly admit that we have no place holding grudges against anyone. Jesus came to bring a humble cleansing to our hearts and to give us a heart of merciful flesh in place of a heart of prideful stone.

Also, are you holding your friends, spouse or children to a standard of graceless perfection that you yourself cannot live up to? You may be able to clean a mean kitchen in a way that they can't, but in truth, those same loved ones in your life have strengths in areas where you are weak. If they are 5 years old, you may not see those strengths playing out in a practical way for a long time. But, just wait for it! Do you show your loved ones the same grace and love in their weaknesses that Jesus showed for you, when he had to carry your burden to the cross without complaining—and with actual joy? How much lighter is the burden we carry when we have to pick up after someone or carry a pair of shoes upstairs with joy? Should we grumble and complain, or carry another's burden with compassion? What about the spouse or needy person who is crippled emotionally? Sometimes, we are called to bear with someone in love and in prayer to bring the power of the gospel to that person with a heart that looks to Jesus as our example— fixing our eyes on him! Others need to see and feel the grace of God. It is oh so easy to bring our own unjustified wrath instead.

> Therefore, since we are surrounded by such a great cloud of witnesses, let us throw off everything that hinders and the sin that so easily entangles. And let us run with perseverance the race marked out for us, fixing our eyes on Jesus, the pioneer and perfecter of faith. For the joy that was set before him he endured the cross, scorning its shame, and sat down at the right hand of the throne of God. Consider him who endured such opposition from sinners, so that you will not grow weary and lose heart. – Hebrews 12:1-3

> For he himself is our peace, who has made the two one and has destroyed the barrier, the dividing wall of hostility, by abolishing in his flesh the law with its commandments and regulations. His purpose was to create in himself one new man out of the two, thus making peace, and in this one body to reconcile both of them to God through the cross, by which he put to death their hostility. He came and preached peace to you who were far away and peace to those who were near. For through him we both have access to the Father by one Spirit. – Ephesians 2:14-18

God is in the business of reconciliation! This reconciliation begins with him SATISFYING his wrath with the blood of his son Jesus Christ. Jesus willingly became our hope in a hopeless situation. We did not deserve his life, his sacrifice, or his love. But, that is what makes it supernatural love and grace. That is what makes it REAL love. Real love gives us hope. We have hope, and trust that we will not be turned away because of our weaknesses, but we are actually saved on the basis of admitting that we are unable to save ourselves, and falling on the mercy of God!

Jesus abolished—in his flesh—the law and commandments that separated us from God and from other people. What are steps to this reconciliation power in your life?

STEPS TO RECONCILIATION

HAVE PEACE WITH GOD. The first step to peace with God is putting faith in Christ's sacrifice for your sins. As believers, every victory we obtain is through the cross and the resurrection. If you haven't put your faith in Christ alone, and you are trying to impress God to get to heaven, you probably are still an enemy of God. The only thing that impresses God is the blood of his Son Jesus. Make sure today that the blood of Jesus has washed away your sins. Do this through prayer, repentance and confessing your faith in Jesus Christ today. Romans 10:9 says, "If you declare with your mouth, 'Jesus is Lord,' and believe in your heart that God raised him from the dead, you will be saved."

BE HONEST WITH GOD and HONEST WITH YOURSELF. We admit our need for God. This is not only our need for eternal salvation by the power of God. But, we also have a need for the Holy Spirit's power and guidance in everyday life, as we work out our salvation with fear and trembling. In this life we need to pray for God to help us to honestly assess our shortcomings, sins and weaknesses. In your relationship with someone else, are you asking God to reveal your weaknesses and areas that you need to repent of? Repentance is turning from sin towards Christ. God showed me personally that deep-rooted bitterness was keeping me from seeing my husband from a place of truthfulness. I was always in a place of defensiveness. Because bitterness was so routine for me, I didn't even realize it was bitterness. Repentance from pride and bitterness was in order and that personal change made all the difference in the relationship!

GIVE GRACE & FORGIVENESS. Have you been sinned against? Do you have a hit list on someone? Time to pray through that hit list and give those personal injuries to God. Pray for God to work in that person's life so they can repent and change. Praying for God to give someone mercy is important. This is not about putting yourself in danger if the person you need to forgive is someone who has abused you. But, it is obedience to God, because God in Christ forgave you. If it is a relationship that God wants to reconcile, he has room to move, when you are cooperating with his Spirit in praying for the person who hurt you. Jesus told Peter in Matthew 18 that he was to forgive a brother who sins against him 70 times 7. Seven is God's number for perfection. Forgiveness is something that Jesus teaches us to live in.

> **TODAY'S BIBLE STUDY TOOL**
>
> **Pray to Forgive.** Bear with each other and forgive one another if any of you has a grievance against someone. Forgive as the Lord forgave you. – Colossians 3:13

PRAY. Go before the throne of God and seek his face for relationships and situations that seem hopeless. Pray by faith, remembering you are seated in the heavenly realms with Christ. Pray by faith, remembering that God already went the distance for you in Christ. Jesus paid it all. His death and resurrection are everything we need for life and godliness.

CONFESS & APOLOGIZE. If there is anything you have done that God brings up in your heart, even if it is being impatient or short tempered, get in the habit of asking God for forgiveness as soon as the Lord convicts you. Confession is spiritual. Instead of just ignoring your sin and "trying to do better next time," a believer confesses that he or she has sinned and submits the sin to Christ. Trying to do better next time, without confession and repentance, is religion and works. If you hurt someone, swallow your pride and do the right thing! Apologize in the same way you would like to be apologized to, without finger pointing or defensiveness. Use a gentle spirit.

Learning to overcome difficulty in relationships is very foreign to people in a society where divorce is the easy way out, and where you just stop talking to people if you have hurt feelings. Brick by brick, hurt by hurt, God wants you to dismantle the anger and resentment between you and others in your life. Are you willing to trust the Lord and allow Jesus to give you the ministry of reconciliation?

Examine the following chart to see how the offenses in our relationships stack up like bricks in a brick wall. You need to dismantle them in Jesus' name through prayer. We do our part through forgiveness and prayer. Another aspect of reconciliation is resting. Rest in the truths of the Lord, even when you don't see immediate results in the relationship. Some of these walls are thick and high, built over decades of offense. Take time to pray through these things, as the Lord leads you, and wait on him patiently for guidance and direction.

GIVING GRACE	DIVIDING WALL of HOSTILITY	RECEIVING GRACE
How much grace have you lived in with God? What has he forgiven you for? Are you giving that grace to other people? Are you holding pain and grudges instead of allowing YOUR mercies to be new every morning? Take time to write down the "bricks" that have built the wall of hostility between you and another. The wall went up brick by brick. Begin—by the resurrection power of Jesus that lives in you—to forgive each and every hurt and offense. This is an act of FAITH and GRACE, not of emotions or circumstances. Prayerfully seek the Holy Spirit's guidance as you create, NOT a hit list, but a GRACE list. A list that you will take before the Father to pray through piece-by-piece, saying, "I forgive this offense, in Jesus' name, because God, in Christ Jesus, forgave me."	What is the dividing wall of HOSTILITY that stands between you and someone you are in a relationship with? Over all the years, what hurts have estranged this relationship brick by brick? Are these hurts any greater than the pain Christ felt when dying for your sin on the cross? Remember the victory we have in Christ and the grace God extends to us.	Remember that grace isn't amazing unless we are honest concerning our need for it. Many times, in broken relationships, both people are contributors to the pain of one another. Sometimes, this is not true, as in cases of abuse. However, in everyday relationships, we frequently offend others, sometimes unknowingly. Pray and ask the Lord if there are any sins you need to ask forgiveness for. Have you wronged someone and need to make it right? This is not time to beat yourself up, but to allow the Holy Spirit to shine his light into your heart, so you can repent of any harm you may have done to another. Ask the Lord for direction in this. Be humble and honest.

Use the space below to write down things you need to pray through, whether it's grievances that you need to forgive, or people you need to ask to forgive you.

BRINGING IT HOME

Are you teaching your children grace and mercy? When your kids get hurt feelings do you teach them how to pray to forgive people, to look at misunderstandings and not judge a person's heart, or do you just fear for their feelings and try to protect them from all harm? (There is a time and a place for protection.) Do you require your children to apologize and ask for forgiveness? We need to teach our children to learn to reconcile, not just run.

Do you practice this in your marriage, or do you ignore things and hope they will blow over?

Do you practice forgiveness in your friendships?

In our time, people are surrounded by hostile conditions at school, work, and even in our family and church. Now, more than ever, we need to up our forgiveness and reconciliation game. Pray for insight into this.

RECONCILIATION
PART 4

CHRIST BRINGS PEACE!

For he himself is our peace, who has made the two groups one and has destroyed the barrier, the dividing wall of hostility. — Ephesians 2:14

NEW PRAYER MEMORY VERSE

We are suddenly blessed with a new prayer from the apostle Paul. Aren't you super stoked to have access to the prayers of the man who wrote a huge portion of the Bible? Since today's study bridges Chapters 2 and 3, I am introducing Paul's second prayer for the Ephesians. You can pray these prayers for your family, friends, and for yourself. It makes me giddy to think of the anointing of God that will come on our lives when we enter into his presence and this study with this type of faith-building prayer! Paul's prayers always are focused on:

• Jesus

• Who we are in Christ

• The power of God to transform

Let's get praying and memorizing!

MEMORY VERSE

[14] For this reason I kneel before the Father, [15] from whom every family in heaven and on earth derives its name. [16] I pray that out of his glorious riches he may strengthen you with power through his Spirit in your inner being, [17] so that Christ may dwell in your hearts through faith. And I pray that you, being rooted and established in love, [18] may have power, together with all the Lord's holy people, to grasp how wide and long and high and deep is the love of Christ, [19] and to know this love that surpasses knowledge – that you may be filled to the measure of all the fullness of God. — Ephesians 3:14-19

READING

Open your Bible and read Ephesians 2:11-3:21.

Paul is developing an important truth so the people of Ephesus can know who they are together with other believers in Christ. Look for this theme throughout your reading. Look for the word "mystery." Hmmmm. This IS a mystery. He keeps using this word throughout Ephesians! What is up with that? Time to ask the Holy Spirit for some wisdom and revelation.

CROSS REFERENCE

After you are done reading the passage, look up the word "mystery" in your Bible concordance or on your Bible app. Find the passages that mention it in Ephesians. Write the references down here:

> **TODAY'S BIBLE STUDY TOOL**
>
> **Cross Reference.** Use a Bible concordance or search your Bible app to find other passages in scripture on the same subject.

LISTEN TO THE WORD

Let's put this puzzle together. Here is your activity for today:

LISTEN to the entire Book of Ephesians aloud. Listening to the Word will activate your faith! You can do this with your Bible app, or just read it aloud to yourself. When you hear the word "mystery," pay attention! Go back in the recording (or your reading) and listen to what is surrounding the word "mystery" in the text.

- Write down your findings here:

> **TODAY'S BIBLE STUDY TOOL**
>
> **Listen to the Word of God.** Recruit your sense of hearing to study the Word of God, too. Read aloud. Have someone read aloud to you. Listen to it from your Bible app. Listen intently!
>
> "So then faith cometh by hearing, and hearing by the word of God." – Romans 10:17 KJV

BRINGING IT HOME

Do you take time to read a passage over and over?

Do you see the difference when you listen to that same passage?

Do you teach your older children how to use these digging tools to look at the passage from different perspectives?

Also, try reading the passage in a different version like NKJV, NASB or NLT.

RECONCILIATION
PART 5

DISCOVERING THE MYSTERY THROUGH REVELATION

MEMORY VERSE

[14] For this reason I kneel before the Father, [15] from whom every family in heaven and on earth derives its name. [16] I pray that out of his glorious riches he may strengthen you with power through his Spirit in your inner being, [17] so that Christ may dwell in your hearts through faith. And I pray that you, being rooted and established in love, [18] may have power, together with all the Lord's holy people, to grasp how wide and long and high and deep is the love of Christ, [19] and to know this love that surpasses knowledge – that you may be filled to the measure of all the fullness of God. — Ephesians 3:14-19

PRAYER

Father God,

Strengthen me with power in my inner being. May your Spirit, Lord Jesus, come in and minister to my spirit, so that you may dwell in my heart by faith. I pray that I can be rooted and established in love and that I will have power, together with all the saints, to grasp how wide and long and high and deep is the love of Christ and to know this love that surpasses knowledge—that I may be filled to the measure of all the fullness of God.

Amen.

WORD STUDY
Mystery

What is the mystery that Paul talks about in Ephesians? Do you know? Do you remember? Get these answers exclusively from our text in Ephesians. Don't fall on what you "think it may mean" or what you've heard others say. We are digging into this part of God's Word and seeking God for answers. Only go to this text for the answers!

> **TODAY'S BIBLE STUDY TOOL**
>
> **Word Study.** Look for context clues to discover the meaning of a word.

In the third chapter of Ephesians, we see the word "mystery" come up four times.

Ephesians 3:1-13

[1] For this reason, I, Paul, the prisoner of Christ Jesus for the sake of you Gentiles –

[2] Surely you have heard about the administration of God's grace that was given to me for you, [3] that is, the **mystery** made known to me by revelation, as I have already written briefly. [4] In reading this, then, you will be able to understand my insight into the **mystery** of Christ, [5] which was not made known to people in other generations as it has now been revealed by the Spirit to God's holy apostles and prophets. [6] This **mystery** is that through the gospel the Gentiles are heirs together with Israel, members together of one body, and sharers together in the promise in Christ Jesus.

[7] I became a servant of this gospel by the gift of God's grace given me through the working of his power. [8] Although I am less than the least of all the Lord's people, this grace was given me: to preach to the Gentiles the boundless riches of Christ, [9] and to make plain to everyone the administration of this **mystery**, which for ages past was kept hidden in God, who created all things. [10] His intent was that now, through the church, the manifold wisdom of God should be made known to the rulers and authorities in the heavenly realms, [11] according to his eternal purpose that he accomplished in Christ Jesus our Lord. [12] In him and through faith in him we may approach God with freedom and confidence. [13] I ask you, therefore, not to be discouraged because of my sufferings for you, which are your glory.

BE A HOLY SPIRIT DETECTIVE

What does the text tell you about the mystery?

You may or may not have come to this conclusion: The mystery is that God takes two hostile people groups who are BOTH spiritually and ethnically different people and makes them ONE group. There are several pictures in Ephesians of what it looks like when the individual believers in the body of Christ come together in faith and Christ dwells in them. What are they?

Read these verses and write your answers.

Ephesians 2:15-16	Ephesians 2:19-21
Ephesians 3:6	Ephesians 3:14-15
Ephesians 4:11-16	Ephesians 5:31-32

Do you think the church is doing a good job living out this revealed mystery of unity? Write your thoughts below.

Before Jesus went to the cross, he spent a special evening in fellowship with his disciples. During this time, he gave many spiritual lessons concerning their oneness with him and with the Father and with one another. Jesus is sharing more than an emotional oneness here. There is something special that he is declaring and revealing to the unaware disciples. During his final prayer, he specifically prays for the disciples and all who will believe in him because of their testimony. Just a thought: Do you ever pray for those who will believe in Christ because of your testimony?

READING

For closing today's study, read John Chapter 17. This chapter is Christ's prayer. He prayed it for you!

BRINGING IT HOME

- When you read God's Word, do you come to it assuming you know what it is saying?

- Do you read the Word in context or pull "sound bites" out of context?

- When you read a Bible story with your children, do you say things like, "What do you think this means?" and "What does this mean to you?"

- Do you ask your children—or those you teach—the erroneous and over-used relative line of questioning that encourages them to believe that the Bible means different things to different people?

OR

- Do you ask, "What is God saying in this story?" and "How do you know?"

- Do you teach your children to ask the Holy Spirit what it means and that they can be a Bible detective?

Ask God to help change your paradigm when it comes to approaching the Word. Ask him to help you seek out his mysteries and to find him!

THE MYSTERY OF GOD'S WILL FOR HIS FAMILY

MEMORY VERSE

[14] For this reason I kneel before the Father, [15] from whom every family in heaven and on earth derives its name. [16] I pray that out of his glorious riches he may strengthen you with power through his Spirit in your inner being, [17] so that Christ may dwell in your hearts through faith. And I pray that you, being rooted and established in love, [18] may have power, together with all the Lord's holy people, to grasp how wide and long and high and deep is the love of Christ, [19] and to know this love that surpasses knowledge – that you may be filled to the measure of all the fullness of God. — Ephesians 3:14-19

PRAYER

Open your study time today by praying the above memory verse. Let's take a few minutes today to settle ourselves into truth through prayer. We have been studying the word "mystery." Since the Garden of Eden, the children of Adam and Eve have fallen into the temptation to believe that God would withhold or hide from them some powerful mystery that they deserve and need to know. Mystery religions, cults and the occult (new age and witchcraft) have drawn people in to seek a power or "revelation" that is hidden and can only be found through incantations and mystical arts. The book of Ephesians reveals to us that God has now unveiled his great mysteries in his son Jesus Christ. God's power is greater than the power of any mystic or fortune teller. God's Spirit will give us everything we need and his Word holds endless spiritual truths to transform our lives in practical and powerful ways. One of the biggest prayer concerns that believers have is wanting to know the "mystery" of God's will for their lives. The mystery is revealed here. God is concerned first and foremost about the state of your relationship with your heavenly Father and others in the family of God. Are you fulfilling your role in his family for today? Don't get side tracked by lofty future goals and ideas. Be faithful in the little things and more will be given to you!

CHALLENGE

Using only our memory verse above, take 5 minutes and write down 5 things you can learn about, 1) the heart of God, 2) your need, and 3) how you are supposed to pray.

35.

36.

37.

38.

39.

READING

Today, we will dig more into the mystery of God! Turn in your Bible and read Ephesians 3:1-13.

At the beginning of Chapter 3, Paul uses the phrase, "For this reason I, Paul...." When you see a phrase like this at the beginning of a passage, be sure to take a peek back at the previous passage to see what the reason or motivation for the next part of his writing is. Another connective phrase you may see is "therefore." When you see "therefore," you always want to ask what it's there for. Paul has laid a solid foundation in Chapter 2 that leads us up to this discussion of mystery and God's family.

Look back at the end of Chapter 2 and then write some of the beautiful and compelling truths Paul taught us in the space below. These are the truths that are the springboard for him to write about the mystery in Chapter 3.

God is revealing to us—his big reveal—that he is on a mission to bring people together! Let's go back to Ephesians 1:7-10 and look at the first time the word "mystery" is introduced in Ephesians.

In the following passage, underline clues to help you understand the mystery.

Ephesians 1:7-10

[7] In him we have redemption through his blood, the forgiveness of sins, in accordance with the riches of God's grace [8] that he lavished on us. With all wisdom and understanding, [9] he made known to us the MYSTERY of his will according to his good pleasure, which he purposed in Christ, [10] to be put into effect when the times reach their fulfillment — to bring unity to all things in heaven and on earth under Christ.

WORD STUDY
Mystery

Below is a study note from the NIV Study Bible. If you have a Study Bible, frequently it will have study tools and helps like this where the translation team has already done some word studies and cross referencing for you. If you are having trouble understanding a word or verse, sometimes this can be helpful. This isn't always the case, and I encourage you to still pray for revelation and direction, because the Lord may lead you to do your own study beyond what you see in the little note. In this situation, I love the insightful hints and cross references. So, I will let you all benefit from it here.

NOTE: mystery—The so-called mystery religions of Paul's day used the Greek word "mysterion" in the sense of something that was to be revealed only to the initiated. Paul himself, however, used it to refer to something formerly hidden or obscure but now revealed by God for all to know and understand. (See Romans 16:25; 1 Cor. 2:7; 4:1, 13:2, 14:2, 15:51, Col. 1:26-27, 2:2, 4:3, and 2 Thess. 2:7, etc.) You may look these verses up for more insight.

The note says that, unlike the pagan religions, the mysteries of Christianity are open and revealed—not concealed! You don't need to go through rituals or pay lots of money to have the insider knowledge or power.

The world is full of chaos and many are searching for peace. In John 14:27, Jesus said, "Peace I leave with you; my peace I give you. I do not give to you as the world gives. Do not let your hearts be troubled and do not be afraid." Christians are searching for peace and unity, even at the expense of sacrificing the truth that Jesus is the only way to the Father. The world tells you that all roads lead to heaven and we won't have peace until we get rid of the idea that Jesus is the only way to heaven. But the truth is that we cannot remove our true peacemaker and expect to be forgiven and accepted by the Father. The sacrifice of Christ and faith in him removes the dividing wall of hostility between us and God AND between us and everyone else in the world. It removes racial, gender and economic walls. True unity comes through the cross.

In my NIV Study Bible, there is a note on verse 9 in Ephesians Chapter 1 that tells me to cross reference Romans 11:25. The following is the passage that was cross-referenced by my NIV Study Bible notes. This powerful scripture dismantles the prideful and racist thoughts that Jews and Gentiles may have which exalt themselves above the knowledge of God's revealed mystery that tells us we are all one in Christ's death and resurrection! To live in God's will we must tear down the lies that bring disunity. always thought relationships could be tough, but I had no idea how much they really are a part of the greatest mystery ever revealed! Turn in your Bible and find this cross reference for yourself. **Read Romans 11:25-36 to grow in your understanding of the mystery.**

Romans 11:25-36 covers some very difficult and confusing stuff. This is because Paul is dismantling racism and long-held, dangerous beliefs that oppose the will of God for unity in the church. Let's start asking questions!

Using Romans 11:25-36, answer the following questions:

40. Why would a believing Gentile be conceited against Israel? (v 25)

41. Why was Israel hardened? (v 25)

42. What does the full number of Gentiles mean? (v 25)

43. Who is Israel an enemy of, on our account, for the gospel? (v 28)

44. Who is Israel loved by, on account of the patriarchs? (v 28)

45. What does the phrase, "the gifts and the call are irrevocable," imply in relationship with Israel? (v 29)

In your own words, write a summary of how Israel's hardening and disobedience leads to the salvation of the Gentile nations. Describe how verse 32 puts us all on equal footing before God.

This passage in Romans quotes prophecies from portions of the Old Testament, including Isaiah 59:20. There is an old saying, "In the Old Testament, Christ is concealed. In the New Testament, Christ is revealed." Apologist Josh McDowell's ministry does an excellent job of teaching how this works. In the blog post *Did Jesus Fulfill Old Testament Prophecy* on josh.org, author Sheri Bell says, "One reason the Bible's Old Testament is so important to Christians is that it contains prophesy—over 300 predictions, in fact—that, like the threads of a tapestry, establish the Messianic credentials of Jesus." (https://www.josh.org/evidence-jesus-lived/)

"Put another way, the Old Testament is like an intricate jigsaw puzzle. The numerous pieces, on their own, are puzzling—until they are assembled enough to fill out the intended picture. Thus, the New Testament is the decryption key for unlocking Old Testament meaning." (www.josh.org/jesus-fulfill-prophesy)

Let's understand how the mystery jigsaw puzzle is being put together in Ephesians and Romans. In Romans 11 Paul says that if non-Jewish believers are ignorant of God's mystery, they will become conceited. Why would they become conceited? Because they can't see the big picture. They can't see that they are just part of the tapestry. They think they are the main event. It says in verses 25-26, "Israel has experienced a hardening in part until the full number of the Gentiles has come in, and in this way all Israel will be saved." Israel rejected the Messiah. Let's just imagine a sibling in a family who is excited when another brother or sister gets in trouble. It's truly not much different! Some non-Jews, knowing that the Jews had hardened their hearts to Jesus, said that God was done with his covenants with Israel and that the Gentiles are the recipients of the new covenant. There is one problem with that. God won't break his promises to Abraham or the Patriarchs! In fact, when non-Jews have a limited view of God's universal plan, they quickly deteriorate into anti-Semitism. Throughout the ages, well-meaning, biblically illiterate—and sadly some biblically literate—people who claimed to be "Christ-followers" persecuted and killed Jews who they slandered as "Christ-killers." Adolf Hitler used this type of rhetoric in his demonically-motivated blood bath across Europe. Does this sound like God's mystery being unveiled? Not at all. When Jesus was on the cross, he prayed for those who killed him, saying, "Father forgive them; for they know not what they do." (Luke 23:34 KJV) Plus, we have to remember that it was truly our sin that nailed Jesus to the cross. Both Romans (Gentiles) and Jews were involved in his crucifixion. And he hung there by his own will and purpose—to redeem all of mankind.

HISTORICAL BACKGROUND
Looking Through the Magnifying Glass at Isaiah

This prophecy from Isaiah 59, which is referenced in Romans 11, spoke to the nation of Israel almost 800 years before the time of Paul about their coming salvation through a deliverer who will bring about a new covenant. I love prophecy! The sheer number of prophecies fulfilled by Christ (all of them!) is proof that he is truly the foretold Messiah. According to Isaiah 6:1, the prophet Isaiah's ministry started in the "year King Uzziah died," 740 years before the birth of Christ, not long before the first destruction of the Northern Kingdom of Israel by the Assyrian Empire. You can find this information in your NIV Study Bible, Introduction to the Book of Isaiah. Northern Israel consisted of ten of the twelve tribes of Israel. The other two tribes, Benjamin, Judah, and some of the Levitical priests (of the tribe of Levi) who were assigned to minister to those two tribes were part of the southern Kingdom of Judah.

When the Assyrians conquered Northern Israel, as we learned in Week Four, they took ten of the twelve tribes and killed most of them. Some people, seeing the deterioration coming, escaped before the siege. Some were left in Samaria and intermarried with the conquering Assyrians. This is why the Jews of Jesus' time hated the Samaritans. They considered them a mixed race of Assyrians and Jews and not "pure" Jewish people. This is why Jesus' story of the good Samaritan astounded so many Jewish listeners. It was a ground-breaking idea, during that time period, for people to reach across racial lines. We may find this to be a no-brainer. Of course we shouldn't be racist! But, Christianity is where the truth about racism being wrong all started. Jesus, the Son of the

Living God, revealed God's will and heart to us about how he does not discriminate among the races, and Paul was reinforcing it to the Ephesians. It was a radical new idea at that time and in many parts of today's world, it still is.

A remnant of the ten tribes, approximately 6,000,000 people, was taken into captivity by Assyria and dispersed around the world. Then, 800 years later, during the time the apostle Paul would write to the Romans and the Ephesians, the ten tribes of Israel were mostly scattered amongst the nations. But, God knew where they were! The DNA of many of the children of Abraham were now mixed into the Gentile races. The only way for all of Israel to be saved was for the Gentiles to be saved—literally! This was the mystery of God's will playing out, as prophesied. Only through the new covenant, which included the Gentiles, could the promises to Abraham and the Jewish people be fulfilled. The jigsaw puzzle of scripture was coming together! Ephesians 3:6 says, "This mystery is that through the gospel the Gentiles are heirs together with Israel, members together of one body, and sharers together in the promise in Christ Jesus."

BIBLE ENCYCLOPEDIA

To learn more background on a subject like this, you can go to biblestudytools. com to do research. In the drop-down menu, you can choose Encyclopedias to do a search of information on "Isaiah" or the "Exile."

> **TODAY'S BIBLE STUDY TOOL**
>
> **Bible Encyclopedia.** Use a Bible encyclopedia to do further research on a topic. If you don't own one, you can use an online encyclopedia such as the one at biblestudytools.com.

TELL ME MORE

The message of salvation for the Gentiles brings redemption to the ends of the earth, even to those Jewish exiles who never came home and to those Gentiles who had not intermarried with Jewish people. And in other prophecies in Isaiah and the Old Testament, we see that the ten tribes will physically come home to Israel in the end of days. We are seeing these prophecies fulfilled even now as Jewish people from around the world return to the country of Israel! And speaking of Adolf Hitler, what the devil intended for evil, God used for good. Because of the Holocaust, at the end of WW II, The United Nations fulfilled prophecies that the kings of the earth would bring the children of Israel back to their land! The physical nation of Israel was established again in 1948, fulfilling more Old Testament prophecies than had been fulfilled since the time of Christ. In 1967 Jerusalem was gained back by the Jews during the Six-Day War. This sent shock waves around the world.

During the time of Darwin in the late 1800s and after, many people fell away from the faith, saying that the Bible must be false, because the physical nation of Israel, which is referred to in all the end times prophecies, hadn't existed for thousands of years. Yet, before the eyes of the world, and out of the great persecution of the Holocaust, God is bringing about what he said in his Word. Now, the puzzle is coming together. We are closer to the return of Christ than we ever have been before. He is returning for this bride, made up of those from all the races and ethnicities of the world who love him and long for his return.

Ladies, God has revealed his mystery to us in his Word! We live in a time in history like none other. We have the complete revelation of God in the Bible. The mystery involves the unified body of Christ, which includes Israel and the Gentile Church—and EVERYONE on the planet who puts their faith in Jesus Christ, for that matter—Jew or Gentile, male, female, black, brown, white, poor, rich, American, immigrant, Baptist, Pentecostal, the list goes on and on. All our pride and walls need to fall! God cares so much about unity and he has made a way for all of us to be part of the same family of God. According to our memory verse prayer shown below, we ALL get our family name from him!

> For this reason I kneel before the Father, from whom his whole family in heaven and on earth derives its name. — Ephesians 3:14-15

QUESTIONS

46. How is all of Israel saved by the full number of Gentiles coming in? (v 26)

47. Some people teach a theology that the nation of Israel no longer matters in God's plan. According to the passages we are studying today, do you think this theology agrees or disagrees with Romans 11 and Ephesians 3? Explain, citing the scripture references you use to support your answer.

BRINGING IT HOME

This mystery we are learning about reveals that God has a long-term plan.

Many times along the road, the plans the Lord has for us may be unfolding, but not clear. It may be confusing. This passage in Romans is a perfect example of how things may or may not seem to make sense up front. However, we CAN know from our prayer today that God's heart for our world and for us is love.

Ask God to help you see with spiritual eyes the things that are difficult. Ask him to open your heart to receive faith from him, to be strengthened in your inner being when things seem confusing and it's hard to see the end game.

Teach your children how God's plan is unfolding in our lives and we can't always see what the end result will be, but we can trust him. He is good and loves us. He is faithful to accomplish his perfect will in our lives.

SPIRITUAL FATHERS & MOTHERS

MEMORY VERSE

[14] For this reason I kneel before the Father, [15] from whom every family in heaven and on earth derives its name. [16] I pray that out of his glorious riches he may strengthen you with power through his Spirit in your inner being, [17] so that Christ may dwell in your hearts through faith. And I pray that you, being rooted and established in love, [18] may have power, together with all the Lord's holy people, to grasp how wide and long and high and deep is the love of Christ, [19] and to know this love that surpasses knowledge – that you may be filled to the measure of all the fullness of God. — Ephesians 3:14-19

PRAYER

Do you ever pray for your inner being to be strengthened? There is a time and place for everything. We spend time strengthening our bodies, feeding ourselves the right food, getting ourselves looking pretty, but do we daily pray for God to strengthen our inner beings so that Christ may dwell in our hearts through faith? We need an increase of faith in our lives. Jesus said, "When I return, will I find faith on earth?" Seriously, Jesus, please find it in me! Please strengthen me and my family with power through your Spirit in our inner beings so that you may dwell in our hearts through faith!

Seek God!

SPIRITUAL FATHERS & MOTHERS

Take a brief inventory of your life. Who is your spiritual father or mother? Do you have someone you answer to, someone like the apostle Paul, who prays for you and holds you accountable? Do you have someone who is responsible before God for what he or she teaches you and how they pray for you? Paul is certainly embracing his "father's heart" for the Ephesians in our memory verse prayer! I wouldn't mind at all if someone like Paul was praying for me on a daily basis. But, Paul is already with the Lord. So, who stands before God for me? My parents and husband do. I answer to them, as well as to some close, trusted friends and the elders of our church. Who stands before God for you?

On the flip side, who do you stand before God for every day? Who do you pray for and plead for? Do you ask for that person to be strengthened in his or her inner being? When we lead someone to Christ or influence someone spiritually, we are like her spiritual parent. Do we take the growth of our spiritual children as seriously as the growth of our biological children? Do we pray for our spiritual children as we hope our spiritual leaders are praying for us? We know that our labors in the Lord are not in vain, especially when we bathe those endeavors in prayer. We know that we were not saved for our own benefit only, but also to carry on the torch to others, who will in turn pass it on to another generation.

In the space below, write the names of people who have spiritual authority in your life to pray for you and hold you accountable before God.

Now, write the names of the people you are accountable before God to pray for and disciple.

READING

Today, your assignment is to re-read Ephesians Chapters 1-3 AFTER you read the directions below. Why would you want to go back and read something you've already studied? Well, when you re-read it after looking at it in detail, you can gain fresh insights. Remember to pray for revelation! Since we are studying spiritual fathers and mothers, we are going to combine this reading with the following word study.

WORD STUDY
Apostles and Prophets

We are going to do a word study in Ephesians Chapters 1-3 to find a theme. We are looking for places in the text where Paul expresses the idea that there is unity among all believers in Christ—himself, the original disciples who became apostles, the Old Testament prophets, and all who have or ever will become believers in Jesus Christ.

- As you read, look for the word "apostle" or the phrase "apostles and prophets." You may want to mark them in a specific way to make them easier to locate for your study.
    - Citing the supporting chapter and verse, record your findings in the space below. *(Remember that context is everything when studying the Bible.)*
    - Record what you learned about
        - the individual believers in the body of Christ
        - the role of the apostle

MY FINDINGS

The following text box contains my own notes I took while doing this activity I just asked you to do. The scriptures included have the words "apostle" or "prophet." First of all, I will list the verses where I found that Paul referenced his role as an apostle and how it relates to the Ephesians and others in the body of Christ. Looking at these scriptures side by side will show us the importance of the calling of an apostle.

Ephesians 1:1 — Paul greets us at the beginning of the letter. It's not just a pleasant greeting. He is showing his authority, gifting and grace as an apostle.

Ephesians 2:19-21 — "Consequently, you are no longer foreigners and aliens, but fellow citizens with God's people and members of God's household, built on the foundations of the apostles and prophets, with Christ Jesus himself as the chief cornerstone, In him the whole building is joined together and rises to become a holy temple in the Lord. And in him you too are being built together to become a dwelling in which God lives by his Holy Spirit."

CITIZENS/CHILDREN — Ephesians 2:19-21 says that the foundations of the household of God are built on the apostles and prophets. How does this work? The phrase "build upon" (according to HELPS™ Word-studies) in the Greek means, *"to build up or edify," or "appropriately build on, following a plan with pre-designed specifications."* We have been learning about revelation and the mystery of God. God chose to reveal his plan to and through the apostles and prophets, so the rest of us could understand his great mystery! They laid the foundation through their obedience and submission to God's plan for them. They also were faithful to teach and carry out the wondrous story of reconciliation we have in Christ. In their obedience, they were foundational in edifying the family of God.

This verse also shows us the unity that Christ brings when it refers to all believers, including the apostles, as citizens and children of God's family. In this spiritual family God is our father, and he also gives authority and responsibility to our spiritual fathers and mothers. They raise us up in Christ and teach us about our place of belonging and what it looks like to be part of this mystery of the unity of Jews and Gentiles.

So, now that you have read my personal notes, from when I did the research, I am going to (hopefully) edify you with insight into this mystery that the apostles unfolded to us! In Israel, being part of the family means being part of the nation. The entire nation of Israel (all Jews in the world) was and is all related through Abraham. We as Gentiles are no longer foreigners of Israel. You are no longer an outcast. No longer separated from the family of God! Did you know God sees YOU as a child of Abraham (the Father of the Jewish nation), as important as a Jewish blood-relative, just because you are trusting in his Son? Ephesians 3:6 says that you are an heir together with Israel. You will inherit all the blessings of Abraham, which are all the blessings that come from being a chosen child of God. We share together in the promise of Christ Jesus. If you want to claim the blessings for a child of Abraham, read Genesis 12:1-3! Be blessed!

BONUS CROSS REFERENCE
For those as excited to learn about your place in God's family as I am!

Let's cross reference to the book of Romans to gain deeper insight into the understanding that this blessing of Abraham is imparted to all who believe in Jesus Christ. What does this have to do with apostles and prophets? They were the ones who unveiled this mystery to us! It was the job of these spiritual leaders to lay the foundation for God's people to understand this new spiritual family.

A person is not a Jew who is one only outwardly, nor is circumcision merely outward and physical. No, a person is a Jew who is one inwardly; and circumcision is circumcision of the heart, by the Spirit, not by the written code. Such a person's praise is not from other people, but from God. – Romans 2:28-29

(Concerning Abraham) So then, he is the father of all who believe but have not been circumcised, in order that righteousness might be credited to them. – Romans 4:11b

FOUNDATION OF THE APOSTLES AND PROPHETS

Let's look at the next place "apostle" shows up! Chapter 3 talks about the spiritual insight that the apostle Paul carried to shine the light of God into the mystery of the gospel so that people could clearly see the revelation of Jesus. A spiritual father or mother helps to open spiritual eyes by communicating God's truth to those in his or her care. Paul did this through his teaching ministry, as well as his ministry through letters, which we also now benefit from!

> In reading this, then, you will be able to understand my insight into the mystery of Christ, which was not made known to men in other generations as it has now been revealed by the Spirit to God's holy apostles and prophets. This mystery is that through the gospel the Gentiles are heirs together with Israel, members together of one body, and sharers together in the promise in Christ Jesus. – Ephesians 3:4-6

Ephesians 2:19-21 tells us that we (the people of God) are built together on the foundation of the apostles and prophets, with Christ Jesus himself as our cornerstone. The apostles, through their teaching, testimony, and sacrificial ministry, carried the truth of Christ and established the foundation of the church, with Christ as the main support and cornerstone. They had great spiritual authority and responsibility. They walked with Christ. They healed people. They raised the dead. They lost everything of this world for everything of the world to come. They were experts on Jesus! We cannot throw away the foundation of truth that we have received from their teaching in scripture. Every good thing we have in Christ, every promise and every word of grace is built on this foundation. In the time we live in, not unlike the time Paul lived in, there are heretics saying that we don't need to take the Word of God as the inspired, God-breathed truth that is still relevant today. Some false teachers use fine sounding arguments to encourage us to justify sin and to believe that spiritual leadership and the authority of the scriptures aren't important. This spirit of error stems from personal pride and a spirit of antichrist that rejects truth. The opposite of pride is humility and submission. True apostles were and are experts on humility and submission.

As we look into the mystery of Christ and the family of God, we need to grasp the concept of humility and servant leadership. In Ephesians Chapter 3, Paul relates to us the weight of the authority and responsibility he carries as an apostle of Jesus Christ. Apostles were required, like the rest of us, to serve God's family with humility. Jesus was a servant leader and he is our example. In Matthew 23:11 Jesus says, "The greatest among you will be your servant." His leaders serve like he did and teach others to walk as servants in Christ.

Being in spiritual leadership is not easy. You commit yourself to serve people who may not always respect your sacrifice—like Jesus did. When you are a servant leader, you can find yourself carrying a lot of the load while other people relax—like Jesus did. It's not too much different from being a mom. Some days your little tribe makes you cry. Some days they make you smile. But you happily die to your own needs to give your children what they need. In fact, part of our sacred identity as women is being like Christ through our daily "dying." It is an honor to bring not only physical life, but emotional and spiritual life to the next generation through our sacrifices. Most of those go unnoticed for the time being, especially when the ugly comes out in those we lead. This is normal. Don't be discouraged. Bear with one another in love while also being honest with those you lead and keeping them accountable. For example, in his first letter to the Corinthians, in Chapter 4, Paul writes to the church using a pretty stern tone compared to the one he uses in the letter he writes to Ephesus. He addresses spiritual cat-fights, division, and general "I'm better than you" attitudes. The Christians in Corinth are not living in the unity that comes from humility and submission to Christ. He uses a bit of spiritual sarcasm and literary wit to call out the Corinthian church on the divisiveness in which they are living and to remind them of the sacrifices he has made in Christ for their spiritual benefit.

Ephesians is such a "feel good" kind of book of the Bible, addressed to people who needed to be encouraged in their place in God's family. However, it is good to read a contrasting passage of scripture, such as the letter to the Corinthians, written by the same author who understands our need for knowing God's lavish love, but also our need for humility. The Corinthians needed to be brought back to the reality of their humble place in the body of Christ. Sometimes we need encouragement and sometimes we need tough love. Servant leaders are sensitive to what those in their care need. This is why we dig deep into scripture—to get the full counsel of God's Word, so we don't become one-sided (with an incomplete understanding of God or a distorted view of ourselves).

CROSS REFERENCE

Let's cross reference this passage to learn a little bit more about humble servanthood and the role of an apostle or "spiritual father" in the church. This time we are going to look for contrasts to see what happens when we don't walk in humility and unity in the body of Christ that Paul talks about in his letter to the Ephesians. **Turn in your Bible to read 1 Corinthians 4.** Get ready. When God's truth clashes with our flesh, it's brutal.

CONTRASTS
Extra Credit

In his letter, Paul contrasts the self-exalting attitude of the Corinthians with the attitude a trained disciple of Jesus Christ should have. Paul is saying all this in love to the Corinthians. God calls all believers to walk like Jesus in humility. The apostles modeled humility and the servant-like attitude of Christ. Paul prayed that each person he shared Christ with would realize that he or she is not above Christ's role as servant leader. Jesus came not to be served, but to serve. Note Jesus' use of contrasts in the following passage of scripture:

> Jesus called them together and said, 'You know that the rulers of the Gentiles lord it over them, and their high officials exercise authority over them. Not so with you. Instead, whoever wants to become great among you must be your servant, and whoever wants to be first must be your slave – just as the Son of Man did not come to be served, but to serve, and to give his life as a ransom for many.' – Matthew 20:25-28

Use the following chart to write a list of things that the apostle Paul says defines the apostles and a list of what he says defines the Corinthians. Paul says the church should strive to be more selfless and sacrificial and less self-important. This is being like Jesus.

APOSTLES	CORINTHIANS
_____	_____
_____	_____
_____	_____
_____	_____
_____	_____
_____	_____

BRINGING IT HOME

As a woman, you make a lot of sacrifices for your friends and family that go unnoticed. Those you are helping may have no idea where they would be if it weren't for you. Paul wants the Corinthians, Ephesians, (and us) to know the power of a good spiritual father (or mother) as an example. We need to know the sacrifices others have made so that we can know Christ and walk in the power of Christ in their footsteps. Ask God if there are any people in your life who are your spiritual fathers or mothers that you have walked through life not noticing. Thank them for the way they have served you and ask them to pray that you will grow in having their selfless, serving attitude toward those in your spiritual care. Pray for them, too! Ask God for a humble attitude so that you may become more like Christ.

During teachable moments with your children, have real conversations with them about your past and how, through the testimony of God's work in your life, they now have the opportunity to live in the faith. They need to understand that they only know Christ because someone else sacrificed and shared Jesus—again, this is a grace and sovereignty moment. Paul shows us through the Ephesians and Corinthians that the different approaches of encouragement and rebuke are necessary with our spiritual and physical children, so they can grow up in Christ.

Finally, are you in a church or body of believers where you are being discipled and are accountable to the leadership? Are you in a church where you are serving in your spiritual gifts or in a church where you are a consumer who comes only for what you can get out of it?

LIVING STONES?

MEMORY VERSE

¹⁴ For this reason I kneel before the Father, ¹⁵ from whom every family in heaven and on earth derives its name. ¹⁶ I pray that out of his glorious riches he may strengthen you with power through his Spirit in your inner being, ¹⁷ so that Christ may dwell in your hearts through faith. And I pray that you, being rooted and established in love, ¹⁸ may have power, together with all the Lord's holy people, to grasp how wide and long and high and deep is the love of Christ, ¹⁹ and to know this love that surpasses knowledge – that you may be filled to the measure of all the fullness of God. — Ephesians 3:14-19

PRAYER

When you approach the throne room today, pray as Paul did, that you can move into a brand-new realm of faith. "…that Christ may dwell in your hearts through faith." If you hear the name Jesus and your heart isn't stirred or strengthened, or if you feel a bit blasé, you need to seek God that he will, out of his glorious riches, strengthen you with power through his Spirit in your inner being, so that Christ may dwell in your heart through faith. AND, this is the BEGINNING! Seek and you find. Ask and it will be given to you. Knock and the door will be opened to you. God wants you to:

- be rooted and established in love

- have power TOGETHER with ALL the saints

- grasp how wide and long and high and deep is the love of Christ

- KNOW this love that surpasses knowledge

- BE FILLED to the measure of all the fullness of God

CONTENTMENT WITH MY DIVINE CALLING AS A LIVING STONE

Yesterday, we searched Ephesians Chapters 1-3 to find God's purpose for the spiritual leadership of the apostles and prophets, those who have passed on into God's presence, and even the spiritual leaders we have in our lives today. We discovered that Jesus modeled servant leadership through humility and sacrifice. As he lowers himself to be our servant, we are taught how to humble ourselves to serve others—even those who are difficult to get along with.

READING

Open your Bible and read Philippians 2:1-18. Savor this beautiful passage that teaches us that our ultimate leader, Jesus, became a servant to all. List all the characteristics of Jesus. List what we are to be like. Contrast this with the ways that we are not to treat others.

JESUS IS	I AM TO BE	AND NOT
_____	_____	_____
_____	_____	_____
_____	_____	_____
_____	_____	_____
_____	_____	_____
_____	_____	_____

SERVANT TO ALL

It is clear from Philippians 2:1-18 that Jesus has every spiritual right and spiritual equality with God, but he did not choose to live exalted. He became a servant to all, because it was the Father's will. The King of kings and Lord of lords became the janitor, so to speak. He made himself nothing. He is an example of divine leadership. When believers who deserve to be exalted lower themselves to exalt others, when they do everything without complaining or arguing, they truly shine as stars in comparison to the darkness of a me-centered world.

Books about achieving greatness fly off the shelves, and speakers who teach you how to make more money and be the best you that you can be are in high demand, but in the kingdom of God, we become great by becoming small. The tension in the kingdom of God is to understand how much we are loved and valued, even when we are small like a stone. We need revelation from the Holy Spirit to understand it. Yesterday, we focused on the accountability that spiritual leaders and teachers have before God for us, and even what servant responsibility we may have for others in our own lives. Let's now look at this section of Ephesians that talks about how we are stones that are fitted together with other believers into a holy temple for the Lord. Even as a small, humble stone, you have belonging. You have purpose. You are needed!

WORD STUDY

In the following passage, highlight the words/phrases that describe you as a believer. Underline the descriptive words/phrases about Jesus.

Ephesians 2:19-22

Consequently, you are no longer foreigners and strangers, but fellow citizens with God's people and also members of his household, built on the foundation of the apostles and prophets, with Christ Jesus himself as the chief cornerstone. In him the whole building is joined together and rises to become a holy temple in the Lord. And in him you too are being built together to become a dwelling in which God lives by his Spirit.

CROSS REFERENCE
The Living Stone & A Chosen People

Let's cross reference another place in scripture that uses this same concept to describe the family of God. **Turn in your Bible to 1 Peter 2:4-10.** Circle the words that describe you as a believer. Underline the descriptive words and phrases about Jesus. If you look in your Bible's footnotes, you will see that Peter is referencing several different Old Testament prophecies, as he writes about Jesus. Peter is helping New Testament believers to understand the greater, foretold mystery of Christ and our role in his body.

There are several word pictures used in these passages from Ephesians 2:19-22 and 1 Peter 2:4-10. They are not just the work of two different writers of these passages using the same metaphors. These word pictures illustrate that the mystery in Ephesians is what is happening in Christ in the supernatural. The first realization is that we are stones. Stones by themselves do not have a great purpose. But, stones that are chosen by a builder are specifically picked for a purpose. Becoming a servant, Christ lowered himself from his majesty to be a stone and then, because of his humility and obedience, he became the chief cornerstone. It says in 1 Peter 2:7-8 that people stumble over this aspect of Jesus' identity—the part where he is a stone. He is fully God, but lowered himself to be fully man and not just a man, but a servant. He submitted himself to death on the cross. It is a great mystery.

Everyone who follows Christ and lowers themselves to be servants will be fitted as a stone in the rising temple of God. This is the second part of the word picture. Single stones united into a great temple—the temple of God. We are actually connected in the Spirit to people we've never met all across the world who are living and who have already gone before us! The apostles and prophets told us with their words and showed us with their actions the goal of God and the mystery—that Jews and Gentiles are unified into one nation and one body, the spiritual house, or temple, of Christ.

This concept of a great temple does not detract from God's care for you as a person. It shows that everyone has belonging. Each individual stone is carefully and lovingly fit together with others in Christ. You are also personally being built up as a home for God. Ephesians 3:16-17 says, "I pray that out of his glorious riches he may strengthen you with power through his Spirit in your inner being, so that Christ may dwell in your hearts through faith." We are strengthened for the purposes of God—to be his dwelling place. As I mull over this idea that we are stones in God's temple, I think of how rough around the edges I am. Then my mind goes to a passage in the Old Testament when the children of God were wandering in the wilderness. When they were bringing an offering to God, he desired an altar built with uncut stones. This was not necessarily an attractive altar, but the uncut stones spoke prophetic volumes. In Exodus 20:25, it says, "If you make an altar of stones for me, do not build it with dressed stones, for you will defile it if you use a tool on it." In the Old Testament, the physical requirements for worship were also a spiritual or prophetic picture of what God desired for his people's hearts. In this case, we are the uncut stones built into God's altar of sacrifice. God wants us to bring ourselves to him as we are. We are not to try to put on spiritual airs and pretend that we have some righteousness from ourselves. Our righteousness comes simply by bringing our broken, rough selves to Jesus and calling on him for redemption. God does the work in us through his Spirit, as we sit there, on the altar, proclaiming our own need. And there we find our value, our belonging and our purpose—to bring glory to God.

> What agreement is there between the temple of God and idols? For we are the temple of the living God. As God has said: 'I will live with them and walk among them, and I will be their God, and they will be my people.' – 2 Corinthians 6:16

> Don't you know that you yourselves are God's temple and that God's Spirit lives among you? – 1 Corinthians 3:16

You are the temple of the Holy Spirit. Ladies, this means that we aren't just here living for the next episode of our favorite Netflix series to come out. We are built into the temple of God that has its foundation on the apostles, but we are the current running season of God's reality show. We are the main characters. We are the actual temple of the Holy Spirit. We are where God is building his kingdom right now!

Are you lonely? Do your days pass quickly by and you feel the futility of the rat race? Do you spend too much time on social media, cleaning, working or waiting for kids to get out of practices feeling like you are a hamster on a wheel? Do you isolate yourself, because the idea of being around others makes you full of anxiety? Do you like a crowd, but find yourself just looking for fun and entertainment instead of a place where you can make a difference in the body of Christ? Are you living with a knowledge of your belonging and your place in the temple of God and your value as someone who carries his life inside of you?

Here is the good news. The stress, loneliness, selfishness and anxiety in your life are all subject to our Living God. If you are in a physically or emotionally bad place, remember that your entire life, as a believer in Jesus, can be transformed. Just think of yourself as an uncut stone in the altar of God, ready and willing to belong to his greater plan and purposes. You were made for relationships! You were made to fellowship with other people in the body of Christ. The enemy wants to divide and conquer us. He wants to keep women away from other women of faith. He wants us to be too busy to connect with others or too paranoid that others are judging us or rejecting us. He wants you to focus on someone else's weaknesses and to get easily annoyed, instead of bearing with one another in love. He wants to isolate members of the body of Christ through busyness, fear, and unforgiveness to keep them from their great calling and purpose in God's kingdom. Jesus said, "If a house is divided against itself, that house cannot stand." (Mark 3:25) Jesus comes to bring his house together and build us up into a great temple for the Lord.

What is your role? Only the Lord can show you. He gives the gifts. He gives the increase. He causes all things to grow. Seek God today. We are part of something much bigger than ourselves. We cannot disconnect ourselves from the bigger picture, no more than our stomach can have a purpose or role separate from our digestive system. We cannot allow fear or bitterness, mistrust or self-centered pursuits to separate us from our mysterious role in the destiny of the body of Christ. We also cannot forget the great and mysterious work of God in our own lives. We are not just "keeping" house. God is making his house a home for his Spirit and we are the building blocks. God is building us. God has a plan that is more beautiful than we can imagine.

Paul wraps it up in Ephesians 3:1-6,

Ephesians 3:1-6

[1] For this reason I, Paul, the prisoner of Christ Jesus for the sake of you Gentiles –

[2] Surely you have heard about the administration of God's grace that was given to me for you, [3] that is, the mystery made known to me by revelation, as I have already written briefly. [4] In reading this, then, you will be able to understand my insight into the mystery of Christ, [5] which was not made known to people in other generations as it has now been revealed by the Spirit to God's holy apostles and prophets. [6] This mystery is that through the gospel the Gentiles are heirs together with Israel, members together of one body, and sharers together in the promise in Christ Jesus.

BRINGING IT HOME

What is your role in the big picture of God's kingdom? What does God want to reveal to you or lay on your heart for the building of his kingdom? Have you asked him?

Is there something that you are "chained" to in life that God has given you to accomplish? Paul reveals to the Ephesians that he is a SERVANT and PRISONER of Christ. Servanthood is a huge responsibility. Paul is not a man with money, power and fame. He is a man who sees his role in the bigger picture of the kingdom of God.

Do you seek God for the role of your children, family and/or friends in the kingdom? Are you just thinking about their careers, sports, music or other physically enriching activities? Since you are built into the kingdom, do you pray for those around you to grow in their knowledge of God's will for their lives? Do you ask God to use your family for his glory and to grow his kingdom in their hearts?

You may feel that life is passing you by, but it's not! Most of the godly men and women of the Bible didn't get their real start until they were in their 40s. Jesus was young when he started in his 30s. Some, like Moses, don't begin their full ministry till they are senior citizens! Start seeking God for wisdom and revelation about what he wants for your life!

SEEK THE HEART OF GOD

MEMORY VERSE

[14] For this reason I kneel before the Father, [15] from whom every family in heaven and on earth derives its name. [16] I pray that out of his glorious riches he may strengthen you with power through his Spirit in your inner being, [17] so that Christ may dwell in your hearts through faith. And I pray that you, being rooted and established in love, [18] may have power, together with all the Lord's holy people, to grasp how wide and long and high and deep is the love of Christ, [19] and to know this love that surpasses knowledge – that you may be filled to the measure of all the fullness of God. — Ephesians 3:14-19

Today, in prayer, we will ask the Father for clarity on what true unity looks like and what it doesn't look like.

PRAYER

Father,

In Jesus' name, I thank you for all the blessings I have in your family! Help me to understand what it means to be a living stone, built together with others into the great temple of God. Help me to understand the difference between true unity and compromise to cover up sin, just to get along with people. Strengthen me in my inner being with power through your Spirit! Increase my faith so I can understand your heart for me and the deep love of Christ. Your love is wider, longer, higher and deeper than I can imagine. Open my understanding through your Spirit so I can know your love and the fullness of that love that comes when your family lives in unity. Speak, oh Lord. Transform me, as I learn of your heart.

In Jesus' name, Amen.

READING

Ephesians 3:7-21

[7] I became a servant of this gospel by the gift of God's grace given me through the working of his power. [8] Although I am less than the least of all the Lord's people, this grace was given me: to preach to the Gentiles the boundless riches of Christ, [9] and to make plain to everyone the administration of this mystery, which for ages past was kept hidden in God, who created all things. [10] His intent was that now, through the church, the manifold wisdom of God should be made known to the rulers and authorities in the heavenly realms, [11] according to his eternal purpose that he accomplished in Christ Jesus

our Lord. [12] In him and through faith in him we may approach God with freedom and confidence. [13] I ask you, therefore, not to be discouraged because of my sufferings for you, which are your glory.

[14] For this reason I kneel before the Father, [15] from whom every family in heaven and on earth derives its name. [16] I pray that out of his glorious riches he may strengthen you with power through his Spirit in your inner being, [17] so that Christ may dwell in your hearts through faith. And I pray that you, being rooted and established in love, [18] may have power, together with all the Lord's holy people, to grasp how wide and long and high and deep is the love of Christ, [19] and to know this love that surpasses knowledge – that you may be filled to the measure of all the fullness of God.

[20] Now to him who is able to do immeasurably more than all we ask or imagine, according to his power that is at work within us, [21] to him be glory in the church and in Christ Jesus throughout all generations, for ever and ever! Amen

RECAP

Yesterday, we discovered that each believer in Jesus is a living stone, rough around the edges, but perfectly fit into the spiritual house of God. God chose the apostles and prophets to be servant leaders and to reveal his mystery to us through his written Word. In this way, we can also learn to be like Christ in humility, putting others before ourselves. When we become part of God's family, we find belonging and purpose alongside others who are also unpolished, living stones. The beautiful part of knowing this mystery is understanding that Christ does the polishing work in each of us, purifying us by his blood and his Word and making us more like him. We also learned in Philippians 2 that the more we become like Jesus in the humility of our attitudes, the more we shine like stars in this crooked and depraved generation. In fact, Ephesians 3:10 says we are examples to the rulers and authorities in the heavenly realms. The devil comes to separate relationships, from our relationship with God to our relationships with each other. When we do everything without complaining and arguing, with Christ-like attitudes, this truth in Ephesians is actualized. We show the devil that he is losing and that in Christ we overcome through the unity of the Spirit.

TRUE UNITY VS FALSE UNITY

This unity is not the fake unity that the world offers. Everyone longs for peace. In response to violence, racism and the separation that comes from other differences of opinions and beliefs, people cry out "Coexist! Coexist!" The peace the world offers implies that deeply held religious beliefs, whether true or false, must be ignored or set aside in the name of unity. Many so-called "Christian" leaders are compromising the gospel of Jesus Christ just to get along, saying that all religions and beliefs lead to heaven. But, how can this be true, if all religions and beliefs don't even believe in a heaven or one supreme Creator-God? And we need to remember the blood that purchased our unmerited salvation. What kind of a good father would God be, if there were another way that led to heaven and he still made Jesus go to the cross? Do you remember Jesus' prayer in the garden of Gethsemane? In Luke 22:42 Jesus prays, "'Father, if you are willing, take this cup from me; yet not my will, but yours be done.'" Was this the first time the Father didn't answer a prayer from his son? That would seem to be so, if we believe the teachers that say there is no hell and everyone gets to go to heaven, even if they don't believe in heaven or Jesus as their Savior. The cross was cruel and horrific. What kind of a father would ask his son to endure that for no reason? Truly, not our heavenly Father.

INCLUSION VS PEACE

True inclusion comes at a price. God knew the price and sent his son to bridge the gap between God and humanity. We are included in the family of God, because Jesus humbled himself to death on a cross and rose again on the third day. When he was raised up, we who believe were raised up with him. True inclusion is not free. True inclusion does not come through disregarding the Word of God.

True inclusion is not possible without Jesus. In John 14:27, Jesus said, "Peace I leave with you; my peace I give you. I do not give to you as the world gives. Do not let your hearts be troubled and do not be afraid." His peace is real, but it is not the temporary, fake peace that comes from compromising with the world. In Daniel Chapter 3, Shadrach, Meshach and Abednego could have existed peacefully in their society if they had agreed to bow down to the 90-foot tall golden idol of King Nebuchadnezzar. These three young men were willing to pay the price for not bowing to a false god. Nowadays, in the United States and other Western countries, you may not be threatened with a physical fiery furnace for not following the protocols of the culture, but you may find yourself in a social media roasting or even a public humiliation fire for not agreeing to bow to the ways of the world. True peace came to the boys in the fire. They weren't exempt from walking through a fire, but they were accompanied by one whom Nebuchadnezzar called, "A son of the gods." Jesus himself was with them in the fire. The peace of God comes to those on whom God's favor rests. At the announcement of his birth in Luke 2:14, the angels of God declared, "'Glory to God in the highest heaven, and on earth peace to those on whom his favour rests.'" We know that favor isn't favor, unless there is an exclusion involved. The exclusion is simply reserved for those who harden their hearts to the truth of Christ and/or are not walking in his redemption power. Favor comes to those who trust in Christ.

PEACE IN THE MIDDLE OF THE STORM

In Luke 12:49-53, Jesus gives us a prophecy that seems at odds with all of this peace and unity talk.

Luke 12:49-53

[49] 'I have come to bring fire on the earth, and how I wish it were already kindled! [50] But I have a baptism to undergo, and what constraint I am under until it is completed! [51] Do you think I came to bring peace on earth? No, I tell you, but division. [52] From now on there will be five in one family divided against each other, three against two and two against three. [53] They will be divided, father against son and son against father, mother against daughter and daughter against mother, mother-in-law against daughter-in-law and daughter-in-law against mother-in-law.'

Does this mean that the Bible contradicts itself? Absolutely not! Jesus is preparing the disciples for persecution within their own family and friend groups. Even when you are humble, loving and kind, many people will "feel" like you are judging them just because you are believing in Jesus and they aren't yet. You cannot avoid it and Jesus promises it will happen. Why? Because those who belong to the world truly hate him first. They may even say with their lips that they are religious or believe in him, but if they are not repentant or willing to admit they are sinners in need of saving, they will inwardly be repulsed by any feelings of conviction of the Holy Spirit concerning their need for Christ. If the Holy Spirit is in you, you may feel like the recipient of the rejection directed at Christ. Now, I am not talking about arguing with family or strife that comes from personality dysfunction, but true persecution for your belief in Jesus. In the middle of all of this, we are offered inner peace from our Savior. Promises like this from John 16:33, "I have told you these things, so that in me you may have peace. In this world you will have trouble. But take heart! I have overcome the world," give us confidence that our outward troubles are momentary and that we are truly stones in the temple of God. When your earthly family rejects you for Christ, your heavenly family has an eternal place for you in his family!

Paul encourages the Ephesians in Chapter 3 verses 12-13, to not be discouraged by his suffering and persecution for Jesus. What does he encourage them with? He reminds them of their position in the family of God and the confidence they should have to go right into the throne room of the Father in prayer for him. He says, "In him and through faith in him we may approach God with freedom and confidence. I ask you, therefore, not to be discouraged because of my sufferings for you, which are your glory." Those of us who live in free countries should be encouraged to pray for our brothers and sisters in Christ who are experiencing persecution, like Paul did. Their persecution is for our glory. We have the glorious opportunity to do our part, lifting them up before the Father. Let's remember that Paul is their spiritual father and example. When our spiritual leaders are in difficulty because of the sacrifices they make for the kingdom, we should not be discouraged; we should pray for them with boldness and confidence the way they have prayed for us! We are the body of Christ. And, much like our own bodies that have cells which work together to create organs, which in turn work in tandem in a physical system, which works in the entire body so the whole being can be sound and functioning, so we as individuals are important to God and to the greater eternal good of the kingdom. Our prayers make a difference and bring God glory!

As I read through Ephesians more and more, I keep seeing a diamond mine. This is a mine of sparkling spiritual truths that shine in the darkness. The deeper we go, the more we will find. This writing of Paul blows away the idea in the body of Christ of the self-centered lifestyle that we value in America. I am not talking about personal responsibility or the value of the individual. However, Paul is making a case for God's intention and plan from the foundations of the world to unify all of us little "rebels" out there, who are intent on making our own lives and following our own dreams, into a revolution against the kingdom of this world—the kingdom and authority of the prince of the power of the air—as we follow our sovereign Lord Jesus to establish the kingdom of heaven in the hearts of people on earth.

From the time we are little children, we think in terms of "me." My toys, my schedule, my life, my purpose, my future. Let's put this into perspective. The individuals in the body of Christ are very important. Individuality is essential. You cannot find your place in God's family, if you don't know how God has called you and gifted you. God cares about your individual needs. He has numbered the hairs on your head and he has written your tears on his scroll. He knows the exact moment of your first heartbeat and he knows the moment of your last. Jesus bore your personal sin and your personal pain and sickness on the cross. But, ultimately, we were made for God and for each other. We were created for relationship. We are redeemed for a relationship with God and we are restored for our relationships with each other, to be part of the unified body of Christ, a spiritual house where he lives.

WORD STUDY

Since Paul's prayers for the Ephesians are for them to know the heart of God, let's do a read through and underline/write notes about ALL the references in Ephesians 1-3 about the INTENT of God and his WILL/PURPOSE.

Write notes and thoughts on what these verses in Ephesians say about God's will and intent.

TODAY'S BIBLE STUDY TOOL

Word Study. The repeated use of words and/or phrases is like a flag signaling us to slow down and think about what the scripture is saying.

Ephesians Chapters 1—3

1:5

_____

1:9

_____

1:11

_____

2:10

_____

2:15

_____

3:10

_____

3:11

_____

Now, when we think of someone's intentions, we usually equate this with character. So, let's draw conclusions—JUST FROM THE TEXT—about the character of God our Father. For each of the verses listed above, ask the Holy Spirit to reveal to you something about the character of God.

Since God _____, he is _____.

Since God _____, he is _____.

Since God _____, he is _____.

Since God _____, he is _____.

Since God _____, he is _____.

Since God _____, he is _____.

Since God _____, he is _____.

Ladies, when I go to this text, all my negative fear of God falls away into a big pile of crumpled-up perfectionism. I always want to be perfect and please God. But, we see here that God's INTENTIONS were to rescue us in the middle of our sin, to show his mercy and his grace. We see his TRUE character displayed here, and it is truly GLORIOUS! He loved us before we loved him. He is a reconciler of relationships. He is a mender of brokenness. He does not delight in our destruction, but he calls us out of darkness and sin and chooses us to be his children. He ordains us from the foundations of the earth to be part of his family, his bride, the body of his Son, whom he loves.

As I write this, the Holy Spirit is bringing up in my heart a passage in the Old Testament. He warned the Israelites not to get conceited about the fact that he chose them from among the nations. Israel was predestined and chosen, because of Abraham's faith. But, God wanted them to remember that it was because of his goodness that they were chosen. They had plenty of flaws. They were stubborn and tended to lose faith and do their own thing. "The Lord did not set his affection on you and choose you because you were more numerous than other peoples, for you were the fewest of all peoples. But it was because the Lord loved you and kept the oath he swore to your ancestors that he brought you out with a mighty hand and redeemed you from the land of slavery, from the power of Pharaoh king of Egypt. Know therefore that the Lord your God is God; he is the faithful God, keeping his covenant of love to a thousand generations of those who love him and keep his commandments." – Deuteronomy 7:7-9

Wow! God's heart is so good and he is so great that even in our wretchedness he loves us and delivers us, when we trust in his son Jesus. In a sermon, the late Bible teacher Derek Prince shared this practical principle on our value with the Lord. When you buy a house, what do you pay for it? You pay what it is worth. If you are selling a house and it is appraised at $250,000, but your top offer is only $200,000, what is it actually worth? Your house is worth what someone will pay for it. In the same way, your life is worth what God paid for it. He valued you at the cost of his very Son. His Son embraced his suffering on the cross and counted it joy to pay for your sin. Your value is very high in the eyes of our Father. You are loved. You belong. Do not reject this wondrous gift or doubt God's intentions for you.

We need to take a long, refreshing drink from this truth. God is good. All the time. He is trustworthy. He is faithful. He keeps his promises and his oaths. We can trust the one who has created us and called us into his glorious kingdom!

Take time to write yourself a letter below. What is the Holy Spirit teaching you about God's intentions for you? What have you personally learned about God's heart? We have been praying to know and understand his heart. I believe, by faith, that God is revealing that to you!

BRINGING IT HOME

When we teach our children about who God is, do we let them know we can't earn his love? We can't earn his love, because it's impossible for him to not love us. We are loved by him, because of his goodness and he truly is love, not because we are really good. Love comes from him. He is love. Remember to teach your children about the intent and heart of God to deliver us and to call us his own.

Are we bringing him glory with our lives? He is glorious! Are we giving him praise? Are we sharing our testimony? Our testimony may not always make us look good, but it will always make God look good and it will bring more people to Jesus.

FREEDOM AND CONFIDENCE

In him and through faith in him we may approach God with freedom and confidence. I ask you, therefore, not to be discouraged because of my sufferings for you, which are your glory. — Ephesians 3:12-13

Since our study today focuses on our attitude of confidence when we go into our Father's presence in prayer, we are adding two more verses to our memory verse passage.

MEMORY VERSE

[14] For this reason I kneel before the Father, [15] from whom every family in heaven and on earth derives its name. [16] I pray that out of his glorious riches he may strengthen you with power through his Spirit in your inner being, [17] so that Christ may dwell in your hearts through faith. And I pray that you, being rooted and established in love, [18] may have power, together with all the Lord's holy people, to grasp how wide and long and high and deep is the love of Christ, [19] and to know this love that surpasses knowledge – that you may be filled to the measure of all the fullness of God.

[20] Now to him who is able to do immeasurably more than all we ask or imagine, according to his power that is at work within us, [21] to him be glory in the church and in Christ Jesus throughout all generations, for ever and ever! Amen. – Ephesians 3:14-21

Have you been learning who you are in Christ? Are you being strengthened? Are you encouraged? Your response to who you are in Christ should be confidence! You could not possibly have more love, acceptance and forgiveness. Let's go into prayer with confidence and freedom!

PRAYER

Father,

In Jesus' name I come into your presence thanking you for the glorious riches in your storehouse which you have opened up to me in Christ! I thank you for your blessings. You can do immeasurably more than I ask or imagine! I eagerly await the work you are going to do in my life and in my family. Thank you, Lord! I thank you that I have freedom to come into your throne room to seek your face. This is all due to your grace and mercy through Jesus Christ my Lord. Take away my timidity in prayer this week, Lord. Fill me with your Holy Spirit and power, as I wait on you. Open the scriptures to me. Give me the Spirit of wisdom and revelation, so I can know you better and walk in hope.

In Jesus' name, Amen.

Spend time worshipping the Lord for who he is!

Dear Friend and Sister in Christ,

We've done a lot of word studies and cross referencing. We have prayed scripture and used our highlighters. We have asked challenging questions, faced our fears and doubted our own faith. Today, I just want to talk to you as a sister in Christ. If you are like me, you know about Jesus. You have heard a lot about him. You have talked to him in desperate times. You have gone days or weeks ignoring him and only giving him a passing glance. You may have enjoyed times of intimacy and prayer with him, promising him you will never slide back into your complacency, only to find yourself a few months later in a bad slump. Today, my friend, I pray that you and I—all of us doing this study in Christ—can find more consistency, confidence and freedom in our relationships with Jesus. I pray that the reality of who we are in Christ comes alive, as our spiritual eyes are opened, so that we can grow in the reality of God's love for us and the belonging that we have in his family.

I spent most of my childhood and life trying to please people. I found that I couldn't please everyone all of the time and I especially found that some people in life would just not like me ever and I would never, ever have the privilege of knowing why. I would often project these fears of failure and rejection onto God, as if he would treat me the way other people had in the past. I didn't even know I was doing it. I just "felt" it. I "felt" like a failure in my marriage, or as a parent, or as a believer in general. This was because my security in my relationship with God was based on my feelings—which at times are insecure—and not the truth of my position in Christ. I was not confident in Christ's love. Even though I knew with my head that his love is unconditional, I didn't believe it with my heart. This gave me a feeling of not belonging to God, even when I did.

Here is what God's Word is teaching all of the women out there who doubt their belonging and have feelings of insecurity or loneliness, instead of confidence and belonging. You are not alone. You are part of the great family of God. You can't always see it every day, or feel its hugs, or have a conversation with it when you need it in the physical realm. The lack we feel in the physical realm reminds us that we were created for more than this life. We were created for our Father in heaven and he has pulled out all the stops to lavish his love upon us. In my normal, practical life I would avoid using an extremely sappy word like lavish, but alas, here it is in the Bible reminding me that God has a deeper, more committed love than I will ever completely understand. His love is deeper than the love of the most sickly-sweet couple I know. And he is jealous for us all. He is jealous of the time we spend on social media. He longs for our hearts and our time. He wants to whisper truth into our hearts and embolden us to be the warrior princesses of God who dismantle the powerful weapons of the enemy that come against those we love.

He has put a fierce love in your heart for those around you. And you may be a bit jaded and feel others aren't responding to that love in the way you would hope. However, let that give you a peek into God's heart. He is a Father longing for his children. He is longing for you. When you grab hold of this love and all of its fullness in a big "A-HA!" moment, you will be more powerful than any devil in hell coming against you or your family.

Today, I implore you to read and memorize this powerful prayer of Paul for the Ephesians and let it soak into your soul. Ask the Father to show you Jesus and all of the love he has for you. You will never see it fully in this life, but just perhaps the grace and love and power of God will compel you to pursue him with a new abandon, to worship with your arms raised high, to forgive the unforgivable and to be willing to believe again in the power of God to heal and change a life, even your deepest pain and your deepest fears.

In Christ's Love,

Briana

CONTRASTS

Take time today to consider your fears and the way you deal with difficulty. Ephesians 3:12-13 addresses contrasting responses.

> **TODAY'S BIBLE STUDY TOOL**
>
> **Contrasts.** Look for contrasts (opposites) in a passage of scripture. The author will use this tool to help paint a more vivid picture for the reader.

"In him and through faith in him we may approach God with freedom and confidence. I ask you, therefore, not to be discouraged because of my sufferings for you, which are your glory." — Ephesians 3:12-13

Can you put those two responses to suffering in your own words below?

Approach #1

In him and through faith in him we:

Approach #2

When we or those we love suffer, we can get:

Approach #2 is complicated because it involves our emotions and does not see the big picture or the spiritual reality. Do you see that big word "therefore"? When you see a "therefore" you should ask what it's there for! That means that there is a reason we should not be discouraged. It is because we can approach God with freedom and confidence!

FREEDOM & CONFIDENCE

Do you pray with FREEDOM and CONFIDENCE or do you just shoot up prayers hoping God hears you? You need to be confident that God hears you. Let's cross reference the word "prayer" to find what another apostle teaches about praying with confidence.

James 5:13-18

[13] Is anyone among you in trouble? Let them pray. Is anyone happy? Let them sing songs of praise. [14] Is anyone among you ill? Let them call the elders of the church to pray over them and anoint them with oil in the name of the Lord. [15] And the prayer offered in faith will make the sick person well; the Lord will raise them up. If they have sinned, they will be forgiven. [16] Therefore confess your sins to each other and pray for each other so that you may be healed. The prayer of a righteous person is powerful and effective.

[17] Elijah was a human being, even as we are. He prayed earnestly that it would not rain, and it did not rain on the land for three and a half years. [18] Again he prayed, and the heavens gave rain, and the earth produced its crops.

Take time to write down what you can learn about prayer from this passage in James.

COMPARE

Compare the James 5:13-18 passage with Ephesians 3:12-13. Write your findings below.

What type of prayer avails much?

_____

What lies from the devil do you believe that keep you from praying fervently and with confidence? Ask the Holy Spirit if there are any lies in the way, blocking your prayer life and your ability to embrace everything God has for you and everything you are in him, as a redeemed daughter of God. YOU have an anointing in Christ through his Spirit! You have Christ! Let's just say, these words need SHOUTING FROM THE ROOFTOP! We have a reason to be confident in Christ! When things look very discouraging, we still have freedom and confidence and a reason to go before our Father with faith. Go back to the beginning of this day of study and read the Ephesians 3 prayer again, with spiritual eyes, asking the Holy Spirit to open your heart and understanding.

Ladies, basically, if you think you know Christ's love, you "ain't seen nothin' yet." There is so much more to find, so much more to know. And through the Holy Spirit, we can know what mortal humankind cannot know in their own minds.

You are not alone. We are together. We can come to a place of knowing and being filled to the measure of all the fullness of God, as a family. I think this is probably a place most people are afraid of going. Prayer is intimacy. Prayer with others is even more intimacy! Sadly, many of you may carry an underlying fear of intimacy with other people and even with God. Intimacy involves closeness, where you cannot hide the vulnerable places of your heart. But—imagine this—the intimacy you have in prayer is with the God who knows each star by name, but still cares about your day. Your tears are written on his scroll. He was with you through every secret and ugly moment of your life and he still loves you. He is our good Father and we are part of a good family. Do not fear the intimacy that comes with this unconditional love, acceptance and forgiveness you have in Christ and in his family. Embrace it!

When you trust in Christ, you are placing no confidence in your flesh or in your own self. You may feel incapable of doing what God has called you to do. You may feel weak or afraid, or even financially limited. These hinderances will not stop the work of God when you pray. Why? Because your confidence is not in yourself. It is in Jesus. Jesus is glorified in our weaknesses. Let's cross reference weakness and see what God has to say about our weaknesses. "But he said to me, 'My grace is sufficient for you, for my power is made perfect in weakness.' Therefore I will boast all the more gladly about my weaknesses, so that Christ's power may rest on me. That is why, for Christ's sake, I delight in weaknesses, in insults, in hardships, in persecutions, in difficulties. For when I am weak, then I am strong." – 2 Corinthians 12:9-10

Our trust is in the Lord's strength and power working mightily in us. Today, as I knelt in prayer by my window, looking out at the beauty of creation, I felt so small for what God has called me to do. When I focused on my smallness, I started to doubt his desire to work in or through me. Then, he reminded me of this truth: "Now to him who is able to do **immeasurably more** than all we **ask or imagine**, according to his power that is at work within us, to him be glory in the church and in Christ Jesus throughout all generations, for ever and ever! Amen."

God can do more than I even think. He is not limited by the things that limit me. He wants me to ask for more blessings, more healing, more freedom, more unity, and more open doors. Simply because my faith is so small, I can't even begin to imagine what he wants to do for me. It is his power, not my power that is at work in me. And for this, I need to ask for more faith, and you do too! In Mark 9:14-29, we see the account of a desperate father who comes to Jesus for his son who is demonically possessed. He can barely ask a very small and desperate, "Help me, if you can." Here is a small excerpt:

[21] Jesus asked the boy's father, 'How long has he been like this?'

'From childhood,' he answered. [22] 'It has often thrown him into fire or water to kill him. But if you can do anything, take pity on us and help us.'

[23] 'If you can"?' said Jesus. 'Everything is possible for one who believes.'

[24] Immediately the boy's father exclaimed, 'I do believe; help me overcome my unbelief!'

How many of us pray, "If you can" prayers, or "If you want to" prayers? More often than not, Jesus wants to and he always is able. I have a theory that we pray small prayers so we aren't disappointed, because we aren't quite sure if God wants to work in our situation or if he will. So, when I feel small and faithless, I pray for more faith! Some examples of this unsure praying would sound something like this, "Dear God, I am afraid. If you see fit, please take away this fear. If you want to and you think it's a good thing, take away my anxiety. If not, help me to live with it." Let me ask you a question. Do your kids have to ask you if they can sleep in their beds at night? Of course not. Because that is part of the package deal for belonging to a family. You get the security of sleeping in a bed. What kind of a parent, who has the money and resources for a bed, would not let their child sleep in a bed? A really bad parent.

There are certain benefits to being God's child. Peace is one of them! When you want to know what your employee benefits are, where do you turn? You go to the benefits manual on the company website. Employers will also hold employee benefits seminars or meetings, to make sure you understand your insurance, retirement and other benefits. I think churches should have benefits classes for new believers. How many people walk through their Christian lives not knowing what amazing benefits are at their disposal? We need basic skills to know how to access the benefits for every child of God. This is why you are doing a Bible study! The Bible is your Christian Benefits Manual. There are many unclaimed believer benefits in the pages of your Bible.

We have freedom and confidence to ask for peace. Jesus is the Prince of Peace. Peace has to do with security and with love. 1 John 4:18 says, "There is no fear in love; but perfect love casts out fear, because fear involves torment. But he who fears has not been made perfect in love." (NKJV) So, why would we doubt whether or not our good Father wants to deliver us from fear and give us peace? God wants his children to be bright-faced and eager to see him work. Instead of giving up on difficult situations, be confident in God's desire to work and intervene, above what you can ask or imagine, in the middle of your need!

BRINGING IT HOME

Get on your knees. Kneel before the Father and pour out your heart. Thank him and go BOLDLY into his throne room asking to understand his love. Also, ask him for those things that have been difficult to ask for—those things you have struggled to believe you could overcome. Go in and ask and receive in faith.

Do you have any unconfessed sin in your life that may be causing sickness or lack of confidence? Only the Holy Spirit can reveal this. Take time to pray and ask God for continued revelation into issues you may be dealing with. If there is sin in your life, "If we confess our sins, he is faithful and just and will forgive us our sins and purify us from all unrighteousness." – 1 John 1:9

Teach your children to pray with confidence!

REAL-LIFE FAITH
HOW IT WORKS

PRAYER

Let's enter God's throne room with confidence and freedom today! Have you knelt before the Father recently, or do you take the American approach that is more laid back in our general veneration of anyone, including God himself? While prayers in the car are a solid practice and praying in your bed at night is scriptural, take time to kneel before God today to bring your confident prayers!

MEMORY VERSE

[14] For this reason **I kneel** before the Father, [15] from whom every family in heaven and on earth derives its name. [16] I pray that out of his glorious riches he may strengthen you with power through his Spirit in your inner being, [17] so that Christ may dwell in your hearts through faith. And I pray that you, being rooted and established in love, [18] may have power, together with all the Lord's holy people, to grasp how wide and long and high and deep is the love of Christ, [19] and to know this love that surpasses knowledge – that you may be filled to the measure of all the fullness of God.

[20] Now to him who is able to do immeasurably more than all we ask or imagine, according to his power that is at work within us, [21] to him be glory in the church and in Christ Jesus throughout all generations, for ever and ever! Amen. – Ephesians 3:14-21

FAITH IN ACTION

While in the first three chapters of Ephesians, Paul spent time giving us illustrious examples of our position in Christ, the power at our disposal that we can't see, the love we need, supernatural strength to know, and the union we have spiritually with other believers, now he is getting down to the brass tacks. Those of you who are realists, detail-oriented and practical people are breathing out a huge sigh of relief. This is a breakdown of how to live out those difficult concepts and truths in our everyday lives, in the power of the Holy Spirit. Turn in your Bible are read Ephesians 4. Ask the Lord to open your spiritual eyes, as you read through the chapter.

WORD SEARCH

Now read through Ephesians 4 a second time. This time search for words that are used repeatedly. Mark them distinctively. You may circle one, underline another, etc.

Get a pen, and let's get busy! List the high frequency words you find.

HIGH-FREQUENCY WORDS

One _____

_____

_____

TODAY'S BIBLE STUDY TOOL
Word Search. When studying the Bible, it is helpful to look for themes and recurring words.

_____

_____

_____

Now write down the themes that seem to be prevalent in Ephesians Chapter 4. If you see a recurring theme from earlier in our study, put a star beside it.

THEMES

Prisoner of the Lord

_____

_____

_____

_____

_____

Living worthy

_____

_____

_____

_____

_____

QUESTIONS

48. According to Ephesians 4:1-5, what are practical ways to live a life worthy of the high calling you have received in Christ?

49. According to Ephesians 4:7-13, does God give grace equally to us? Yes or No? Support your answer with the passage.

50. Ephesians 4:14 starts with a connecting word THEN. This word shows something happening in a chronological order. Can you write a few sentences describing what comes in the previous paragraph that this word THEN is referring to and how that benefits us in verses 14-16?

51. What does verse 22 tell us about how our old self is corrupted?

52. Verse 25 starts with the word "therefore." What is it there for? What comes before this verse that prepares us for what comes after the word "therefore"?

OUTLINING SCRIPTURE

Make your own outline of Chapter 4. What are the main topics addressed? What are the smaller points? There is so much in this chapter about how believers should treat each other. If you take time to flesh it out, the Father can reveal even more to you! Ask him for help.

TODAY'S BIBLE STUDY TOOL
Outlining Scripture. This helps you see the main point(s) the author is trying to convey to his readers. It also gives you a synopsis of the passage and helps you to understand and remember it.

BRINGING IT HOME

Sometimes "doing our homework" can feel like a chore. Are you remembering to invite the Holy Spirit in to enlighten the eyes of your heart as you search the scriptures?

- Read a passage of scripture to your children and ask them questions that they can ONLY answer WITH THE TEXT.

- For older children, have them do "Sword Drills" where they have to race to look up the passages you will read (example: Ephesians 3:24-32). Children need to learn to look up scripture and to find the chapters and verses, too!

I find, when teaching children and even teens, that this is a skill that they are sorely lacking. Children should be very familiar with reading the Bible. It should feel like coming home!

GOD'S ESTABLISHED FAMILY
PART 1

HOPE FOR RELATIONSHIPS

MEMORY VERSE

14 For this reason I kneel before the Father, 15 from whom every family in heaven and on earth derives its name. 16 I pray that out of his glorious riches he may strengthen you with power through his Spirit in your inner being, 17 so that Christ may dwell in your hearts through faith. And I pray that you, being rooted and established in love, 18 may have power, together with all the Lord's holy people, to grasp how wide and long and high and deep is the love of Christ, 19 and to know this love that surpasses knowledge – that you may be filled to the measure of all the fullness of God.

20 Now to him who is able to do immeasurably more than all we ask or imagine, according to his power that is at work within us, 21 to him be glory in the church and in Christ Jesus throughout all generations, for ever and ever! Amen. – Ephesians 3:14-21

As we all know, families can have conflict. The body of Christ is no different. Conflict is not always unhealthy, if it is part of growing together and learning to handle differences in relationships in a Christ-like way. Let's start our prayer today asking the Lord to teach us how to handle conflicts with others.

PRAYER

Father,

In Jesus' name I thank you for who you have created me to be in Jesus. I know that you care about my brothers and sisters in Christ, even the ones I disagree with or have conflict with. You know our hearts and the root of the problems in my relationship conflicts. Please reveal truth to me about the source of the conflicts in my life. I pray that you prepare my heart to be open to what you want to teach me. Even if it hurts, help me to see where I have sin in my relationships. Show me where I need to forgive others. Give me the spiritual tenacity to forgive every time I am hurt. May your love and compassion fill me so much that it overflows to others around me. Break the cycles of unforgiveness, suspicion and fear in my relationship with _____.

In Jesus' name, Amen.

TO GOD BE THE GLORY

At the end of Paul's prayer in Chapter 3, he says the end result of God doing immeasurably more than we can ask or imagine in our lives is:

- That he is glorified in the church and in Christ Jesus.
- That he is glorified in future generations.

Usually when reading, I hurriedly blow past a passage like verse 21 as if it were just a flowery sentence. But, after reading Paul's prayer in Chapter 3 over and over and praying about it, this just jumped out at me! When we pray with faith and confidence in God, he moves and is glorified in the church and in Christ and in our children and grandchildren. God's kingdom comes and God's will is done in our communities and in our families! Ultimately, God is exalted when we walk in unity in our relationships. This is easier said than done, especially in a family situation. But, if God says that he can do more than we ask or imagine in the church and in all generations, he means it!

The very popular 23rd Psalm says, "He leadeth me in the paths of righteousness for his name's sake."

The paths God leads us in bring his name glory. When the Holy Spirit works in our lives and transforms us, making us more like Christ, the world sees Jesus in our testimonies and glorifies his name! When we don't walk in God's truth and power, when we go our own ways, he cannot do immeasurably more than we ask or imagine. It actually can hinder the prayers we pray, except the prayer of repentance. For example: Malachi 2:13-15 tells us that God does not hear our prayers when we live in adultery. "Another thing you do: you flood the Lord's altar with tears. You weep and wail because he no longer looks with favour on your offerings or accepts them with pleasure from your hands. You ask, 'Why?' It is because the Lord is the witness between you and the wife of your youth. You have been unfaithful to her, though she is your partner, the wife of your marriage covenant. Has not the one God made you? You belong to him in body and spirit. And what does the one God seek? Godly offspring. So be on your guard, and do not be unfaithful to the wife of your youth."

It is easy to think that marriage is all about being happy. It is the way of the world to run from situations when happiness is scarce. Marriage can bring happiness and it can bring joy; however, it also has rough patches—or even years—where the couple needs to grow and learn to walk in oneness together. Ephesians Chapter 4 talks a lot about what oneness looks like.

What does Malachi say about God's purpose in bringing oneness through marriage? (v15)

When you are in a crisis in your marriage, or in a relationship with another believer and everything is breaking loose, what is your goal? Is your goal to be understood? Is your goal to be vindicated? Or, is your goal the preservation and security of your relationship? When husbands and wives make the security of the relationship their goal, the children will be able to live in security and safety and ultimately glorify God. Your children know whether or not your spiritual walk is legitimate or a sham. If they see you are weak, but humble and willing to grow and change, they will see the light of the gospel of Jesus Christ. They will see that Jesus saves sinners, of whom I am the worst. They will learn that through perseverance and submission to God, believers become more and more like Jesus. They will see your testimony, slowly and steadily, played out in front of them, declaring the glory of God. However, if they see you put on a show for other Christians at church, but behind closed doors there is no humility or confession of sin and growth, they will smell a rat and possibly think all Christians are hiding the dark secrets that go on behind the doors of their homes.

If your marriage is on the rocks, remember your children are on the boat that is being dashed against the rocks by the waves of the storm. Instead of the captain and the navigator fighting each other or each doing their own thing, they need to realize the grave situation and begin to work together. Don't start thinking, 'If I just jump ship and maybe look for another man, my life will straighten out.' Adultery is the surest way to drown the power of your prayers. Remember, the precious cargo in the boat—the children—will greatly benefit from an end to the mutiny. How do you begin to put the relationship first and not only come to a truce, but also start to find the light from the lighthouse in the middle of the storm?

If your goal is the growth and security of the relationship, you will take several of the steps indicated by the apostle Paul in Ephesians 4:2. Below, I use biblehub.com to find some amazing details on this passage from HELPS™ Word-Studies. Gary Hill, translator of The Discovery Bible and HELPS™ Word-Studies, has done decades of work to develop software which aids in understanding the nuances of Greek and Hebrew that are hard to translate into English. Look at what we can find out on the Bible Hub website!

Be completely humble. What does the word "humble" mean in the Greek? According to HELPS™ Word-Studies (visit http://biblehub.com/greek/5012.htm):

> "Humility is an inside-out virtue produced by comparing ourselves to the Lord (rather than to others). This brings behavior into alignment with this inner revelation to keep one from being self-exalting (self-determining, self-inflated). For the believer, … tapeinophrosýnē ("humility") means living in complete dependence on the Lord, i.e. with no reliance on self (the flesh)."

Usually, when we are angry with someone, it is because we are offended. We didn't get what we wanted. Someone did something to us that caused an offense. They may or may not know it. We start getting puffed up and comparing our behavior to theirs, instead of to Jesus. Even if you have been legitimately hurt, humility will bring you closer to resolving the relationship or issue.

- Come to the conversation without assuming the worst about the other person.

- Come to the conversation after praying for the relationship and for the other person.

- Come to the conversation to resolve the conflict, not to prove the other person wrong.

- Commit yourself to listen to understand. Don't prepare your answer as the person is talking. Ask questions to help clarify what the other person is saying. Don't jump to conclusions or make assumptions.

- Make sure the other person knows you care about him or her and that love is your motivation. If it is not your motivation, go back and pray some more. Repent for not caring and having a hard and prideful heart.

- Admit where you are wrong.

- Be willing to apologize for hurting the other person—if that person is hurt—even if you think it is silly. (ie. Your personality may think that some issue the other person thinks is important is frivolous and vice versa. Be humble and allow that person the right to what he or she feels is important, as long as it is not sin.) Make sure the apology is sincere and not flippant. Apologize the way you would want to be apologized to.

Be gentle. The Greek word for gentle is not weakness. It is meekness, which expresses "power with reserve." (visit http://biblehub.com/greek/4240.htm) The classical Greek word for meekness referred to a horse who had been tamed and bridled. This gives us a picture of power under the control of a master. Jesus is our master! When you are in a tough situation, it's easy to allow anger to seethe underneath the surface. It's easy to laugh at the other person, to yell at them, or just ignore them. Are you gentle in your approach to your relationships? This does not

---

TODAY'S BIBLE STUDY TOOL

Greek Word Study. Dig deeper into the meaning of a word by learning the intent of the original language. Some underlying meaning may have been lost in translation.

---

mean pretending you aren't hurt. This does not mean brushing your feelings under the rug. It means ask the Holy Spirit to give you gentleness. It has to come from him! Ask the Holy Spirit to give you wisdom and revelation on this. Let Jesus be the master of your emotions and reactions. Jesus' transformation of our character is a refining process—the process of "meeking."

Be patient. HELPS™ Word-studies found at biblehub.com says:

> … the word for patience in the Greek, "embraces steadfastness and staying-power. If in English we had an adjective 'long-tempered' as a counterpart to 'short-tempered,' then makrothymia could be called the quality of being 'long-tempered' … which is a quality of God …"

It's easy to get impatient when dealing with something that annoys you. One of the things God has convicted me of over the years is that getting easily annoyed is not loving and not of God. Being easily annoyed is very self-centered and may be a signal that something else is going on under the surface.

Do not take today's study as telling you to stuff your feelings and put on a smile. This is not about behavior modification. I am writing about praying for the Holy Spirit to transform your heart by his power and forgiveness, and with his indwelling.

PRAY INSTEAD OF FRET, THEN PRAY TOGETHER!

Instead of complaining about your husband or nagging him—let's be honest, if complaining and nagging hasn't helped yet, how can we keep doing the same thing over and over and expect different results—try praying! You are seated with Christ in heavenly realms. Get busy! Begin praying for your spouse's heart and for your own heart. Ask God to change you both. Ask Jesus to intervene. Do spiritual warfare for your spouse. How many fretful hours have you wasted just worrying and resenting, instead of praying and breaking through a problem? Probably too many to count for all of us.

Look back at the memory verse prayer. God intends us to experience the fullness of Christ through our unity in the Spirit with others. There is a fullness of God's presence that we experience in unified prayer, when we begin to go before the Father with our spouse or other believers for the issues that are overwhelming us. When you begin to walk in the humility of Christ, you will experience more and more unity and oneness in your marriage. The results? Your prayers will be infused and emboldened with faith and confidence. If your spouse is willing, ask him to pray with you for the situation you are facing, either in your marriage or in one of your children. Warning—don't criticize his praying. Just be thankful for the time together and be sure that you pray, too. He will grow in his ability to pray, the more you pray together. If you criticize his prayers, he will probably never want to do that together again! Would you?

CROSS REFERENCE

1 Corinthians 13:4-7

[4] Love is patient, love is kind. It does not envy, it does not boast, it is not proud. [5] It does not dishonour others, it is not self-seeking, it is not easily angered, it keeps no record of wrongs. [6] Love does not delight in evil but rejoices with the truth. [7] It always protects, always trusts, always hopes, always perseveres.

> **TODAY'S BIBLE STUDY TOOL**
>
> **Cross Reference.** Use a Bible concordance or search your Bible app to find other passages in scripture on the same subject.

If we allow ourselves the right to be annoyed with people frequently, we are certainly not allowing Christ to reign and rule in our attitudes and hearts in patience. Some things may be extra difficult to bear, but bearing with someone in LOVE does not mean eye rolling, constant sarcasm, put-downs or ignoring. Can you see Jesus doing this to you? Hopefully, not!

Now, if you are feeling condemned by this, remember that God does not reject you when you struggle with sin. Your sin does not define you. CHRIST defines who you are, not your habits, or the way you were raised to treat people. If you are not demonstrating all the fruit of the Spirit in your life, what needs to happen? Repent and ask for revelation. Ask God to open the eyes of your heart that you may know the HOPE to which you have been called. That HOPE is in the power of Christ and the authority of Christ to not only help you overcome sin, but to conquer it under your feet and to establish his character in your heart. Remember:

> You cannot change anyone else,
> but you can let Christ change you.

So, you can either be irritable, annoyed, overwhelmed and angry with someone whom you cannot change, OR you can allow the Holy Spirit to show you why it is happening and to change your heart to be humble, patient and gentle. So, whether that person changes or not, you will be at peace!

PRACTICAL APPLICATION
Dealing with Pain

Let's talk about pain. When I address irritability and impatience, I am not saying that the pain you feel in a relationship is sin. Pain is different than sin. Pain needs to be dealt with through forgiveness on a regular basis, and also through prayer for healing and restoration. When you are overwhelmed with pain and even irritability, take it to the Lord in prayer—are you seeing a pattern here? This is about asking GOD to change your heart, and fill you with the Spirit of wisdom and revelation to know him better in this area of your life.

> **TODAY'S BIBLE STUDY TOOL**
>
> **Practical Application.** How can I personally apply this scripture to my life today? What changes do I need to make? What prayer should I pray?
>
> Don't forget to ask the Holy Spirit for help!

GET OFF THE CRAZY TRAIN

Does being hurt by someone imply the person who offended you isn't a true believer? Sometimes yes. Sometimes no. Only God knows the heart. It very well can mean they are being a self-centered believer who is not living according to the principles of God's Word, a.k.a. sinning. It could also mean that—as God has shown me about myself in the past—it is very possible that the injured party is being "paranoid" or oversensitive, allowing self-centeredness, personal preference or the pain of the past to be projected onto someone who had no intention of doing any harm. Unforgiveness and bitterness can cause quick "knee jerk" reactions like these. This is what my friend calls "The Crazy Train." You probably know the drill. The Crazy Train is something you get on with a person you have history with. Maybe you've been on it with your mother, mother-in-law, father, sibling, or your husband. Sometimes, you've been on The Crazy Train so many times, you even pull innocent bystanders onto it, accusing other people of being just like so and so, because you assume that all people will hurt you like so and so has. How did you acquire this ticket for The Crazy Train? Through hurts that were never forgiven, through bad habits that were formed in pain, through always putting your expectations ahead of the value of a person—that's how you got this ticket. This is why we need to take everything to the Lord in prayer and be led by the Spirit and not by our gut reactions when dealing with others. The enemy will do everything he can to divide and conquer believers. Remember that he is known as "the accuser of the brethren." He is constantly accusing believers to one another and to God. Do not allow yourself to be manipulated by the enemy of your soul! Do not allow yourself to be manipulated by your pain. Jesus lives in you and in the other believer you may be at odds with.

I remember reading *Farmer Boy* by Laura Ingalls Wilder to my children. I highly recommend this reading for your children. In the story, 9-year-old Almanzo so desperately wanted to pet the colts that his father was carefully training. His father would not allow him near the young horses, because he didn't want him to "spoil" them. One fright could cause his future, powerful driving horses to become skittish and unpredictable. These powerful horses could be trained up to be meek and obedient, or unreliable, easily triggered by any little sound. We are the same way. Old memories and hurts can be triggered at any time by new reminders. Thankfully, in Christ Jesus, we can be given a meek nature. Our trainer can help us to unlearn our old reactive ways and come under submission to his voice and gentle hand. No more trigger!

When you have a ticket to The Crazy Train, you need to spend extended and frequent time in prayer. Ask the Lord for revelation to understand what is causing you to overreact, or what is causing the blow ups in general. What behavior or sin in the other person triggers fear or anger in you? What do you need to forgive? Maybe you personally have a behavior or sin that causes the other person to overreact. I know that fear was one of my biggest triggers in my relationship with my husband. If there was a past hurt, even if I forgave it, if some similar circumstance started to make me afraid that I would experience the hurt again, I would get afraid and overreact. These emotional land mines can come in different sizes, like a pair of shoes left in the middle of the floor. A major holiday can carry the pain of rejection and disappointment. Vacations can also become these types of emotional traps. If you have pain around a certain holiday, God can break those emotional patterns and give you freedom from blow-ups and overreactions.

Maybe you don't overreact, but you under-react. You may pride yourself in not blowing up or yelling. When you get afraid or angry, you may withdraw and not talk to your spouse or friend. Silence actually can be deeply painful, because it is often received as a form of deep rejection. If you have these types of reactions from fear or pain, take them to the Lord and forgive again. Ask the Lord to break the chains and strongholds of old emotional habits, and help you to walk in what the apostle Paul describes in Ephesians 4:1-5,

> As a prisoner for the Lord, then, I urge you to live a life worthy of the calling you have received. Be completely humble and gentle; be patient, bearing with one another in love. Make every effort to keep the unity of the Spirit through the bond of peace. There is one body and one Spirit, just as you were called to one hope when you were called; one Lord, one faith, one baptism; — Ephesians 4:1-5

On a personal note, this is something the Lord has taught me. I tend to get into self-pity when I am in a place of pain or weakness. People DO hurt us! People DO reject us. Even physical pain can wear me down and bring an overall feeling of hopelessness and self-pity. However, truly, the Lord has spoken to my heart in days of pain and whispered, "Self-pity—you are walking in self-pity." I remember a time when I didn't listen and I stayed in my little personal pity party with my little rain cloud following me around for the day. I ended up hurting my husband very much by ignoring the Holy Spirit's gentle wisdom. I kept focusing on all the things from the past that had hurt me in our relationship. I began to recount them to him when he asked what was wrong. I replayed disappointments in my head—wrongs that were resolved and forgiven. Now ladies, I don't need to state the obvious, but I can't tell you how upset I would be if he did that to me. He did bear with me in love that day when I wallowed in self-pity and weakness. I chose to walk in my flesh and not the Spirit. I know I hurt him. The funny thing is this—when my rain cloud started pouring on him, it made mud for both of us. After I was completely covered in mud from head to toe, I finally decided to stand my ground against the fiery darts of the enemy. I stopped everything, asked my husband to forgive me, asked God to forgive me and did war against the enemy. I rebuked a spirit of self-pity and commanded it to leave, in Jesus' name. And you know what? It did leave. It took its fiery darts and went home, rain cloud and all. A lesson in listening to the Lord.

BRINGING IT HOME

The adults in the home set the atmosphere of the home.

Our children are little hidden cameras ready to play back with precision the behavior we have modeled for them. You may not fall on the floor and scream when you don't get your way, but do your children see your own adult version of "protesting"?

Do you model humility for them in giving genuine apologies, or do you show them defensiveness and pride?

Take this to the Lord in prayer.

GOD'S ESTABLISHED FAMILY
PART 2

HANDLING NECESSARY CONFLICT

PRAYER

Even though we started a new memory verse and prayer last week, let's not forget to ask our Glorious Father to fill us with the Spirit of wisdom and revelation to know him better, every day! It may take a bit more time to work through both prayers, but you can be led by the Spirit of God as you pray. It's always important to invite the Holy Spirit daily to speak to you and to open your heart to hear from him. Here is the memory verse from Week One.

Ephesians 1:17-23

[17] I keep asking that the God of our Lord Jesus Christ, the glorious Father, may give you the Spirit of wisdom and revelation, so that you may know him better. [18] I pray that the eyes of your heart may be enlightened in order that you may know the hope to which he has called you, the riches of his glorious inheritance in his holy people, [19] and his incomparably great power for us who believe. That power is the same as the mighty strength [20] he exerted when he raised Christ from the dead and seated him at his right hand in the heavenly realms, [21] far above all rule and authority, power and dominion, and every name that is invoked, not only in the present age but also in the one to come. [22] And God placed all things under his feet and appointed him to be head over everything for the church, [23] which is his body, the fullness of him who fills everything in every way.

Speaking of memory verses …

How are you doing with our new memory verse? One of my sons told me, "Mom, I am so bad at memorizing!" My question to him was, "What do you think being good at memorizing looks like?" Memorization is a skill you can develop, the way we can develop any other skill.

IDEAS FOR SUCCESSFUL MEMORIZATION

53. **Ask yourself what you are memorizing.** What does it mean? Mull it over. Don't just get the words—understand the context! Ask the Holy Spirit for revelation.

54. **Write it down.** Spend time writing down the text on 3x5 cards. Maybe even do a little "verse graph" to show what words are related to what concepts and other truths.

55. **Record yourself reading it aloud slowly.** Listen to it while you drive.

56. **Review it at night before you sleep.** Let it be one of the last things you think about at night.

57. **Work on it with a friend.**

MEMORY VERSE

[14] For this reason I kneel before the Father, [15] from whom every family in heaven and on earth derives its name. [16] I pray that out of his glorious riches he may strengthen you with power through his Spirit in your inner being, [17] so that Christ may dwell in your hearts through faith. And I pray that you, being rooted and established in love, [18] may have power, together with all the Lord's holy people, to grasp how wide and long and high and deep is the love of Christ, [19] and to know this love that surpasses knowledge – that you may be filled to the measure of all the fullness of God.

[20] Now to him who is able to do immeasurably more than all we ask or imagine, according to his power that is at work within us, [21] to him be glory in the church and in Christ Jesus throughout all generations, for ever and ever! Amen. – Ephesians 3:14-21

READING

As we look at dealing with difficult relationships, take a few minutes to read all of Ephesians Chapter 4 again.

Now, let's examine what the apostle Paul has already revealed to us in scripture about how relationships in the body of Christ work, by asking some questions.

QUESTIONS

58. What does Paul encourage us to do in verse 1? How do we do that, according to verse 2?

59. How does God want us to live in our relationships? Look at verses 2-4 for the answer.

60. Why does this matter? (vs 4-6)

61. In Ephesians 4:3, what does the apostle Paul say we need to make every effort to do? Every effort sounds important.

62. What in the world does "keep the unity of the Spirit" mean? Let's look back to verse 2. It says:

- Be completely humble and gentle

- Be patient

- Bearing with one another in love. Strong's Concordance says this means: "to hold oneself up against, i.e. (figuratively) put up with—bear with, endure, forbear, suffer."

Think of a difficult relationship pain that is super hard to bear. Here in Ephesians, God, through the apostle Paul, tells you to bear with that person in love. Strong's Concordance says "bearing with" is, "to hold oneself up against." Love is a decision. God gives us the strength, in difficult relationship moments, to walk in the decision to love someone who is unlovable. In this way, we are held up by love when we walk through pain and conflict—love holds us up against the pain and against the temptation to run away from the relationship. What does that look like? Think about how you feel when you hear words like humble, gentle, patient and love. I usually get warm fuzzies because I imagine those words coming toward me personally. I would love someone to be humble, gentle, patient and loving towards me! This is how I want to be treated. But, the context of this passage is for me to have these attributes toward those around me who are difficult to live with. Verse 3 says to make every effort to keep the unity of the Spirit through the bond of peace. If I have to make every effort, that means it may be a bit of a struggle, correct?

Good feeling's gone! This does not sound fun or pretty, does it? It may make a girl want to ask, "What right does the apostle Paul have to tell me to do this difficult 'bearing with one another in love'?" What does Paul know about suffering and putting up with others who hurt him? Well, do you remember the Corinthian church we learned about last week on Day 3? Remember how Paul thought they needed to learn some humility in Christ? Well, open your Bible to the second letter to the Corinthians, Chapter 11. Yes, he needed to write another strong letter to them to challenge them on bad attitudes and following false teachers.

CROSS REFERENCE

Take time to read 2 Corinthians Chapter 11. We will see how Paul "bears" with their weaknesses in this relationship.

HANDLING CONFLICT IN LOVE

Wow! Paul definitely has earned the right to speak to us about walking in Christ through suffering! Let's answer some questions about the passage to get a better understanding of it.

63. Why is Paul jealous? Is jealousy in this situation a sin?

64. In verse 2, what does he compare the Corinthians' error with?

65. In verses 5 and 12-15, he tells us how the people who are seducing the church with false doctrine are presenting themselves. List the two ways here.

66. Why do you think Paul is boasting in all of his suffering and weaknesses? What is he contrasting that with?

67. What does Paul remind the Corinthian church about godly leadership? (Remember our lesson from last week?)

True leaders will boast in their weaknesses, not in their successes, so that Christ will be glorified in any of their accomplishments. Mature, Christ-like leaders will not promote their affluence and strength as bait to get you to give them more money—aka for a ministry jet—in hopes God will also bless you the same (see verse 7). The passage seems to indicate that the false teachers are soaking the Corinthians monetarily and they are putting up with it. They are rejecting the free gospel for a false gospel that is costing them dearly—spiritually and physically. This is different from giving to the poor or giving generously to your church to support the work of God through tithes and offerings. This is also different than a minister having a living wage that allows him to live in the area his church is in, which is also biblical.

These false teachers outwardly look like they have it all together and are seducing the Corinthians away from the true gospel and from their relationship with Paul, who is their spiritual father. The other men seem like well-polished professionals, so to speak, and in comparison, Paul's response is to bear with the Corinthians in love. This involves a bit of a conflict. He confronts them about their wrongdoing because he loves them and cares deeply that they are turning away from the gospel of Jesus to follow people who are convincing speakers and seem to be servants of righteousness.

IS IT WORTH IT?

The conflict that Paul is addressing is of great spiritual urgency. It is not petty, physical or self-centered. He is not going to battle over the color of carpet in the church, who gets more time singing on the worship rotation, or even political differences. There are really silly and inconsequential issues that people get emotionally divided over. On the other hand, modern-day believers find it easy to close their eyes to whether or not someone is going to hell or leading people to hell. For example, I have seen well-meaning college students at a Christian college protest vigorously when a professor was let go for teaching heresy and refusing to step down from his philosophies that denied God's inherent qualities of omnipotence and omniscience. The students made t-shirts to protest and called for the college to save his job. They thought firing a family man was so unloving and un-Christlike of the college leaders. Were these students right or wrong?

Ephesians 4:3-6 shows us that there are core issues of our faith that we do not compromise on. These very elements unite us and give us belonging in the body of Christ. "Make every effort to keep the unity of the Spirit through the bond of peace. There is one body and one Spirit, just as you were called to one hope when you were called; one Lord, one faith, one baptism; one God and Father of all, who is over all and through all and in all."

We are one with the others who put their faith in Jesus. We serve the same Lord. His qualities do not change depending on our emotions or ideas. We have the same faith. It is a faith handed down to us in a sacred trust. We are all baptized into the same baptism. We are in one family with one God and Father. We cannot allow people to infiltrate the body of Christ with heresy that destroys the foundation of everything that actually gives the body of Christ unity.

I asked one teenager, "Why do you think the college should retain this man who is teaching people that God can't be all-knowing and all-powerful?"

"Because!" she replied. "The professor has a family. It's so unloving. What will happen to his family?"

"That is a great question," I replied. "The people who fired him are asking the exact same question. He was hired to teach the truth and character of God to the future pastors, youth pastors, missionaries, and leaders of the church and prepare them for ministry. What are the implications, if they allow him to stay because they feel sorry for him? What will happen to God's family? When the college students he taught graduate and go out teaching heresy, how many people will be led to hell in churches all over the world? What will happen to the family of God?"

She sat in silence for a minute. "I guess I never thought of it that way."

The man or woman teaching heresy is the one responsible for what happens to his or her family, when they are trading the truth of Christ for a lie. That person will answer to God for that, as well as for all the people led astray by the false teaching. Individually, we are responsible for our own circle of influence. The college leaders were responsible for the lives and minds entrusted to them. We will all be judged on whether we stand our ground for Jesus or follow the crowd by making emotional decisions.

In his response to the church leaders putting up with the false teachers in the letter to Corinth, Paul is frustrated with them. He doesn't seem patient at all! Is this conflicting with his other teaching? Well, let's think through this. A phrase that is popular amongst mothers is "choose your battles." This is a battle Paul is willing to die fighting. Literally. He eventually is beheaded in Rome, because he will not back down from the truth of who Jesus Christ is. This is the same man who, before his conversion, vehemently persecuted Christians, because he thought Christians were in error and leading people against God. But, when he met Jesus face-to-face on the Damascus road, he discovered that everything he believed was a lie. He was willing to die for Jesus and for those people he formerly persecuted. We live in a time where truth is considered relative. Live and let live, some will say. However, Paul knows that "letting them live" the way they wanted in this situation meant "letting them die" spiritually. He loved them too much to keep quiet.

PRACTICAL APPLICATION
Addressing Conflicts in Everyday Relationships

In cases where we are not talking about false doctrine, the source of conflict between believers can be found in Ephesians 4:20-24. "That, however, is not the way of life you learned when you heard about Christ and were taught in him in accordance with the truth that is in Jesus. You were taught, with regard to your former way of life, to put off your old self, which is being corrupted by its deceitful desires; to be made new in the attitude of your minds; and to put on the new self, created to be like God in true righteousness and holiness."

Our old self is full of deceitful desires. It comes from our own inner greed. "Do not let any unwholesome talk come out of your mouths, but only what is helpful for building others up according to their needs, that it may benefit those who listen. And do not grieve the Holy Spirit of God, with whom you were sealed for the day of redemption. Get rid of all bitterness, rage and anger, brawling and slander, along with every form of malice. Be kind and compassionate to one another, forgiving each other, just as in Christ God forgave you."

When we refuse to treat another person with respect and honor, gentleness and love, we offend and grieve the Holy Spirit of God, with whom we are sealed. And yes, when someone else in God's family sins against you, God is very much grieved and concerned.

Conflict can feel yucky. We may long for happy feelings to return, but conflict needs to be resolved, not suspended indefinitely with false peace and avoidance. Being patient and bearing with someone means not walking away in the middle of trouble. Bearing with someone in love means working through an issue and communicating with open hearts and open ears. It is a selfless confrontation, not a selfish one. Healthy conflict involves using words, not giving the silent treatment to punish someone, in hopes they will know why you are upset. When you know someone is in spiritual danger, or a relationship is on the rocks, the best order of business is honesty and communication with the relationship in mind. The people in Corinth are worth too much to Jesus and to Paul for him to pretend these issues do not matter. Paul could just simply walk away and let the whole city of Corinth go to hell in a hand basket. Literally. If he leaves them to the false prophets and false apostles who are twisting and tainting the true gospel of Jesus Christ, they will go to hell.

> **TODAY'S BIBLE STUDY TOOL**
>
> **Practical Application.** How can I personally apply this scripture to my life today? What changes do I need to make? What prayer should I pray?
>
> Don't forget to ask the Holy Spirit for help!

True love doesn't give up on someone who is struggling, but it is willing to navigate difficult waters for resolution. True godly love looks at a person, or even a group of people, and sees the potential in the middle of the crisis or chaos. True love has grit. Paul has focused love and patience that isn't a fake kind of unity like we see in the world today. Paul's strong words are not an argument where he is trying to be justified. He knows he is right. He isn't trying to prove himself. He is trying to help the Corinthians. His goal is the reconciliation of the relationship. What are your goals? Are your goals for your relationships God's goals?

BRINGING IT HOME

In a conflict situation, many people have either a "fight or flight" response. What is your response to a conflict?

- Do you retaliate and say hurtful things?
- Do you avoid people or make assumptions about them?

or

- Do you engage them and ask questions to resolve the issue?
- Do you bear with others in love, by the power of the Holy Spirit?

This does not mean you pretend that hurt isn't happening! No! This means, again, asking the Holy Spirit for revelation for how to deal with a situation and how to love a person that is difficult to love, forgiving them in Jesus' name. Ask God for spiritual eyes to see what is going on. The ultimate goal of our Father is for the church to be united and for marriages to be united. Is the unity of the body of Christ, including your personal relationships, a goal in your life?

CHRIST IS VICTORIOUS
OVER OUR CAPTORS OF SIN & DEATH!

In the past two years, I have attended way too many funerals for teenagers or even adults taken before their time. Honestly, there are days when I will forget about the end-game and the hope we have in Christ. The here-and-now seems so urgent and so real, because it is. But, even more real and more permanent is the future eternity we will step into when we take our final breath. When we read the Word of God, especially passages like today's reading in Ephesians 4, our hearts can be strengthened to face the despair that seems to come, more often than not, in the form of bad news. There is a lot of scripture in today's study, so please sit back and allow it to go down deep into your being and give you hope. Also, remember that we approach scripture and difficulty by inviting the Holy Spirit to fill us with wisdom and revelation, so we can have the mind of Christ to understand from God's perspective.

PRAYER

Father,

In Jesus' name, I pray that you will fill me with the Spirit of wisdom and revelation, so that I can have spiritual understanding of your Word today. Enlighten my heart to know the hope of my calling and all of the riches available to me in Christ. Speak to my heart. I no longer want to rely on my physical mind or reason accompanied by doubts as I navigate difficult waters. Strengthen me with power in my inner being so that Christ can dwell in my heart through faith. I need faith and a change of heart so that I can live in your love, know your love, and walk in your love in a tangible way. May I be rooted and established in love, in Jesus' name. Help all of us in the kingdom of God, all your holy people, to learn your love and walk in the power to grasp what this love of Christ is like.

God, it's hard to love people. They get on my nerves, they hurt me, they ask me to do things I don't want to do, they overwhelm me—they ignore me, and use me, and cause me distress, in general. But, I am believing that I will see you do immeasurably more than I can ask or imagine, because of your power in me. I want my life to give you glory. I want to be your hands and feet to the world. I want to live in healing and freedom and power.

I invite you to fill me today, Holy Spirit! Come in and anoint my life today. Work a mighty work in my life, Lord Jesus.

Amen!

MEMORY VERSE

[14] For this reason I kneel before the Father, [15] from whom every family in heaven and on earth derives its name. [16] I pray that out of his glorious riches he may strengthen you with power through his Spirit in your inner being, [17] so that Christ may dwell in your hearts through faith. And I pray that you, being rooted and established in love, [18] may have power, together

with all the Lord's holy people, to grasp how wide and long and high and deep is the love of Christ, [19] and to know this love that surpasses knowledge – that you may be filled to the measure of all the fullness of God.

[20] Now to him who is able to do immeasurably more than all we ask or imagine, according to his power that is at work within us, [21] to him be glory in the church and in Christ Jesus throughout all generations, for ever and ever! Amen. – Ephesians 3:14-21

READING
Why So Many Translations?

Today's reading passage is presented here in the New King James Version of the Bible. All the reliable Bible versions are carefully translated from the oldest ancient Greek and Hebrew texts. Some translators have chosen slightly different renderings of the same passage. This is because some translations take a word-by-word approach, like the NASB or NKJV. In word-by-word versions— as you may assume—the words are generally translated from one word in the ancient language to one word in the English language. If there is something implied in the Greek and it is difficult to translate it directly into one English word, a word may be added to express the biblical text's intention completely. You may see those extra words in italics, as in the Amplified Bible or NASB. Sometimes the word-by-word translation is difficult for modern English readers to follow, since our sentences are ordered with different grammatical structures and linguistic flow than that of the ancient Hebrew, Greek, Aramaic, or English, for that matter. Other translations, like the NIV, use a thought-by-thought combined with a word-by-word technique to help put the words in the most readable syntax, which communicates the complete meaning in a way that flows best in the language of the reader. If it is a reliable translation, one that uses the oldest manuscripts for translation, you can still see some slight differences, because there may not be an English word that perfectly expresses the Greek or Hebrew phrase. So, translators do their best, working on teams, to carefully pick the English phrases and words and express them in a way that captures the original meaning. When you read in a different reliable translation, you can see the passage with new eyes, seeing things expressed in a fresh way from another translation team.

Ephesians 4:7-16 New King James Version (NKJV)

[7] But to each one of us grace was given according to the measure of Christ's gift. [8] Therefore He says:

> "When He ascended on high,
> He led captivity captive,
> And gave gifts to men."

[9] (Now this, "He ascended"—what does it mean but that He also first descended into the lower parts of the earth? [10] He who descended is also the One who ascended far above all the heavens, that He might fill all things.)

[11] And He Himself gave some to be apostles, some prophets, some evangelists, and some pastors and teachers, [12] for the equipping of the saints for the work of ministry, for the edifying of the body of Christ, [13] till we all come to the unity of the faith and of the knowledge of the Son of God, to a perfect man, to the measure of the stature of the fullness of Christ; [14] that we should no longer be children, tossed to and fro and carried about with every wind of doctrine, by the trickery of men, in the cunning craftiness of deceitful plotting, [15] but, speaking the truth in love, may grow up in all things into Him who is the head—Christ— [16] from whom the whole body, joined and knit together by what every joint supplies, according to the effective working by which every part does its share, causes growth of the body for the edifying of itself in love.

What has Christ given to you, according to verse 7?

If you said grace, you are correct! Grace in this context refers to spiritual gifts. Remember that we need to read the Word of God in context! Often times, without reading in context, we erroneously LIMIT grace to a "free pass" to sin or a "free ticket" to heaven.

Without grace, we would not have spiritual gifts, freedom or power. Grace is the power to OVERCOME and BE EDIFIED in the body of Christ. When we overcome, we mature and grow up, so to speak. By grace, we conquer sin and death.

We are going to break down this passage today and look at it from a bird's-eye view.

- God gives each of us spiritual gifts, freely by the authority of his grace. (Different than the natural gifting, talents and abilities he gives us at birth.)

- Jesus became a man—lowered himself to our position (coming down as a baby from the heavenly realms we learned about in the earlier weeks) in order to release us from the captivity and bondage of sin.

- Jesus took CAPTIVITY captive! (Old Testament prophecy fulfilled by Christ in Psalm 68:18-19)

Psalm 68:18-19 New King James Version (NKJV)

[18] You have ascended on high,
You have led captivity captive;
You have received gifts among men,
Even from the rebellious,
That the Lord God might dwell there.
[19] Blessed be the Lord,
Who daily loads us with benefits,
The God of our salvation! Selah

Jesus breaks our chains, and in the Book of Revelation—New Testament prophecy to be fulfilled at the end of time—we see DEATH AND HELL in CHAINS thrown into the lake of fire! Our very captors—Satan, Death and Hades are held captive by Christ!

Let's take a look at our future in Christ and the VICTORY for the body of Christ, when God takes the very spiritual beings captive that held us captive and throws them into the lake of fire! This is exhilarating. Truly. I once heard the saying, "When the devil reminds you of your past, remind him of his future." Love it! **Turn to Revelation 20:7-15 to read this New Testament prophecy to be fulfilled at the end of time.**

Isn't this amazing!? Jesus didn't just die for our sins—he is so much more than the Final Sacrifice. He has vanquished our greatest enemies and set us free! Do you believe it? Jesus not only died, but was resurrected and ascended into heaven to his proper place at the head of the kingdom of God. He is the Head of the Body, the Final Authority, and is now able to fill the whole heavens with his power, because he has overcome! Death does not have the final say.

Not only did Christ overcome, but he leads us in a victorious life. Romans 8:37-39 says that when we face persecution and abandonment,

No, in all these things we are more than conquerors through him who loved us. For I am convinced that neither death nor life, neither angels nor demons, neither the present nor the future, nor any power, neither height nor depth, nor anything else in all creation, will be able to separate us from the love of God in Christ Jesus our Lord. – Romans 8:37-39

In Exodus, when God led his people out of Egypt, he allowed them to plunder the Egyptians. The Egyptians begged them to leave and gave them lavish gifts of gold and other articles of wealth. This was a prophetic foreshadowing of what God would do for those who would trust in his precious son Jesus. Jesus not only leads us out of slavery to our past and our sin, but he also brings us into a spiritual promised land, loaded down with benefits—the milk and honey or fruit and gifts of the Holy Spirit. He gives us spiritual gifts in our own lives, but also gives us spiritual gifts in the lives of our brothers and sisters in Christ, so we will truly experience the unifying, life-giving power of Christ as we are knit together with other believers, whom we will need to rely on to participate in the fullness of our walk with God. In this way, we truly go from being held captive to abandonment, loneliness, rebellion, and separation to living freely in acceptance, love, submission, and family. Next week, we will explore this family more!

BRINGING IT HOME

Find time to talk to your children about death at a time that is not stressful or fearful. Give them a chance to hear about the good news of what God will do to Death and Hades in the end.

Ask them, "Does this give you hope?"

Make sure your children know that it is through faith in Christ that we will be on the winning side. It is not by works, but through Christ alone; otherwise, they may get hopeless when life gets tough.

Is *your* hope built on nothing less than Jesus' blood and righteousness?

CHRIST SETS UP HOUSE
PART 1

SPIRITUAL OFFICES AND GIFTS IN THE BODY OF CHRIST

PRAYER

Today, let's use our memory verse to help enrich our time with the Lord. Praying the truths of scripture over your life is like taking a coupon to the store and redeeming something you have a right to. Or another picture of prayer is a child coming home from school and raiding the refrigerator. It would be rude if he or she went into someone else's house and took food without asking. But, my children know that they have full access to the snacks in the cabinet or the leftovers or lunch meat in the fridge! In fact, after they eat, they usually ask what's for dinner. They know that I will prepare for them something that they cannot make on their own. But, they do have access to that food, unashamedly, through asking. Also, sometimes when it gets close to grocery day and my family does their daily kitchen raid, they can't imagine what in the world I will make. But, it delights me to no end to whip up something amazing for them from nothing. That is what it is like in the family of God. Go right into his throne room, through prayer, and take what is rightfully yours. You can ask, but you can also just take what he has already given you with a great, big thank you! For example, "Thank you, God, for being a good Father! Thank you for your love, which is beyond knowing. It says in your Word that I can know this love supernaturally. Reveal it to me through your Holy Spirit, in Jesus' name. Help me to grow up into my role in the family of God and to respect others in your family." Today we will learn about all the different leadership roles in the family of God. Take time to thank God for leaders in your life. Ask God to build them up and how you can work alongside them to further the kingdom of God. If you are a leader, ask the Lord to continue to fill you with his Spirit for greater insight, power and victory as you serve the people of God.

MEMORY VERSE

[14] For this reason I kneel before the Father, [15] from whom every family in heaven and on earth derives its name. [16] I pray that out of his glorious riches he may strengthen you with power through his Spirit in your inner being, [17] so that Christ may dwell in your hearts through faith. And I pray that you, being rooted and established in love, [18] may have power, together with all the Lord's holy people, to grasp how wide and long and high and deep is the love of Christ, [19] and to know this love that surpasses knowledge – that you may be filled to the measure of all the fullness of God.

[20] Now to him who is able to do immeasurably more than all we ask or imagine, according to his power that is at work within us, [21] to him be glory in the church and in Christ Jesus throughout all generations, for ever and ever! Amen. – Ephesians 3:14-21

Let's think of this week's study as our "power week," kind of like leg day at the gym. It's a little bit longer than normal, because there is so much to cover, but I promise to give you some "recovery" days after our big workout!

After he rose from the dead, Christ set up house! Jesus wanted to make sure his Body was taken care of by people who walk in the gifts of the Spirit and the calling of God for the purpose of edifying the church—true bodybuilding! It was so very important to Jesus. Why? Because Jesus loves his people. In John 21, on a beach after his resurrection, he asked Simon Peter, "Do you love me?" Peter was hurt, but Jesus asked two more times and reiterated, "Feed my sheep." True love expressed to God is done through using our gifts to nurture the people of God and bring about his kingdom here on earth.

READING A PARALLEL VERSION

This week's reading is taken from the New King James Version.

Ephesians 4:7-16 New King James Version (NKJV)

[7] But to each one of us grace was given according to the measure of Christ's gift. [8] Therefore He says:

> "When He ascended on high,
> He led captivity captive,
> And gave gifts to men."

[9] (Now this, "He ascended"—what does it mean but that He also first descended into the lower parts of the earth? [10] He who descended is also the One who ascended far above all the heavens, that He might fill all things.)

[11] And He Himself gave some to be apostles, some prophets, some evangelists, and some pastors and teachers, [12] for the equipping of the saints for the work of ministry, for the edifying of the body of Christ, [13] till we all come to the unity of the faith and of the knowledge of the Son of God, to a perfect man, to the measure of the stature of the fullness of Christ; [14] that we should no longer be children, tossed to and fro and carried about with every wind of doctrine, by the trickery of men, in the cunning craftiness of deceitful plotting, [15] but, speaking the truth in love, may grow up in all things into Him who is the head—Christ— [16] from whom the whole body, joined and knit together by what every joint supplies, according to the effective working by which every part does its share, causes growth of the body for the edifying of itself in love.

Can you list in the space below the five offices of the church found in Ephesians 4:7-16 (also referred to as the 5-fold ministries)?

Now, fill in the blanks to show the purposes for the 5-fold ministries. (hint: verses 12-13)

_____ of the _____ for the

_____ of the _____ till we all

_____ to _____ and of the

_____ of the Son of God, to be a _____ man, to the

_____ of the _____ of the fullness of Christ.

Notice the passage above doesn't list college degrees or job titles. Jesus' disciples went to the "University of the Master" where they lived, ate, and breathed real-life ministry with Jesus. These are God-ordained positions for Spirit-filled ministry. Hebrews 5:3, in referring to positions of ministry, in particular the priesthood, says, "And no one takes this honour on himself, but he receives it when called by God, just as Aaron was." Incredibly enough, as believers, we are all called to be priests—or ministers—of God. We will explore how we all have important, functioning roles in Jesus' body while digging into Ephesians 4. Some believers are also called to fill one of these five offices or positions of leadership with specific callings and anointings to serve, teach, lead, pray for, and protect the church of God. They are positions with great responsibility and calling by the Lord, since the rest of the body of Christ thrives or wanes based on the leaders' faithfulness to either teach, evangelize, prophecy, pray, or protect the flock.

APOSTLE

We've already talked about the office of apostle in previous weeks, so let's examine three of the four remaining offices God created for building his body in more detail today. Tomorrow we will examine the fifth office of Teacher.

EVANGELIST

Evangelists are exclusively gifted by the Holy Spirit, through grace, to share the gospel—which means good news—of Christ and to lead the lost to make a commitment to follow Jesus by faith. Greg Laurie, Greg Stier, and the late Billy Graham are excellent examples of men in the office of Evangelist. They aren't the only people who are, or were, expected to evangelize—share the death and resurrection of Jesus with the lost—but they have such a strong anointing and calling for this that they not only have led many to Christ, but they encourage believers to evangelize and teach the body how to do it.

PROPHET

Joel prophesies that in the end times, everyday men AND women will be anointed with prophecy. Scripture says this began at Pentecost, in Acts. Notice that it says both sons and daughters will prophesy, which means speak in church a message God has for the church. This does not exclusively refer to predicting future events. Prophesying can also be the anointed act of speaking a timely message about sin or repentance that the Lord gives a person. It is an anointed declaration. We see an example of prophesying when Mary, the mother of Jesus greets Elizabeth, who was carrying John the Baptist. Mary prophesies, giving the Lord glory and declaring his magnificence. She also praises him for what he has declared over her life and future.

> Joel 2:28 – 'And afterwards, I will pour out my Spirit on all people. Your sons and daughters will prophesy, your old men will dream dreams, your young men will see visions.'

In turn, the prophets are charged with sharing the Lord's plan with God's people.

> Amos 3:7 – Surely the Sovereign Lord does nothing without revealing his plan to his servants the prophets.

Jesus discusses how the spiritual offices bless those who participate in the ministry.

> Matthew 10:41 – Whoever welcomes a prophet will receive a prophet's reward, and whoever welcomes a righteous person as a righteous person will receive a righteous person's reward.

The apostle Paul describes how prophecy works to bring people to Christ.

> 1 Corinthians 14:24-2 – But if an unbeliever or an enquirer comes in while everyone is prophesying, they are convicted of sin and are brought under judgment by all, as the secrets of their hearts are laid bare. So they will fall down and worship God, exclaiming 'God is really among you!'

Prophecy isn't weird or scary. A prophet can receive a message from the Lord through the Holy Spirit, pray about it and give that message to the church in an orderly fashion. Also, this shows that people can "quench" the Spirit by not obeying the Lord when he gives them something to share with someone. The spiritual gift of prophecy can be used at the person's discretion, as specified in scripture.

> 1 Corinthians 14:32 – The spirits of the prophets are subject to the control of the prophet.

Paul realizes there are people who will be afraid of these supernatural gifts and will try to restrict them, and there are also people who will not use their gifts in an orderly way and others who will pretend they have a particular gift to try to gain attention for themselves or even control the body of believers. He shows there is a balance. See the above scripture from verse 32 where Paul reveals that people with spiritual gifts have the ability to freely use these gifts at any time. Using a gift does not happen when you have a crazy experience where you get worked up into a frenzy. A gift is a gift. We just need to use them in an orderly way, as specified in scripture.

> 1 Corinthians 14:39 – Therefore, my brothers and sisters, be eager to prophesy, and do not forbid speaking in tongues. But everything should be done in a fitting and orderly way.

There are people who claim to have dreams and prophecies from God who are false prophets. Anyone who contradicts scripture, preaches another gospel or denies the divinity of Christ is a false prophet. Paul said, "But even if we or an angel from heaven should preach a gospel other than the one we preached to you, let them be under God's curse!" (Gal 1:8) Paul warns in advance of spiritual or supernatural encounters that deny the gospel of grace. We see this happen with Mormonism and Islam. Both religions offer foundational stories of angelic beings that deny the biblical, triune divinity of Christ. Jesus warned about the abundance of false prophets in the end times. He did not say there would be no true prophets. He said there would be lots of false prophets. It's BIBLICAL to "test" the word of a person who says he or she is a prophet!

> 1 John 4:1 – Dear friends, do not believe every spirit, but test the spirits to see whether they are from God, because many false prophets have gone out into the world.

Jesus was rejected in his hometown. Many times people will see someone they grew up with and think there is no way that God could use him or her. They are seen as a "normal, everyday Joe or Mary." God can take everyday people and use them to his glory as prophets.

> Luke 4:24 – 'Truly I tell you,' he continued, 'no prophet is accepted in his home town.'

TRUE PROPHECY VS FALSE PROPHECY

A prophet is not a fortune teller or mystical seer. Prophecy is listed as an office of the church and was never intended to be something to go by the wayside when the church canonized scripture, as some people assert when they take 1 Corinthians 13 out of context. In the New Testament, we see men and women, young and old functioning in prophecy. A prophet is not just someone who sees the future. A prophet is not someone who will tell you how to get rich or prophecy generic messages of good times now—example: "Send me your $1000 *seed* check and God will give you $10,000"—um, no. A prophet will never be able to tell you the exact day of the return of Christ. Jesus said that no one would know the hour or the day—not even he himself, nor the angels in heaven—only the Father. If you happen to see a Youtuber with a video about how Jesus appeared to him and showed him the exact day of the end of the world, just click off of the video. That person may have seen a spirit, but it certainly wasn't Jesus! A true prophet WILL know the signs of the times—as we all should—and hear from the Lord things that the body of Christ needs to know for the season they are walking through, including the end times. The role of the prophet is not to be our only connection to hear from God. God can speak to us through others, but a prophet will not replace your own personal relationship with God through the Holy Spirit. A true prophet will lead you to hear from the Lord and walk closely with him, instead of needing the prophet to tell you everything you need to know about God. People are flawed. While we can and should learn from spiritual leaders in the church, exclusive dependency on someone else instead of God is dangerous.

Prophets in the Old Testament and New Testament are known for speaking God's truth to his people. Prophets call people to repent and turn back to the Lord. They are called to say tough things in obedience to the Lord. Think about it. When our hearts are hardened to the Holy Spirit, the Holy Spirit may need to use another mouth to speak to us. Or if our hearts are discouraged and beaten down, the Holy Spirit may refresh us through the words of a prophet. Frequently, this will come with sharing, like Jonah shared with Nineveh the consequences to be visited on the people, if the people do not turn back to the Lord. In the Old Testament, prophets also communicated God's heart and love for the people. Even the prophets with fiery messages against sin knew the heart of God and his love for his people. Repentance messages are messages of love! Turn back to God before it's too late—God loves you! A prophetic person will carry a heavy burden, like Jonah did, which was to deliver hard words to people, urging them to turn back to God. When Jonah ran from his calling, he found that he couldn't run from what the Lord had for him. Even in his running from

God, he became the prophetic symbol of Christ's resurrection—the sign of Jonah. (Jonah was in the belly of the big fish for three days before being spit out to continue his God-assigned work just as Christ was in the earth three days before being resurrected to continue his work for his Father.) Ha ha! God says, "Jonah, you can run, but you can't hide! I will make your whole escape plan a prophetic picture for the Jewish people and the world!" God sent Jonah, because he cared for the thousands of people in Nineveh.

In the church, a prophet will hear from the Lord in a special way that prepares the body of Christ for his work, including calling them to repentance and directing them to know what God wants them to know. I was once in a prayer meeting where God told one of the believers that the devil would use the strategy of divide and conquer to destroy the group of believers. In this case, it was a preemptive call to repent from divisiveness that the enemy could use to attack the work of the Lord and to be aware of the enemy's tactics.

A true prophetic word will never ever contradict the Bible and will always come to pass. Sometimes, a future looking word will take decades—or hundreds of years to come to pass! This is true of many Old Testament prophecies. Most of them took many years to come to pass. If someone is a prophet and gives a "Thus saith the Lord" statement, this must come to pass in the prophet's lifetime or in the future after his or her death, or they are not speaking from God. Having a word from God does not mean that a prophet will have the whole picture or complete understanding of what God is saying. Sometimes the person will just have something God spoke to him or her. For example, Daniel received dreams from the Lord and was perplexed about what they meant. The Lord explained to Daniel what some of his dreams meant. Concerning other parts of the same dream he said,

> Go your way, Daniel, because the words are rolled up and sealed until the time of the end. Many will be purified, made spotless and refined, but the wicked will continue to be wicked. None of the wicked will understand, but those who are wise will understand. – Daniel 12:9-10

Do not expect a prophet to be a mind reader or to know everything. This is not scriptural. It is a mystical, superstitious misunderstanding of prophecy. A prophet is simply called to be obedient in sharing what the Lord gives. Again, the purpose of prophecy is to build up the body of Christ and prepare it for the works of the Lord. If you would like to know more about the role of a prophet, I encourage you to do a word study on the word "prophet" or "prophecy." You will find this word making abundant appearances in the teachings of Christ, as well as in the rest of the New Testament.

PASTOR

In Ephesians 4, the word for pastor in the Greek is shepherd. Just as David fought lions and bears when he was a shepherd, a pastor will daily fight off spiritual attacks coming against the people in his flock. He leads them to still waters, to green pastures to eat, and ultimately directs them to follow the True Shepherd—Jesus. This can be accomplished through giving the congregation consistent, healthy teaching from God's Word, as well as through counseling and prayer. A pastor's position is one of long-term commitment to the people of God, as opposed to an evangelist's role to travel more frequently to share the gospel. A pastor will often do the work of an evangelist, teacher, and sometimes a prophet, which is a spiritual gifting. Most churches in America have a pastor that ministers in a paid position, which is biblical. However, this man may erroneously be expected—with the average American mentality—to do all the ministry of God in a church. That's like expecting the mom to do all the housework, because that's her "job." Really, one of a mom's many jobs is to equip her family to work with their hands and find manageable, age-appropriate responsibilities for children to grow into. Congregations who expect that the pastor is the only one who ministers may think they pay him to have funny illustrations, to draw a crowd, to do all the leg work. In fact, you may have heard people say, "What are we paying that pastor for? What is being done with OUR money, anyways?" Don't forget that when we give to the Lord, it is God's money! It's not ours anymore. Its purpose is to build the kingdom. And God wants more than your tithes and offerings. He wants you! He wants your servant heart. You are part of the team! P.S.—Your pastor is required to give generously to the Lord, too. We are all to give and serve together joyfully.

Remember, your pastor is uniquely called by the Lord and has his own special personality, gifting and calling. Don't try to compare your pastor or any other church leader with another church's pastor or even your favorite mega church pastor/teacher. It's simply not biblical or fair. Some pastors will be musical, others spiritually gifted as teachers, others gifted in counseling and prayer, others in acts of service. Some are introverted, others extroverted. There is no right and wrong in this, as long as the person is called by God. But, remember, if the person is called by God, God will equip this person with all the appropriate gifts needed for ministering in this role. Paul told Timothy to "…fan into flame the gift of God, which is in you through the laying on of my hands." Pastoral gifts can be received by the laying on of hands and pastors can fan those gifts into flame through prayer, faith and use of the gifts.

ARE THEY BUSINESS LEADERS?

These five different positions of spiritual headship for the church are not a business model. The church is not a business. Businesses are about increasing revenue. Churches are about building the kingdom of God in the hearts of people, through the power of the Spirit. Here in Ephesians, it says that the reason that these five offices exist is to equip the saints for the work of ministry, so the body of Christ can be edified! The goal of someone in a pastoral position is to equip his people for the work of the Lord—not to carry the load himself. We all work together! Do not expect your pastor to be the only one who visits the sick in the hospital or leads people to Christ. Do expect your pastor to create an atmosphere where the men and women in the church can grow into Jesus' gifts for them, so that everyone is working together to the glory of Christ in love.

In my church, there are several qualified lay people who are ready and spiritually equipped to step into the pulpit to preach a Spirit-filled message. You would think they are "paid staff" by the quality of their messages. But, the quality of the message is actually from the anointing of the Holy Spirit and a heart that is in the Word, not from that person's paid staff position. There are many lay-believers who can come beside a wounded soul and give godly counsel, operating in gifts of knowledge, wisdom, and discernment between spirits. There are encouragers and generous people who mercifully pour themselves out for the Lord. Some are gifted with hospitality. When I was recovering from appendicitis and my husband was out of town for ministry, the women in our ministry team and church came around me, providing meals, prayer, transportation, and even selfless cleaning! God used these women to show me his love and to bring his comfort in my time of need. The job of the leaders is to equip these wonderful people of God to minister like Jesus.

This is why the 5-fold offices are given by the Lord, so more and more followers of Christ can gain confidence in who they are in Christ and step into the power of God for their lives, which results in gloriously reaching more souls for the kingdom. One of my prayers for our church is, "Lord, put meat on our bones." The Lord wants to bring muscle to the framework of the body of Christ. He wants prayer warriors, helpers, teachers, and servant-hearted people who are loving others and are kingdom-minded! He also wants the muscles on the body to get a work out and grow in strength! If I imagine the pastor's job as the body part of the mouth, but a church expects him to do the work of the feet, hands, hamstrings—most of the spiritual ministry—it creates this image in my mind of an atrophied person, lying in bed powerless. How silly. Let's get the whole body up, moving and getting stronger!

> … until we all reach unity in the faith and in the knowledge of the Son of God and become mature, attaining to the whole measure of the fullness of Christ. – Ephesians 4:13

BRINGING IT HOME

I just got home from the hospital where my father had a stroke. Watching the people of God work together to help each other, pray for each other, and minister to each other is awe-inspiring. We hurt together and we pray together. We overcome together and when we do, we are strengthened together.

Are you a part of a body of believers where you are a functioning member, providing support, love, and hope? Are you able to receive these things from other believers at your church? Have you been living in the idea that the paid staff are the ones who are supposed to minister? Are you ready to receive from God his truth for your position in the body of Christ?

Have you been in prayer before the Lord, asking him to equip you and use you by his Holy Spirit? God is waiting for you to be willing for him to use you powerfully.

CHRIST SETS UP HOUSE
PART 2

SPIRITUAL OFFICES AND GIFTS IN THE BODY OF CHRIST

PRAYER

Today, we are going to learn about walking in truth as we follow godly men and women who are teachers. We need discernment to avoid the trap of deception. Spend time praying today that the Lord will fill you with truth and protect you from false leaders who would lead you astray. Pray for the Lord to reveal his day-to-day purposes for your life. These are the seemingly mundane things that a believer can do with joy and anointing, like teaching Sunday School or bringing your children security by doing their laundry or cooking. There are other purposes in life that we are called to that will change the course of a person's life forever, like leading someone to Christ, praying in faith for a person who needs victory over depression, giving generously to someone in need or supporting a ministry. Whatever we do, we should do it as if we are doing it to the Lord. Pray that God gives you eternal perspective today, as you walk through life and serve him. Ask him how he wants you to serve at church. Ask him to be Lord of your weekends and evenings—all the valuable down time you love. Pray that the will of God will be done, even on a Friday night or as you turn your laundry day into a day of tearing down strongholds in the laundry room! Allow the love of God to transform every part of you by faith. Think on these things, as you go before the Lord today praying your memory verse.

MEMORY VERSE

[14] For this reason I kneel before the Father, [15] from whom every family in heaven and on earth derives its name. [16] I pray that out of his glorious riches he may strengthen you with power through his Spirit in your inner being, [17] so that Christ may dwell in your hearts through faith. And I pray that you, being rooted and established in love, [18] may have power, together with all the Lord's holy people, to grasp how wide and long and high and deep is the love of Christ, [19] and to know this love that surpasses knowledge – that you may be filled to the measure of all the fullness of God.

[20] Now to him who is able to do immeasurably more than all we ask or imagine, according to his power that is at work within us, [21] to him be glory in the church and in Christ Jesus throughout all generations, for ever and ever! Amen. – Ephesians 3:14-21

READING

Today, let's dig deeper into Ephesians 4:7-16. We want to see and understand why Paul writes these words about the body of Christ and the reason God gave the church positions of authority. What is the purpose of the Lord for this body of believers, his church? How do we accomplish this purpose?

CONJUNCTION SEARCH

As you read the following passage,

- underline the conjunctions or connecting words (example: so, that, then, instead, as). Doing so will help you see more of the richness of the passage.

- after underlining them, draw an arrow to connect the phrases that reveal the intent of the passages before and after the conjunction.

For example:

> 13 till we all come to the unity of the faith and of the knowledge of the Son of God, to a perfect man, to the measure of the stature of the fullness of Christ;
>
> 14 that we should no longer be children, tossed to and fro and carried about with every wind of doctrine…"

PARALLEL VERSION

This week's reading is taken from the New King James Version.

Ephesians 4:7-16 (NKJV)

7 But to each one of us grace was given according to the measure of Christ's gift. 8 Therefore He says:

> "When He ascended on high,
> He led captivity captive,
> And gave gifts to men."

TODAY'S BIBLE STUDY TOOL

Conjunction Search. Underlining conjunctions or words that connect phrases will help you see the conclusion the author is drawing.

---

9 (Now this, "He ascended"—what does it mean but that He also first descended into the lower parts of the earth? 10 He who descended is also the One who ascended far above all the heavens, that He might fill all things.)

11 And He Himself gave some to be apostles, some prophets, some evangelists, and some pastors and teachers, 12 for the equipping of the saints for the work of ministry, for the edifying of the body of Christ, 13 till we all come to the unity of the faith and of the knowledge of the Son of God, to a perfect man, to the measure of the stature of the fullness of Christ; 14 that we should no longer be children, tossed to and fro and carried about with every wind of doctrine, by the trickery of men, in the cunning craftiness of deceitful plotting, 15 but, speaking the truth in love, may grow up in all things into Him who is the head—Christ— 16 from whom the whole body, joined and knit together by what every joint supplies, according to the effective working by which every part does its share, causes growth of the body for the edifying of itself in love.

ASK QUESTIONS

Now that you have done this activity, record your discoveries below. Using your own words AND the words from this passage, write what God's purpose for the body of Christ is. We will ask WHO, WHAT, WHY, WHEN and HOW to discover this.

68. WHO is involved?

69. WHAT is the purpose?

70. WHY is this the will of God for the body of Christ?

71. WHEN will the will of God for the church happen, according to this passage?

72. HOW does God accomplish his will for the body of Christ, according to this passage?

TEACHERS

Now let's discuss the last of the 5-fold ministries—the special anointing and calling of the teacher.

Luke 6:40 – The student is not above his teacher, but everyone who is fully trained will be like their teacher.

James 3:1 – Not many of you should become teachers, my fellow believers, because you know that we who teach will be judged more strictly.

Matthew 13:52 – He said to them, 'Therefore every teacher of the law who has become a disciple in the kingdom of heaven is like the owner of a house who brings out of his storeroom new treasures as well as old.'

1 Corinthians 10:32-11:1 – Do not cause anyone to stumble, whether Jews, Greeks or the church of God — even as I try to please everyone in every way. For I am not seeking my own good but the good of many, so that they may be saved. Follow my example, as I follow the example of Christ.

Teaching is a very important gifting from the Lord, which comes with a great responsibility. Teachers protect God's people from heresy by teaching biblical truth about Jesus. Teachers help facilitate growing faith, because the scripture says, "So then faith cometh by hearing and hearing by the Word of God." (KJV) If the scripture says that believers must study to show themselves approved unto God, how much more are teachers responsible to do this, as they strengthen us through what God teaches them. In fact, I would encourage everyone to read the book of 1 Timothy to see Paul's encouragement to Timothy as a pastor and teacher. Timothy is told to stay in Ephesus, because there are false teachers rising up among the believers there, leading people astray. That is probably why Paul emphatically teaches the Ephesians that the role of the 5-fold ministries is to mature the body of Christ into fullness, so they will not be blown about by every teaching that breezes their way like the wind. He warns them in Ephesians 4 not to follow teachers that contradict the truth of the gospel or the precedents given by the apostles for the people of God.

Study to shew thyself approved unto God, a workman that needeth not to be ashamed, rightly dividing the word of truth. – 2 Timothy 2:15 (KJV)

The Word of God is so powerful and important in the life of a believer, so a teacher is responsible to God for how he or she handles the scriptures. Scripture brings life. It is spiritually discerned. It is eternal. The Bible is the Word of Christ and it's the Sword of the Spirit, our weapon against the devil. Because of its power, its teacher needs to be someone who studies God's Word, knows it, can apply it, and is called by God to teach it. A teacher can be a man or a woman. Titus 2:3-4 says that it is good for older women to encourage and teach younger women. Notice that the scripture does not say a teacher needs to be talented or creative. Those are things the Holy Spirit will develop supernaturally in someone whom he calls to teach. God really just requires obedience when he calls, studying God's Word—which hopefully we are all doing anyway—and living a Spirit-filled life, the way he calls all born-again believers to live.

Look back at the passages listed above. A teacher is held to a higher standard of judgment with God. Why? Because God's goal is that the student become like the teacher. When one is teaching spiritually, students are not looking to that person to just fill their mind with facts, but to reveal to them what living in a relationship with Jesus looks like. In Jesus' time, a Jewish person who was following a teacher, would literally follow him! The student wanted to know how the Rabbi prayed and how he handled the most intimate parts of his life. We want to know that about the person who is teaching us too, right? How do I parent this teenager in

Christ, when he is different than my other teen? How do I walk with God through loss? How do I reconcile a damaged relationship? Is the person teaching you living what he or she is teaching?

Once I got a call from a woman whom God had delivered out of extreme anxiety. She related to me how she cried through a church service where the guest speaker "taught" that anxiety and depression are emotional conditions that you can never be delivered from. The speaker pushed back against the teachings that someone should pray to find freedom. To him, it was only discouraging and made the depressed person more depressed.

She said, "I know exactly how he feels. I used to think the way he thinks. But there is so much freedom in Christ that it makes me cry to think of what he is going through. I also think it's so dangerous to teach people that there is no hope in God for anxiety and depression. People were crying all around me. Some were cheering. He made it sound so spiritual and mature, but it was really hopeless and he is at least twice my age. He has lived in that bondage for so long. The whole thing was so sad."

This is an example of how the position of teacher carries a weighty load. In this example, of course, deliverance from anxiety is comprised of more than just praying for God to take it away. It is a great battle. There is so much that the Lord will lead you through, as you learn the Word and God's promises. Direction from the Word will increase our faith and bring healing. The devil and his lies need to be dealt with—rebuked and commanded to leave. New truth needs to replace life-long-held lies, bitterness, and pain. Healing needs to be ministered through prayer and counseling. Depressed people need the love, support, and encouragement of the body of Christ. To put this process in a few sentences here is not sufficient. But, sitting under a teacher who walks in freedom or has helped people find Christ's deliverance in the middle of the depression is truly "finding a treasure" from someone's storehouse. Hope is a treasure! We have already learned in Ephesians that the Spirit needs to open our eyes to see this hope.

THE USE AND MISUSE OF THE 5-FOLD MINISTRIES

The Word is alive and active and it should be alive in the lives of leaders first and then the rest of the church. This does not mean that teachers, pastors, evangelists, apostles, or prophets have arrived, but they are living in an alive, active, healthy, and obedient walk with the Lord that others can model their lives after. That is why the scripture requires elders and leaders to have their personal life in order. (See 1 Peter 5:1-4 and 2 Timothy 2:1-7, 14-26)

In a day and time when headlines are filled with sickening story after discouraging story of another fallen man of God who succumbed to financial or sexual sin, there is no better time to understand this important scriptural concept. The standards for a person in ministry are very high, because so much is at stake—the soundness of the whole body is at stake! The scripture says in 1 Timothy 5:22, "Do not be hasty in the laying on of hands, and do not share in the sins of others. Keep yourself pure." The church is commended to be very careful when giving authority in the church, especially when commissioning men or women for ministry or missions work. Also, we see precedent for accountability. Is it possible for someone to lead God's church with purity? The answer is a resounding YES! In fact, these positions are specifically designed for the protection of the body from those who would exploit it. There is nothing more that the enemy would like to do other than to destroy a church or ministry by attacking the leaders with scandals and sinful pitfalls, which can be avoided! "And they overcame him by the blood of the Lamb, and by the word of their testimony..." (Revelation 12:11 KJV) However, we can have hope, because the true church is designed by God to be protected from this when those given the callings of the 5-fold ministries use them in openness and honesty before God and those they serve.

Paul expounds on this: that we should no longer be children, tossed to and fro and carried about with every wind of doctrine, by the trickery of men, in the cunning craftiness of deceitful plotting — Ephesians 4:14

This is the end-all purpose of the leadership of Christ—to build up and grow believers in the body of Christ and to PROTECT it—the church—from EVIL SCHEMERS! This sounds like a conspiracy, but in Paul's time, and how much more now, there were men trying to get people to follow them personally, instead of Jesus. Recently, there was a shameful article about a pastor of a mega church who was found guilty of committing adultery. He defiantly stood before his congregation and told them he wouldn't step down from the calling of God. This was met with applause! It sounds spiritual for him to say he won't step down from God's ministry, but when he made his compromises, he already had stepped down. This behavior is really shaking his fist in God's face, taking advantage of women, destroying his family and the family of God, and dragging the name of Jesus through the mud.

Schemers may sound good, "smart" or "spiritual." They may just be subconsciously scheming to get more people in their ministry so they can get more money and recognition or consider themselves successful. God knows the heart, so we cannot make this assumption. It's not always obvious. A schemer may compromise the message he or she preaches to make more people happy in order to get more money or accolades, but this person could actually believe that this wrong teaching is true, because he or she has given into temptation and is deceived. Obedient teachers will unselfishly teach the Word, uncompromised, promote good relationships in the body of Christ, and protect those under his or her teaching.

Let's compare the behavior of the adulterous pastor/teacher to that of evangelist Billy Graham, who died at 99 after a scandal-free ministry. His world-wide teaching impacted millions of people for the kingdom of God. At the beginning of his ministry, he sat down with men in his ministry team and created a set of guidelines to prevent sin from staining his ministry with scandals. Billy would never, ever be alone with a woman, except his wife. His humble leadership shaped the entire organization and built a wall of protection around his own family and around every family that was won to Christ by his evangelism. His consistent example and scandal-free ministry really built a wall around the world-wide body of Christ and showed the world what happens when people follow the biblical precedents set out for leaders in the body of Christ. ...till we all come to the unity of the faith and of the knowledge of the Son of God, to a perfect man, to the measure of the stature of the fullness of Christ; – Ephesians 4:13

BRINGING IT HOME

Has it been on your heart to teach, maybe even starting with children's church? It is a noble task and something to not be taken lightly. Do not let this study on teaching scare you away from serving the Lord as a teacher in the body of Christ! If God calls you, he will qualify you. Remember that being a teacher is a gift and office of the Holy Spirit. The Spirit of God will help you in your weaknesses. Seek his face, because his grace and his Spirit will more than make up for your inadequacy.

On the flip side, are you leading or teaching, but struggling with serious sin and temptation? There is absolutely nothing wrong—and everything right—with taking a sabbatical to get your house in order, before the enemy can attack you and use your sin to destroy you and the church. Find accountability from someone who has already removed the "log from his or her own eye" so they can help you remove the speck from your eye.

Even though we are not all teachers, we are all called to teach our children about God at home. Start teaching them by reading God's Word with your children and discussing it. In Deuteronomy 6:4-7, God teaches us how to teach our children, 4 Hear, O Israel: the Lord our God, the Lord is one. 5 Love the Lord your God with all your heart and with all your soul and with all your strength. 6 These commandments that I give you today are to be on your hearts. 7 Impress them on your children. Talk about them when you sit at home and when you walk along the road, when you lie down and when you get up.

The more you are filled with the Word and the more you are filled with the Spirit, the more God will use you to grow and expand his kingdom.

EXTRAVAGANT EVENT
WHAT ARE YOU BRINGING?

PRAYER

Today, let's combine the spiritual truths in our Ephesians 1 prayer and our Ephesians 3 prayer.

Glorious Father and God of our Lord Jesus Christ,

Give me the Spirit of wisdom and revelation so that I can know you better. Give me revelation to understand the mystery of Christ and the power of your work to bring people together. Open my spiritual eyes to know you and the hope to which you have called me—hope for my relationships, hope for my future, hope for the difficulties and sin I struggle with.

I know that I am seated with you in heavenly realms and I want to walk in victory in my position in you, Lord God. I know that the same power that raised Jesus from the dead is in my life, is in me by the Holy Spirit. I pray that you will strengthen me with this power by your Spirit in my inner being. Fill me with faith. Help me to know, beyond a shadow of a doubt, who Christ is and your desire to work in my life.

I pray that you will root me and establish my life in love. I need your power to comprehend your love. Jesus, give me a deep and personal relationship with you to know your love and its width, length, height and depth.

Fill me to all the fullness of God and do more in my life than I can ask or imagine, according to your power that is at work in me. Glorify yourself in my life, and in my family, and in the generations that will come from me, in Jesus' name. I pray that my children and my children's children will know you by your Spirit and that your name and your renown will go forward from my line forever.

In Jesus' name. Amen

MEMORY VERSE

[14] For this reason I kneel before the Father, [15] from whom every family in heaven and on earth derives its name. [16] I pray that out of his glorious riches he may strengthen you with power through his Spirit in your inner being, [17] so that Christ may dwell in your hearts through faith. And I pray that you, being rooted and established in love, [18] may have power, together with all the Lord's holy people, to grasp how wide and long and high and deep is the love of Christ, [19] and to know this love that surpasses knowledge – that you may be filled to the measure of all the fullness of God.

20 Now to him who is able to do immeasurably more than all we ask or imagine, according to his power that is at work within us, 21 to him be glory in the church and in Christ Jesus throughout all generations, for ever and ever! Amen. – Ephesians 3:14-21

Today's lesson will explore some verses in scripture that describe the different roles in the body of Christ. This theme occurs throughout Ephesians, but today we will look at it from a fresh, more detailed angle. The world tells us we need to be independent and not rely on anyone. Honestly, who really believes that? With your head, it may make sense, especially if you have been hurt by people close to you. But, our hearts are yearning for relationships, to be needed, and to have a purpose and a place with loved ones.

As women, we raise our children to be independent. We often equate independence with strength, freedom, and the ability to navigate life, which are all essential human needs. However, this sprint for independence can be accompanied by isolation and loneliness. Our society places value on work, money, and success. All of these pursuits take up copious amounts of time. This usually comes at the expense of relationships and the healthy balance they bring to life.

In the family of God, each person is important and has a role within the body. The church isn't an organization like a football league or PTO. It is a spiritual family—actually the manifest presence of Christ himself in people on earth—where everyone matters and everyone contributes. God has delivered you from sin, rejection, and a life separated from him, and he has adopted you into his family. What is your role in your local church body? Have you discovered it yet?

We are the body of Christ! When you think of the body of Christ, what do you think of? Write your thoughts below.

CROSS REFERENCE

Let's do a cross reference check on the phrase "body of Christ." If you look it up in your Bible app, you can find lots of scripture pertaining to what we are studying in Ephesians 4. Turn to 1 Corinthians 12:12-20 to read one famous passage.

1 Corinthians 12:12-20 discusses the roles of the independent parts of the body, but it also clearly states that each part is created to need other parts, in order to function. Ephesians 4:15-16 says,

> **TODAY'S BIBLE STUDY TOOL**
>
> **Cross Reference.** When you want to dig deeper into a topic and make sure you don't take it out of context, consult the full counsel of the Word of God. Look up other passages in scripture with the same phrases and words and read them in context.

Instead, speaking the truth in love, we will grow to become in every respect the mature body of him who is the head, that is, Christ. From him the whole body, joined and held together by every supporting ligament, grows and builds itself up in love, as each part does its work. – Ephesians 4:15-16

PARALLEL VERSIONS

When reading these two verses in the New King James Version, I suddenly was caught off guard by the wording. Here it is:

but, speaking the truth in love, may grow up in all things into Him who is the head—Christ— 16 from whom the whole body, **joined and knit together by what every joint supplies,** according to the effective working by which every part does its share, causes growth of the body for the edifying of itself in love. – Ephesians 4:15-16 (NKJV) *(emphasis mine)*

It says in verse 16 we are joined and knit together by what every joint supplies. I was reading this passage aloud to my husband and daughter one evening and we all took pause at this section.

"What did that say?" my husband asked, curiously.

"I know, let's read it again," I said, trying to wrap my mind around it. "Lord, give us understanding," I muttered under my breath. "It says, '… may grow up in all things into Him who is the head—Christ—from whom the whole body, joined and knit together by what every joint supplies, according to the effective working by which every part does its share, causes growth of the body for the edifying of itself in love.' So, it's saying that the body of Christ is held together—joined—knit together by what every joint supplies. That means that we are designed to hold each other together—but not just by being there—but also by what we supply, right?"

"That's what it sounds like," he mused.

My daughter, an athletic training major who spent the last year studying human anatomy, looked intrigued. "This year we learned so much about the joints and muscles and how each part affects each other. We are taught over and over again that if you are treating the point of pain in the body, you are probably not treating the problem. Something as simple as an ankle that is lacking range of motion, could be the cause of chronic back pain, even if the individual is unaware of the ankle problem. The back pain won't stop until the ankle is adjusted to restore full range of motion. It's mind-blowing."

"So, if one part of the body isn't doing its part, it can cause extreme pain in other parts of the body?" I asked, thinking through all the aches and pains I've endured through the years and wondering what the real problem was. My mind also went to different times over the years when ministries or churches I have been in have not had enough workers to carry the load of the ministry. There were lots of people there to attend the service, but not lots of available or willing hands and feet to do the work. Jesus said in Luke 10:2, "The harvest is plentiful, but the workers are few. Ask the Lord of the harvest, therefore, to send out workers into his harvest field." My daughter's reminiscing helped me to see some more crazy connections between "body life" and actual bodies.

She continued, "Remember when I was in track in high school and was having foot pain when I ran? Well, the physical therapist analyzed my run with computer technology to find out that a weakness in my hip muscles was causing me to run incorrectly, which in turn caused the foot pain. When I strengthened my hips through exercise, my foot pain left and I greatly shortened my running by a couple seconds."

GREEK WORD STUDY

So, each little joint and muscle is important to the maturity and functionality of the body of Christ! I was curious. What does "supplies" mean in the Greek? I didn't know what to expect. I thought it would be obvious. But, I was truly blown away by what was revealed when I went to biblehub.com, typed in Ephesians 4:16, and clicked on the Greek HELPS™ Word-studies for the word "supply." Check out this screenshot from my phone of a truly jaw-dropping revelation from the Greek word study!

> **TODAY'S BIBLE STUDY TOOL**
>
> **Greek Word Study.** Dig deeper into the meaning of a word by learning the intent of the original language. Some underlying meaning may have been lost in translation.

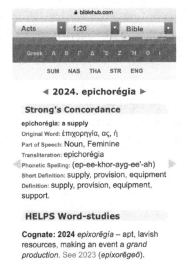

The word "supply" here in the Greek isn't just your run of the mill office supplies, but when you look down to the word-studies, you can get a clearer picture of the usage. It means "lavish resources" making an event a grand production!

Immediately, my mind shot back several months to our Revealed Women's Ministry team—which, at the time, didn't have an official title—when we worked together to put on the first *Revealed: The Great Mystery* Ladies' Conference. It was literally like a beautiful theatrical production unfolding, and I am not talking about the event. The Lord used each woman, in her gifting, to lavish on the ministry weekend everything from prayer, to administrative work, to hospitality, creativity, teaching, music, organization, generosity, encouragement and more than I can articulate here. All the beautiful women, young and old, bringing their gifts, and supplying the body of Christ with lavish resources, made the weekend of teaching, worship, deliverance, and prayer truly an extravagant event! I can't imagine if any one of those women were not on the planning and ministry team. We really would have suffered the loss of spiritual provision that the women contributed to make our weekend a grand event!

Even more so in the grand event of everyday life of the body of Christ, we can see the parts working together. An older woman encourages a young mom, whose estranged relationship with her own mother makes navigating the storms of life a bit blinding and scary. Strong backs and arms set up church Sunday after Sunday for a mobile church that meets in a school. Tender and gracious, mercy-laden hearts listen to the broken and downcast sinners, who feel there is no hope. These same patience-filled, warm faces cry tears of empathy and smile, speaking words of grace and life. Prayer warriors go before the throne of grace with confidence, lift up and fight for the persecuted church, for the pastors rotting in prison across the world, wondering if anyone remembers or knows that they are alive.

This is a reflection of what our Father in heaven does for us, when in all his goodness, grace and mercy, he lavishes redemption upon us. Our Father does not hold back from his children! Remember what Ephesians 1:7-10 says?

Ephesians 1:7-10

[7] In him we have redemption through his blood, the forgiveness of sins, in accordance with the riches of God's grace [8] that he **lavished on us**. With all wisdom and understanding, [9] he made known to us the mystery of his will according to his good pleasure, which he purposed in Christ, [10] to be put into effect when the times reach their fulfilment – to bring unity to all things in heaven and on earth under Christ. (emphasis mine)

Because we are the children of God, when we walk in the Spirit, we will look and act like we belong to him—a chip off the old block, so to speak.

Everything we need for life and godliness we truly have in Christ Jesus—including the revelation we need to understand this mystery of our purpose in Christ—so that we can all be a part of the unification of everything in heaven and on earth under Christ! When we look all through Ephesians, we see these themes of unity over and over, but unity is more than a word that means to come together or to be in agreement. It is not a fake unity, like the Unity "church" that welcomes every wind of doctrine, false belief or religion. It is only in Christ that true spiritual unity occurs, because it is a unity of the Spirit, not a relational unity of people just getting together physically. In Ephesians, the Father's heart is shown, beating for his children, that his family will be truly one. This is just as Christ prayed in the garden of Gethsemane. He prayed that we would be one, as he and the Father are one! And how did God answer this prayer, which surely Christ prayed in submission to the Father's will?

When you study a book of the Bible, it's like looking for a treasure. Have you ever lost something in your house and you know, beyond a shadow of a doubt, it is in a certain room, but you simply cannot find it? Months later, you may find it, just out of sight, in the very room you had combed over and over, to no avail. Dumbfounded, you stand there wondering how you overlooked it this whole time! That is exactly what we are going to do right now! Not lose something—FIND something right under our noses!

Let's examine Ephesians 4:12b-13 further. I mulled over this passage in two different translations of the Bible.

… till we all come to the unity of the faith and of the knowledge of the Son of God, to a perfect man, to the **measure of the stature of the fullness of Christ;** – Ephesians 4:12b-13 (NKJV)

… so that the body of Christ may be built up until we all reach unity in the faith and in the knowledge of the Son of God and become mature, **attaining to the whole measure of the fullness of Christ.** – Ephesians 4:12b-13 (NIV)

For many years, I have read this phrase at different times, wondering what it means to attain to the whole measure of the fullness of Christ. The phrase sounds a bit redundant. Why would the Holy Spirit inspire Paul to use this wording? What does *"whole measure of the fullness"* mean? I would pray about it and imagine that it referred to someone like Paul the apostle who raised the dead, wrote most of the New Testament, and spread the gospel of Christ to the Gentiles. Definitely HE walked in the fullness of Christ. But, the problem was, I was taking it out of CONTEXT. Context. Context. Context! The context is that the phrase, *"attaining to the whole measure of the fullness of Christ,"* refers to the entire body of Christ in unity. We know that while the body of Christ can refer to an individual church or small group of believers, it ultimately includes the people of God all over the world from the time of the early church until Christ returns. Have you ever heard this phrase "fullness of Christ" anywhere else in the Bible? Let's look it up! Following is a screenshot of my search of the phrase, "fullness of Christ," in my Bible app.

Hmmmmm…. Here we are again! Just like looking up the phrase "heavenly realms" or the word "mystery," we find a recurring theme in Ephesians for the phrase "fullness of Christ." And God placed all things under his feet and appointed him to be head over everything for the church, which is his body, the fullness of him who fills everything in every way. – Ephesians 1:22-23

This refers to Christ's authority over the church, but also says that the church is the fullness of Christ. What does that mean? Ephesians 3:16-19, our memory verse and prayer says:

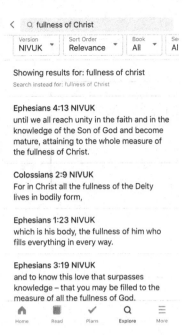

I pray that out of his glorious riches he may strengthen you with power through his Spirit in your inner being, so that Christ may dwell in your hearts through faith. And I pray that you, being rooted and established in love, may have power, together with all the Lord's holy people, to grasp how wide and long and high and deep is the love of Christ, and to know this love that surpasses knowledge – **that you may be filled to the measure of all the fullness of God.**

So, Paul's prayer is not a rambling sentence of spiritual platitudes strung together. It is a prayer that petitions the Lord to allow what needs to happen so the body of Christ may be filled to the measure of all the fullness of God—TOGETHER! This revelation shook me to my core. I was stunned. All this time, all my life I have run a race in pursuit of Christ that was even more individualistic than I realized. It is impossible for me to walk in the full measure of the fullness of Christ alone. It can only be experienced within unity in the body—in love and power together! This is why it may hurt so badly when the people of God are not walking in love and unity and why God may feel so distant at those times of discord. When we work together, in love and unity for the common goal of the gospel, we experience the power and presence of God in a fuller way. How does this work and can we back this up with more scriptures other than Ephesians?

Matthew 18:15-20 is a great example of Christ teaching on life in a body of believers. In verse 15, he deals with confronting someone in sin, who is a believer. The actual context of Matthew 18 is Christ speaking of unity in the church. So, since we are in context, we know we are on the right track! Jesus goes on to talk about the power in corporate—or unified—prayer. Corporate prayer is when two or more people pray together. ¹⁸ 'Truly I tell you, whatever you bind on earth will be bound in heaven, and whatever you loose on earth will be loosed in heaven. ¹⁹ 'Again, truly I tell you that if two of you on earth agree about anything they ask for, it will be done for them by my Father in heaven. ²⁰ For where two or three gather in my name, there am I with them.'

Jesus explains it is very important and powerful for two or more people to gather together in prayer. There is something "extra" about this type of prayer that manifests the presence of Christ even more than the prayer of a faithful person by him or herself. God loves it when believers come together in unity, so he gives extra power when people agree together in prayer! God chooses his glory to be manifest in unity! One of the hardest things to do in a church is to get people to a prayer meeting. I am not sure how many people understand the power of meeting together with other believers in prayer. It is a promise from Christ that he will not only be there, but that he will do for us what we ask in unity and agreement!

I want to challenge you today. The scripture is clear. Each of us has an important role in his body. It is also clear we need to grow up into our role, to mature with other believers, drawing close to Christ, with each part doing its job. Have you asked God what your role is? Are you too busy to participate in the body life, or are you actively seeking God's direction for you? If you are sitting on the sidelines, just taking in the sermon, then heading for the door, I guarantee everyone else is missing what your lavish gifts will bring to the party! Prayerfully seek the Lord and ask him to fill you with his Holy Spirit to do the work he has called you to. He has a purpose for your life, and I guarantee—according to Ephesians 3 and 4—you will experience more of the fullness of God and his presence in your life, when you start to walk in obedience in the areas of your gifting and calling.

BRINGING IT HOME

Do you know what your spiritual gifts are?

Are you attending a church where you can sit as a consumer and sneak out the door, trying to avoid getting involved in the work of God's kingdom?

Do you criticize those who are leading and working in the church, but do not take a role yourself—aka analyzing the pastor's sermon, or the worship, or complaining about the lack of ministries—and are not offering your own gifts and talents?

If you are doing God's work, are you praying for a fresh infilling of his Spirit daily? Are you asking the Lord how your gifts fit in with other people's gifts? Are you working together with others and benefiting from the holy relationships in the body of Christ?

Do not allow the enemy to discredit what God has placed inside of you to contribute to the body of Christ! You are important!

SHARING IN HIS GLORY

How many times a day do you go to Siri or Alexa—I am sure this question will date this book in a few years—to gain knowledge of some sort? Today, let's discover a more glorious search engine for the great enigmas in life: the glory of God revealed through the body of Christ. I hope this teaching will help demolish strongholds of fear and guilt you may live in. I say this because, as I studied the topic of the body of Christ in Ephesians 4, the Lord deconstructed lies I believed, along with guilt and fear I lived in. It's incredible how healthy we become, inside and out, when we live in the way the Lord designed us to live.

PRAYER

Today, take time to talk to your heavenly Father about your gifts and what he wants to do in you and through you to bring fullness to the body of Christ. Here is an example of a prayer, taken from our verse.

Father,

Forgive me for undervaluing my role in the body of Christ. I have a limited view of everything you have given me in Christ. I struggle with the idea of how it looks to function in the family of God in my role. Deliver me from my fears of being inadequate. Fill me with your love by your Spirit. Strengthen me with power in my inner being that Christ can dwell in my heart through faith. Let me remember that it is not my own talents or abilities that I give to you, but that I also surrender my fears and weaknesses, so that Jesus can show himself strong in me. Help me to find a way and a place to glorify you in my giftings. Fill me with your Spirit and bring an increase in my spiritual gifts and anointing so that others will be strengthened and encouraged by your work in me. I eagerly desire you. I desire your presence. I desire your work in my life. Move in me in a fresh, new way.

In Jesus' name, Amen.

MEMORY VERSE

[14] For this reason I kneel before the Father, [15] from whom every family in heaven and on earth derives its name. [16] I pray that out of his glorious riches he may strengthen you with power through his Spirit in your inner being, [17] so that Christ may dwell in your hearts through faith. And I pray that you, being rooted and established in love, [18] may have power, together with all the Lord's holy people, to grasp how wide and long and high and deep is the love of Christ, [19] and to know this love that surpasses knowledge – that you may be filled to the measure of all the fullness of God.

[20] Now to him who is able to do immeasurably more than all we ask or imagine, according to his power that is at work within us, [21] to him be glory in the church and in Christ Jesus throughout all generations, for ever and ever! Amen. – Ephesians 3:14-21

READING

2 Corinthians 3:18

And we all, who with unveiled faces contemplate the Lord's glory, are being transformed into his image with ever-increasing glory, which comes from the Lord, who is the Spirit.

Turn in your Bible to read Ephesians 4:7-16.

GOD REVEALS HIMSELF TO HIS PEOPLE

When I started to dig into Ephesians 4, the Lord laid a profound statement on my heart. "The weight of God's glory is distributed throughout his body." I immediately had a picture of a healthy, strong person standing straight and tall. The energy and weight of every step is absorbed through the feet, ankles and legs. Since the Holy Spirit spoke so directly to my heart concerning this, I spent a couple weeks praying over it in the car on my way to work, talking to other mature believers about it, and praying about it more when I was cooking dinner or doing anything where my mind was free. I went to scripture to confirm it. The more I studied, the more the Lord revealed to me. It is so important to seek the Lord, when you believe he lays something on your heart. First of all, the Lord promises to speak to us, but like we studied a couple days ago, his Spirit will never contradict what he has already spoken in his Word, the Bible. After all, his Word is the sword of the Spirit. His Word is breathed by the Spirit. So, when the Holy Spirit speaks to a believer, he will be in complete agreement with the Word.

Never be afraid of God speaking to you and never be afraid of asking him to speak to you. The Bible teaches that the Lord reveals himself to his people. It is normal. It is not scary, freaky, weird or any other synonym of your choice. Also, when another believer says the Lord spoke to him or her, do not be afraid. Just go to the Word to confirm it and go to the Lord in prayer. Why confirm it? On the flip side, people can deeply believe God is leading them when it's their flesh, like the five little boys in middle school who confessed their love to my daughter, each one confirming God's assurance of their future marriage—I use a safe example here. That is why we approach everything with, you guessed it again, the Word and prayer. This is business as usual for the body of Christ. Christ is the head of the body and the head sends messages to the rest of the body. This is called revelation. It is how God speaks to his people.

> **TODAY'S BIBLE STUDY TOOL**
>
> **Prayer.** Pray for the Holy Spirit's wisdom and revelation as you read God's Word. Every time!

Some may say, "God has said everything he needs to say in his Word. He is done speaking." However, this is simply not what the Bible teaches. He said the promised Holy Spirit would lead us into all truth. What the Spirit speaks to us will never contradict the Word of God, but through the Holy Spirit, we understand the Word more deeply as it applies to us in a practical way. The Word will not change, but we can have a deeper understanding of it through the Spirit. God is still speaking, but he will never go against what he has already said in his Word. In Greek, the name for the Holy Spirit is Paraclete, which means comforter or advocate. Para, in the Greek, means close beside—very close. So, let's explore what the Word says about this phrase the Lord spoke to my heart: "The weight of my glory is distributed throughout my body."

GLORY REVEALED

We need to grasp exactly what the glory of God is, before we understand how incredible it is that God allows us to share in this life with other believers. According to my Bible Hub app, the Greek word for glory is "kabowd," which means:

- abundance, riches

- honor, splendour,

- glory of external circumstances: of men, of things or of God

- honor ascribed to God, a parent or an object of honor

> **TODAY'S BIBLE STUDY TOOL**
>
> **Word Study.** Take time to look up the meaning of a word. You can use an online Bible dictionary or concordance.

Strong's Concordance says "kabowd" can also mean properly, weight, but only figuratively in a good sense, splendor or copiousness.

The glory of God is what we can see and experience of the triune God—his power, abundance, life, blessing, splendor, honor, knowledge and wisdom, when God reveals it to us. Often times you will hear people refer to the manifest glory of God. This simply means that our walk of faith is given eyes for a moment, so we can see God in this physical realm.

In the Old Testament, when the Israelites were led by God's presence, it was an earth-shattering experience. Fire and smoke appeared on the top of Mt. Sinai, revealing God's glory. The glory of the Lord appeared as a fire by night and a cloud of covering from the sun by day. These are examples of God showing himself to his people, so they can put their trust in him. After Moses led the children of Israel out of Egypt, while fasting and seeking the Lord before receiving the Ten Commandments, there was a pivotal moment when Moses asked the Lord to please not leave them, but to let his presence go with them.

Exodus 33:12-23

[12] Moses said to the Lord, 'You have been telling me, "Lead these people," but you have not let me know whom you will send with me. You have said, "I know you by name and you have found favour with me." [13] If you are pleased with me, teach me your ways so I may know you and continue to find favour with you. Remember that this nation is your people.'

[14] The Lord replied, 'My Presence will go with you, and I will give you rest.'

[15] Then Moses said to him, 'If your Presence does not go with us, do not send us up from here. [16] How will anyone know that you are pleased with me and with your people unless you go with us? What else will distinguish me and your people from all the other people on the face of the earth?'

[17] And the Lord said to Moses, 'I will do the very thing you have asked, because I am pleased with you and I know you by name.'

[18] Then Moses said, 'Now show me your glory.'

[19] And the Lord said, 'I will cause all my goodness to pass in front of you, and I will proclaim my name, the Lord, in your presence. I will have mercy on whom I will have mercy, and I will have compassion on whom I will have compassion. [20] But,' he said, 'you cannot see my face, for no one may see me and live.'

[21] Then the Lord said, 'There is a place near me where you may stand on a rock. [22] When my glory passes by, I will put you in a cleft in the rock and cover you with my hand until I have passed by. [23] Then I will remove my hand and you will see my back; but my face must not be seen.'

Moses was the only person who ever spoke with the Lord face to face. He performed miracles by the power of the Spirit, yet Moses wanted more. He wanted to see God's glory. I love Moses' prayer of desperation. He cries out to the Lord to not leave him and to let the presence of God be the sign, or revelation, that the Israelites are God's chosen people. God promised his presence would go with Moses, but Moses asks something daring. Differentiating between God's presence and his glory, he implores the Lord to allow him a glimpse of God's glory. This prayer for revelation is something we should model our prayers after. The Lord, with Moses' protection in mind, agrees with conditions. So there is no fear that the Lord will harm us. God is a good Father. In Luke 11:11-13, Jesus teaches his disciples on prayer saying,

'Which of you fathers, if your son asks for a fish, will give him a snake instead? Or if he asks for an egg, will give him a scorpion? If you then, though you are evil, know how to give good gifts to your children, how much more will your Father in heaven give the Holy Spirit to those who ask him!' – Luke 11:11-13

God's glory is so great, God had to hide Moses in the cleft of the rock to protect him from his glory, just to give him a glimpse of himself from the back. If you read Exodus 34, you will see the next chapter is where the Lord gave Moses the Ten Commandments. When Moses finished 40 days receiving revelation from the Lord—are you seeing a theme here—he came down the mountain radiating the glory of God so intensely that the Israelites were afraid of him and asked him to put a veil on his face. The Lord's glory is so holy, even a reflection of his glory is overwhelming for human eyes. God's glory is only seen when God chooses to reveal it. God revealed his law to Moses. This time of revelation with God allowed Moses' face to shine, so the Israelites, who had not been in close proximity with the Lord would get their own glimpse of who God is. But, their response was fear. They didn't want revelation. This fear brought judgment on their children's children, so they could not hear from God, even when they read his Word, or when he was manifesting himself through miracles. In 2 Corinthians 3:7-18, Paul shared the following story of Moses with the Corinthian church.

2 Corinthians 3:7-18

[7] Now if the ministry that brought death, which was engraved in letters on stone, came with **glory**, so that the Israelites could not look steadily at the face of Moses because of its **glory**, transitory though it was, [8] will not the ministry of the Spirit be even more **glorious**? [9] If the ministry that brought condemnation was **glorious**, how much more **glorious** is the ministry that brings righteousness! [10] For what was glorious has no **glory** now in comparison with the surpassing glory. [11] And if what was transitory came with **glory**, how much greater is the **glory** of that which lasts!

[12] Therefore, since we have such a hope, we are very bold. [13] We are not like Moses, who would put a veil over his face to prevent the Israelites from seeing the end of what was passing away. [14] But their minds were made dull, for to this day the same veil remains when the old covenant is read. It has not been removed, because only in Christ is it taken away. [15] Even to this day when Moses is read, a veil covers their hearts. [16] But whenever anyone turns to the Lord, the veil is taken away. [17] Now the Lord is the Spirit, and where the Spirit of the Lord is, there is freedom. [18] And we all, who with unveiled faces contemplate the Lord's **glory**, are being transformed into his image with ever-increasing **glory**, which comes from the Lord, who is the Spirit.

The Lord's revelation through Christ allows us to contemplate his glory! As our spiritual faces are unveiled, through our faith in Christ, who removed our veil of a darkened understanding when he died and rose again, we are transformed into his image with ever-increasing glory. We now can see and understand the glory of God, revealed in Christ. We reflect the glory of God to those around us, the way that Moses reflected the glory of God to Israel. Our transformation, or metamorphosis experience, brings the glory of God and the revelation of Christ to the world! Revelation can only come from the Lord, who is the Spirit! That is why Paul prays continually for the Spirit of wisdom and revelation. "Show us your glory, oh Lord! Give us the ability to contemplate you, to dwell on you, and to reflect you to the world with hope and boldness!"

CHRIST DISTRIBUTES HIS GLORY TO HIS BODY

Jesus left his glory in heaven, to take on human flesh, as the incarnate Son of God. Many cults, such as Mormons and Jehovah's Witnesses say that Jesus couldn't be divine, because how could God's glory be contained in human flesh. Philippians 2 teaches Jesus gave up the fullness of his glory to accomplish the Father's mission. However, the Father allowed him to be glorified on the Mount of Transfiguration. Do you remember the story of the transfiguration in Matthew 17, when Jesus shone like the sun? Three of his disciples were allowed to see him have a holy conversation with Moses and Elijah in this glorified state. The transfiguration was a moment of revelation. Jesus was revealed as the powerful Son of Man, as described in Daniel—the Messiah—and John the Baptist was revealed to be the Elijah that was to come. This momentary revelation was for the sake of the disciples, so they would know and trust God's plan. Why? They were chosen to carry the weight of revealing God's good news to the world. Wisdom and revelation carry responsibility. Jesus told them not to tell anyone what they had seen, but to wait. Sometimes the Lord will give you a glimpse of his glory for a personal understanding and not for sharing. Be very careful not to make assumptions about what the Lord gives you! Take everything to the Lord in prayer. If he reveals something to you, it is for a purpose. For example, he may reveal to you the root of a personal weakness in your spouse or another believer so you can pray for them. He probably will not want you to take that knowledge and use it against them in an argument, or in gossip, or to confront them with it as a way of telling them where they need to change and "pulling power" on them. Of course, he may at some point direct you to share this with them gently and lovingly as part of your personal, confidential relationship with them. But, all personal revelation of this nature needs extra prayer and direction before you take any action on it to be sure you are acting in the best interest of the person you are talking to and not out of pride, revenge or manipulation.

God is very deliberate and purposeful in his relationship with his children. It is our responsibility to seek, ask, knock, and then find what he wants us to find. This is one way the weight of God's glory is being distributed through his body. The weight is the great responsibility that comes with the revelation he gives us.

After the shining light faded away, Jesus still had the full power and presence of the Holy Spirit, even though it wasn't as visibly obvious to the naked eye. We know this, because John the Baptist testified, saying,

> "For the one whom God has sent speaks the words of God, for God gives the Spirit without limit. The Father loves the Son and has placed everything in his hands." – John 3:34-35

God's Spirit resides in Christ without limit and we are the body of Christ. I am not the body of Christ alone by myself. I am part of the body. God's presence filled his temple. In the Old Testament, the temple was made of stone. Today, the temple is made of flesh and bone. He is filling his temple right here and right now—the living stones of his temple! We are the new, eternal temple of God, filled with his glory.

John 2:18-20

[18] The Jews then responded to him, 'What sign can you show us to prove your authority to do all this?'

> **The Pharisees couldn't see what was right in front of their faces.** This is because they didn't have the revelation from God of who Christ was. His glory was hidden from them by the veil of Moses.

[19] Jesus answered them, 'Destroy this temple, and I will raise it again in three days.'

[20] They replied, 'It has taken forty-six years to build this temple, and you are going to raise it in three days?' [21] But the temple he had spoken of was his body. [22] After he was raised from the dead, his disciples recalled what he had said. Then they believed the scripture and the words that Jesus had spoken.

I used to think this prophecy of Christ referred to the resurrection of Jesus's physical body alone. But, truly, when Christ's body was crucified, we all died with him. When he was raised up, we were all raised up with him. He raised the new temple—the body of Christ —in three days, hallelujah! And the final part of this glorious mission was to fill the temple with his presence and his glory.

This brings us back to Ephesians 4:7-9:

Ephesians 4:7-9

[7] But to each one of us grace was given according to the measure of Christ's gift. [8] Therefore He says:

> "When He ascended on high,
> He led captivity captive,
> And gave gifts to men."

[9] (Now this, "He ascended"—what does it mean but that He also first descended into the lower parts of the earth? [10] He who descended is also the One who ascended far above all the heavens, that He might fill all things.)

At his ascension, he apportioned or measured out grace to each part of his body! Every wonderful, born-again woman reading this text was personally "fitted" for her spiritual gifts by the Lord Jesus. When someone walks in the Holy Spirit, the fruit of the Spirit and the gifts begin to manifest in power, and the glory of God is revealed little by little in this person's life and testimonies. This glory of God is intensified and multiplied as more and more individuals in the body of Christ walk this way and manifest the glory of God together, so that the corporate body of Christ is filled with God's glory. One person cannot contain it all. The highest heavens cannot contain the Lord. King Solomon declared this truth in several places in the Old Testament, when he was charged to build the first temple for the Most High God.

> 'The temple I am going to build will be great, because our God is greater than all other gods. But who is able to build a temple for him, since the heavens, even the highest heavens, cannot contain him? Who then am I to build a temple for him, except as a place to burn sacrifices before him? – 2 Chronicles 2:5-6

And truly, God is building his body, his temple, that no man or woman can build. We are all the bricks and mortar. We are the beams and floors. We bear the weight of his glory—all together. The joints must all bring their lavish supply, empowered by the

Spirit, growing together into the full measure of the fullness of God. And in our lives, we also are living sacrifices, before the Lord, to bring him glory.

WHAT DOES THIS HAVE TO DO WITH ME?!!

First of all, you, my sweet woman of God, have access to the Holy Spirit of the living God, and his glory is being revealed to you, as you seek it. Anything you need, as a child of God, you have at your disposal. Do you need marriage help? Do you need direction for a job? Do you need to understand a Bible passage that confuses you? God wants to speak to you through his Word, by his Spirit. Secondly, the way the Lord choses to reveal his glory to us is through other believers. The body works together.

Once I texted a sister in Christ, when I was sick and stressed out about finishing something for ministry. I asked for prayer. She texted back, "God showed me you are being harassed by a spirit of self-pity. It is coming against you." The healing must have occurred between the time I texted her and the time I received a reply. I knew her prayers and warfare for me worked powerfully! The Lord glorified himself through my friend, who received a revelation from him about my situation. She did spiritual warfare for me and relayed the message. Right then, God began to pour out his truth to me. He reminded me of time after time when I lived in self-pity. I was driven by it in my marriage, at work, with my responsibilities at home or anything in general. The enemy used self-pity to constantly derail me and to get me into anger, bitterness and depression. I repented on my face until God gave me release. The moral of the story? God used my friend to tell me something he needed to tell me. It was so direct and obvious, yet he chose to use her. He gave her discernment between spirits—1 Corinthians 12:10—to minister to me. Through this revelation he was glorified in both of our lives, together. I was healed and set free.

> Now to each one the manifestation of the Spirit is given for the common good. – 1 Corinthians 12:7

> All these are the work of one and the same Spirit, and he distributes them to each one, just as he determines. – 1 Corinthians 12:11

There are so many extensive, beautiful passages about the glory of God at work in us—together. Please take time to read all of 1 Corinthians 12, so that you will not be uninformed about the workings of the Spirit. You don't have to be a great speaker, singer, artist or even articulate to function in your role in the body of Christ. You may be physically weak or feel untalented, but do not let this depress you into thinking you have nothing to offer God! Every part of the body is equipped by God to do his work and express his glory. You are included!

> The eye cannot say to the hand, 'I don't need you!' And the head cannot say to the feet, 'I don't need you!' On the contrary, those parts of the body that seem to be weaker are indispensable, and the parts that we think are less honourable we treat with special honour. And the parts that are unpresentable are treated with special modesty. – 1 Corinthians 12:21-23

This is why we do not need to fear. Every woman in our society—especially believing women—feel this need to be everything. You have probably heard the hilariously sad statement that goes something like: 'It's hard to be a woman. One must think like a man, act like a lady, look like a young girl, and work like a horse.' And all God's people said, "Amen!" Just say this after me right now, "I don't have all the answers, but that's okay—God does! I need my friends and family in the body of Christ and I don't need to be ashamed to ask for help."

We need to acknowledge that all of God's glory is not contained in my little, beautiful life. I am sharing it with others. God has given my brothers and sisters in Christ, all over the world, and all through eternity their own share. There is no place for jealousy or feeling inadequate. You may desire to see your entire life perfectly under control, but you will surely fall short every day. Remember, we all fall short of the glory of God. BUT, we are justified freely by his grace through redemption that came by Christ Jesus. The redemption that came by Christ and the free justification by his grace include the "grace apportioned" to us for every difficulty and every shortcoming. One of God's greatest ways of meeting our needs and shortcomings is through others in the church. But, for many reasons—fear, personal roadblocks, busyness, apathy, or a general ignorance of their own place in the body—people aren't always willing or able to step up into their role. Maybe you were hurt when you relied on someone who wasn't there for you. This is where the comfort of the Holy Spirit leads us into forgiveness. Remember, we are all human and we must bear with one another's weaknesses in love. Instead of living in reaction to what others have done or not done for you, pray for the Lord to help you to trust him and to show you who to trust. If you live in unforgiveness and fear, you will never trust anyone. You will cut yourself off from the fullness of God that you can only experience in unity with others in the body.

Not trusting other believers stems from a very subtle twisting of truth that the enemy engages in to isolate believers from experiencing 'the whole measure of the fullness of Christ.' He will tell you that you should be able to rely on God alone by yourself. "You don't need to go to counseling with your pastor. If God wants to tell you something, he'll tell you himself." Or you may hear, "You don't need to bother that person with a prayer request. They are too busy. Besides, if you can't pray to God on your own, what kind of a Christian are you, anyways?" A friend recently told me that she had a strong 'feeling' that God was calling her to pull away from other believers and rely on him only. She didn't need other believers as a crutch. After she verbalized it to me and we discussed what scripture said, she realized that the enemy was disguising himself to deceive her and to keep her from the help she needed. She laughed after the fact and realized that she was truly being deceived in a time of difficulty when she needed accountability.

BRINGING IT HOME
Prayer to Bring Unity to the Family of God

Father,

In Jesus' name, reveal your glory to me. Reveal it in my life and in my church. Teach me to walk in the truth that I need other people in your family. Forgive me for pride and for control that keeps me from opening myself to others for help. Lord, help me to forgive those who have hurt me, broken my trust or have not been there for me. I give these people to you, in Jesus' name. Please uproot bitterness from my life concerning the times I did not experience the love and glory of God from the body of Christ. I pray for those people now. Convict them of sin, lift their burdens, reveal yourself to them by your Spirit, so they can repent and learn to hear from you. If they are overwhelmed personally, please deliver them. Help me, oh Lord, to walk in the power of your Holy Spirit. Fill me with your Holy Spirit and power, so I can hear from you, walk in your power and live in the fruit of your Spirit. I want to experience true unity in the church, Lord. Please reveal that to me, to my church, and to the believers in my area and around the world.

In Jesus' name, Amen.

TODAY'S BIBLE STUDY TOOL
Cross Reference
Contrast & Comparison | Word Study

PUTTING ON THE NEW SELF
WHAT ARE YOU WEARING TODAY?

PRAYER

Today, our prayer time will focus on giving God our misconceptions about what the body of Christ should look like and how it should function. Ask for clarity, wisdom and revelation to understand this. Give God any pain that you may have received at the hands of imperfect people who love God. Forgive those who have injured you. Pray that the Lord will remove any lies of the devil concerning the church and God himself that you may have believed due to sin in the body of Christ. If someone has hurt you, it can really affect how you feel in church or around believers. It can also put up walls to the movement of the Spirit and the glory of God being revealed through the unity of the body of Christ. Pray for God to fill you with his Spirit so that the world can see and understand him. As you are strengthened in your inner being, the Lord gives you more faith. The more faith you have, the more you can understand God and trust him. It is the gift that keeps on giving! Use our memory verse today to ask the Lord for his love to be built in you. More love! More family! More unity! More forgiveness! More power, Lord!

MEMORY VERSE

[14] For this reason I kneel before the Father, [15] from whom every family in heaven and on earth derives its name. [16] I pray that out of his glorious riches he may strengthen you with power through his Spirit in your inner being, [17] so that Christ may dwell in your hearts through faith. And I pray that you, **being rooted and established in love, [18] may have power, together with all the Lord's holy people**, to grasp how wide and long and high and deep is the love of Christ, [19] and to know this love that surpasses knowledge – that you may be filled to the measure of all the fullness of God.

[20] Now to him who is able to do immeasurably more than all we ask or imagine, according to his power that is at work within us, [21] to him be glory in the church and in Christ Jesus throughout all generations, for ever and ever! Amen. – Ephesians 3:14-21

Our memory verse from Ephesians 3 reminds us that we receive power from God when we are rooted and established in love. The more we are rooted in LOVE, the more fear RUNS AWAY! Fear is a faith stealer. We need more love, not because it's the sugary-sweet version of Christianity, but because it is the pulse and the heartbeat of Christianity. Without love, there is no cross. Without love, there is no forgiveness. Without love, there is no grace. Without love, there is no relationship. Since our study today is about "putting off" our old self and "putting on" our new self, let's do a cross reference to see what happens when we put on love.

CROSS REFERENCE

Turn in your Bible to 1 John 4:7-21. This is a key scripture that we will be referencing again in our spiritual warfare section at the end of the book. Love is an important part of putting off fear.

In our reading today, we are moving on to a new part of Ephesians 4. This new passage is teaching us how to live in the way of the Spirit, from the inside out, with changed hearts and minds, transformed by the power of Christ. This is what it looks like to be a part of the body of Christ. When our hearts are changed, it affects everything, especially how we relate to one another.

READING

Ephesians 4:17-22

[17] So I tell you this, and insist on it in the Lord, that you must no longer live as the Gentiles do, in the futility of their thinking. [18] They are darkened in their understanding and separated from the life of God because of the ignorance that is in them due to the hardening of their hearts. [19] Having lost all sensitivity, they have given themselves over to sensuality so as to indulge in every kind of impurity, and they are full of greed.

[20] That, however, is not the way of life you learned [21] when you heard about Christ and were taught in him in accordance with the truth that is in Jesus. [22] You were taught, with regard to your former way of life, to put off your old self, which is being corrupted by its deceitful desires; [23] to be made new in the attitude of your minds; [24] and to put on the new self, created to be like God in true righteousness and holiness.

[25] Therefore each of you must put off falsehood and speak truthfully to your neighbour, for we are all members of one body. [26] 'In your anger do not sin': do not let the sun go down while you are still angry, [27] and do not give the devil a foothold. [28] Anyone who has been stealing must steal no longer, but must work, doing something useful with their own hands, that they may have something to share with those in need.

[29] Do not let any unwholesome talk come out of your mouths, but only what is helpful for building others up according to their needs, that it may benefit those who listen. [30] And do not grieve the Holy Spirit of God, with whom you were sealed for the day of redemption. [31] Get rid of all bitterness, rage and anger, brawling and slander, along with every form of malice. [32] Be kind and compassionate to one another, forgiving each other, just as in Christ God forgave you.

We've all heard of keeping skeletons in the closet. Jesus wants to do some spring cleaning and remove the skeletons from the closet of your heart. Your closet may be so full of junk that it is falling out and the door is hard to close! When your heart is full, it will overflow—whether its contents are good or bad. The "skeletons" are the attitudes and mind frames or ways of "stinkin' thinkin'" that have ruled your life up to this point. Are you an emotional pack-rat? Have you been wounded, rejected or abandoned in your past, and now you carry that with you everywhere you go? Are you easily offended and always on the defense, because your heart has never fully healed from major conflict or pain from the past? Do you put on fear of rejection every morning when you wake up? Do you put on defensiveness and and a harsh demeanor, because you have learned to live life as a "tough girl?" Imagine never going shopping for yourself. Imagine still wearing old clothes from high school, or even from 10 years ago. The clothes are old and comfy, but they are really unbecoming. They may not even fit. They are worn out and thread bare and really out of style! Everyone needs time to grab some trash bags, open the closet door and make room for a new wardrobe! When was the last time you "put off" your old ways of thinking and "put on" new spiritual thinking and living? Let's invite Jesus to help us do inventory and clean out our closets today, ladies!

CONTRAST & COMPARISON
Cleaning Out Your Closet & Getting a New Wardrobe

In order to make room for our new spiritual wardrobe, let's give our old spiritual wardrobe to Jesus. He took these sinful attitudes and behaviors to the cross and left them in the tomb when he rose again!

Read Ephesians 4:17-32 above and using the passage, write all the ungodly behaviors that believers need to "put off" under the GENTILES column. Write all the items for your new wardrobe in the BELIEVERS column. This is a contrast and comparison activity that helps us to better understand God's Word. As you dwell on the Word, it will make its way deep down into your heart. Ask the Lord to speak to your heart and reveal to you anything he wants to do in you, as you do this activity.

GENTILES   BELIEVERS

_____   _____

_____   _____

_____   _____

METAMORPHOSIS
Out with the Caterpillar, In with the Butterfly!

There is such a huge difference between a caterpillar and a glorious butterfly. Second graders in Virginia are required to learn all about the life cycle of the Monarch butterfly and it is truly fascinating. What a beautiful prophetic picture the Lord gives us with butterflies! Metamorphosis is a picture of the work God does in the heart of a person who comes to Christ. When we trust in Christ, we die with him. We are buried in the tomb through baptism and, just like a butterfly coming out of its cocoon, we come out of the grave with him transformed into a new creation! The old is gone and the new is come! We just compared and contrasted life before and after Christ and read what that new life should look like. Let's dig into that more. In Ephesians 4:17, Paul makes a case that the Gentiles, the unsaved masses of the world, are corrupted by the futility of their thinking and the hardening of their hearts. What does futility mean? Let's do a word study!

WORD STUDY

fu·til·i·ty

NOUN: pointlessness or uselessness. "the horror and futility of war"

SYNONYMS: **fruitlessness**, vanity, pointlessness
              uselessness, worthlessness, ineffectuality, ineffectiveness, inefficacy
              failure, unproductiveness, barrenness, unprofitability, abortiveness
              impotence, hollowness, emptiness, meaningless, forlornness, hopelessness, sterility, valuelessness

According to the English Oxford Living Dictionaries at http://www.en.oxforddictionaries.com, the meaning of futility implies that the thinking of mankind is full of pointlessness, uselessness, fruitlessness, vanity, ineffectiveness, and impotence or a lack of power. This is because of a darkness, or blindness, in their understanding. When a person is born again, yet lives in unforgiveness or continues to function out of the pain of his or her past, instead of in the resurrection power of Christ through the Holy Spirit, this is truly futile. Living in bitterness has no power to change the person's situation. You may think that by living in fear, anger, defensiveness and gossip, or even by lying to protect yourself you are safe, but you are really walking in spiritual darkness. Someone who is used to living in this manner needs illumination and power from God to find healing and transformation from the inside out! Remember our prayer in Ephesians 1? What does Paul pray for the Ephesians? He asks the Holy Spirit to open the eyes of their hearts that they can know the hope to which they have been called. We need spiritual revelation and wisdom to transform our hearts and minds. What else does he say in verse 18? He says that the unbelieving Gentiles are ignorant. Here is the definition from English Oxford Living Dictionaries:

ig·nor·ant

ADJECTIVE: *[predicative]* Lacking knowledge, information, or awareness about a particular thing.

SYNONYMS: **uneducated,** unknowledgeable, untaught, unschooled, untutored, untrained, illiterate, unlettered, unlearned, unread, uninformed, unenlightened, unscholarly, unqualified, benighted, backward

People without God are ignorant of life in Christ, because they have hardened their hearts against God. Someone may be a genius and have knowledge and expertise in many fields of discipline. He or she may know every law of science, but be ignorant, or uneducated concerning the laws of the spirit realm. Closing yourself off to the God who created you, and choosing to neglect his spiritual wisdom is the epitome of ignorance. Hardening of the heart is deadly spiritually. Even believers can harden their hearts by ignoring the convicting voice of the Holy Spirit. Many self-proclaimed Christians mock and argue with non-believers on social media, while truly living in the futility and ignorance of a non-believer in their own personal lives. When you are being invited to a "bitterness party," do not be tempted to go to your old wardrobe. Clothe yourself in the Spirit.

Hebrews 3:12-15

[12] See to it, brothers and sisters, that none of you has a sinful, unbelieving heart that turns away from the living God. [13] But encourage one another daily, as long as it is called 'Today', so that none of you may be hardened by sin's deceitfulness. [14] We have come to share in Christ, if indeed we hold our original conviction firmly to the very end. [15] As has just been said:

> 'Today, if you hear his voice,
>   do not harden your hearts
>   as you did in the rebellion.'

How do we know what is in someone's heart? Jesus said that what comes out of our mouths is a good gauge for what is in our hearts.

Matthew 15:10-20

[10] Jesus called the crowd to him and said, 'Listen and understand. [11] What goes into someone's mouth does not defile them, but what comes out of their mouth, that is what defiles them.'

[12] Then the disciples came to him and asked, 'Do you know that the Pharisees were offended when they heard this?'

[13] He replied, 'Every plant that my heavenly Father has not planted will be pulled up by the roots. [14] Leave them; they are blind guides. If the blind lead the blind, both will fall into a pit.'

[15] Peter said, 'Explain the parable to us.'

[16] 'Are you still so dull?' Jesus asked them. [17] 'Don't you see that whatever enters the mouth goes into the stomach and then out of the body? [18] But the things that come out of a person's mouth come from the heart, and these defile them. [19] For out of the heart come evil thoughts – murder, adultery, sexual immorality, theft, false testimony, slander. [20] These are what defile a person; but eating with unwashed hands does not defile them.'

Here Jesus declares that sinful thoughts, actions and words spring up from sinful hearts, where sin is rooted. The more we harden our hearts against the Lord, the more sin we will feel free to do. There is just a continual lust for more. Our consciences will not stop us.

The following passage in Jeremiah is a dialogue God has with his children—not pagan nations—about how they enjoy sin so much that they refuse to blush. This is what a hardened heart looks like. Someone in this condition may even think people who blush at sin are 'prudes.' Notice what the Lord says about these people whose hearts are hardened? He says they are praying people. They prayed for rain in a famine. They couldn't understand why the Lord wouldn't hear their prayers—he explains, "This is how you talk, but you do all the evil you can."

Jeremiah 3:2-5

> [2] 'Look up to the barren heights and see.
>   Is there any place where you have not been ravished?
> By the roadside you sat waiting for lovers,
>   sat like a nomad in the desert.
> You have defiled the land
>   with your prostitution and wickedness.

³ Therefore the showers have been withheld,
and no spring rains have fallen.
Yet you have the brazen look of a prostitute;
you refuse to blush with shame.
⁴ Have you not just called to me:
"My Father, my friend from my youth,
⁵ will you always be angry?
Will your wrath continue for ever?"
This is how you talk,
but you do all the evil you can.'

When we have said NO to the Holy Spirit and to our God-given innocence from childhood and embraced whatever we want, there is no conscience anymore concerning issues where the heart is hardened. People who are hardened will participate in behaviors that are completely ungodly and have no problem with it. Why? Because they have lost the ability to "feel" like it is wrong. There is nothing in their flesh or conscience that stops them in their tracks. This is why we can't trust our feelings or even our conscience! Our feelings are, according to Ephesians 4, being corrupted by our evil desires. This is also why Paul teaches the Ephesians—and us—to PUT OFF our old self and our old ways of life and PUT ON the NEW.

Do not conform to the pattern of this world, but be transformed by the renewing of your mind. Then you will be able to test and approve what God's will is – his good, pleasing and perfect will. — Romans 12:2

The word "transformed" here in Romans is from the Greek root for metamorphosis. When you think of metamorphosis, do you imagine a butterfly? The butterfly can never enter into its God-given destiny while it is still in the form of a caterpillar. We must also be born again and transformed by the renewing of our minds. God wants to renew our thoughts and our hearts. We are active participants in this process, as we PUT OFF our old self. 2 Corinthians says:

We demolish arguments and every pretension that sets itself up against the knowledge of God, and we take captive every thought to make it obedient to Christ. – 2 Corinthians 10:12

If you want to be transformed by Christ, invite him to be Lord of your heart and mind. Instead of allowing old thought patterns to reign free—thoughts of lust, or critical thinking against others, thoughts of doubts, constant fearful thoughts, cursing in your heart or even with your mouth—take your thoughts captive in Jesus' name and put your mind under the authority of Christ. Old habits die hard, so if you want a transformation from the Lord, you need to be willing to walk daily in his truth and the correction of his Word by the direction of his Spirit. Remember that your feelings may not line up with what you read in the Bible, if you are in a hardened state. If you have to decide to follow Jesus anyway, then your heart will change. Do you remember Week Three and Week Four where we discussed the truth that we are positioned in Christ and that we are a slave to the one we obey, whether a slave to sin which leads to death or a slave to Christ which leads to righteousness? When we take authority over our thoughts in the name of Jesus and submit our minds to obey the truth, the Holy Spirit can work and bring renewal. Here is a promise from Ezekiel,

I will give you a new heart and put a new spirit in you; I will remove from you your heart of stone and give you a heart of flesh. – Ezekiel 36:26

Paul's prayer for the Ephesians is so on point in Chapter 1. He prays that they will have the Spirit of wisdom and revelation to know God better—that is an inside-out spiritual understanding. This knowledge is not in the flesh, but in the spirit, in the inner being, which he also prays to be strengthened so that Christ can dwell in our hearts through faith. Today, put off your old self. Take captive every thought that exalts itself against Christ and bring it under the authority of the cross.

PRAYER TO TAKE THOUGHTS CAPTIVE

Father,

Fill me with your wisdom and revelation through the Holy Spirit. I am struggling with sin (name the sin). Please forgive me, but also, Lord, do not let me be deceived by the evil desires in my heart. Give me a new heart and put a new spirit in me.

Remove my heart of stone and give me a heart of flesh. I know that I need you to protect me from lies. I ask in Jesus' name that you reveal to me truth by your Spirit and give me knowledge of lies that I need to take authority over in Jesus' name.

I rebuke the lies of the enemy that are coming against me in Jesus' name. I renounce anxious thoughts and fears that are waging war against me in Jesus' name. I rebuke Satan's attacks against my mind. I cast them down in Jesus' name. Fill me with your love and the peace that comes from knowing Christ. I want Christ to live in my heart through faith.

Forgive me for dwelling on lustful and sensual thoughts. I rebuke lust in Jesus' name. I know there is a time and a place where I am to live in intimacy and that it is not healthy for me to be full of lust or impure thoughts. Jesus, I give you my mind. Fill my mind with your Spirit. Replace wicked and impure thoughts with the newness of Christ. Remove the evil and replace it with your truth and your purity and your love and your Spirit, in Jesus' name!

Create in me a clean heart, oh Lord, and renew a right spirit within me. Father, do a new work in my mind. Cleanse my mind. Remove futility and ignorance and replace it with your truth and understanding. I want to walk in the Spirit and not in my flesh.

In Jesus' name, Amen.

BRINGING IT HOME

Is your faith in Christ life-changing? Do you teach your children the transforming power of Christ that cleanses you from the inside out?

Many people focus on either "faith" or "loving God" but are missing the outward change that happens when Christ changes our hearts. Others just try to make their outward actions all look good and even fake it to try to fit in at church. This is not a true relationship with God. This is trying to impress others for your own glory. The true walk is faith and love walked out in obedience. It is a balancing act that requires keeping your eyes on Jesus. Just like walking on a balance beam, you will fall off if you don't keep your focus straight ahead.

Living a life of holiness before God is all about the work of Christ to change a heart. It is also about crucifying our flesh with Christ. Our flesh won't always want to do the right thing. Our flesh may want to rebel with everything inside of us, but that is when we need to submit, or humble ourselves to Christ. We do this in the power of the Holy Spirit and full of the knowledge of the love of Christ. We "put on" the truth and the new life in Christ!

WEEK EIGHT

DAY 1

TODAY'S BIBLE STUDY TOOL

Cross Reference
Word Study | Bible Commentary

DEALING WITH ANGER & THE DEVIL

PRAYER

In order to put on these new behaviors in Christ, we truly need God to cleanse our hearts. For many of us, our old behaviors, attitudes and even emotional habits or patterns are learned and very familiar friends. Apart from Christ, it's impossible to even want to part ways with a behavior or way of thinking that has been a close companion all your life. Today, we will dig into how to deal with some of these sticky issues, such as anger. Let's start with our prayer and then I am introducing a new memory verse!

Ephesians 3:14-21

[14] For this reason I kneel before the Father, [15] from whom every family in heaven and on earth derives its name. [16] I pray that out of his glorious riches he may strengthen you with power through his Spirit in your inner being, [17] so that Christ may dwell in your hearts through faith. And I pray that you, being rooted and established in love, [18] may have power, together with all the Lord's holy people, to grasp how wide and long and high and deep is the love of Christ, [19] and to know this love that surpasses knowledge – that you may be filled to the measure of all the fullness of God.

[20] Now to him who is able to do immeasurably more than all we ask or imagine, according to his power that is at work within us, [21] to him be glory in the church and in Christ Jesus throughout all generations, for ever and ever! Amen.

This week you have a very short memory verse! When you commit the Word to your heart, God will bring that passage back to your mind later, at a time when you need it the most. I'll never forget the day when I was newly married and was angry with my husband. I was running my mouth a mile a minute as we drove down the road. God kept quietly running a verse about anger through my mind on a repeated loop. I kept ignoring it, in my indignation. Finally, as we drove by a church, the marquee starkly proclaimed the same exact verse in black and white. I realized I had committed a huge sin in ignoring the Holy Spirit! Thank God he mercifully arranged for the church to display just the right verse that day to stop me in my tracks. I've come a long way over the years. God's Word will transform your life, as you commit yourself to follow and obey him.

MEMORY VERSE

[26] 'In your anger do not sin': do not let the sun go down while you are still angry, [27] and do not give the devil a foothold. – Ephesians 4:26-27

READING

Ephesians 4:28-32

[28] Anyone who has been stealing must steal no longer, but must work, doing something useful with their own hands, that they may have something to share with those in need.

[29] Do not let any unwholesome talk come out of your mouths, but only what is helpful for building others up according to their needs, that it may benefit those who listen. [30] And do not grieve the Holy Spirit of God, with whom you were sealed for the day of redemption. [31] Get rid of all bitterness, rage and anger, brawling and slander, along with every form of malice. [32] Be kind and compassionate to one another, forgiving each other, just as in Christ God forgave you.

CROSS REFERENCE

James 1:19-27

[19] My dear brothers and sisters, take note of this: everyone should be quick to listen, slow to speak and slow to become angry, [20] because human anger does not produce the righteousness that God desires. [21] Therefore, get rid of all moral filth and the evil that is so prevalent, and humbly accept the word planted in you, which can save you.

[22] **Do not merely listen to the word, and so deceive yourselves. Do what it says.** [23] Anyone who listens to the word but does not do what it says is like someone who looks at his face in a mirror [24] and, after looking at himself, goes away and immediately forgets what he looks like. [25] But whoever looks intently into the perfect law that gives freedom and continues in it – not forgetting what they have heard but doing it – they will be blessed in what they do.

[26] Those who consider themselves religious and yet do not keep a tight rein on their tongues deceive themselves, and their religion is worthless. [27] Religion that God our Father accepts as pure and faultless is this: to look after orphans and widows in their distress and to keep oneself from being polluted by the world.

Ladies, at first glance, the end of Ephesians 4 and the beginning of Ephesians 5 read a bit like a buffet-style spiritual meal. There are lists of dos and don'ts. However, remember that it all comes back to the greatest commandment. Jesus told us what it is,

Matthew 22:36-40

[36] 'Teacher, which is the greatest commandment in the Law?'

[37] Jesus replied: '"Love the Lord your God with all your heart and with all your soul and with all your mind." [38] This is the first and greatest commandment. [39] And the second is like it: "Love your neighbour as yourself." [40] All the Law and the Prophets hang on these two commandments.'

During these passages in Ephesians, Paul details what love in action looks like as we walk in our Christian lives in our relationships, lest we deceive ourselves. Are you struggling with anger, distress or division in your life or your household? If you are, and you are a Christ-follower who is full of the Holy Spirit, this will be very perplexing and defeating. You know that God wants you to live in unity and love, but it seems elusive, like trying to capture the wind.

When you look back at Ephesians Chapters 1-4, remember the case Paul builds—our relationship with Christ impacts our relationships with others. We cannot separate our spiritual life with God from others and keep it in a little box for ourselves. One of the most difficult aspects of this spiritual journey is the intricate dance we have with other believers. It's tough not to step on one another's toes. It's easy to get your own toes stepped on and react! This is why in Ephesians Chapter 5, Paul talks about submission. When we submit to one another in Christ, we are giving the other person permission to lead—like in ballroom dancing. To submit is to lower the priority of our own needs so that the other person's needs can be met. Without mutual submission, conflict can easily arise in any relationship.

What are some of the causes of discord in relationships? Let's turn in our Bibles to look at what **James 4:1-12** says concerning this issue. Take time to underline all the causes of anger in this passage. Circle the solutions James gives to overcome the devil's strongholds rooted in anger and bitterness.

[1] What causes fights and quarrels among you? Don't they come from your desires that battle within you? [2] You desire but do not have, so you kill. You covet but you cannot get what you want, so you quarrel and fight. You do not have because you do not ask God. [3] When you ask, you do not receive, because you ask with wrong motives, that you may spend what you get on your pleasures.

[4] You adulterous people, don't you know that friendship with the world means enmity against God? Therefore, anyone who chooses to be a friend of the world becomes an enemy of God. [5] Or do you think Scripture says without reason that he jealously longs for the spirit he has caused to dwell in us? [6] But he gives us more grace. That is why Scripture says:

> 'God opposes the proud
> but shows favour to the humble.'

[7] Submit yourselves, then, to God. Resist the devil, and he will flee from you. [8] Come near to God and he will come near to you. Wash your hands, you sinners, and purify your hearts, you double-minded. [9] Grieve, mourn and wail. Change your laughter to mourning and your joy to gloom. [10] Humble yourselves before the Lord, and he will lift you up.

[11] Brothers and sisters, do not slander one another. Anyone who speaks against a brother or sister or judges them speaks against the law and judges it. When you judge the law, you are not keeping it, but sitting in judgment on it. [12] There is only one Lawgiver and Judge, the one who is able to save and destroy. But you – who are you to judge your neighbour?

Sinning in anger is one of the issues addressed in Ephesians 4. It is a major tool the enemy can use to take you captive and to get a "foothold" in your life and relationships. What does this word foothold in Ephesians 4:27 mean and how does it develop through anger? Let's do a word study on FOOTHOLD and an ancient language study on the rest of Ephesians 4:26-27!

WORD STUDY

I went to Ephesians 4 on biblehub.com to look up the word "foothold" in the Greek. This is something you can do, too! http://biblehub.com/commentaries/bengel/ephesians/4.htm

Ephesians 4:27

Neither give place to the devil.

Ephesians 4:27. **Μήτε**, *Neither*) Place is given to the devil by persisting in anger, especially during the night; comp. [*the Rulers*] *of the darkness*, ch. Ephesians 6:12.[74]—**μήτε** is used as *ΚΑΊ ΜΉ*, Ephesians 4:30.

[74] This reference also implies that Beng. takes *the night*, during which anger is retained, as figurative of *the darkness* over which the *devil* is prince. This does not exclude the literal sense. The literal keeping of anger during the night is typical of spiritual giving place to the devil, the ruler of darkness.—ED.

Strong's Concordance
topos: a place
    Original Word: τόπος, ου, ὁ
    Part of Speech: Noun, Masculine
    Transliteration: topos
    Phonetic Spelling: (top'-os)
    Short Definition: a place
    Definition: a place, region, seat; an opportunity.

There are different scenarios that present you with the temptation to sin in anger which opens a door for the devil to have authority in your life. One situation occurs when we experience trauma, pain or rejection at the hands of another. The shock of the wounding can make it very difficult to forgive. You become vulnerable to the enemy's temptation not to forgive. Not forgiving even a grievous offense can make it impossible to find healing. Another more common situation happens when you continue not to submit to God and to another person in love, forgiveness, and reconciliation. This is what I would call a dripping faucet of offense. In these cases, where love and patience are scarce and pain and irritation build up over time, it is easy to sin in anger. When these offenses happen and you do not release the offenders to the Lord through forgiveness, or repent and make things right before the day is over, you can open up the door of your home and life for the devil to gain entry. You give the devil a "place to live." Literally, you unintentionally invite him to be a permanent guest in your home. This means that you may try to command the devil to leave out the front door, but you leave the back door open for him to come right back in.

Some people will contend this is not possible, because we are in Christ. However, in Ephesians 4:27 the very apostle Paul, who taught us the power of the grace and authority of Christ, teaches us that the devil CAN, INDEED, gain access, power and authority in our lives, when we live in the willful sin of unresolved anger. When we are full of bitterness, we cannot be full of the Spirit. Sister, it is impossible to defeat the devil in our own strength. We are only victorious over Satan when we are what?

Can you list what James says in verses 7-10 that we need to do to overcome the evil one?

Do you see that what James prescribes for victory is the fruit of a changed life, not religious ritual? When we live in this submitted manner, the devil must flee!

Note, this passage does not say that anger is a sin. It says, IN your anger, DO NOT SIN. So, when the feelings of injustice and anger come over you, take heed to what James 1:19 says.

> My dear brothers and sisters, take note of this: everyone should be quick to listen, slow to speak and slow to become angry. – James 1:19

On the following lines, write down the three things we are commanded to "be" in James 1:19.

Be _____ to _____.

Be _____ to _____.

Be _____ to _____.

Do not be deceived by the desire to justify yourself. If you are used to living in bitterness and holding grudges, it will be very, very easy for you to fall into this behavior again. In fact, the devil MAY have a stronghold of anger in your life or in your family. If you are praying to forgive and can't seem to get over the anger, it is very possible that you may need to ask the Holy Spirit to show you if the devil has a foothold in your life.

WORD STUDY
Anger or Irritation?

When I feel curious about a passage and want to understand it more deeply, I will do a word study on the word that I have questions about in the text. So, as I have done throughout this book, I use biblehub.com. It seems to be the one stop shop for finding everything you need to know about a passage.

The first step is to enter the verse you are studying in the search bar. That way, you won't get lost in the website, since it has so much information. Always type the specific reference into the search bar first. In this case, the word "anger" is from Ephesians 4:26, so you would enter Ephesians 4:26. When you want to hone in on the word and see the Greek meaning as well as the commentary on it, you click on the word GREEK in the bar above the scripture. Doing this will take you to a chart of the Greek translation of the words in the verse. There you will see the Strong's Concordance catalog numbers listed in the far left-hand column. Click on the catalog number that corresponds to the word you are looking for. In this case, the number for "anger" is number 3950 which is also the number for the Greek word "parorgismos."

What I found, when I began reading the Greek definition and commentary on the word "anger," was very astonishing to me! Strong's Concordance translates it as, "exasperation, wrath, irritation and indignation." Hmmm. Exasperation and irritation. This isn't just a generic "anger" anymore. Let's scroll down and see what HELP'S Word-Studies says.

HELPS™ Word-studies

Cognate: 3950 *parorgismós* (from <u>3949</u> */parorgízō*, see there) – irritation (exasperation, bitterness) which is provoked, i.e. by someone causing a personal ("up-close") sense of anger (R. Trench, 127). <u>3950</u> */parorgismós* ("slowly built-up provocation") is only used in Eph 4:26. <u>See 3949</u> (*parorgízō*).

BIBLE COMMENTARY

I dug a little further, by looking up the same passage under the commentator Bengel Gnomon on biblehub.com. His opinion is that the translation of the Greek word parorgismós to the English word "wrath" or anger LOSES the implication that irritation is included. Often times, when translating from the Ancient Greek language to another, there isn't a word that exactly fits the meaning of the original word. The translation team does its best. However, in this case, the Greek meaning includes irritation and exasperation. I don't know about you, but I can get irritated VERY easily! This look into the ancient languages shows me that my irritation is not honoring God nor is it beneficial to my relationships. If I go to bed without resolving my irritation with a person, I am giving the devil a foothold. It's easy to pass over this word "wrath" and think, "Well, I'm not a wrathful person." But, looking through the lens of this commentary, written by a Greek scholar, our eyes are opened to the truth that the word actually can mean irritated. Have you ever considered that the living God knows there are many personalities in the world and they all manifest anger in different ways? It is important to ask the Lord if your behavior when you are angry is sinful. Do not just assume it is pure as the wind-driven snow. It is also important to ask God if your purpose for being angry is just or motivated by sin. Scripture does not allow any type of sinning in anger off the hook, whether it is overt "wrath" or more passive "irritation and exasperation." Praise the Lord!

1 Corinthians 13 says that love keeps no record of wrongs. If we are holding irritation or anger in our hearts towards another, it is truly sinning against that person and against God. Sometimes my irritation is rooted in unforgiveness, and sometimes it is rooted in pride or selfishness. Think of when you feel disappointed, because someone didn't do something you asked to be done in a certain time frame. This is from selfishness. Disappointment is a natural response when you feel let down. But, do you turn that into sin by the way you treat the person who disappointed you? Another root cause of irritation is pride. When you look down on someone, it is easy to be irritated with them. They get on your nerves. This is from pride. Whether anger or irritation is from unforgiveness, pride, selfishness or any other cause, let's remember that sinning in our anger is not only a sin, but a sin that can give the devil a foothold. Let us also put this to the Jesus test. Jesus said,

"So in everything, do to others what you would have them do to you, for this sums up the Law and the Prophets." – Matthew 7:12

How do you feel when someone is irritated with you or always exasperated? On the flip side, how do you feel when someone is patient with you, bearing with your weaknesses in love?

About ten years ago, I was struggling with a lot of anger. I was constantly at odds with one of my children, even though she was young. I felt like every single interaction was full of tension and emotion. During this time, the Lord allowed me to end up in the hospital with my infant son while he was having breathing issues. Lying there on the couch in the hospital room in the middle of the night, while my new baby was in an oxygen tent, the Lord dealt with me concerning my anger with my daughter. He led me to pray to forgive her (as silly as it sounds to need to forgive a little child) and to pray that the Lord would literally "remove" anger from me, from her and from our home. I knew it was more than an emotion that I was praying about. I was under the influence of the enemy who had gained access to my home through my unchecked anger. After that night in the hospital, my baby quickly improved and we came home the next day. When the house was empty, I prayed strongly and rebuked the devil, commanding him to leave my home and to leave my child alone. Immediately, the great heaviness lifted and I felt the freedom of the Lord. When the children came home from school that day, the excessive arguing and bickering stopped. It was that simple.

Before we move on to Chapter 5 of Ephesians, take a spiritual inventory before the Lord. You can only live in the behaviors commanded by God in Chapters 4 and 5 through the power of the Spirit living in you. If you have given the keys of your spiritual house to the enemy, through anger, deception and bitterness, the Holy Spirit cannot move in your life to help resolve relationship issues. You first need to take focused time to repent of bitterness, irritation and unforgiveness.

PRAYER TO FORGIVE OFFENSES

If you are living a forgiving lifestyle, this will be a fairly easy prayer. If not, this prayer may take some time and could very possibly be something that evokes much pain or emotion. Take your time with it. Don't be afraid of strong feelings or even physical responses. Jesus is with you. He took this pain to the cross. If pain is that deeply embedded in your soul, this is all the more reason to deal with it.

Father,

Is there anywhere in my life that I am harboring anger against anyone? Please root it out of me, in Jesus' name. Open the eyes of my heart to see where I am angry. Help me to give my anger up to you. Holy and gracious Father, fill me with the Spirit of wisdom and revelation so that I can know your will for me and that I can see where there is anger inside of my life or my relationships, in Jesus' name.

In Jesus' name, I forgive _____ for these offenses:

(List the offenses here)

Father, I forgive _____ for the pain he/she has caused me, in Jesus' name. I release this person to you, Lord. I pray for _____ to be touched by you and delivered from all trials, forgiven of sins and set free, in Jesus' name. Set me free, also, oh Lord. Forgive me for self-pity, pride and selfishness. Father, fill my home and my life with your Holy Spirit. Deliver me, cleanse me, fill me, in Jesus' name.

I rebuke a spirit of anger, resentment, division, confusion or any other stronghold from the devil that made its place in my life and home through my unrepented sin of unforgiveness, in Jesus' name. I uproot bitterness from my heart and cast it out, in Jesus' name. I command the enemy the devil to leave my home and my family and my life, in Jesus' name!

Teach me to walk in the freedom that comes from a heart submitted to you. Please, God, show me where I need to change and repent in my relationships. I release these people *(name them here)* from my judgment, in the name of Jesus. I ask you to fill my home with your Holy Spirit and fill my life and my spouse/children, etc. with your powerful Spirit.

In Jesus' name! Amen.

BRINGING IT HOME

Is forgiveness a habit of obedience in your home and relationships? Do you wait till you "feel it" to apologize and ask for forgiveness or do you obey the Lord and work to resolve the issues as soon as you can?

Teach your children to forgive right away. We require our children to speak truth, even when they don't feel it. We live by faith and not feelings. Forgiveness is not a feeling; it is an action that we take in Jesus' name. Teach your children to apologize and to receive apologies. "I'm sorry" and "I forgive you." Powerful, real words and real habits!

FINDING JOY IN FOLLOWING GOD'S EXAMPLE
PUTTING OTHERS FIRST

Today, we will learn about finding true joy in serving others. We will also discover what behavior grieves the Holy Spirit and how to replace this behavior with the fruit of the Spirit.

PRAYER

Adapting the prayer from Ephesians 3:14-21

Father,

I kneel before you. I praise your holy name! Your whole family in heaven and on earth derives its name from you. Help me to put others in your family first, following you as an example. I pray that out of your glorious riches you will strengthen me with power through your Spirit in my inner being, so that Christ may dwell in my heart through faith. And I pray that I, being rooted and established in love, may have power, together with all the Lord's holy people, to grasp how wide and long and high and deep is the love of Christ, and to know this love that surpasses knowledge—that I may be filled to the measure of all the fullness of God. Help me to live in the joy of this reality with other believers, Lord. You can do immeasurably more than all I ask or imagine, Lord, according to your power that is at work within me! Help me to believe this. To you be glory in the church and in Christ Jesus throughout all generations, for ever and ever!

In Jesus' name, Amen.

MEMORY VERSE

26 'In your anger do not sin': do not let the sun go down while you are still angry, 27 and do not give the devil a foothold. – Ephesians 4:26-27

READING

Turn in your Bible and read Ephesians 4:23-32.

As you read and prayerfully reflect on this passage, can you tell that all of the sinful behavior we need to "put off" is rooted in selfishness? This is the opposite of the life of love God has called us to in Christ. Look at verse 32 in Ephesians 4. Where does our power to live outside of our own interests come from? It comes from Jesus Christ, our great example, who demonstrated his love for us in this:'While we were still sinners, Christ died for us!'—Romans 5:8b

GETTING TO THE ROOT OF THE PROBLEM

In Week Seven, Day 5, we read Jesus' explanation concerning the root of sinful behavior. Our words and our actions come up from what is in our hearts. (Matthew 15:10-20) It is honestly easier to try to look good on the outside than to deal with what is really in our hearts. All of our bad behavior is rooted in some kind of sin or pain. "Woe to you, teachers of the law and Pharisees, you hypocrites! You are like whitewashed tombs, which look beautiful on the outside but on the inside are full of the bones of the dead and everything unclean." — Matthew 23:27

What does Jesus compare the Pharisees to? Why?

The Pharisees were good at looking beautiful and religious on the outside, but the Lord knew what was on the inside, and the inside was full of death. The goal of every believer should be to please the Lord from the inside out. A teachable heart and mind, surrendered to God, will always please the Lord.

When you are full of God and his love, his compassion, and his forgiveness, there is less room for you to be full of yourself. When the Holy Spirit is in the house, conviction will come on you when you sin. It is difficult for someone who is full of God to walk in sin without feeling very uncomfortable. In Christ, the liar becomes the truth teller, the adulterer becomes faithful, the thief becomes a generous giver. Why? Because in Jesus, you come from death to life. The old man is replaced by the new. You now belong to a father who takes care of you. You can trust God to provide for your needs and even give you the power to work hard to give to others in need! A friend of mine is married to one of the most generous men I know. One day, I told her how amazing it is to watch him freely give to others. She said the interesting part of his story is how he was the opposite of generous before he came to Christ—he was stingy! After submitting to Christ, when the Holy Spirit came to live in him, he gave to everyone all the time, and still does. This is the work of God. When we allow the Holy Spirit to move in our hearts, we are able to find true JOY!

Jesus first

Others next

You last

This is how the thief can become a philanthropist and the person who is dishonest and a slanderer can become trustworthy and an encourager. What God does in our hearts, through the grace of Christ, should fill us with awe and wonder!

CONTRAST & COMPARISON

Write down all the "others-centered" phrases in Ephesians 4:23-32.

Does what comes out of your mouth build up others? Is it beneficial? Do you look out for the needs of others, or do you think of your own needs most? Are there any areas of your life, that Ephesians 4:23-34 shines a light on, where the Lord wants you to grow and change?

Years ago, when praying for a person with whom I had underlying conflict and needed to forgive, the Spirit of God showed me that I was praying selfishly. My prayers were just "help me get by" and "help me to forgive." I was defensive and full of self-pity when talking to the Lord about the relationship. God directed me to pray faith-filled, proactive prayers to build this person up. My attitude needed to change so I could see myself not as a victim, but as a positive contributor to the relationship, working towards reconciliation. He wanted me to pray in an others-centered way, for the other person's heart to change. I did. Guess what? It didn't happen overnight, or on my time table at all—but he redeemed the situation, doing more than I could ask or imagine! Let's pray down blessings on our enemies, just as Jesus taught us to do. Remember that while we were yet sinners, Christ died for us. Oh what joy comes, when we trust the Lord and he surprises us with his work!

BRINGING THE HOLY SPIRIT JOY INSTEAD OF GRIEF

When we are others-centered, we—and the Lord—are filled with JOY. When we are self-centered, we fill the Holy Spirit—and others—with grief. Let's think about this. The Holy Spirit is God himself. He is not a metaphor, a feeling, or an emotional high. He chooses to live in us. All the time. This is because Jesus promised us that he would never leave us or forsake us. He is in it for the long-haul, through good times and bad, to comfort us, to empower us, to guide us and to lead us into all truth. He never sleeps or slumbers. He is not far away. He is very close to you. He lives in you.

CROSS REFERENCE

Let's cross reference with John 14:15-19 to understand the role of the Holy Spirit in our lives. Underline all the names that Jesus gives the Holy Spirit. Circle his roles.

John 14:15-19

15 'If you love me, keep my commands. 16 And I will ask the Father, and he will give you another advocate to help you and be with you for ever – 17 the Spirit of truth. The world cannot accept him, because it neither sees him nor knows him. But you know him, for he lives with you and will be in you. 18 I will not leave you as orphans; I will come to you. 19 Before long, the world will not see me any more, but you will see me. Because I live, you also will live.

UNDERSTANDING THE HOLY SPIRIT'S WORK

After Jesus ascended into heaven, the Father sent the Holy Spirit at Pentecost to live inside of the disciples. However, the Spirit was already at work alongside the disciples before Jesus' death and resurrection. Here, in John 14:17 Jesus says,

"But you know him, for he lives with you and will be in you." – John 14:17

The Spirit was with the disciples. I have heard many people refer to the work of the Holy Spirit in their lives before they were saved. They will give accounts of God drawing them and speaking to them. Conviction, protection and revelation are definitely works of the Spirit, which can happen to a non-believer. How else could you get saved, if the Spirit didn't reveal Jesus to you? But, this is completely different from being a temple of the Holy Spirit and having the Spirit of Christ living inside of you, communing with your spirit, filling you with power and giving you gifts. The Holy Spirit comes into a person when he or she is saved. This is the deposit of the promised inheritance that we discussed in Week Two, Day 1.

FRUIT

Out of all of the benefits the Holy Spirit brings to believers, today our reading from Ephesians focuses on one: fruit. Fruit is the natural way a tree brings life. Your life is, spiritually speaking, a tree. In fact, in his teachings, Jesus frequently referred to a person's spiritual life as a tree. (Matthew 3:10, 7:17-19, 12:33) The roots of your life will produce the fruit of your life. When you are in God's word—like you are learning to be with this study—and submitting to God's Spirit, your life will produce the fruit of the Spirit of God. Let's cross reference to Psalms Chapter 1, where David compares a spiritual life, rooted in the Word of God, to a fruit tree.

> Blessed is the one who does not walk in step with the wicked, or stand in the way that sinners take, or sit in the company of mockers, but whose delight is in the law of the Lord, and who meditates on his law day and night. That person is like a tree planted by streams of water, which yields its fruit in season, and whose leaf does not wither – whatever they do prospers. – Psalms 1:1-3

There are two responses a believer can have to the Holy Spirit that can stop the move of God in his or her life: grieving and quenching. Grieving the Holy Spirit means going forward with sin when the Holy Spirit says stop. Ephesians 4:30 says,

> And do not grieve the Holy Spirit of God, with whom you were sealed for the day of redemption. – Ephesians 4:30

In context, this verse specifically refers to grieving the Holy Spirit in our relationships with one another. Quenching the Holy Spirit is saying no, when the Holy Spirit gives you the urging and anointing to do something. 1 Thessalonians 5:19 says, "Do not quench the Spirit." Grieving the Spirit results in a life producing rotten fruit. Quenching the Holy Spirit results in a life without power. Today, we are going to discuss how the first response, grieving the Holy Spirit, affects the Lord. Yes. I said affects the Lord.

I know the tiny house movement is really big right now, but imagine living in a cluttered tiny house. Since he lives inside of us, the Holy Spirit has to live in a messy home, when we allow sin in our lives. We always talk about the sacrifice of Jesus, but let's meditate on the sacrifice of the Holy Spirit. Meditate on the fact that living in communion with a believer is utter joy for the Holy Spirit. He loves you. His goal is relational intimacy with you. He wants to hear from you, and to enjoy everything he is there to do for you in the relationship—the way you might plan or do something special for a friend or even for a spouse or child—he is a person. He has a personality and a heart. This is why verbally thanking the Lord and testifying to his goodness are so important. It really shows the quality of your own heart, when you react to his work in you. When we don't obey his prompting or conviction, we can grieve him.

GREEK WORD STUDY
Grieve

Let's do a word study to see what the Greek word for "grieve" means. Just on a side note, I love my handy-dandy Bible Hub app, but there is a lot more detail available online when you look up a passage or do a word study through the website on a computer. Again, HELPS™ Word-studies comes to our rescue in this passage, to give us a deeper understanding of the original language. The Greek word for "grieve" is lupeo. Wow. If this screen shot doesn't drop your jaw, I don't know what will. After reading this, I realize sometimes, subconsciously, I think of the Holy Spirit as an impersonal force, even though I know the truth of his personhood.

TODAY'S BIBLE STUDY TOOL

Greek Word Study. Dig deeper into the meaning of a word by learning the intent of the original language. Some underlying meaning may have been lost in translation.

Strong's Concordance

lupeó: to distress, to grieve
Original Word: λυπέω
Part of Speech: Verb
Transliteration: lupeó
Phonetic Spelling: (loo-peh'-o)
Short Definition: I pain, grieve, vex
Definition: I pain, grieve, vex.

HELPS Word-studies

Cognate: 3076 lypéō (from 3077 /lýpē, "deep grief") – to experience deep, emotional pain (sadness), i.e. *severe sorrow* (grief). 3076 (lypéō) is very intense and hence even used of *the pain of childbirth* (see Gen 3:16, *LXX*). See 3077 (lypē).

The idea that my selfishness and sin can cause him deep, emotional pain and severe sorrow—similar to the intensity of childbirth pain—is a bit stunning. I don't know if I can actually take it in. This is where I truly need him to explain it to me, through revelation. Most of what I hear from other people, or even if I admit it, from deep in my heart, is the perception of God's response to sin being only anger. Here we see his grief. It may be difficult to understand God's grief for your soul. He longs for you, jealous for your companionship. You were bought with a price, for the purpose of fellowship and relationship with the Lord Jesus Christ.

After running in "Christian circles" my entire life, I have the impression most believers just think of sin in terms of whether or not it will keep them out of heaven. I also have the impression that church-goers see Jesus as this unfazed, unemotional tough guy who took our sin to the cross and eats nails for breakfast. Don't get me wrong. No one is more powerful or tough than the source of all power, Jesus our Lord. However, he doesn't just wink at sin, as if to say, "This one's on me! I am paying for whatever sin you feel like doing tonight," as if he is buying everyone a round of drinks at the bar.

Jesus is the perfect example of power and strength accompanied by a tender, caring heart. Our Lord was a man of sorrows and acquainted with grief. He bore our sorrows. He was happy to do it. He did it with joy—the joy of putting his Father's will and others first. He did not do it to facilitate unbridled sin, bad attitudes, avarice, sexual immorality and unchecked self-centeredness. His Spirit is grieved by our unrepented sin.

When we sin in our relationships it truly grieves him. Have you ever been around a couple who argues in front of others? It is one of the most awkward situations on the planet. The pair in conflict is so caught up in the bitterness, it is impossible for them to consider the feelings of uncomfortable bystanders. What about children who are exposed to parents fighting all the time? Unless you have been around it or have grown up with it, you may not have a full understanding of the pain this can cause a child. Imagine the Holy Spirit, who loves you so much, listening to all of your complaining, gossiping and arguing. Imagine him watching every movie you watch, and listening to the music you listen to. He knows you are in Christ. He knows all the potential you were made to live in. He knows all the riches at your disposal, through his generosity and power. But, he lives among roots of bitterness cluttering up the floor and the smell of pride wafting through the house. He is there to make your body his home, to pull up the old foundations, and reset the house on Christ. He redecorates the rooms and puts his personal touches on the walls of your heart. But, bitterness, anger, gossip, complaining, brawling and dirty talk have destroyed his clean-up work in the home faster than a group of preschoolers on a playdate. Let's cross reference to Galatians to understand how the Spirit of God can help us to put off the old self and put on the new.

Let's cross reference to Galatians 5:13-26 to understand how the Spirit of God can help us to put off the old self and put on the new. Open your Bible and make notes as you read.

If you want to live and walk in JOY, start by having an attitude like Christ, putting God first, others second and yourself last. When you walk in truth and obedience to the Lord, you will produce good fruit and God's power will flow through your life. As we obey the Lord, even through suffering in difficult relationships, we become more like Christ and we please him in every way and bring him joy, instead of grief.

In closing, remember that one of the reasons the Holy Spirit is in you is to assure you of your place in God's family. He speaks to you about your brothers and sisters, reminds you of how to love and gives you power to walk where he leads you to walk. Our hearts can rest in this: if we have confidence in our walk with the Lord, he will hear our prayers. He loves to answer our prayers, the way you love to bless your children—especially when there is no issue of discipline at the moment. He hears our prayers and answers them!

BRINGING IT HOME

Do you walk in selflessness with others, with a heart of joy before the Lord?

Do you model selflessness for your children? Good! But, remember that children have a selfish, sinful nature that will most likely need a verbal teaching on the topic of selflessness. Don't just assume that they will take your lead and be sacrificial. They may be little heathens like I was and just think that is "Mom or Dad's job!" Teach them about it with gentleness and respect. (Unless they are unresponsive to gentleness and are taking it as a weakness in you. In that case, you may need to teach them with a little bit more strength. Remember that God deals with us with patience and with strength! God disciplines those he loves.) Let them know that God cares about our attitudes and about everything we say and do.

DISMANTLING THE CAIN RESPONSE

Today, we will learn about the mystery of our lives being a fragrant offering to the Lord. What does it mean to be a living, fragrant offering? Let's find out! First, let's take time to pray the prayer from the third chapter of Ephesians. This passage has timeless truths that can be applied to different situations in your life. For example, I can learn from Ephesians 3:14-21 that it is out of God's glorious riches that we have access to being strengthened by his Spirit in our inner beings. So, I know that I can praise God for his glorious riches. I know that he has so many resources, not just for my physical needs, but for the needs I have deep inside my soul. This is called a transferable concept. The truth that God will always have enough—more than enough—for any deficit I experience in my life can be transferred and applied to all situations in my life. Everything I need, in my mind/thoughts or in my insecurity or in a relationship that needs healing and reconciliation, is found in God's treasure house of love and power. I can pray with thanksgiving for these treasures that he lavishes upon me! Whenever I have a need, a weakness or a trial, I can call on the Lord who gives liberally to all who ask. Close your eyes and meditate on the goodness of the Lord. Ask him to show you an area of your life that you haven't considered giving to him before. Ask the Lord to provide you with strength for whatever he brings to your heart, out of his glorious riches.

Another transferable concept in this prayer is the truth that the Spirit does the work inside of us, communing with our own spirits! We are not alone inside. We have a close counselor and personal trainer to help us grow in power. Our personal trainer at the gym challenges us with exercises that seem difficult as they break down our muscles. But, the next day, our muscles are even stronger. In the same way, the Holy Spirit strengthens us, walking with us through trials, helping us to endure, coaching us in how to handle what we walk through and giving us great strength and motivation. With this in mind today, go to the Lord in prayer, seeking his strength and personal training to deal with whatever he shows you today as you grow in the Lord and his grace!

PRAYER

Ephesians 3:14-21

[14] For this reason I kneel before the Father, [15] from whom every family in heaven and on earth derives its name. [16] I pray that out of his glorious riches he may **strengthen you with power through his Spirit in your inner being**, [17] so that Christ may dwell in your hearts through faith. And I pray that you, being rooted and established in love, [18] may have power, together with all the Lord's holy people, to grasp how wide and long and high and deep is the love of Christ, [19] and to know this love that surpasses knowledge – that you may be filled to the measure of all the fullness of God.

[20] Now to him who is able to do immeasurably more than all we ask or imagine, according to his power that is at work within us, [21] to him be glory in the church and in Christ Jesus throughout all generations, for ever and ever! Amen.

MEMORY VERSE

[26] 'In your anger do not sin': do not let the sun go down while you are still angry, [27] and do not give the devil a foothold. – Ephesians 4:26-27

READING

Today, let's read for content. As you read, underline repeated words and themes, and anything that jumps out at you!

Ephesians 5:1-21

Follow God's example, therefore, as dearly loved children [2] and live a life of love, just as Christ loved us and gave himself up for us as a fragrant offering and sacrifice to God.

[3] But among you there must not be even a hint of sexual immorality, or of any kind of impurity, or of greed, because these are improper for God's holy people. [4] Nor should there be obscenity, foolish talk or coarse joking, which are out of place, but rather thanksgiving. [5] For of this you can be sure: no immoral, impure or greedy person – such a person is an idolater – has any inheritance in the kingdom of Christ and of God. [6] Let no one deceive you with empty words, for because of such things God's wrath comes on those who are disobedient. [7] Therefore do not be partners with them.

[8] For you were once darkness, but now you are light in the Lord. Live as children of light [9] (for the fruit of the light consists in all goodness, righteousness and truth) [10] and find out what pleases the Lord. [11] Have nothing to do with the fruitless deeds of darkness, but rather expose them. [12] It is shameful even to mention what the disobedient do in secret. [13] But everything exposed by the light becomes visible – and everything that is illuminated becomes a light. [14] This is why it is said:

> 'Wake up, sleeper,
>   rise from the dead,
>   and Christ will shine on you.'

[15] Be very careful, then, how you live – not as unwise but as wise, [16] making the most of every opportunity, because the days are evil. [17] Therefore do not be foolish, but understand what the Lord's will is. [18] Do not get drunk on wine, which leads to debauchery. Instead, be filled with the Spirit, [19] speaking to one another with psalms, hymns, and songs from the Spirit. Sing and make music from your heart to the Lord, [20] always giving thanks to God the Father for everything, in the name of our Lord Jesus Christ.

[21] Submit to one another out of reverence for Christ.

> ### TODAY'S BIBLE STUDY TOOL
>
> **Reading for Content.** Ask the Holy Spirit to speak to you as you read through a passage of scripture. This is just for a general overview, but be looking for repetition of words which may indicate the development of a theme that the author is trying to convey.

◄ 3860. paradidómi ►

Strong's Concordance

paradidómi: to hand over, to give or deliver over, to betray
Original Word: παραδίδωμι
Part of Speech: Verb
Transliteration: paradidómi
Phonetic Spelling: (par-ad-id'-o-mee)
Short Definition: I hand over, deliver, betray
Definition: I hand over, pledge, hand down, deliver, commit, commend, betray, abandon.

HELPS Word-studies

3860 paradídōmi (from 3844 /pará, "from close-beside" and 1325 /dídōmi, "give") – properly, to give (turn) over; "hand over from," i.e. to deliver over with a sense of close (personal) involvement.

In Ephesians 5:2 it says Christ "gave himself up" for us as a fragrant offering. What does that mean? Let's do an online search on biblehub.com and look at the original word for "gave up."

Wow! Christ gave himself up! He betrayed his own personal interests in submission to the will of the Father. He delivered, committed, commended, and abandoned himself over to our well-being. There is no self-protection in this. HELPS™ Word-studies says that the language implies that he did this with a sense of close, personal involvement. His love for the Father and for us compelled him! Let's see what else we can find about the next part of this sentence.

Copyright © 1987, 2011 by Helps Ministries, Inc.

HELPS™ Word-studies

CROSS REFERENCE
Fragrant Offering

Can you do a cross reference in your Bible app to see where else scripture refers to a fragrant offering? In the space below, detail what you learn about fragrant offerings.

THE FIRST ACCEPTABLE OFFERING
& the First Unacceptable Offering

Where in scripture do we see the first "offering" to God? It would be after the first sin, of course. Read below.

Genesis 4:3-5

³ In the course of time Cain brought some of the fruits of the soil as an offering to the Lord. ⁴ But Abel also brought an offering – fat portions from some of the firstborn of his flock. The Lord looked with favour on Abel and his offering, ⁵ but on Cain and his offering he did not look with favour. So Cain was very angry, and his face was downcast.

Here, not long after the first sin, we have the first written account of a sacrifice or offering made by men for their sins. God sacrificed the first animals to cover Adam and Eve's sin and clothe their nakedness. But, this is the first time we read about people sacrificing to God. Both brothers were hoping to please the Lord with their offerings.

Cain and Abel are old enough to have full-time occupations. I am sure this is not the first time they have brought a sacrifice before the Lord. Why did they have to bring an offering? God told Adam and Eve before they sinned that the day they sinned they would surely die. The punishment for sin is death. From the very beginning, God allows a substitutionary sacrifice for sin. The offering that pleases the Lord is the offering of a true sacrifice, the death of a perfect animal to be our stand-in or replacement. For sin to be covered, the blood of an animal had to be shed and the body was burnt as an offering. The fragrance would ascend before the Lord. (This is similar to the fragrances we experience at a cookout. In fact, in the Old Testament, they would indeed partake of the sacrificial animal and share portions with the priests.)

Did Cain know this was required? I am sure that he did, given the ensuing situation. Also, God walked with Adam in the cool of the day. There was a lot of openness and communication between God and the first family. For some reason, on this infamous day, Cain decided that he would give what HE felt was a reasonable sacrifice. This is different from the acceptable sacrifice that God required for sin. The first fruits of his field had just come in. Maybe he got excited about the harvest. Maybe he didn't have time after harvesting to go ask Abel for an animal to sacrifice. He definitely could have bartered with Abel, since Cain had just harvested. Maybe he was too prideful to ask his brother? Too lazy? Maybe he was already angry with his brother? Maybe he thought it should be good enough, because God knew he had worked hard all day. Cain justified his choice enough to get upset by God's reaction. God did not accept Cain's sacrifice, because it wasn't a blood sacrifice. Cain was angry. Very angry. God warned Cain. "Then the Lord said to Cain, 'Why are you angry? Why is your face downcast? If you do what is right, will you not be accepted? But if you do not do what is right, sin is crouching at your door; it desires to have you, but you must rule over it.' "– Genesis 4:6-7 The direct words of the Lord were ignored. Cain was offended with God when God was not pleased and he was angry enough to kill his brother. And sadly, he did.

- What does this have to do with us today?

- What does this have to do with Ephesians 5?

Today, in Christ, we have the same expectation from the Lord, that we should live lives that are pleasing and fragrant offerings to him. He has laid out in scripture what this life of love in Christ looks like. We follow Christ, who gave himself selflessly. We have the same clear warnings like Cain was given, that personify sin as an attacking animal—Romans 6 speaks of the *body of sin*—it is hiding in the bushes outside of our doors, ready to pounce on us. Master it! The door represents the entry way to our spiritual houses.

Ephesians 5 starts with a picture for the believer that we are to live a sacrificial life of love in the family of God, the way that our big brother, our Lord and Savior Jesus Christ, lived and died for us. He was the perfect sacrifice for our sins. Many people erroneously say, "Jesus was perfect so that we don't have to be." The correct way to word the sentiment they are expressing is that "Jesus was perfect, because we cannot be perfect in our flesh. He came to do what we simply cannot do." We DO have to be perfect, BUT we cannot be so in our flesh. However, after we confess and repent of our sins and accept Christ's blood sacrifice for our sins, we have the Holy Spirit who allows us to live a life that pleases God through his power, as we submit to him in humility. It is through the Spirit that we live in God's holy family. We live with one another and bring our own sacrifices of holy and pure lives lived out for Jesus alongside our own brothers and sisters in Christ.

Ephesians 5 begins to lay out what God himself looks upon as an acceptable sacrifice. These are the ways to live that honor him and his name in the family of God. List some of the lifestyles in Ephesians 5 that God sees as a fragrant offering in the life of a believer.

List some of the behaviors in Ephesians 5 that God sees as unacceptable behaviors. These are behaviors that people in the family of God should avoid at all cost!

OPPOSITES
Light vs Darkness

In Ephesians 5, Paul lists behaviors that are unacceptable offerings to God; he doesn't just say to stop using coarse joking or obscenity, but he uses the word "rather." He reveals what the sin should be replaced with in the heart—thanksgiving. When we are religious and not relational with God, we try to do outward things to please God. God desires a change of heart that transforms us from the inside out. This is an acceptable, fragrant sacrifice to God.

Write in the godly corresponding opposites to the sinful behaviors listed in Ephesians 5.

LIGHT		DARKNESS
_____	not	obscenity, foolish talk, coarse joking
_____	not	darkness
_____	not	unwise
_____	not	foolish
_____	not	drunkenness and debauchery

Cain's jealousy and anger with God projected onto his brother. He knew he wasn't doing the right thing, but he still wanted to be justified. In a culture where everyone wants to be right and to feel good about the way they are living, do you see this cycle playing out? Instead of mastering the sin of jealousy and anger, and the desire to justify their sins, many believers find it easier to turn against brothers or sisters in Christ who remind them of their own perceived failures. There is also a lie a person can believe concerning sin. The lie goes something like this: "What my brothers and sisters are calling a sin is part of my own identity and that situation can never change." This is not true. God claims our identity. Our power to change is in Christ, through his Spirit. Again, friends, this is all about family life in the body of Christ. Are we living in defeat, jealousy, pride? Are we willing to admit that some of our lifestyle choices need an inside-out makeover? Will we allow Jesus, through the Holy Spirit with whom we are sealed, to teach us a new way?

Even after a direct conversation with God, Cain killed Abel. God was patient. God was kind. God was loving to this soon-to-be killer. Cain didn't listen to God's patient and loving correction, which is a characteristic of people who are not submitted to God in their hearts. God also speaks to you today when you are faced with difficult temptation and jealousy. Are you listening? How are you responding?

BRINGING IT HOME

Read your children the story of Cain and Abel. Ask them why they think Cain was upset with Abel for doing something good that God required of him. Can they think of any examples in their own life when they have gotten upset with someone for doing something good for God? Has anyone gotten angry with your children for being good? Talk with your kids about the beauty of a life lived as a fragrant offering.

NOT A HINT
PART 1

WHAT'S FLAVORING YOUR LIFE?

There are many subliminal messages in our society that tell women that our value lies in sexuality and in physical appearance. Many women subconsciously measure their worth in inches and pounds, feeling emotionally up or down based on whether they feel attractive that day. Today, we will learn that our value and worth is so much deeper. We are valued in God's family. We should not strive to find fulfillment in who the world says we are—sex objects, but what God says we are—daughters of the King.

PRAYER

Father,

In Jesus' name, I thank you that your whole family in heaven and on earth derives its name from you. I am named for you. I pray that my life will bring your name glory, as a daughter of the King. I pray that out of your glorious riches you may strengthen me with power through your Spirit in my inner being, so that Christ may dwell in my heart through faith. And I pray that this faith will transform my life to bring your family and your name glory. You are able to do immeasurably more than all I can ask or imagine, according to your power that is at work within me. Transform me so that there will not be a hint of anything in my life that brings discredit to your name and your family. Cleanse me from the inside out, Lord.

In Jesus' name. Amen.

(adapted from Ephesians 3:14-21)

MEMORY VERSE

[26] 'In your anger do not sin': do not let the sun go down while you are still angry, [27] and do not give the devil a foothold. – Ephesians 4:26-27

REVIEW OF EPHESIANS

When Paul wrote the letter to the church in Ephesus, he painted a beautiful picture of who we are in Christ. Let's review what we've learned so far from a bird's-eye view.

CHAPTER 1
New Identity

Paul begins Chapter 1 with reminders of our past identity and how it was replaced with a new identity in the family of God. The old is gone, the new is come! He pens a prayer with such incredible power, insight and anointing, and gives us an inside look into the Apostle's own prayer life. Paul teaches us the Holy Spirit's role in our lives and our need for our own spiritual eyes to be open, so that we can see all the riches of our inheritance in Christ Jesus.

CHAPTER 2
Unity

After reminding us all how individually we are sought after, loved, and saved, Paul begins to challenge us and reveal to us that the things that separate us from other believers in Christ fall away at the cross. No racial divisions, no cultural differences, no sin can separate us from our destiny to be united in Christ. We are all woven together into the DNA of Christ, building blocks of the body of Christ —a holy temple for the living God.

CHAPTER 3
Family

Paul unravels the mystery for us. It's no longer a secret! We are all unified in the family of God. If you don't feel more secure in the knowledge of who you are in Christ by the end of Chapter 3, you need to go back and pray for spiritual revelation and healing by the Holy Spirit. Paul unveils another prayer as an example for how to pray, teaching us to pray to be strengthened in our inner beings so that we can comprehend the love of God. His prayer also mysteriously teaches us of the deeper things of God, concerning our unity in the body of Christ, and the fullness we experience in Christ together.

CHAPTER 4
Spiritual Gifts & Relationships in the Church

Paul shows us our need for order and authority in the church. He talks about why God gives different gifts and callings to believers and explains how we are to live with one another.

CHAPTER 5
Getting Personal

Paul starts Chapter 5 talking about our past personal sins, and our redemption, and takes us on a tour of our authority, our belonging in the family of God, and our need for each other. Now, he touches the most personal, deep parts of our lives when he discusses how being a believer should transform our private relationships—our sexuality and marriage.

Before we dig into an area that can potentially evoke strong feelings of shame, defensiveness, and guilt, let's remember some things that Paul has already covered in the first four chapters of Ephesians.

- **You are loved by God.** No matter what your past sin or present struggles, the blood of Jesus has never failed you. God loves you in the middle of your sin. He doesn't wait till you are perfect. If he did, none of us would ever be saved!

- **In Christ, you BELONG!** You belong to our Holy Father in heaven. You are his beloved daughter, for whom his beloved Son died, to save you from the power and penalty of your sin. He prepared, in advance, many great things for you to do and experience through him and in his family.

- **You have unlimited resources in Christ for everything you experience and face.** The same power that raised Jesus from the dead lives in you!

- **You are part of the eternal, timeless, world-wide family of God.** You have support from all over the world. Christ is teaching you to function in a healthy family, even if you didn't grow up in one and have no idea what it looks like.

READING

Let's open our Bibles and read the beginning of Ephesians Chapter 5. Look for similarities in verses 3 and 5. Paul makes a list. What are the three things listed that are repeated in both places?

83. _____ 84. _____ 85. _____

Ephesians 5:1-5

¹ Follow God's example, therefore, as dearly loved children ² and live a life of love, just as Christ loved us and gave himself up for us as a fragrant offering and sacrifice to God.

³ But among you there must not be even a hint of sexual immorality, or of any kind of impurity, or of greed, because these are improper for God's holy people. ⁴ Nor should there be obscenity, foolish talk or coarse joking, which are out of place, but rather thanksgiving. ⁵ For of this you can be sure: no immoral, impure or greedy person – such a person is an idolater – has any inheritance in the kingdom of Christ and of God.

When I read this passage, I just think it's incredible how rampant sexual immorality is in the body of Christ with this clear mandate that does not stand alone in the Bible. Paul is NOT addressing past immorality. If you were a prostitute or promiscuous before coming to Christ, and have repented, turning from your sin, you are NO LONGER held accountable before God for what you did. The purpose of this passage is to entreat believers not to be led astray or deceived by false teachers with empty words who teach that the grace of God is a license to sin. There is no place for sexual sin in a believer's life. So, let's break it down, just to be clear.

TODAY'S BIBLE STUDY TOOL

Greek Word Study. Dig deeper into the meaning of a word by learning the intent of the original language. Some underlying meaning may have been lost in translation.

But among you there **must not be even a hint** of sexual immorality, or of any kind of impurity, or of greed, because these are improper for God's holy people. — Ephesians 5:3

What exactly does NOT A HINT mean? Let's go to biblehub.com, type Ephesians 5:3 in the search bar, then click on GREEK and find this scripture verse. This seems pretty clear, but is it? I know the human tendency will be to challenge the meaning of this to try to justify behavior, so I want to look it up!

WHAT IS SEASONING YOUR LIFE?

So, the word for "hint" is Onomazo in the Greek, which means to be named for something. In this case, it means to be named for sexual immorality. How does this work?

When I am eating at a nice restaurant, one of my favorite things to do is to guess what is in the dish I am eating. Being a cook, I like to imagine what it would take to reproduce in my own kitchen what I am tasting at a gourmet venue! If there is a hint of garlic, oregano and basil, usually I am naming that dish an Italian or Mediterranean dish. If I am drinking my water infused with a hint of lemon, it's usually called lemon water. The smallest amount of seasoning can work its way through a whole dish and affect the taste. Take salt, for instance. An inexperienced cook who over-salts in the beginning stage of preparing a soup, may unknowingly ruin the whole pot. Also, if you use table salt, it takes more time to work its seasoning through the dish than perhaps a kosher salt

◄ **3687. onomazó** ►

Strong's Concordance

onomazó: to name, to give a name
Original Word: ὀνομάζω
Part of Speech: Verb
Transliteration: onomazó
Phonetic Spelling: (on-om-ad'-zo)
Short Definition: I give a name to, mention
Definition: I give a name to, mention, call upon the name of.

NAS Exhaustive Concordance

Word Origin

from onoma

Definition

to name, to give a name

NASB Translation

derives its name (1), name (1), named (5), names (1), so-called (1).

would take; thus over-salting can occur. And, if you add a little too much salt before the taste is evident, you may be puckering up and grabbing your water at dinner time. Another example from cooking is my husband's dislike for cilantro. Even though I really enjoy this fresh Latin herb, he would rather me not put even a hint of cilantro in his guacamole. He feels that it ruins his experience!

In this next passage of scripture, Paul uses a kitchen analogy to share how a little bit of yeast is all that it takes to make bread rise. He uses this baking example to not only remind us of the dangers of sexual immorality in our lives, but also to tell us how to handle it when we see it in the body of Christ.

CROSS REFERENCE

1 Corinthians 5:1-12

[1] It is actually reported that there is sexual immorality among you, and of a kind that even pagans do not tolerate: a man is sleeping with his father's wife. [2] And you are proud! Shouldn't you rather have gone into mourning and have put out of your fellowship the man who has been doing this? [3] For my part, even though I am not physically present, I am with you in spirit. As one who is present with you in this way, I have already passed judgment in the name of our Lord Jesus on the one who has been doing this. [4] So when you are assembled and I am with you in spirit, and the power of our Lord Jesus is present, [5] hand this man over to Satan for the destruction of the flesh, so that his spirit may be saved on the day of the Lord.

[6] Your boasting is not good. **Don't you know that a little yeast leavens the whole batch of dough?** [7] Get rid of the old yeast, so that you may be a new unleavened batch – as you really are. For Christ, our Passover lamb, has been sacrificed. [8] Therefore let us keep the Festival, not with the old bread leavened with malice and wickedness, but with the unleavened bread of sincerity and truth.

[9] I wrote to you in my letter not to associate with sexually immoral people – [10] not at all meaning the people of this world who are immoral, or the greedy and swindlers, or idolaters. In that case you would have to leave this world. [11] But now I am writing to you that you must not associate with anyone who claims to be a brother or sister but is sexually immoral or greedy, an idolater or slanderer, a drunkard or swindler. Do not even eat with such people.

[12] What business is it of mine to judge those outside the church? Are you not to judge those inside?

If you have been named for something, you are known for it. Even though it was only one man participating in this behavior, the whole church in Corinth was "named" for it! In fact, even though Paul wasn't in Corinth, he says in this passage that word of this immorality has reached his ears. If you are known for a sin, it is something that most people have a "hint" that you participate in. It becomes your identity. Our identity as believers is in Christ. How can someone named for Christ also be named for sexual immorality?

Thinking about this Greek word for NAMED led me to ask the question, "In Paul's prayer for the Ephesians in Chapter 3, it says that the Father's whole family in heaven and on earth derives its name from him. Is this the same Greek word 'Onomazo' used in Ephesians 5:3?"

So, I looked it up. YES! IT IS! We are named and known for being children of God! How can we also be named as people who are sexually immoral? People in God's house follow the rules of God's house, and sexual immorality is a sin against the very body of Christ. "By his power God raised the Lord from the dead, and he will raise us also. Do you not know that your bodies are members of Christ himself? Shall I then take the members of Christ and unite them with a prostitute? Never! Do you not know that he who unites himself with a prostitute is one with her in body? For it is said, 'The two will become one flesh.'" – 1 Corinthians 6:14-16

BRINGING IT HOME

- What is flavoring your life? Do you allow yourself a little guilty pleasure here and there in this area?

- Do you expect purity from your teens, or do you just expect that teens will be teens?

- Are you allowing thoughts about someone other than your spouse to creep into your mind?

- Is there anything in your social media messages that would make you squirm if someone else read them? Do you habitually bring sexual immorality into your home through TV shows, sitcoms, and movies that you watch and even fantasize about? What about the books you read?

- In what ways do you find yourself allowing "hints" of immorality into your life?

Spend time asking the Lord why this is something you are struggling with. If you are living in sin, the correct response is to repent! Don't just try to "do better." Give God your heart and ask him to cleanse your life of anything that would bring him dishonor. If you are wrestling with a temptation, tell a trusted friend and ask for accountability! Get it out into the open so you won't be caught in the devil's trap.

WEEK EIGHT
DAY 5

TODAY'S BIBLE STUDY TOOL
Greek Word Study

NOT A HINT
PART 2

PROTECTING YOUR FAMILY FROM IMMORALITY

PRAYER

Ephesians 3:14-21

[14] For this reason I kneel before the Father, [15] from whom every family in heaven and on earth derives its name. [16] I pray that out of his glorious riches he may **strengthen you with power through his Spirit in your inner being**, [17] so that Christ may dwell in your hearts through faith. And I pray that you, being rooted and established in love, [18] may have power, together with all the Lord's holy people, to grasp how wide and long and high and deep is the love of Christ, [19] and to know this love that surpasses knowledge – that you may be filled to the measure of all the fullness of God.

[20] Now to him who is able to do immeasurably more than all we ask or imagine, according to his power that is at work within us, [21] to him be glory in the church and in Christ Jesus throughout all generations, for ever and ever! Amen.

Heavenly Father,

I kneel before you, thanking you for changing my name and adopting me into your family. I praise you for delivering me from the wages of my sin and writing my name in the Lamb's Book of Life! May others see Christ in me. Strengthen me with power through your Spirit in my inner being. Out of your glorious riches, give me the ability to overcome the sin in my life that may be tainting the life you have called me to in Christ Jesus.

Root and establish me in love to have power to grasp your love. I don't completely understand the height, depth, length and width of your love for me. I need your revelation and wisdom of your Spirit to understand it! Fill me with your love, oh Lord, so that I will not be tempted to run after the things of the world. The world is all around me and can tempt me and my family in so many ways. Lead us not into temptation, but deliver us from evil! Please allow the revelation of your love to overpower me. Do immeasurably more than I can think to ask or imagine in my life, in Jesus' name!

May your glory shine in my life, in Jesus' name, Amen!

[26] 'In your anger do not sin': do not let the sun go down while you are still angry, [27] and do not give the devil a foothold. – Ephesians 4:26-27

Today, ladies, as we read about protecting ourselves and our families from immorality, let's be sure to be open to the Holy Spirit's revelation and wisdom. We work so hard to do the best for our lives and our families. If you are like me, you strive to be all that you can be, to make those around you happy, to obey the Lord, and to love your friends, husband and children and to honor them. Let's get to one of the roots of the problem of immorality in our culture today and how we can protect ourselves and our family from it.

READING

Ephesians 5:1-16

[1] Follow God's example, therefore, as dearly loved children [2] and live a life of love, just as Christ loved us and gave himself up for us as a fragrant offering and sacrifice to God.

[3] But among you there must not be even a hint of sexual immorality, or of any kind of impurity, or of greed, because these are improper for God's holy people. [4] Nor should there be obscenity, foolish talk or coarse joking, which are out of place, but rather thanksgiving. [5] For of this you can be sure: no immoral, impure or greedy person – such a person is an idolater – has any inheritance in the kingdom of Christ and of God. [6] Let no one deceive you with empty words, for because of such things God's wrath comes on those who are disobedient. [7] Therefore do not be partners with them.

[8] For you were once darkness, but now you are light in the Lord. Live as children of light [9] (for the fruit of the light consists in all goodness, righteousness and truth) [10] and find out what pleases the Lord. [11] Have nothing to do with the fruitless deeds of darkness, but rather expose them. [12] It is shameful even to mention what the disobedient do in secret. [13] But everything exposed by the light becomes visible – and everything that is illuminated becomes a light. [14] This is why it is said:

> 'Wake up, sleeper,
> rise from the dead,
> and Christ will shine on you.'

[15] Be very careful, then, how you live – not as unwise but as wise, [16] making the most of every opportunity, because the days are evil.

Ephesians 5:3-5 lists three things that are out of place or improper for God's holy people. What word in the list seems to be out place, at first glance?

[3] But among you there must not be even a hint of sexual immorality, or of any kind of impurity, or of greed, because these are improper for God's holy people. [4] Nor should there be obscenity, foolish talk or coarse joking, which are out of place, but rather thanksgiving. [5] For of this you can be sure: no immoral, impure or greedy person – such a person is an idolater – has any inheritance in the kingdom of Christ and of God.

Do you see the word "greed"? Does that fit in with the theme of immorality in the passage, or is it just a randomly listed word? Why would the Holy Spirit lead Paul to write this into his letter to the Ephesians, combining it twice with two other words in verses 3 and 5? What does greed have to do with impurity and immorality?

A man who came out of over a decade of addiction to internet pornography privately related his testimony to our family. I have permission to put it in this book, in order to possibly help someone. This is an intense addiction that seems almost impossible to overcome. Most people feel completely defeated by it, whether they have the addiction, or their spouse or a child has the addiction. But remember, God is faithful. This man shared what God revealed to him about himself, after years of seeking God and struggling with the temptation. The Lord showed him why he was so prone to this addiction.

"The Lord showed me that I was just greedy or gluttonous. I couldn't just be satisfied with what God had given me in my wife. It wasn't because she wasn't beautiful, or everything I needed. I just wanted more than I needed. I was afraid there was something I was missing out there. That was the lie. I was trapped by my greed and gluttony."

Greed is very intricately tied in with the sin of immorality. Have you ever heard the phrase, "Appetite for sin?" Our flesh always wants more than it needs. Adam and Eve literally had a hunger for the very fruit that God forbade them to eat. The devil lied to them and tempted them to doubt God's law and God's plan for them. The devil implied that God was keeping something good from them. It seemed that maybe the devil was right. They landed in the wrong place. They landed in the lie of the devil and the consequences have meant death and misery for billions of people since death entered the world because of Adam and Eve's greed.

This man who overcame the lies of the devil and pornography received the personal wisdom and revelation he needed from the Spirit of God to help him deal with his sin, repent and conquer it. When we open the scriptures and seek God's face on an area of weakness, he will always reveal himself to us. It may take some time to get all of what God is saying, mostly because we are weak in our natural selves. But you can be confident that God will work with you over the long haul to overcome the power of this sin.

The lie of greed, or our appetite for more, is in direct conflict with what is actually good and spiritually healthy for us. Our own flesh can deceive us so that when we read scriptures like Ephesians 5, instead of accepting the truth with an open heart, we may ask questions like, "What does sexual immorality mean, exactly?" This would be done to justify ourselves, of course. Well, we need to know what it means to God. We don't need to know what it means to me, or to you, or to your favorite internet preacher, or meme theologian. If I ask myself what it means to me, then my appetite for more sin can get in the way and deceive me!

A whole line of questioning that happens in way too many Christian small groups goes something like this, "Let's read this passage together. Okay. What does sexual immorality mean to you?" Well, it doesn't matter what it means to you, unless you want to be like Cain and offer up an unacceptable offering to a holy and mighty God. So, let's check the Greek.

GREEK WORD STUDY
Sexual Immorality

You can find the entire page of information on this at: http://biblehub.com/greek/4202.htm

Strong's Concordance
porneia: fornication

Original Word: πορνεία, ας, ἡ
Part of Speech: Noun, Feminine
Transliteration: porneia
Phonetic Spelling: (por-ni'-ah)
Short Definition: fornication, idolatry
Definition: fornication, whoredom; met: idolatry.

> **TODAY'S BIBLE STUDY TOOL**
>
> **Greek Word Study.** Dig deeper into the meaning of a word by learning the intent of the original language. Some underlying meaning may have been lost in translation.

HELPS™ Word-studies

4202 *porneía* (the root of the English terms "pornography, pornographic"; cf. 4205 /*pórnos*) which is derived from *pernaō*, "to sell off") – properly, a *selling off* (surrendering) of sexual purity; *promiscuity* of any (every) type.

Let's take a look at a real-life example of a "what's right for me" conversation from a high school birthday sleepover.

A girl, eager to know what everyone else thinks, asks how old her girlfriends think a teen needs to be before she has sex. Several of the girls seem to have ideas from their mothers, others from movies and social media. With much self-justification and a sense of impending adulthood, one girl says, "Sixteen." One brave girl, who is a Christian, chimes in that it is a sin to have sex before marriage and that God tells them to wait—party pooper, right? Looks of incredulity come over their faces, as they stare at her as if she just told them that the earth was flat. This is very much a Cain response—a "what is right for me" response. They look at her in disgust, and the challenge immediately begins. One girl says, "The Bible talks about adultery. That's different. That's what my mom says. There is nothing wrong about having sex when you are 16. That seems like the right age."

Again, you see the line of reasoning here? The girls were instructed by their mothers—and probably online bloggers, snap chat, and Hollywood—on what was right and wrong. They WERE concerned about what the Bible said, but they actually didn't know what it says. People in authority, like parents, Bible teachers, pastors, and public figures will answer to God for what they do or don't teach children.

The word "pornea" means sexual promiscuity of every type. We get the word "pornography" from it. It refers to fornication, which is any kind of sexual impurity. So, ask yourself and pray and ask God, "What does it mean to be pure? Is sleeping with your boyfriend or girlfriend pure? Is sexting pure? What makes something a 'selling off or surrendering' of sexual purity? What does it mean to be promiscuous?"

One of the issues that really has me up in arms lately is the crisis concerning our teens—and even young children—having access to all kinds of unlimited filth online. I personally believe that, as adults, we have no real idea what goes on in the Instagram, Snap Chat, Facebook private or direct messaging world with teen-to-teen or even adult-to-adult conversation. Many teens and even tweens are getting pulled into a very twisted world that may shock you.

The Bible teaches us that the flesh is greedy. The greed for more voyeuristic experience keeps calling while seeds of lust are built into the hearts of our children, even at their youngest, as they are just developing physically, emotionally, and mentally. Since across the board, unlimited internet access to sexual content via smartphone has hardly been around for a decade, at the writing of this book, the long-term consequences—as in lifetime consequences—have yet to be seen from the effects of technology and social media on children who grow up with it. But, one doesn't have to guess why depression is skyrocketing in young people. There are some recent studies that show the short-term effects of unlimited anonymous access to porn online. The following excerpt from *The Impact of Pornography on Children* is from that article on the website of the American College of Pediatrics. It details the harrowing effects that viewing pornographic materials has on young people.

"Grade school children are sometimes exposed to pornography accidentally when they view material on the Internet. They may also come into contact with a parent's or close adult's pornographic material. Sexual predators have purposefully exposed young children to pornography for the purpose of grooming the children for sexual exploitation. Pornography exposure at these young ages often results in anxiety for the child. Children also report feelings of disgust, shock, embarrassment, anger, fear, and sadness after viewing pornography. These children can suffer all of the symptoms of anxiety and depression. They may become obsessed with acting out adult sexual acts that they have seen, and this can be very disruptive and disturbing to the child's peers who witness or are victimized by this behavior. Children under twelve years old who have viewed pornography are statistically more likely to sexually assault their peers. In sum, children exposed to pornographic material are at risk for a broad range of maladaptive behaviors and psychopathology."

Also, concerning young adults, this report revealed:

"The following observations were noted regarding young adults exposed to pornography compared to the control group:

o   Male subjects demonstrated increased callousness toward women.

o   Subjects considered the crime of rape less serious.

o   Subjects were more accepting of non-marital sexual activity and non-coital sexual practices such as oral and anal sex.

o   Subjects became more interested in more extreme and deviant forms of pornography.

o   Subjects were more likely to say they were dissatisfied with their sexual partner.

o   Subjects were more accepting of sexual infidelity in a relationship.

o   Subjects valued marriage less and were twice as likely to believe marriage may become obsolete.

o   Men experienced a decreased desire for children, and women experienced a decreased desire to have a daughter.

o   Subjects showed a greater acceptance of female promiscuity."

The full article is here: https://www.acpeds.org/the-college-speaks/position-statements/the-impact-of-pornography-on-children.

Young men and women are being exposed to more than a human being should ever be exposed to. We are not just talking about hard core materials here—which is what most parents fear, but about an appetite for lust and sensuality being developed. Online conversations with another curious peer that start very harmlessly, or even anonymously, quickly can escalate. The temptation is so great and their emotional immaturity level is so high. The brains of teens are simply not equipped to handle the constant dripping of harsh bullying or sexual comments, pictures, and videos from friends all day long, and way into the night, after parents think they are sleeping.

Social media is a world of virtual reality that most parents have no control over. Most adults have no idea of what is happening there. Teens may think that what they are dabbling in is just satisfying a curiosity that all kids have when they hit puberty. Instead of just asking friends questions at a sleepover, they are asking Siri to educate them. They may think this virtually sensual world is not the same as actually committing fornication, so they keep filling up their appetite for racy dialogues, and swapping sensual swimsuit pictures and videos, not thinking there is anyone who knows. Children should not be trusted with this type of internet responsibility. They are unable to protect themselves from themselves.

Forget about the stereotypical scenario you are always given of the sleazy 60-year-old man who is pretending to be a 13-year-old boy or girl. Our children have sin natures just like everyone else. If we trust what God says about human nature, we should know that our children need protection from themselves, not just from strangers online. It is the responsibility of the parents to teach their children how to honestly deal with their sin nature, or even curiosity/temptation, before the Lord. It is also parents' or guardians' responsibility to build a wall of purity and protection around their children's hearts until they develop emotionally and spiritually to the place where they can handle the responsibility themselves. Even then, as adults, many men and some women need help with accountability. It has been said that up to 80% of pastors have an addiction to pornography. This is a serious situation.

This may seem overwhelming to think about, and I know sometimes I just want to shut my eyes and close my ears because there seems to be no way to get hold of this beast. But there are very solid ways to protect your child. Jesus said that it is better to have a millstone tied around your neck and to be thrown into the sea than to cause a little one to stumble. When we close our eyes and ears to the serious dangers of technology in the lives of our children, we are allowing the power of death to rule in their lives, and to put it mildly, causing them to stumble. Another thing Jesus told his disciples was if your hand causes you to sin, cut it off. Or if your eye causes you to sin, pluck it out. It's better to enter eternity maimed than to go into hell with a whole body. How much more do we need that proverbial cutting off of the things that cause sin in our lives or in our children and to teach them to do this for themselves as they grow older?

One night, I had a dream. In the dream, I saw our family had adopted a cute little lion cub. The little cub was so cute, and my children fell in love with it. As the dream went on, I started to panic as the lion grew and grew. I knew that it was going to turn on my children one day and destroy them if I didn't get rid of it, but they loved him so much I knew it would be a fight. I woke up in a panic with a clear realization that the Lord was telling me that I needed to fight this fight. Soon afterwards, we researched software to secure our electronic devices and found ways to block social media use. There are also ways to make sure all of our children's texts come through our phones.

There are many resources available to parents to help monitor online behavior for children. Our family uses Net Nanny and also utilizes the general settings restrictions on our children's devices to lock out websites and apps with mature content. You will need to create a password your child can't crack, and you can take YouTube, FaceTime and other apps off of their phones. You also can remove the App store and the ability to install and delete apps, so they cannot hide sneaky behavior behind your back. Most importantly, any protective software will not replace the regular conversations, interactions and oversight that you should be initiating with your children. If they push back against it and say that you are "in their space" or "making them uncomfortable," remember that you are their parent, not their best friend. It's okay if they feel a little uncomfortable. Hopefully, these conversations can be open and helpful, but don't be surprised if they occasionally are emotional.

Most likely, you will be fighting a battle with your older children who either do not understand the dangers of the world, or who want to have the freedom to do what they want to do. It is your place as a parent to stand your ground in love and protect your children. Your consistent love and accountability in this area will communicate to your children what is important. Do not give up in your vigilance as watchman over your house! Get support from other parents who have walked through the battle. I have heard a very wise saying quoted concerning child rearing—"Choose your battles carefully." This is a battle you want to choose. Your children will know what is important in life depending on what you stand your ground on. Do you value purity? Are they worth it? Rhetorical questions, I know.

BRINGING IT HOME

If you don't have children, have a candid conversation with the Lord and with a good friend to know if there is anything you should be doing in your own life. Learn how to protect yourself and/or a relationship with your spouse from the immorality in our online culture. Don't assume that just because you don't struggle, your spouse is in the clear.

If you have children, make it a priority to educate yourself on protecting your children from the online world, as well as from themselves. Pray for your children. Have candid, age-appropriate conversations with them to help them understand the importance of having a pure and honest heart before God.

Our children need to know that every person has a heart that is inclined to turn from the Lord. They need to know that your job, as a parent, is to protect them and to teach them to seek the Lord with all of their heart, mind, soul and strength.

Avoid angry overreactions if you find something shocking on your child's device. Even if what you have discovered is scary and overwhelming, anger does not communicate God's grace and forgiveness. The shame they will feel will be a heavy-enough burden. They will need to know how to surrender their sin and shame and to find mercy at the cross. Ask the Lord for grace. They will know you are serious when you stand your ground and create a safe environment for them to live in as a young person.

Be proactive. Read up on the legal ramifications for texting, viewing, and opening inappropriate materials when it comes to underage kids. It is in your best interest to know how to handle that if anyone has sent your child anything questionable. The laws are actually complicated, and in some ways, are less intuitive than they should be on this issue. In some situations, they can do more harm than good. Usually, companies like Net Nanny, Covenant Eyes, or ministries like Focus on the Family will have email newsletters with up-to-date information about new cyber threats or apps that are unhealthy for your children. They try to give you simple direction to keep your child safe. You don't have to look far to find support! Once you are armed with information, you will feel much more confident in helping your child and family navigate online territory. There may be a learning curve, but as in any valuable thing in life—the protection of your children—anything worth having is worth working for. Remember that God loves your children and he is on your side. When you seek his guidance in this area, as in any area, he will not fail you.

NOT A HINT
PART 3

ARE YOU SURE THAT'S IMMORAL?

PRAYER

Ephesians 3:14-21

[14] For this reason I kneel before the Father, [15] from whom every family in heaven and on earth derives its name. [16] I pray that out of his glorious riches he may **strengthen you with power through his Spirit in your inner being**, [17] so that Christ may dwell in your hearts through faith. And I pray that you, being rooted and established in love, [18] may have power, together with all the Lord's holy people, to grasp how wide and long and high and deep is the love of Christ, [19] and to know this love that surpasses knowledge – that you may be filled to the measure of all the fullness of God.

[20] Now to him who is able to do immeasurably more than all we ask or imagine, according to his power that is at work within us, [21] to him be glory in the church and in Christ Jesus throughout all generations, for ever and ever! Amen.

Heavenly Father,

I kneel before you thanking you for changing my name and adopting me into your family. I praise you for delivering me from the wages of my sin and writing my name in the Lamb's book of life! May others see Christ in me. Strengthen me with power, through your Spirit, in my inner being. Out of your glorious riches, give me the ability to overcome the sin that taints the life you have called me to in Christ Jesus. Root and establish me in love, so I can understand it. I need your revelation and wisdom of your Spirit to understand it! Fill me with your love, oh Lord, so I will not be tempted to run after the things of the world. The world is all around me and tempts me in so many ways. Lead me not into temptation, but deliver me from evil! Please allow the revelation of your love to overpower me. Do immeasurably more than I can think to ask or imagine in my life, in Jesus' name! May your glory shine in my life.

In Jesus' name, Amen!

NEW MEMORY VERSE

We have a new verse starting today to help us focus our hearts and minds on our purpose as believers—to do everything to the glory of God. Instead of looking at our walk with the Lord as a life of restriction with a big fat NO over everything fun, we need to focus our lives on bringing the Lord joy and also reflecting well on his name. There is a great deal of question and consternation in

2018 concerning the great falling away of young adults who were raised in the church. Many of these young people see Christianity through the prism of hypocrisy. They know what is right and wrong. They see professing believers partying on a Saturday night, sleeping around and then going to the church on Sunday with their eyes closed during worship—and it's not because they are praying! It seems to them that no one is living out authentic Christianity, that no one is the real deal. Everyone lives for themselves and what feels good. When someone who is part of God's family lives a selfish, self-serving life, it reflects very poorly on God and can be a stumbling block to others. But, as we focus this week on purity, relationships and marriage, and keep our hearts and eyes focused on doing everything to bring God glory, others will want to glorify him, as they see our authentic faith lived out before their eyes.

MEMORY VERSE

[31] So whether you eat or drink or whatever you do, do it all for the glory of God. [32] Do not cause anyone to stumble. – 1 Corinthians 10:31-32a

READING

Turn in your Bible and read Ephesians 5:1-20.

GREEK WORD STUDY

These *Not A Hint* lessons have been hard-hitting! It is necessary, as a believing woman, to allow God's Word to set our standards of purity, not the world. Let's do a brief review of the Greek word for immorality:

> **Strong's Concordance**
> **porneia: fornication**
> Original Word: πορνεία, ας, ἡ
> Short Definition: fornication, idolatry

Do you notice that one of the uses for porneia is idolatry? Why is this word used in scriptures that reference idolatry? Because in the Old Testament, worshipping other gods or idols was considered adultery or breaking the relationship with God, the way that one would in an adulterous situation. We will read later in Ephesians 5 that God's relationship with Israel and the church is that of a husband with his bride. Is the activity you are involved in "cheating on God"? Or, are you, by his Spirit, remaining faithful?

Some of you may be still hanging on by a thread to this study. When challenged on watching sensual movies, dabbling in erotic talk on social messaging, or reading *50 Shades of Grey*, you may be cringing. You may be wanting some more proof that these modern-day topics are covered in the Bible. So, let's look at the phrase: "any kind of impurity" in Ephesians 5:3. What does the word "impurity" mean in the Greek? Let's see! "But among you there must not be even a hint of sexual immorality, or of any kind of impurity, or of greed, because these are improper for God's holy people." – Ephesians 5:3

> **Strong's Concordance**
> **akatharsia: uncleanness**
> Original Word: ἀκαθαρσία, ας, ἡ
> Part of Speech: Noun, Feminine
> Transliteration: akatharsia
> Phonetic Spelling: (ak-ath-ar-see'-ah)
> Short Definition: uncleanness, impurity
> Definition: uncleanness, impurity.

> **HELPS™ Word-studies**
> **Cognate: 167** *akatharsía* (from 1 /A "not" and 2513 /katharós, "clean because unmixed, pure") – ritual *impurity*, caused by leprosy, open infection, child birth, touching a corpse, etc. See 169 (*akathartos*).
> [This use of 167 /*akatharsía* occurs in the *LXX* (see Lev 9:6, 12:5, 13:11, etc.).]

THAYER'S GREEK LEXICON
STRONGS NT 167: ἀκαθαρσία

ἀκαθαρσία, (ας, ἡ (ἀκάθαρτος) (from Hippocrates down), **uncleanness;**
a. physical: <u>Matthew 23:27</u>.
b. in a moral sense, the impurity of lustful, luxurious, profligate living: <u>Romans 1:24</u>; <u>Romans 6:19</u>; <u>2 Corinthians 12:21</u>; <u>Galatians 5:19</u>; <u>Ephesians 4:19</u>; <u>Ephesians 5:3</u>; <u>Colossians 3:5</u>; <u>1 Thessalonians 4:7</u>; used of impure motives in <u>1 Thessalonians 2:3</u>. (Demosthenes, p. 553, 12.) Cf. Tittmann i., p. 150f.

The Greek word for impurity in Ephesians 5:3 has connotations of an Old Testament principle that refers to the spiritual state of a person who touched a dead body or had leprosy. The same use is found in the New Testament to describe our lives or even our bodies when we "touch" spiritually unclean things. What entertainment do you allow in your home? Is it something you would watch with Jesus? What do you allow in your mind? Do you allow a hint of sexual immorality or impurity?

CROSS REFERENCE
Hosea

In the Old Testament, the word "idolatry" is interchanged with adultery to emphasize Israel's relationship with the Lord, being like a husband and wife. The entire fourteen-chapter book of Hosea is an account of God commanding the prophet Hosea to take a wife who is a prostitute. Hosea experiences the pain of loving a wife who is unfaithful, never staying at home. This gave Hosea an empathetic look into the heart of God when his people go astray from their relationship with him.

The following subtitles are some of the verses referenced in Thayer's Greek Lexicon as being AKATHARSIA or unclean.

HOMOSEXUALITY

Therefore God gave them over in the sinful desires of their hearts to sexual impurity for the degrading of their bodies with one another. — Romans 1:24

In Romans 1:24, homosexuality is referred to using the same Greek word that is referenced in Ephesians 5. It is considered impure. This is a touchy topic in our society, but remember that has only been the way of thinking for the past few years, very recently. Compromising leaders in some pulpits and podcasts are deceiving many by saying that homosexuality is not a sin, as long as you are in a committed relationship or a marriage. There is a lot of confusion and turmoil over this issue, because it involves real people whom many of us care for deeply. The reason there is confusion is shown to us in Ephesians 4:14-15: Then we will no longer be infants, **tossed back and forth** by the waves, and **blown here and there** by every wind of teaching and by the cunning and craftiness of people in their deceitful scheming. Instead, **speaking the truth in love**, we will grow to become in every respect the mature body of him who is the head, that is, Christ. – Ephesians 4:14-15

When spiritual teachers, pastors, prophets and leaders are doing their job, you will no longer feel tossed about by the waves of society and blown about by the wind of every blogger, every opinion on YouTube, or every social media meme. Everyone has an agenda. Our agenda should be to love the Lord, know his will, obey him and follow him with all of our hearts and to love our neighbors as ourselves. So, let us dig into what the Lord says! In Ephesians 4:15 he says we are to speak the truth in love. So, even on hard matters like homosexuality, we speak the truth in love. The love of God is what leads people to repentance. The love of God compels us. No matter what tough conversation you have, it should always be framed in love with care for the person you are talking to.

Perhaps that is why those pastors and bloggers teaching error about this issue are so compelling. They distort the truth by saying all that matters is that the people involved love one another. Since love is from God, those distorting God's word say that we have no right to say homosexual love is a sin. Remember, Paul warned the Ephesians that false teachers would arise to lead people astray and that those in spiritual offices were to correctly lead and teach the church, so the people of God would not be led into sin. This is a prime example of this false teaching contradicting the Word of God. It is deceiving, because the word "love" is used and taken out of context from the full counsel of the Bible. The devil always will deceive God's people by taking the Lord's words and twisting them and taking them out of context.

Let's use a different example of when "love" may be a sin. What if I am married and "fall in love" with another man? That's still a sin, right? Yep. The world's definition of love focuses on feelings. God's definition is much different. The world's definition should not be the standard believers measure their lives against. Our standard is God's standard. Our standard is Jesus. Here, in Romans 1:24, the word "akatharsia" is used to describe homosexual relationships. Paul says in Ephesians 5:6 not to let "anyone deceive you with empty words, for because of such things God's wrath comes on those who are disobedient."

Remember to take all things to the Lord in prayer. Like any other sin with strong urges and desires, this sin or "impurity" can be cleansed and forgiven by Jesus. He loves people while they are yet sinners. Do not be deceived into thinking that God cannot change or heal someone with homosexual desires, or even that homosexual sin is their worst sin. Rosaria Butterfield, a former lesbian college professor who authored *The Secret Thoughts of an Unlikely Convert* testifies that her worst sin was unbelief. When a pastor and his wife opened their home to her and began to love her, showing her who Jesus is, her spiritual eyes began to open to her need for God. She was confronted with Jesus and his love and the outflow of that was repentance. If God can heal the person addicted to pornography, if God can heal the suicidal person, if God can bring the wayward husband or wife home and make them satisfied with their spouse, if God can heal the abused and the neglected and bring them into newness of life, God can do the same for those who do not feel aligned with their birth gender or who have unnatural desires for the same gender. Jesus died to save us and rose again to deliver us. Do not allow the devil to "rob" the cross of Christ of its power in your heart and mind. I can't possibly address this exhaustively here, but I recommend reading Butterfield's book *The Secret Thoughts of an Unlikely Convert* for unpacking this topic.

LUST

Colossians 3:1-6

[1] Since, then, you have been raised with Christ, set your hearts on things above, where Christ is, seated at the right hand of God. [2] Set your minds on things above, not on earthly things. [3] For you died, and your life is now hidden with Christ in God. [4] When Christ, who is your life, appears, then you also will appear with him in glory.

[5] Put to death, therefore, whatever belongs to your earthly nature: sexual immorality, impurity, lust, evil desires and greed, which is idolatry. [6] Because of these, the wrath of God is coming.

Again, here we have sexual immorality paired with impurity and lust. Deceivers would tell you pornography is okay, because you aren't hurting anyone. Sister, it is a sin. *50 Shades of Grey* is a book full of lust and perversions. You do not need to spice up your love life by reading a twisted person's fantasy, and then superimpose those ideas or thoughts onto your own marriage. That is defiling your marriage bed. Did you know you can defile your marriage bed? Hebrews 13:4 says, "Marriage should be honoured by all, and the marriage bed kept pure, for God will judge the adulterer and all the sexually immoral." Notice that the writer of Hebrews does not only list adultery as defiling the marriage bed. He also says sexual immorality can defile it.

Pornography is a form of prostitution. You pay money to be able to participate. Even when the model, writer, or actor is a willing, consenting adult, that does not cancel out the fact that you are sinning by lusting after them, their lusty tales, or their bodies. Need to spice up your love life? God wants you to do something daring. Bring the Holy Spirit in to heal your marriage so you can learn to enjoy each other without shame, distraction, ghosts from your past, perverted and unhealthy sexual acts, and unforgiveness.

Colossians 3:5 says that we need to put to death our earthly nature, because we are destined for glory! When I think of putting to death, a couple of pictures come to mind. One is starvation. If you do not feed your flesh, you will die physically. If you do not feed your sinful nature, your sinful nature will die. If you put restrictions on your life, not allowing a hint of immorality in your internet, social media use, movie consumption, or real life, you will start to starve your old self. Let's look at what Jesus said concerning lust.

'You have heard that it was said, "You shall not commit adultery." But I tell you that anyone who looks at a woman lustfully has already committed adultery with her in his heart. If your right eye causes you to stumble, gouge it out and throw it away. It is better for you to lose one part of your body than for your whole body to be thrown into hell. And if your right hand causes you to stumble, cut it off and throw it away. It is better for you to lose one part of your body than for your whole body to go into hell. – Matthew 5:27-30

You must replace old habits that led you into temptation with new habits and with being built up in your inner person by the Holy Spirit. We live by the Spirit, so we do not indulge the sinful nature. Ask the Lord to fill you with his Spirit, and to give you direction in taking positive steps to healing. Here are some basic ideas for cutting off things from your life that grieve or quench the Spirit and adding things that fan the Spirit into flame in your life.

It is easy for believers to point their fingers at others and say, "Well, at least I am not doing THAT sin!" We first need to get our own hearts in order, before we can pick the speck out of our brother's or sister's eye. If we don't, we may just end up bringing shame on the name of Jesus! When our hearts are in order and our thoughts and actions are submitted to the Lord, we will have the right and authority to help others walk out of temptation. But, when you do help others, make sure you don't fall yourself.

CUTTING OFF

- Repent from sin.

- Confess sin to the appropriate person.

- Do spiritual warfare, cutting off the devil's access to your life in these areas. Scripture refers to unclean spirits that can get a foothold in your life when you sin.

- Remove social media apps where you may be tempted to message people you shouldn't be talking to.

- Purge your house and accounts of movies you should not be watching. Get rid of cable, if that is a problem for you.

- End relationships that are unhealthy.

PUTTING ON

- Ask the Lord to change your heart.

- Ask the Lord to fill you with his Holy Spirit. You need to be continually filled with the Spirit of God. Your only power over things that control you is being filled with God.

- Combine social media account access with your spouse or a close friend you trust to hold you accountable.

- Get suggestions from friends of good movies. Get the Plugged In app by Focus on the Family to review movies and shows before watching.

- Seek out healthy relationships with believers who are like-minded about purity to hold each other accountable.

CROSS REFERENCE
Impure

1 Thessalonians 4:3-8

[3] It is God's will that you should be sanctified: that you should avoid sexual immorality; [4] that each of you should learn to control your own body in a way that is holy and honourable, [5] not in passionate lust like the pagans, who do not know God; [6] and that in this matter no one should wrong or take advantage of a brother or sister. The Lord will punish all those who commit such sins, as we told you and warned you before. [7] For God did not call us to be impure, but to live a holy life. [8] Therefore, anyone who rejects this instruction does not reject a human being but God, the very God who gives you his Holy Spirit.

BRINGING IT HOME

What do you teach your kids about purity? What do you expect from them? What do you expect from yourself?

Are you saying no to the Holy Spirit when it comes to your thoughts and the things you entertain in your heart? Have you been deceived into thinking that some forms of entertainment that are "hot and heavy" are actually okay for adults? Paul says that, as believers, we should not be identified with this.

Do you allow God's Word to frame your understanding of sexual purity, or the world?

Do your kids think, "Well, I will be able to watch nudity and sex scenes when I grow up?" Is this honoring Christ?

Take time to ask the Holy Spirit for wisdom and revelation into this subject area. Ask him to reveal to you the lies of the enemy that are filling your mind and heart to lead you astray.

ADDENDUM

I need to close out this section of study with this letter from the apostles in the early church to the Gentile believers. The letter is in response to those who are trying to force the Gentiles to follow the law of Moses, in order to be saved. Hopefully, this content in the book will debunk the false teachings from different camps, who may try to confuse you. One camp says that you can live however you want, sexually speaking, because we are not under the law, but under grace. The other camp says you have to follow the Jewish dietary laws in order to be saved. This is not a requirement from the scriptures. So, if you are in doubt, even if someone does Bible gymnastics and contorts the Bible every which way to make it seem to agree with his or her stance, you cannot dispute this entire letter from every apostle of Jesus and all the additional leaders in the Jerusalem church. Selah.

Acts 15:23b-29

The apostles and elders, your brothers,

To the Gentile believers in Antioch, Syria and Cilicia:

Greetings.

[24] We have heard that some went out from us without our authorisation and disturbed you, troubling your minds by what they said. [25] So we all agreed to choose some men and send them to you with our dear friends Barnabas and Paul – [26] men who have risked their lives for the name of our Lord Jesus Christ. [27] Therefore we are sending Judas and Silas to confirm by word of mouth what we are writing. [28] It seemed good to the Holy Spirit and to us not to burden you with anything beyond the following requirements: [29] You are to abstain from food sacrificed to idols, from blood, from the meat of strangled animals and from sexual immorality. You will do well to avoid these things.

Farewell.

TODAY'S BIBLE STUDY TOOL

Greek Word Study
Cross Reference

MARRIAGE RELATIONSHIPS:
WHAT IS SUBMISSION?

PRAYER

We've been studying through Ephesians and learning about unity in the body of Christ. We are about to learn from the person who created marriage how to experience unity in marriage. I implore you to pray and go into this section of the study with an open heart before the Lord. Trust that the same God who created the universe created marriage and knows your heart and your every need. Let's go before our good and glorious Father!

Father,

In the name of Jesus Christ your Son, who submitted himself to your will, I come before you in prayer. Even though Jesus was equal with you, he did not consider equality with God something to be grasped, but took on the nature of a servant. Give me your Spirit of wisdom and revelation that I can know your heart for marriage and understand the truths in this scripture. Open the eyes of my heart that I can see the hope to which you have called me and the glorious inheritance I have with all the saints. I declare right now, in the name of Jesus, that the same power that raised Jesus from the dead lives inside of me through your Spirit. I declare that I was raised up with Christ and seated with him in heavenly realms. Strengthen me in my inner being, oh Lord. Let my spirit grow and be strengthened by your power that I can be secure in my faith and in your love for me. Let those I love experience this strengthening in their inner beings, as well. Challenge them, Lord, and grow them by your Spirit, that we can all grow up in Christ together.

In Jesus' name, Amen.

Compilation of Philippians 2:6, Ephesians 1:18-20; 3:16

Today, as you meditate on our new memory verse, ask the Lord if your relationships bring God glory. Ask him how you can bring him glory, even in the little things in your relationships, as you strive to do everything to his glory.

MEMORY VERSE

[31] So whether you eat or drink or whatever you do, do it all for the glory of God. [32] Do not cause anyone to stumble. – 1 Corinthians 10:31-32a

When we talk about cooking our family delicious and healthy food that can feed their bodies and souls, we are usually thinking of things like chicken stock, broccoli, protein, garlic and other foods that build our cells, muscles and immune system. Our children don't always understand why they need to eat vegetables. They may not even like them, but if we don't encourage our children to develop an appetite for good foods when they are young, then when they are older, they will reject the idea of trying new foods that are healing and strengthening.

Let's apply this to God's Word. The verses we are about to read may be akin to learning to eat your spinach. Your children may turn their noses up at spinach, just because it's green. In fact, those bright colored vegetables probably get lots of reactions that include scrunched up faces, puckered lips and pouty eyebrows. But, it is the strong and beautiful colors that have the most nutrition. And, the less processed those veggies are, the better they can deliver the nutrition to your cells!

The strength of this passage in Ephesians may jump off the page at you with boldness that will make you recoil. You may rather just read a nice marriage book that has distilled down all of these truths into something that seems easier on the eyes. But, let's just trust the Lord and HIS ability to make these truths viable for the health of our relationships. Let's prayerfully and with open hearts read this passage! We will be doing lots of cross referencing to see how these verses stack up against other passages, too!

READING
Thirteen Verses to Heal a Marriage

Ephesians 5:21-33

²¹ Submit to one another out of reverence for Christ.

²² Wives, submit yourselves to your own husbands as you do to the Lord. ²³ For the husband is the head of the wife as Christ is the head of the church, his body, of which he is the Saviour. ²⁴ Now as the church submits to Christ, so also wives should submit to their husbands in everything.

²⁵ Husbands, love your wives, just as Christ loved the church and gave himself up for her ²⁶ to make her holy, cleansing her by the washing with water through the word, ²⁷ and to present her to himself as a radiant church, without stain or wrinkle or any other blemish, but holy and blameless. ²⁸ In this same way, husbands ought to love their wives as their own bodies. He who loves his wife loves himself. ²⁹ After all, no one ever hated their own body, but they feed and care for their body, just as Christ does the church – ³⁰ for we are members of his body. ³¹ 'For this reason a man will leave his father and mother and be united to his wife, and the two will become one flesh.' ³² This is a profound mystery – but I am talking about Christ and the church. ³³ However, each one of you also must love his wife as he loves himself, and the wife must respect her husband.

As we read this passage, there is a word that I am sure is jumping out at you: SUBMIT. Hmmmm. I am sure you are asking, "What exactly does that mean?" We should never make assumptions! We prayerfully read the text in context. In fact, verse 21 says, "Submit to one another out of reverence for Christ." So, today, we are going to do some word studies.

GREEK WORD STUDY

Let's go to biblehub.com and look up the definition of the Greek word for each of the following words or phrases in verse 21. Write that definition beside each word or phrase.

73. Submit yourselves _____

74. to one another _____

75. in _____

76. reverence _____

77. for Christ _____

Using the definitions from the Greek, can you make your own translation, freshly worded, using descriptive words that are true to the original Greek?

Our command from the Lord, in light of everything we have been learning, is not surprising. We are in relationship with one another and it requires a servant-like attitude. The idea communicated in this first verse that segues into marriage is that we are to lower ourselves into a position or attitude of respect and obedience to one another. This attitude is commanded within the body of Christ, and it is also to happen within our marriages. There is nothing in this verse in particular that says only wives must submit. It says everyone must submit to each other. It does specify a wife's role later in the chapter, but this verse says that we ALL must submit to each other. To put it more simply, we must all live less for ourselves and more for others.

Let's think deeper on this, using the Greek word study we just did.

78. Who is verse 21 talking about?

79. What are we supposed to do?

80. Why are we motivated to do this?

81. How are we supposed to do this?

The reason we need to dig deeper when we study is because there is so much more that God wants to teach us. He doesn't want us to make assumptions with our minds and put up walls because of our culture or upbringing. I call this living in revelation instead of living in reaction. We need more of God's leading through his Spirit and scripture, and less of our own reasoning based on personal reactions to people who put a bad taste in our mouths. Coming to grips with a scriptural truth is important, because our faith in his Word means trusting our good Father in heaven. We want to understand why he designed this truth for us and what it looks like. Since submission is one of those topics, I decided to dig deeper! When I did the word study, I wasn't surprised by the definition of the word "submit." I was surprised by the phrase "reverence for Christ."

Let's look at the word reverence.

> **Strong's Concordance**
> **phobos: panic flight, fear, the causing of fear, terror**
> Original Word: φόβος, ου, ὁ
> Part of Speech: Noun, Masculine
> Transliteration: phobos
> Phonetic Spelling: (fob'-os)
> Short Definition: fear, terror, reverence
> Definition: (a) fear, terror, alarm, (b) the object or cause of fear, (c) reverence, respect.

The first thing I notice is the root word phobos. Definitely this is the root of our English word phobia. When I think of the word "reverence," I think of respect. However, the root seems to indicate fear. The New American Standard Exhaustive Concordance says that the word origin is phebomai, which means "to be put to flight." The question is, do we have a healthy fear of the Lord in our relationships, and what does that look like concerning submission? The story that comes to mind is the parable of the unforgiving servant. Jesus told this story.

CROSS REFERENCE
Example of "Fear of the Lord"

Open your Bible to Matthew 18:21-35 and read the parable.

The servant who took the master's grace lightly and with personal arrogance and NO FEAR of what the master would do, since his debt was forgiven, held bitterness and contempt for his fellow servant who owed him LESS than he had owed the master. God expects us to walk in a healthy fear of him in our relationships with our fellow human beings. We are not to lord it over others who have wronged us, just as the Lord does not lord it over us but forgives us our great debt of sin. He set us free, and now we live in submission to one another, the way that Christ lowered himself to become a sacrifice for our sins which he was not responsible for. He is our example. We live in such a huge debt to Christ, and what he asks us to do is to live in love and in submission to one another, to show we are God's children.

Notice that there is a punishment involved for the servant who sinned by not forgiving the debt owed to him. He is to be handed over to the jailers to be tortured, until he should pay back all he owed. We have already studied in Ephesians that if we allow the sun to go down on our wrath, anger, or irritation—without forgiving—that we make room for the devil. What is the purpose of God allowing this intrusion of the enemy into a believer's life? We see the reason here. It is for the end game of driving the servant to pay back his debt. What is his debt? His debt is to forgive, out of love and reverence for his master. Now, like the servant in the story, our only debt is to forgive those who have hurt us, out of love and reverence for Christ.

> Let no debt remain outstanding, except the continuing debt to love one another, for whoever loves others has fulfilled the law. – Romans 13:8

> Love is patient, love is kind. It does not envy, it does not boast, it is not proud. It does not dishonour others, it is not self-seeking, it is not easily angered, it keeps no record of wrongs. Love does not delight in evil but rejoices with the truth. It always protects, always trusts, always hopes, always perseveres. Love never fails. – 1 Corinthians 13:4-8a

Submitting to one another out of reverence for Christ means loving others the way Christ loves us. Ask yourself—am I impatient? Am I unkind? Am I dishonoring my spouse? Am I seeking my own gain? Am I easily angered—even if it is merely displayed with eye rolling, the silent treatment or ignoring? Am I keeping a record of wrongs? Do I delight secretly when my spouse 'gets what he deserves'? If I am living in these ways, I am not living in submission to my spouse out of reverence for Christ.

We all know that some spouses are difficult to live with! (Aren't we all?) Remember that the fellow servant of the unmerciful servant owed him a debt. He wasn't a perfect person who owed nothing to the first servant. The point is that as a forgiven servant of the Lord, you need to make sure that you are walking in love and forgiveness. If you have not chosen to do this, not only is God unable to forgive you of your sins, but you also may be living in a certain measure of captivity, spiritually speaking. You may be bound up in depression, fear, anger, bitterness or hatred and unable to love. One woman I know, who has been to hell and back in her personal family relationships, told me this: "Living in bitterness and unforgiveness is like drinking poison and expecting someone else to die." God doesn't want any of his children chained up in unforgiveness. The purpose of the master's edict is to drive the servant back to the master's heart. Our God is a God of forgiveness and love. Jesus sacrificed and submitted to his Father's will to build us up. He became a suffering servant to bring us freedom and life. A wife can choose to build up her husband or to tear him down. Submission is a building up.

When you first fall in love and are getting to know each other, you always put your best foot forward. The guy and girl try to impress each other and are looking for the best in the potential spouse. However, after some time, life, children and reality hit. Disappointments, discouragement and other downers drip, drip, drip onto our lives like Chinese water torture. Before you know it, bitterness has a foothold in your relationship. This is all rooted in the unforgiveness of those things that make you feel bitter.

Most people sweep things under the rug to keep the peace, but the piles accumulate, anyway. This is why you start to resent when the other person needs you because your needs aren't being met. To fear the Lord and to live in reverence for him, as we submit to one another, is to take the advice of the parable of the unforgiving servant that Jesus told us.

Instead of fighting to get our way, Jesus wants us to love one another and defer to each other with grace and mercy. Instead of wanting to be first, he wants us to volunteer to be last, as he was! Jesus is our example. Jesus is Lord of the universe. If submission to my needs and to the will of the Father is the best for the King of kings and Lord of lords, it's the best for me.

Here is a famous story of a rich man who really seems eager to follow Jesus. He has everything he wants in this world, but wants to make sure he is set for eternity, too. Jesus wants to see where his heart is and if he truly wants to follow God. He ends this story with the famous verse, "Many who are first will be last, and the last will be first."

Open your Bible to Mark 10:17-31 to read this second parable of Jesus on our relationships with one another.

When we lay down our own wants and needs and put others first, for the sake of Christ and the kingdom, that is true love. I think our marriages would be much, much better if we all decided to do what is best for our husbands, even if hubby isn't in a good mood or if the sacrifice hurts. Sacrifice is something that we give up to God, with no expectations of reward or compensation. Ask the Lord today if your heart is open to taking on Christ's attitude. Becoming more like Christ is reward or compensation in itself and is enough!

BRINGING IT HOME

Do you teach submission in your home? Do you submit to others in your home to lift them up? Jesus was a servant leader. He led by example. He washed his disciples' feet. The Ultimate Servant was the real-life Undercover Boss. The one who deserved to be venerated asks only that we venerate him by washing each other's feet and living lives of submission and humility toward one another.

SUBMISSION WITHOUT FEAR

PRAYER

I kneel before you, Father in heaven, from whom your whole family in heaven and on earth derives its name. My family derives its name from you. May we live for you and in your truth, Lord. I pray that out of your glorious riches you may strengthen me with power through your Spirit in my inner being, so that Christ may dwell in my heart through faith. Give me faith to trust your plan for marriage and for relationships. Take away my pride and help me to put others first, instead of living in selfishness, the way that Jesus put me first and died for all of my sin. I pray that my family, being rooted and established in love, may have power, together with all the Lord's holy people, to grasp how wide and long and high and deep is the love of Christ, and to know this love that surpasses knowledge—that we may be filled to the measure of all the fullness of God. May we live in this fullness of unity, Lord. May we walk in the power of submission and humility. Now to him who is able to do immeasurably more than all we ask or imagine, according to his power that is at work within us, to him be glory in the church and in Christ Jesus throughout all generations, for ever and ever!

Amen.

Adapted from Ephesians 3:14-21

MEMORY VERSE

[31] So whether you eat or drink or whatever you do, do it all for the glory of God. [32] Do not cause anyone to stumble. – 1 Corinthians 10:31-32a

READING

Ephesians 5:21-33

[21] Submit to one another out of reverence for Christ.

[22] Wives, submit yourselves to your own husbands as you do to the Lord. [23] For the husband is the head of the wife as Christ is the head of the church, his body, of which he is the Saviour. [24] Now as the church submits to Christ, so also wives should submit to their husbands in everything.

[25] Husbands, love your wives, just as Christ loved the church and gave himself up for her [26] to make her holy, cleansing her by the washing with water through the word, [27] and to present her to himself as a radiant church, without stain or wrinkle or any other blemish, but holy and blameless. [28] In this same way, husbands ought to love their wives as their own bodies. He who loves his wife loves himself. [29] After all, no one ever hated their own body, but they feed and care for their body, just as Christ does the church – [30] for we are members of his body. [31] 'For this reason a man will leave his father and mother and be united to his wife, and the two will become one flesh.' [32] This is a profound mystery – but I am talking about Christ and the church. [33] However, each one of you also must love his wife as he loves himself, and the wife must respect her husband.

Why are we scared when we read a passage like this? Whether it is the woman or the man, no one wants to read it! I just heard a sermon where the pastor said that as a young believer, he was mortified to read that God expected his love for his wife to be the same as Christ's sacrificial love for the church. So, whether you are the woman or the man, most people recoil at the thought of their own responsibility before the Lord. These reactions are rooted in pride and fear. No one wants to end up with the short end of the stick. Everyone wants their needs met, and I believe that we end up in fear when we think that God wants us to be short-changed and miserable. God has the best for you! He created marriage so that we wouldn't be alone, not so that we could be suffering slaves.

I have to say that writing this day of study is not an easy one for me. I have a strong personality and learning how to submit the personality God gave me in the way that God requires in relationships has been a long walk. I think that God did a lot of work in me as a teenager, when I would not want to submit to my parents. Thank the Lord, he gave me a dad who could stand up to my defiant attitude, and earn my respect in the process. As a teen, I was mostly concerned with whether or not I thought everything was fair. I have always had a high sense of justice. As an adult, I know that God has the highest sense of justice, and he is the perfect judge. He created marriage to be a union and a partnership of love, balance, sharing and sacrifice. Learning to love and submit to each other's needs is not a loss; it is a win. In marriage, the husband and wife are one in God's eyes. He created this oneness and the balances within it for our own enjoyment and security. Do not be afraid of God's plan.

CONTRAST & COMPARISON

Let's look, without fear, into the perfect law of the Lord! Let's compare and contrast the expectations of Wives vs Husbands in this passage.

WIVES	HUSBANDS
_____	_____
_____	_____
_____	_____
_____	_____
_____	_____

So, now that the tally is added up, which person seems to have the greatest burden from God in the relationship? It seems pretty much hands down to be the husband who is carrying the biggest burden from the Lord. He is to be willing to sacrificially love his wife as Christ loved the Church and lay his life down for her.

Paul sets husbands beside Jesus as an example of the positive power a man has to build up his wife. In verses 26-27 what does Jesus do for his bride? What does Jesus do to make his bride holy?

Here we see the power of the Word of God to wash us—men and women. We are all part of the bride of Christ. This is one powerful picture of why we need to read the Bible in a prayerful, interactive way with Jesus. As we prayerfully read the scriptures, his Word washes us, making us radiant.

In the same way, I have seen godly men take this calling to be like Christ to their families very seriously. I am so proud of my two brothers. Both have young families and make it a priority to read the scriptures daily aloud to their wives and children. It is not a religious ritual, but I know they both believe that it is their responsibility to encourage and support their families with the Word of

God. They both saw strong, loving, servant spiritual headship modeled by our father and they are passing this heritage on to their families. If you are not married to a man who is willing to do this, you are able to read the Word of God to your children on your own. Jesus is the one who will wash them with the Word. You just need to get that Word into your children. Create a love in them for it!

I have recently read some shocking materials from certain Christian sects that imply that women cannot understand the Word of God without their husbands or fathers to teach it to them. That is not scriptural. It is a twisting of scriptural truths concerning spiritual authority and completely ignores other scriptures. Should husbands and fathers be teaching scripture to their families? Yes! Do their wives and daughters have the Holy Spirit to direct them and minds able to understand God's Word if their husbands and fathers aren't doing a good job leading spiritually? Double Yes! Should women and children seek the scriptures with confidence, because God wants a personal relationship with each person, where he reveals his truth to the individual freely? Yes. This is how Jesus washes the bride of Christ with the water of the Word. The godly husband functions as a type of Christ—this means he represents Christ—in the marriage relationship to reflect the loving, servant-like, spiritual headship that Jesus has over the church.

The husband is expected by God to actually be willing to die for his wife and children. This is not just talking about physical death, but also to work hard for them and to sacrifice himself for their physical, emotional, mental and spiritual needs. THIS IS ALSO SUBMISSION. When we think about this role, it mirrors what Jesus did for us. He traded his life for our lives. Of course, we should be willing to honor our husbands, if they are required by God to die for us. Paul also seems to detail more of the expectations on husbands to be spiritual leaders and protectors, as well as to show genuine love. We will look at this more tomorrow.

CROSS REFERENCE
Wives

Now, let's do a cross reference to see what other scriptures speak to a wife's role in the marriage. Read the following passage.

1 Peter 3:1-6 (NASB)

[1] In the same way, you wives, be submissive to your own husbands so that even if any of them are disobedient to the word, they may be won without a word by the behavior of their wives, [2] as they observe your chaste and respectful behavior. [3] Your adornment must not be merely external—braiding the hair, and wearing gold jewelry, or putting on dresses; [4] but let it be the hidden person of the heart, with the imperishable quality of a gentle and quiet spirit, which is precious in the sight of God. [5] For in this way in former times the holy women also, who hoped in God, used to adorn themselves, being submissive to their own husbands; [6] just as Sarah obeyed Abraham, calling him lord, and you have become her children if you do what is right without being frightened by any fear.

82. <u>Underline</u> all the words/phrases that show WHY women are to submit to their husbands.

83. Circle all the POSITIVE attributes that God sees in a woman who loves him. These are attributes that you would also hope your son would look for in a woman.

All of these types of verses may seem to go against what our current culture teaches us. But, maybe, just maybe, since the Bible is the inspired Word of God, and it's been around longer than our culture, we could assert that our culture is against the Word of God. But, let's dig deeper!

God is calling the wife to enter into a relationship with her husband who is expected to lay down his life for her. Men are supposed to love their wives the way that Christ loved the church and laid his life down for her. This means that men aren't supposed to consider their authority as something to "lord over" their wives. They are to operate in humility and mutual submission to their wives in love. Our response as women should be to give our husbands the same respect that we give Jesus. Instead of walking all over Jesus' submission and his gift of grace, we venerate him and respect his gift by obeying his commandments. Another word that may help you better than commandments is "will." When you know what someone you respect cares about, you know their will, and because you respect them so much, you will be committed to making sure that their will happens, within godly boundaries. If your husband is against you being a Christian or going to church, you are not required to submit to his will that you disobey the Lord. If he asks you to watch pornography to spice up your married life, you do not need to submit to that sin.

A positive example of godly submission would be dealing with finances. My husband and I both work. We both make money. He happens to currently be the one who is in charge of keeping the books. There were other times I was in charge of it. However, whatever happens in our budget is something that we pray about and discuss together. We listen to each other. Sometimes we come to an impasse. We try to work around it. However, there are times when I just need to defer to him on some things. Honestly, someone has to give. Often times, he will hear me out and sacrifice to make something happen that is important to me. Other times, I have to sacrifice. But, again, if there is an impasse, I try to submit to his will. This allows the blessing of God to rest on me, because by submitting to my husband's authority, I am submitting to God's authority.

Now, I personally have not seen a healthy Christian relationship where the husband is giving out harsh commands to the wife. If he is walking in what the Lord requires of him, he will not behave like that. But, the wife should know what things matter to her husband and respect his needs and desires, the way that the husband should love his wife and take care for her needs and desires. My husband may call and ask me to make sure something gets done at home before he gets off of work. But, of course, I, in turn, ask him to go out of his way to run an errand on the way home. We should cheerfully serve one another!

Contrary to popular new public opinion, men and women are different. They are created differently by God. There is certainly space for personality variations, tastes and other unique qualities within each gender; however, there are distinct differences. Men have the God-given need to be respected. Women have the God-given need to be loved. We both need love and respect, but there is a spiritual truth in God's Word that teaches us that husbands specifically need respect. Even so, given all the different personality types out there, each marriage can look very different from house to house and still be godly. So, don't get caught in the comparison/jealousy game. Some people have stronger personalities and others are more laid back. God calls everyone, no matter what their strengths or weaknesses to submit the entirety of their personality to the Lord so that he can work mightily in every marriage and bless it.

Are we afraid of respecting our husbands? Are we afraid of giving up ourselves and not getting in return what God says is due to us? At the end of this passage in Peter, it says that, "Sarah obeyed Abraham, calling him lord, and you have become her children, if you do what is right without being frightened by fear." Fear is one of the biggest stumbling blocks to our faith. I don't think that it's just women who are afraid. I think men become afraid, too. We are all afraid to do what God requires of us. What are we afraid will happen? Are we afraid that if we respect someone or love someone sacrificially that we won't have our needs met? Are we afraid of being used? Are we afraid of being demeaned? Are we afraid of not getting our way? Are we afraid of always being miserable and never being happy? Do we trust God to be our source of joy, even during the times when our husbands are not living up to their end of the bargain?

Happiness is fleeting, when it is based upon circumstances. Feelings can be up one day and down the next. If I decided to base all my relationship decisions upon my feelings, I would feel like I live on a yo-yo. I am not saying this hypothetically. I am saying this after 21 years of marriage. Many of those years were lived in obedience to my emotional frame of mind and not to Christ's truth. The emotional vortex I live in at times can be influenced by hormones, pressures at work, lack of sleep, anxieties about my children, or on the flip side, an abundance of great coffee, time with friends, and feeling like I've lost weight and gotten a lot of de-cluttering done around the house! Happiness is never listed as a fruit of the Spirit, but many Christian women are looking for this as a thermometer to gauge the progress or status of their marriage.

What is the fruit of the Spirit we should look for in our relationship with God and with one another? We find out about this fruit in Galatians 5. "But the fruit of the Spirit is love, joy, peace, forbearance, kindness, goodness, faithfulness, gentleness and self-control. Against such things there is no law. Those who belong to Christ Jesus have crucified the flesh with its passions and desires. Since we live by the Spirit, let us keep in step with the Spirit. Let us not become conceited, provoking and envying each other." – Galatians 5:22-26

When we walk in submission to the Spirit of God, the result will be love, joy, peace, patience, kindness, goodness, faithfulness, gentleness and self-control. You can get your way every day of the year and not walk in peace. You can have everything you want and not have joy or love. These are qualities that most people are seeking in their lives. Celebrities at the top of their career have come out saying that you can have everything you ever wanted in life and still be miserable. The fulfilled life is life in Christ. It is a life of humility that tells the hungry, dissatisfied parts of our soul to be filled with Jesus. There is so much peace when we submit our lives and our marriages to the way the Lord calls us to live. Peace doesn't come all at once. It is acquired through a daily process of walking in the Lord and learning to be like Jesus.

BRINGING IT HOME

Today, if you are struggling with this concept of submission, take time to seek God and ask him to REVEAL to you, by his Spirit, what is standing in the way of your receiving this truth. You may need to ask him to reveal to you worldly mind frames that need uprooting so that you can walk in freedom in your marriage. Pray for God to remove the fear and other stormy things in your soul that need replaced by tranquility.

TRICKY SUBMISSION SITUATIONS
ABUSE, SIN, CONFLICT

PRAYER

Father,

I ask you to give me the Spirit of wisdom and revelation that I can understand the deep things of God. I want hope for my relationships in Christ. I know that when I talk to you, you hear me and you are mighty to save and to bring to pass all that I need. Teach me the difference between respecting authority and not condoning abuse. Help me to know the difference between a relationship that is struggling and one that is truly abusive. I need revelation on this, Lord. Teach me your ways.

In Jesus' name, Amen.

Adapted from Ephesians 1:17-18

MEMORY VERSE

[31] So whether you eat or drink or whatever you do, do it all for the glory of God. [32] Do not cause anyone to stumble. – 1 Corinthians 10:31-32a

Look at our prayer from Ephesians Chapter 3:

For this reason I kneel before the Father, from whom every family in heaven and on earth derives its name. – Ephesians 3:14-15

The whole family derives its name from the Father in heaven. There is authority in a name. There is power in a name. Just like our Father in heaven has authority and power over his family, which he sent his Son to die for and redeem, he has given authority to people in the family, and in the church. He has given spiritual authority to men over their households. He has given parents authority over their children and even children have authority over sin and the devil. When we buck the authority of the family, we are sinning against God, and we undercut our own position and power. We reject God's plan. Now spiritual authority is not the same as just any old kind of earthly authority. It is powerful. We want to benefit from the blessings of our husbands' authority. We want to pray for and boost up our husbands. You are his warrior princess, fighting the good fight of the faith beside him. Together, defend your family, your communities and the very souls of your children from the enemy's tactics! What God has brought together, let no man put asunder.

In spite of all of this, sometimes, men and women use the authority God has given them to sin through abusing the people under their authority. The results can be devastating. What does a person do, when he or she is trapped in a situation where sin is abounding in a place of authority?

READING

Open your Bible and read Ephesians 5:21-33

1 Peter 3:1-7 (NASB)

[1] In the same way, you wives, be submissive to your own husbands so that even if any of them are disobedient to the word, they may be won without a word by the behavior of their wives, [2] as they observe your chaste and respectful behavior. [3] Your adornment must not be merely external—braiding the hair, and wearing gold jewelry, or putting on dresses; [4] but let it be the hidden person of the heart, with the imperishable quality of a gentle and quiet spirit, which is precious in the sight of God. [5] For in this way in former times the holy women also, who hoped in God, used to adorn themselves, being submissive to their own husbands; [6] just as Sarah obeyed Abraham, calling him lord, and you have become her children if you do what is right without being frightened by any fear.

[7] You husbands in the same way, live with your wives in an understanding way, as with someone weaker, since she is a woman; and show her honor as a fellow heir of the grace of life, so that your prayers will not be hindered.

84. What does 1 Peter 3:7 say will happen to the husband who does not live with his wife in an understanding way?

85. What happens to him if he takes advantage of her physical weakness, or does not honor the fact that he is stronger than she is, or doesn't treat her as a fellow heir of grace and of life?

86. 1 Peter 3:3-4 says women need reminded of where their beauty comes from. Where does it come from?

ABUSE? NO WAY!

Does being submissive mean that you give in to sin or abuse? No. I do not see that here and I do not see any scripture that agrees with that. Even children are not required to obey parents that are asking them to sin or disobey God.

Children, obey your parents in the Lord, for this is right. – Ephesians 6:1

But, that is not what this passage is speaking to. It is not asking you to submit to abuse. You do need to forgive the abuser, so you can walk in freedom. Forgiving an abuser does NOT mean you go back to him. Doing that is not love and it is not a sign of forgiveness. Love does not enable abusive or damaging patterns of behavior. If you are in a physically or emotionally abusive situation, please get help immediately! Break the chains of sin in your family by getting help. In situations of physical abuse, get help by taking yourself and any children you have to a safe place like a women's shelter or a safe home of a family or friend.

CROSS REFERENCE
1 Samuel 25

1 Samuel 25 gives us a riveting example from the Bible of a beautiful, righteous woman dealing with an out of control and abusive husband. 1 Samuel 25:3b says, "She was an intelligent and beautiful woman, but her husband was surly and mean in his dealings."

This chapter in the Old Testament tells the tale of a beautiful and intelligent wife who almost loses her life due to her husband's crass and wicked behavior. Take time to read this account of how Abigail saved her own life and the lives of hundreds of people—including her family—by going against her husband's wishes.

Background information—David was anointed by the prophet Samuel to succeed King Saul as King of Israel. David loved Saul and his family. He was married to Saul's daughter. However, Saul turned from God and grew bitter and full of demonic rage. He tried to kill David and even took his wife away from him. David is on the run from Saul with 400 fighting men who are loyal to him. They spend their time protecting Israel's borders and running from Saul. David doesn't try to engage Saul in battle or take the throne by force. David is waiting for God's justice and doesn't want to "touch God's anointed," even though he is anointed himself. He has shown incredible self-control and is a man after God's heart. Even though David was not in a marriage relationship with Saul, submission is a transferable concept. David was in a position of submission to a wicked, angry king who happened to be his father-in-law. This is an example of a man honoring another man's authority while running from his abuse. He didn't stay in the palace. He ran. He got help by inviting other men to come alongside his cause. He honored the King's anointed position by refraining from killing Saul with his own hands when he had an opportunity. This is an example of what a wife should do if she is in an abusive situation in her home. She is free to run from it and get help. No one should ever tell you to stay in a situation or to go back to a situation where you are in danger.

When we come upon this story of Abigail, David's men are protecting her husband's extensive property for free, out of the goodness of their hearts. Open your Bible and read 1 Samuel Chapter 25.

ASK QUESTIONS

87. Why are Nabel's actions considered wicked?

88. Why is Abigail's action considered righteous?

89. How does Abigail keep David from sinning?

90. Does Abigail try to hide her actions from Nabel?

91. Is Abigail being dishonoring to her husband?

92. Abigail calls David master. Why?

93. Does the Bible picture her as a "low-life" servant? She calls herself a servant. Does she seem to be thinking poorly about herself? How would you describe the way she is portrayed in this story?

TODAY'S BIBLE STUDY TOOL

Ask Questions. Lots of questions. Have you ever noticed that this is one way that small children learn about their world? This is the beginning of your discovery about the facts of the passage you are reading. Why? Who? When? How?

What about other situations that aren't so severe, like being married to a non-believer who isn't into the whole loving-you-like-Christ thing? Or, what if you are married to a believer and he sins against you by not loving you the way that Christ loved the church? This is not an abuse situation, but just a failure to love, or harshness, or selfishness. Gotta admit it, we all struggle in these ways sometimes, right? Selfishness manifests in many different ways. Let's explore this!

PRACTICAL APPLICATION
Conflict from Everyday Sin

Let's first address the believing man who hasn't matured in Christ in the area of loving you the way you need to be loved. Maybe he is demanding, lazy, impatient or harsh. Are you still required to obey Christ by showing him respect? You tell me. Does his sin or weakness justify my sin? No, it doesn't. I will only be held accountable for my own personal behavior. I can't control my spouse, but I CAN control myself! Boy, this is hard!

Imagine times when you have been impatient or harsh with your husband. Don't you appreciate when he is gracious to you in the middle of your weaknesses? When I personally think of these times in my marriage, I know that I need to give my husband grace in his weaknesses the way he gives me grace in my weaknesses. If you do not have a husband who gives you grace in your weaknesses, then you need to look to Christ as your example. (Well, we all need to do that in the first place!) Christ gives you grace in the middle of your sin. Romans 5 says, "While we were yet sinners, Christ died for us." When I remember my debt to the Lord and his grace towards me, it helps me to forgive those who are in debt to me. Now I can pray for him and I can definitely have constructive conversations with him about my feelings. There is nothing in scripture that prohibits a wife from challenging her husband in love. Just be careful how you do it. Pray about it first. Don't be surprised, if you challenge or disrespect your husband in front of the kids, that your children will take it as a green light to do the same to you. Also, disrespecting a man in front of his children is akin to a declaration of war. He may even see certain things as disrespect or embarrassment that you will not view the same way. This is where submission is required. Do unto others, as you would have them do unto you. Think of when your husband may think you are over-reacting to a situation. Do you wish he would simply be sensitive to your needs, even if he doesn't understand? This is the same courtesy you should give your husband, when you don't understand his needs. Give him the grace you want extended to you. Back to the timing of addressing a conflict, remember how Abigail waited for the right time to talk to her husband? She didn't talk to him when he was drunk, but she was completely up front with him when it was time to talk. She didn't try to hide, or lie, or sneak around. When a woman or man is afraid of conflict and being honest

> **TODAY'S BIBLE STUDY TOOL**
>
> **Practical Application.** How can I personally apply this scripture to my life today? What changes do I need to make? What prayer should I pray? Don't forget to ask the Holy Spirit for help!

with those they are in relationship with, the weakness can lead to a tendency to lie or be dishonest in order to keep the other person from being angry. The enemy can even lie to you to make you believe that your spouse will react in a way you loathe, to help you justify lying or hiding. This will subtly teach your children that lying is appropriate, when it suits your needs. You may wake up to find yourself with children who have learned to sneak, hide, or be one person to your face and another person behind your back.

WHAT IF YOUR KIDS SEE AN ARGUMENT?

It's not ideal, but God established marriage as a greenhouse to raise godly children in. Godly children need to understand that healthy marriages have obstacles to overcome. He establishes the authority of the father and mother in the home. If one of the spouses disrespects the other's authority in front of the children, this is a double whammy. I once heard John and Lisa Bevere say that if they ever fight in front of their children, their children have to see them apologize and make up! It's only fair that if they see the transgression, they then see the redemption! We say, "I'm sorry for sinning against Mommy or Daddy by being harsh or disrespectful. The way we talked didn't honor God or each other and it put you in a bad situation, when you had to listen to it. Will you please forgive us? We will pray and work together to make sure this doesn't happen again." The children learn to reciprocate by saying, "We forgive you." In this way, they learn humility and that forgiveness is done with our will, not our emotions. They also see that you are human. Adults sin. Adults can also grow in Christ and in relationships through confession, repentance and forgiveness. This is, perhaps, the most important lesson you can model for your children.

Conflict is a normal part of home life. Human beings tend to have differences of opinions, personality conflicts, selfishness and weaknesses. Learning to submit to your husband means learning how to handle conflict in a way that is healthy. Instead of demeaning him and disrespecting him, pray about how to approach conflict in a loving and prayerful way. You will definitely need the Holy Spirit on this. It's impossible to be loving when you are angry and hurt. This needs a supernatural intervention! When we pray, we bring Jesus into the situation. When we pray for revelation, the Holy Spirit can soften our hearts and maybe even show us the other person's perspective!

BRINGING IT HOME

Remember that if we love Jesus Christ, all things are possible for our marriages. God can bring health and balance back to our relationships in a way that we never thought possible. There are issues you may feel alone in, but remember that with Jesus you are never alone. Jesus is in your marriage with you, whether you are married to a believer or a non-believer. Either way, you have the ear of the Father. You are seated in heavenly realms with him. He is ready to go to battle for you and for your family!

WITHOUT A WORD
A TRANQUIL SPIRIT

PRAYER
Prayer for Your Spouse

I keep asking you, God of our Lord Jesus Christ, the glorious Father, that you may give me your Spirit of wisdom and revelation, so that I may know you better.

I ask that you will also reach into my husband's heart with your Spirit of wisdom and revelation, and speak truth and conviction to him, in Jesus' name. I pray that you will wake him from death to life. Let him see Jesus. I pray also that the eyes of his heart may be enlightened in order that he may know the hope he has in Christ. Let him see that he needs you in everything. Lord, let him hear your call and respond, in Jesus' name.

May my husband be a partaker in the riches of the glorious inheritance in the saints. May he value your riches more than the riches of this world. I declare that this same incomparably great power that is in me, is right now convicting him and drawing him by your love. That power is like the working of your mighty strength, which you exerted in Christ when you raised him from the dead and seated him at your right hand in the heavenly realms, far above all rule and authority, power and dominion and every title that can be given, not only in the present life but also in the one to come. Raise up my husband in Christ, in Jesus' name. Raise him up, Lord. Call him up into his purpose for your kingdom. And place my husband's life, destiny, heart, spirit, and very being under your feet. Christ, be head over my husband. Include him in your body, the fullness of him who fills everything in every way.

Amen.

Adapted from Ephesians 1:17-23

MEMORY VERSE

[31] So whether you eat or drink or whatever you do, do it all for the glory of God. [32] Do not cause anyone to stumble. – 1 Corinthians 10:31-32a

READING

1 Peter 3:1-7 (NASB)

[1] In the same way, you wives, be submissive to your own husbands so that even if any of them are disobedient to the word, they may be won without a word by the behavior of their wives, [2] as they observe your chaste and respectful behavior. [3] Your adornment must not be merely external—braiding the hair, and wearing gold jewelry, or putting on dresses; [4] but let it be the hidden person of the heart, with the imperishable quality of a gentle and quiet spirit, which is precious in the sight of God. [5] For in this way in former times the holy women also, who hoped in God, used to adorn themselves, being submissive to their own husbands; [6] just as Sarah obeyed Abraham, calling him lord, and you have become her children if you do what is right without being frightened by any fear.

[7] You husbands in the same way, live with your wives in an understanding way, as with someone weaker, since she is a woman; and show her honor as a fellow heir of the grace of life, so that your prayers will not be hindered.

WITHOUT A WORD?

Many women bristle at the wording in 1 Peter 3 when it describes submissive behavior as doing so "without a word" (v1), "not merely external" (v3), "gentle and quiet spirit" (v4), and "calling him lord" (v6). Should our initial reaction be to dismiss—as old-fashioned and cultural—God's Word and the writings in it by the apostle Peter who lived with Jesus for three years, who heard all of his teachings and saw all of his miracles, who raised the dead himself, and ultimately was crucified upside down on a burning cross for Christ? I would encourage you to take the alternative route of prayer and deeper study to help you find what God is saying through the apostle Peter to women here.

Let's pray and then look at the contrasts between what God says we should do versus what he says we shouldn't do. Some of the verses will have clear, stated contrasts. Some of the positive behaviors listed have implied negative contrasts that aren't stated. Ask yourself and the Lord what some of these contrasts may be in your life, if you are married. If you aren't married, you can still prayerfully ask the Lord to give you insight into this.

	DO	DON'T
Verse 1		
Verse 2		
Verse 3		
Verse 4		
Verse 5		
Verse 6		

Do you interpret the phrase "without a word," and the phrases about clothing and jewelry as prohibiting women from having equal standing with men? If that were true, Peter wouldn't instruct the husband to honor his wife's femininity and treat her as a fellow heir of the grace of life. The teaching is clear that BOTH the man AND the woman should value the inner person of the woman—not just look at her as a physical being who is only valuable for physical intimacy and beauty.

In a world that increasingly brings confusion to the value and place of a woman, this clearly gives us a breath of fresh air. The world says women now need to work like a man all day long, come home and have the house beautiful, the kids well-educated and well-rounded, make as much money as a man, bear the emotional weight of the household, be in perfect health and physical shape, and dress like a sex object. There is utter confusion abounding about gender roles, and the demands on women are overwhelming. This passage clears the air.

What is valuable in a woman in God's sight? A spirit that is at peace—an inner life with God that shines with more beauty than you can buy at any salon, gym or jewelry store. That is what really makes the difference in your relationships. The word "quiet spirit" in the Greek actually means tranquility. God desires our hearts and homes to be full of tranquility. When we work to create a tranquil home, full of respect where individuals are honored and not put down, even a man who is living in disobedience to God notices the difference—this can be a believer who is not obeying God or a non-believer. The power of Christ in a woman can move mountains!

As for the verse about the woman being weaker, let's dig into this! God wants our husbands to lift our burden in areas we are lacking. Guys don't like to show weakness, but God is letting a man know that it is A-OK for him to acknowledge and honor any areas where his wife may need help and give her that help. This may mean helping her by dealing with a rebellious teenage son, carrying that heavy load of laundry up the stairs—even if you are strong and in great shape, changing a dirty diaper, unloading the dishwasher, driving kids to sports activities or getting out of the car in the rain and changing that tire on the side of the road. Our society would say it is demeaning to the woman to imply she can't do these things, but I would like to know who decided that serving someone is demeaning to the person being served?

God gave our husbands to us to honor us and love us. Once, when an old woman was talking to a sweet younger woman who did not grow up with a father, the young lady relayed her hesitations about her new Christian boyfriend buying her flowers and paying for her expenses on dates. The elderly lady listened prayerfully and intently as the college girl espoused what the world had told her—that this was demeaning and somehow showed that she wasn't an equal. Then the Lord showed her what to share to encourage her young friend.

> "God loves you so much. He loves you in many ways. One of the ways that he chooses to show us love is through the men in our lives. You were never loved by a father, but God is now showing you what it is to be loved by a man. God requires godly men to honor and serve their wives the way Christ loved the church. When you deny this young man the ability to lift you up the way Christ lifts you up, you deny him the right to obey God, and you also reject the love God is giving you through him."

The young woman's eyes grew big and round. She gave me a big hug. So simple and so beautiful, yet this truth is rejected by the world. The more our world rejects Christ, the more unhealthy our relationships become.

Let's look at how God commands a man to love his wife. In the following passage,

- Circle every command to husbands.

- Underline any similes that compare the husband's role to Christ's role.

Ephesians 5:25-33

[25] Husbands, love your wives, just as Christ loved the church and gave himself up for her [26] to make her holy, cleansing her by the washing with water through the word, [27] and to present her to himself as a radiant church, without stain or wrinkle or any other blemish, but holy and blameless. [28] In this same way, husbands ought to love their wives as their own bodies. He who loves his wife loves himself. [29] After all, no one ever hated their own body, but they feed and care for their body, just as Christ does the church – [30] for we are members of his body. [31] 'For this reason a man will leave his father and mother and be united to his wife, and the two will become one flesh.' [32] This is a profound mystery – but I am talking about Christ and the church. [33] However, each one of you also must love his wife as he loves himself, and the wife must respect her husband.

Christ builds up his bride. Christ eliminates anything that keeps his bride from becoming everything she was created to be. Christ sacrifices.

My father always says that it is a man's role to create an atmosphere in the home, both spiritual and emotional, in which his wife can become everything God has created her to be. This is a big job, and since I am not a man, I can only imagine the weight of this responsibility. If a man is not following God's will and seeking the Lord, it is felt by the whole family. When a man starts to turn his life over to Christ, the whole family feels the refreshing cleansing it creates in the home. Selfishness starts to be exchanged for selflessness. It doesn't happen overnight. It is a process of growth for both spouses. Each person learns how to submit to one another, respect one another and love one another.

TRANQUILITY VS SELF PITY

When I imagine a tranquil pool, I think of the glassy, undisturbed surface that reflects everything around it. Contrast this with a stormy body of water raging from the elements blowing against it, with strong riptides pulling unsuspecting swimmers into imminent danger. Once at the beach, there was a big storm coming up the coast. It wasn't anywhere near us, yet, but the waves were getting bigger and bigger. I parked my children right in front of the life guard that day to be safe. My youngest, a toddler, took off running as fast as he could on his tripping toes down the beach. Putting one chubby foot in front of the other to keep from falling on his face, he made excellent time maneuvering around sand castles and towels. Even though I was only gone a few seconds to grab him, in that fateful window of time, the life guard walked down the beach and my 8-year old son Ellis got sucked out to sea, just two dark, breaking waves from the shore line. Adults had lined up watching the developing emergency, as I grabbed a body board, attached the Velcro strap to my wrist and dove into the crashing waves to rescue him. We both tumbled around, but I reached him, after braving two very scary waves. Once back on the shore, we sat stunned at what had transpired.

Even though a storm of life can be far behind you, even years ago, its after-effects can pull you under into a dangerous situation. Self-pity and bitterness act as an internal storm that sucks the thanksgiving and the beauty out of life's best moments. You may keep an internal hit list of everything you have been deprived of in your marriage, while coveting another woman's life. You may feel self-pity every time you go to a wedding, just remembering how your wedding wasn't as perfect. Self-pity will create a storm out of nowhere. It can cause you to overreact to a simple question, because you are reacting with all the pain from your past. Self-pity makes you a martyr, and it is never satisfied. It makes your spouse your enemy, even when he is doing nothing wrong. I know this battle very intimately, because God delivered me from a spirit of self-pity and showed me how I indulged thoughts and feelings of self-pity to the detriment of my marriage and our joy.

A tranquil spirit in a woman protects her from the internal forces pulling and pushing in her life. As a believer, unforgiveness, bitterness and self-pity can cause more storms in your marriage than actual everyday life. Ask the Lord to deliver you from self-pity and anything else that comes in to rob your personal tranquility.

BRINGING IT HOME

Pray and ask the Lord to bring tranquility to your heart.

Do you have inner turmoil that is causing fights and quarrels? You cannot change this simply by just changing your behavior; you need an inner transformation that comes through forgiveness and agreeing with God's plan for your life.

Have you submitted to the Lord's plan for your marriage?

TODAY'S BIBLE STUDY TOOL
Online Bible Dictionary & Encyclopedia

THE TWO WILL BECOME ONE
THE MYSTERY

MEMORY VERSE REVIEW
& Prayer for Your Marriage

I keep asking you, God of our Lord Jesus Christ, the glorious Father, that you may give US the Spirit of wisdom and revelation, so that we may know you better. I ask that you will reach into the heart of our marriage with this same Spirit of wisdom and revelation and speak truth and conviction, and teach us about intimacy, in Jesus' name. I pray that you will wake our marriage from death to life.

Let us see Jesus. I pray also that the eyes of our hearts may be enlightened in order that we may know hope in Christ for our present life and our future together. May we see the riches of our glorious inheritance in the saints.

I declare that this same incomparably great power that is in me, is right now working in him and drawing us together, by your love. That power is like the working of your mighty strength, which you exerted in Christ when you raised him from the dead and seated him at your right hand in the heavenly realms, far above all rule and authority, power and dominion and every title that can be given, not only in the present life but also in the one to come.

Raise up my marriage in Christ, in Jesus' name. Raise us up, Lord. And place our marriage, life, destiny, heart, spirit, and very being under your feet. Christ, be head over my marriage. Let us be the manifest presence of your body, the fullness of him who fills everything in every way.

Amen.

Adapted from Ephesians 1:17-23

READING

Ephesians 5:31-33

[31] 'For this reason a man will leave his father and mother and be united to his wife, and the two will become one flesh.' [32] This is a profound **mystery** – but I am talking about Christ and the church. [33] However, each one of you also must love his wife as he loves himself, and the wife must respect her husband.

Today, we get to step back and look at a final piece in the "mystery" puzzle that the apostle Paul writes about so frequently in his letter to the Ephesians. It is found in these three verses about marriage. Let's review what we have read in Ephesians concerning the body of Christ. In what other chapter did we read about the word "mystery"? Do a quick phrase search in your Bible app! Type "mystery" into the search bar to see where that word is found in the book of Ephesians.

- Ephesians 3:6 — This **mystery** is that through the gospel the Gentiles are heirs together with Israel, **members together of one body**, and sharers together in the promise in Christ Jesus.

- Ephesians 1:7-10 — [7] In him we have redemption through his blood, the forgiveness of sins, in accordance with the riches of God's grace [8] that he lavished on us. With all wisdom and understanding, [9] he made known to us the **mystery of his will** according to his good pleasure, which he purposed in Christ, [10] to be put into effect when the times reach their fulfilment – **to bring unity to all things in heaven and on earth under Christ**.

Here are two places in Ephesians that speak of the mystery unfolding. Two becoming one. The Gentile church and the Jewish church, the people of God all over the world are united spiritually into one flesh—the body of Christ. Generations past and generations to come are one in Christ. Ladies, God takes those who were called rejected and transforms them in Christ, into an accepted, beloved child in his family! The Gentiles, before Christ, could not participate in the inheritance of God. They were on the outside of the clique looking in. However, God's endgame, the whole time, was to bring all of humanity, who trust in his Son, those who were near and those who were far away, together as the bride of Christ!

In Ephesians 5, Paul takes it to another level. He reveals that God sees marriage between a man and a woman in the same way. Marriage manifests what happens in the body of Christ spiritually. We see two separate people from two different backgrounds coming together, blending their lives under the lordship of Christ. Then we mature. Maturing in Christ and in marriage takes time. We grow together into the healthy and strong marriage God desires for us, in grace and mercy. We are no longer just a guy and a girl who fell in love and live together in a house. We learn to submit to one another in love. We put aside the selfishness that separates us and we live for the other person as strongly as we live for ourselves. We love with purpose. In our purposeful, focused, intentional love, we create a family that we bring children into.

Our children become the genetic and spiritual manifestation of this union. Our DNA is wound up tightly inside of them. They manifest our strengths and our weaknesses. In the same way, we are the DNA of the body of Christ. Every one of us is built into Christ and who he is. We are included in the mystery. Have you ever read Jesus' genealogy? Look it up in Matthew or Luke. You will find included in his family line, his blood line, are sinners, saints, Jews AND Gentiles. HIS very DNA in his physical body included what would happen in the spiritual realm, because of his death and resurrection. We should no longer live for ourselves. We cannot separate ourselves from each other. God sees us as one.

About a year ago, God started convicting me over a very small thing. Whenever I would refer to my son or my daughter, the Holy Spirit would say, "OUR son" or "OUR daughter." Even in the smallest wordings, God wants our hearts to be united. It's easy for our hearts to want to claim our own little corner and to stand in it, taking claim for our child's strengths as from "my side of the family"

and his or her weaknesses as being from "your side of the family." Even in this way we divide ourselves. What are some ways that a man and woman can be intentional to create oneness in the home? Do you take time for one another to talk on deep levels? This doesn't mean discussing the budget or even the kids. What about hopes and dreams?

Here is a visual aid which my father, Mike Dean, uses in marriage counseling. God is at the top of the triangle. The husband and wife are at the bottom corners and the children are in the center. When the spouses both move up the triangle, closer to the Lord in their own personal relationships, they will move closer to each other. The children are in the middle of the relationship. They have no choice. They are born into the family and the role of the parents is to create an atmosphere of grace, security, love, acceptance and forgiveness for the children to safely grow and mature in. When one parent attacks another parent, whether it is in front of the children or not, it is "taking out" your children's line of defense. They are supposed to be safe inside a haven of harmony. On that note, let's think about what harmony is. Harmony doesn't happen when each note is the same; it happens when two or more notes complement each other, working together in the music to create a pleasing sonic structure.

The husband has spiritual headship over the household. This means that he is the first line of spiritual defense for you and for your children. If he is not doing his job of spiritually protecting the family, or if he is doing things that negatively affect the family, then you are probably in a red-alert status in your marriage. However, you and your children still have you as a second line of defense. The enemy cannot bring the full onslaught he would like to bring against your children, if you are walking with the Lord and standing for them in prayer, even if your spouse isn't doing his part. However, if you join forces with the enemy and begin to attack your spouse, to allow resentment to seethe under the surface, to speak curses against him about what a terrible man he is, then the battle is over. The enemy has won. No one is left standing to protect your children. God cannot forgive you if you refuse to forgive, and, as we learned in Week Eight, Day 1, you are making a special guest room for the devil in your life and your home.

If you are in a situation where your husband is not a believer, or if he is a believer, but is walking a spiritually lazy life or even a sinful life, you have other alternatives to hating him and speaking curses over him. Proverbs 18:21 says, "The tongue has the power of life and death, and those who love it will eat its fruit." If you speak negativity, death and curses over your own husband, you are cursing your own household, your own protection and your own children. In the same way, if the husband does not value his wife, but harms her with neglect or with his words, he is ignoring his greatest asset in life. He also will swiftly find the one who should 'have his back' attacking him from the back. It all is so futile. Try praying that the Lord will teach you to love your husband the way he needs to be loved and to intercede for your husband the way he needs to be prayed for. Speak life over your husband. Forgive your husband the way Christ forgives you. I am not asserting that you should never challenge a man in sin. I am saying that you need to deal with your own heart before the Lord. No matter how much you wish, you cannot separate yourself from the spiritual oneness with your spouse. If you are not married yet, take this into account when you think about whom you are dating. Is this a man who would be a strong spiritual covering for your home? Is this a man you want to be united with spiritually for the rest of your life?

If you come from a background of divorce, separation and infidelity in your family history, you may find yourself on a heated battleground, fighting for the oneness of your marriage union. Do not be deceived by the devil into a life of self-pity and resentment. Do not agree with the things the devil wants you to agree with. You will have to decide that you will stand your ground in the day of evil. Forgive. Bless. Love well. Entrust your heart to the Lord. You are in a special position in your spouse's life. You have authority and power to pray for him like no one else can. You see his weaknesses. You see his day in and day out. You are entrusted with a sacred honor to lift up this man, when he is down. When he is unlovable, you are trusted to love him. We all have our unlovable times, when we are stressed out and weak. My points of stress may not make sense to my husband. They are not his points of weakness, but he still prays for me and bears with me in love. My weaknesses are not the same as my husband's, but God forgive me if I ever have a haughty heart against his vulnerable places, because I do not have the same vulnerabilities as he does.

PRAYER FOR ONENESS

Father,

In Jesus' name, forgive me for the times I have rejected your plan for marriage. I know I am one with my husband, but we haven't been acting like it. There is bitterness, resentment and even hatred. (Pray to forgive specific sins against you.) I have allowed Satan a foothold in my home through anger. I have spoken evil over my husband, by grumbling and muttering, by nagging, complaining and back-biting. I have made him feel like he can never please me. I have attacked him. Right now, forgive me, Jesus. I break off every curse I have spoken over my husband, in Jesus' name. I pray that my sin will not pass on to my children. Do not hold this against them. Bring blessing instead of strife to my husband, in Jesus' name. Allow the fruit of my lips to be pleasant. I rebuke and renounce the resentment, hatred, bitterness and anger that I have harbored, in Jesus' name. I command these to leave my life, my marriage and my home, in Jesus' name. I pray that you forgive me for pride, Lord Jesus. There is no place for pride in marriage, because we are on the same team. Remove a spirit of pride from me and from my spouse, in Jesus' name. Teach us to walk in the gentleness and humility of your Holy Spirit. Fill our marriage with your presence, oh Lord. Give us a heart of flesh, in place of our heart of stone. Let us walk in oneness.

In Jesus' name, Amen!

This prayer example has transferable concepts for every area of your life. For more prayers like this, please refer to the Prayer Index in the back of the book.

IDEAS FOR FOSTERING ONENESS IN THE HOME

Even if you are single, it is good to pray for a future spouse that you can do these things with.

1. **Pray together.** Do you spend time together on your knees praying for your children and other burdens?

2. **Pray for one another.** Take time to put your hand on your husband's shoulder and pray over him. Pray for the cares of his heart and pray with all your might!

3. **"What I love about you."** This is a great activity for a date. You can also use it for birthdays. Take turns telling the person what you love about them. It can include physical traits, but mostly it should be things about their personality. Keep it real and free from any little hurtful jabs or sarcasm. This was a family tradition I grew up with. My father and mother were very good at creating a loving atmosphere of building one another up. I introduced it to my husband when we got married. At first he felt uncomfortable giving words to his emotions in front of a group. But, slowly he got better at it. It took him several years to become an old pro. Now all of our children are very good at letting someone know why they are important to them. We both model this verbal affirmation!

4. **Exercise together.** This is something we started in the past couple of years. I used to really dislike running. However, I have found that it is a great way to do "shoulder to shoulder" activity with my husband. We both run in silence. Sometimes, he runs in the opposite direction of me, because he needs to run faster. Then he will turn around and run back to me to find me and run at my pace. We usually end the time with walking for a mile and talking about life.

5. **Non-sexual physical contact.** This is very important to women. Back rubs, holding hands and hugs are very important!

6. **Make time for one another.** Life gets crazy, especially when you start adding children. The whole family rises and falls on the foundation of the parents. Be sure to make time for each other every week! You can do it!

7. **Play games.** Playing a game as a family around the table is a great way to have fun and connect.

8. **Cook and eat meals together around the table.** Creating meal routines is essential for healthy family time.

9. **Physical intimacy.** Be sure not to freeze your husband out. As much as it may sound terribly distasteful to a woman who has been in a cycle of arguments or just living in tension with her husband for days, coming together physically can actually be a huge spiritual warfare weapon.

10. **Help one another.** What is important to your spouse? Make it a priority. It's easy for irritation to enter in when your spouse starts talking about something that he loves, if you feel like you are not getting the appreciation you need or the help you need. Try showing interest in his areas of interest. Do you loathe sports, but that is all he talks about? Try watching a game with him while you spend time on Instagram. He may even rub your feet—I have a friend who has a great arrangement with her husband that she will watch soccer with him, and he rubs her feet. Sign me up! Is eating a good meal really important to your husband, but you hate to cook? Learn some of his favorite recipes and become a pro at making them! Do you hate to clean, but your husband is OCD? Even though you may fear that it won't ever be good enough—LOL—find a cleaning blog or system that will help you start making strides in the areas that are important to him.

11. **Meet him halfway!** I heard one testimonial from a wise woman who said that she was so lonely, because all her husband did was play golf. She could have chosen bitterness, whining and nagging. Instead, she learned to play golf. Now they spend time together talking every day on the golf course. When you show love to someone and meet his or her needs, then it paves the way for that person to desire to meet your needs. Both partners need to be all in—100%!

12. **Worship together.** Be sure to attend church together with your husband. Serve the Lord together. Model faithfulness and putting God first to the next generation!

BRINGING IT HOME

Take time to start thanking God for your spouse. Thank God for your union. Is there some small part of your heart that you reserve for yourself and keep back from entering into what God has for you completely?

PASSING THE TORCH TO YOUR CHILDREN

MEMORY VERSE

[10] Finally, be strong in the Lord and in his mighty power. [11] Put on the full armour of God, so that you can take your stand against the devil's schemes. [12] For our struggle is not against flesh and blood, but against the rulers, against the authorities, against the powers of this dark world and against the spiritual forces of evil in the heavenly realms. [13] Therefore put on the full armour of God, so that when the day of evil comes, you may be able to stand your ground, and after you have done everything, to stand. – Ephesians 6:10-13

PRAYER FOR YOUR CHILDREN

Father,

In Jesus' name, I come to you for my children—even those who are yet to be born. I pray my children will know you and walk with you all the days of their lives. Today, Lord, I ask you to give my children the Spirit of wisdom and revelation that they will know you and the hope you have called them to in Christ. Protect my children from deception, in Jesus' name. Please speak to their hearts, convict them of sin, and give them a hunger for your Word. May your light so shine in their hearts, that they may bring hope to many. Lead my children not into temptation, but deliver them from the evil one, in Jesus' name. Give me teachable moments with my children, so I can share my personal testimonies with them. Lead me, as I lead them.

In Jesus' name, Amen.

READING

Today we begin the final chapter of Ephesians. Remember that when Paul wrote this, he didn't put in chapters and verses. Those were added later. Moving onto a new chapter does not necessarily mean that his train of thought from Chapter 5 is finished. In fact, he is now moving through a well-developed teaching on our identity in Christ—how that identity, power and position play out in real life. In this chapter he addresses children, slavery and spiritual warfare. It is truly full of hot-button topics for the time we live in! As we read, let us keep all this in context with everything we've already read in Ephesians to better understand God's heart and will for us. Remember, this is all done through WISDOM and REVELATION from the Holy Spirit. We invited him to speak to us in today's prayer.

[1] Children, obey your parents in the Lord, for this is right. [2] 'Honour your father and mother'– which is the first commandment with a promise – [3] 'so that it may go well with you and that you may enjoy long life on the earth.'

[4] Fathers, do not exasperate your children; instead, bring them up in the training and instruction of the Lord.

[5] Slaves, obey your earthly masters with respect and fear, and with sincerity of heart, just as you would obey Christ. [6] Obey them not only to win their favour when their eye is on you, but as slaves of Christ, doing the will of God from your heart. [7] Serve wholeheartedly, as if you were serving the Lord, not people, [8] because you know that the Lord will reward each one for whatever good they do, whether they are slave or free.

[9] And masters, treat your slaves in the same way. Do not threaten them, since you know that he who is both their Master and yours is in heaven, and there is no favouritism with him.

CONTRAST & COMPARISON

In the above passage, Paul is addressing four groups of people. Two of those are subordinate in this world. Two have headship or authority over the other two. Let's see what God's commands are for each of these groups by contrasting them in lists. Write your findings in the following chart.

CHILDREN	FATHERS
Do	Do
	Do not

SLAVES	MASTERS
Do	Do
	Do not

Notice that in both situations of children and slaves, all the advice Paul gives to them is proactive. There is a lack of negatives or DO NOT commands. The focus, when a person is in a lower position of submitting to someone, is on a positive heart of submission to Christ.

To those in authority, Paul specifically gives both the DOs and the DO NOTs. Why? They need to see there is a limit to their authority, and a right and wrong way to use that authority.

To children, Paul references a promise of God found in the Ten Commandments. Let's cross reference the Ten Commandments in the book of Deuteronomy to see the context. **Feel free to open your Bible and read all of Deuteronomy 5 to get the full effect of the passage.**

Honor your father and your mother, as the Lord your God has commanded you, so that you may live long and that it may go well with you in the land the Lord your God is giving you. – Deuteronomy 5:16

What is the promise to children who honor their parents? Write it here:

Our children need joyfully reminded that God gives them a promise in the Ten Commandments. God does not break his promises! Here is a guarantee of that! To find scriptures on God's promises, I looked up the word "promise" in my Bible app—something you can do, too. Look at this gem of a scripture. It ties into Ephesians 1 also. This discovery makes me giddy! We belong to God the Father. He owns us. We are sealed! "For no matter how many promises God has made, they are 'Yes' in Christ. And so through him the 'Amen' is spoken by us to the glory of God. Now it is God who makes both us and you stand firm in Christ. He anointed us, set his seal of ownership on us, and put his Spirit in our hearts as a deposit, guaranteeing what is to come." – 2 Corinthians 1:20-22

The promise in Ephesians 6 teaches us two things:

94. When children heed their parent's advice and counsel, they are wise and will succeed in life. The parent's real-life experience helps the child avoid pitfalls and dangers. If a child honors the parent's counsel, he or she will avoid the same pitfalls and do well. This is common sense, really.

95. There is a spiritual blessing and promise from God for people who live in obedience and honor for their parents. We can count on this promise and even pray this promise in faith, the way we pray other scripture! For example: "Lord, you promise in your Word that I will enjoy a long life on the earth, if I obey and honor my parents in the Lord. I claim this promise in Jesus' name and thank you that you keep your promises!"

This promise is a great passage to have your children memorize! It helps kids to see that the Bible tells them to honor and obey their parents for their own good. There is a reward involved! A child needs to know the character of God and the nature of God. He always is concerned about the next generation. The goal is not to subjugate them, but to bless them and to establish a deep relationship with them. Also, when children submit to and obey their parents, they are learning to submit to and obey the Lord. God revealed this to me with my first born, when I struggled with taking her to the grocery store at two years old. She didn't always want to sit in the grocery cart seat. She was excited to be there and wanted to buy everything she saw advertised on television! Ariel, a strong, independent toddler, liked to walk by the cart. She never liked being restricted. I tried to allow her to be a big girl and walk, but occasionally, she would dart away and I would have to chase her down the aisle. Then came the task of trying to thread her wriggling, kicking legs back through the holes in the child seat in the cart, as she stiffened her back saying, "No, Mother! I want to walk!" Yes, she called me mother. No, I didn't ask her to. As this process continued to frustrate me, the Lord spoke to my heart that I was training her up to listen to him. God wanted me to talk to her about his desire to speak to her heart, even at two years old. I pushed the cart down the aisle at Wal-Mart, after having secured her back in the seat.

"Ariel, God wants you to obey Mommy. That is how you will learn to listen to him. Every time Mommy tells you something, it is to keep you safe, because I love you. God is the same way. Whenever you obey Mommy, you are practicing listening to God."

She did listen intently and, being the great talker she was at that age, we had a nice little conversation about it. God makes it very clear in Deuteronomy that children need to be reminded constantly, throughout the day, of their parents' testimony and how to walk with God. As children get older, they need a different level of real-life instruction. Deuteronomy 11 teaches us that children may not understand what you require of them completely, because they do not know your past history with the Lord. They do not know what God delivered you from.

Deuteronomy 11:2-3a, 5, 7, 18-19

Remember today that your children were not the ones who saw and experienced the discipline of the Lord your God: his majesty, his mighty hand, his outstretched arm; the signs he performed and the things he did in the heart of Egypt…

It was not your children who saw what he did for you in the wilderness until you arrived at this place…

But it was your own eyes that saw all these great things the Lord has done.

Fix these words of mine in your hearts and minds; tie them as symbols on your hands and bind them on your foreheads. Teach them to your children, talking about them when you sit at home and when you walk along the road, when you lie down and when you get up.

When I was a child, I was born into a loving Christian home. I was sheltered from brokenness and sorrow. However, my parents often times told me the wonderful story of Christ's redemption of our family and what he brought them out of in Christ. These stories meant so much to me. They were my testimony, too! On my parent's 40th anniversary, we held a wonderful celebration. I found out that the minister who married my parents and who discipled my father as a new believer, Reverend Harold Myers, was living within a two-hour drive of their home. I wanted to surprise my parents by inviting him and his wife to attend. When I called his church office to talk to him personally, I found myself weeping on the phone. I am not sure he even knew who I was at first! I was talking to the man whose work in God's kingdom delivered my parents and set my feet on a path of righteousness in Christ. I was overwhelmed.

Do your children know your story? Are you hiding it from them to protect them? If so, you are actually disarming them of a great spiritual weapon that would help them to overcome, when they fight their own spiritual battles in the future. It says in Revelation 12:11, "They triumphed over him by the blood of the Lamb, and by the word of their testimony." Our testimony of God's deliverance and work in our family is how we overcome the devil's attacks in our lives.

Children do not only need to "mind" their parents, but they need to know the Lord and to love him with all of their heart, mind, soul and strength. It is our job to teach them and to lead them in a life that honors God. I tell my children that they are passing the baton in the great relay of life. They bear the torch. For my sons, I want them to seriously consider that the woman each of them will choose to marry will be instructing their children in the Lord. Is she of godly character? Will their wives teach their children in the Lord's way? As mothers, we give our children the foundation of their relationship with God. We want them to know that when they obey and honor us, they will be able to participate in this awesome promise of long life.

This promise is also for us, as adults. We all have parents—living or not—and are still required to honor them. Jesus was angry with the Pharisees who did not honor their parents financially. Jesus said,

5 "But you say that if anyone declares that what might have been used to help their father or mother is "devoted to God," 6 they are not to "honour their father or mother" with it. Thus you nullify the word of God for the sake of your tradition. 7 You hypocrites! Isaiah was right when he prophesied about you: 8 "'These people honour me with their lips, but their hearts are far from me. 9 They worship me in vain; their teachings are merely human rules.'" – Matthew 15:5-9

In other words, the Pharisee who dishonored his aged parents would avoid helping them by announcing that he couldn't give them financial assistance, as he was doing something "holy" by putting the money he would have otherwise given his parents into the temple offering. God says that giving to your parents is giving to him, when they are truly in need in their old age.

INSTRUCTION FOR FATHERS

Fathers, do not exasperate your children; instead, bring them up in the training and instruction of the Lord. — Ephesians 6:4

What does exasperate mean? Let's look up the Greek word for exasperate on biblehub.com.

Strong's Concordance
parorgizó: to provoke to anger

Original Word: παροργίζω
Part of Speech: Verb
Transliteration: parorgizó
Phonetic Spelling: (par-org-id'-zo)
Short Definition: I provoke to anger, exasperate
Definition: I provoke to anger, exasperate.

HELPS™ Word-studies

3949 *parorgízō* (from <u>3844</u> /*pará*, "from close-beside" and <u>3710</u> /*orgízō*, "become angry") – properly, rouse someone to anger; to *provoke* in a way that "really pushes someone's buttons," i.e. to "*really get to them*" in an "up-close-and-personal" way (because so near, literally "close beside").

When you are in a family situation, you are, as this Greek word "para" indicates, very close in someone's space. As a parent, you cannot hide your weaknesses or pretend that you never make mistakes with a "do what I say and not as I do" attitude. As we have learned in Ephesians about all of our relationships, our relationship with our children must be loving, graceful, and careful. They are under your authority. You can either abuse this authority and "lord" over them, or you can use this authority to build them up and train them in godly love.

Mean joking and harsh teasing, mocking, or shaming children in order to manipulate them, or even just for some fun, is off limits for godly fathers, who are to be the earthly example of God to his children. This scripture gives the image of a father strengthening his children. If a child has no grace and love in his or her instruction, and sees no humility from parents who make mistakes, that child will become angry or afraid, feeling like he or she can never please the father, nor Father God. Sometimes fathers tend to think it is their job to make their sons or daughters "tougher" by withholding things from them such as love and tenderness or even withholding the instruction and teaching they need to overcome a situation. The mentality that children will "figure it out" on their own can be very detrimental and is a form of spiritual and emotional neglect. A godly father will give grace, instructing and building up his children without intentionally provoking them to anger.

A modern example of provoking your children to anger is the new social media shaming of children. Shaving a child's head publicly for the world to see, or making a post about how disrespectful your child is will definitely teach the child a lesson—a lesson in shaming! If you wouldn't want your boss or spouse to publicly shame you when you make a mistake, then think twice about publicly shaming your child. My mother refers to this type of discipline as "emotional discipline." We should not allow our emotions to get in the way. It's not about us. Our goal, as parents, is to build our children up and to discipline them for their own good, with a clear head. 1 Peter 4:8 says, "Above all, love each other deeply; love covers over a multitude of sins." Love protects, even in discipline. I am not advocating letting your children get away with disrespect or disobedience. I am advocating teaching them respect through modeling how to act with respect, even when you are angry. There are many ways to discipline your children without wounding a spirit. Always use the Jesus test. "Do unto others, as you would have them do unto you." If your child needs grounded, by all means ground him or her! If you need to correct, correct. If you need to take away a privilege like electronics, by all means, do it! Just pray about not allowing shaming, put-downs and spirit-wounding into your discipline.

Many Christian young people are turning away from the faith today. Is some of this due to a spiritual imbalance in the home? The father and the mother can give their children a view of God that is either healthy or erroneous. It is truly sad to see a parent give a child a wrong perception of God by talking all about God when in public, yet filling his or her private home with strife. If you grew up in a graceless home where your father did not model Christ for you, or if your spouse is not doing a stellar job of building up your children in Christ, do not despair. Focus your energy on praying for our good Father God to give you revelation to know his love. Pray to forgive those who have hurt you. Pray for your spouse, that God would transform his heart and give him a desire to seek God on how to be a good father. Pray that the Lord turns his heart towards his children, as it says in Malachi 4:5-6. If you are single and plan to marry someday, pray that God will send you a man who can be taught by the Lord and is open to learning and changing when the Holy Spirit speaks to his heart. Godliness is more valuable than any other character trait a man may have. Investing in your children is more important than investing in work, a good house, or a great retirement fund. Investing in your children is investing in eternity.

BRINGING IT HOME

Teach your children to memorize Ephesians 6:1-3:

Ephesians 6:1-3

[1] Children, obey your parents in the Lord, for this is right. [2] 'Honour your father and mother'– which is the first commandment with a promise – [3] 'so that it may go well with you and that you may enjoy long life on the earth.'

Let them know that by obeying and honoring their parents, they are promised by God a great reward in this life. There is a difference between just living a long life and enjoying a long life on the earth. The ability to enjoy life comes from God. Teach your children to pray and claim this promise, in Jesus' name.

NEITHER SLAVE NOR FREE

MEMORY VERSE

[10] Finally, be strong in the Lord and in his mighty power. [11] Put on the full armour of God, so that you can take your stand against the devil's schemes. [12] For our struggle is not against flesh and blood, but against the rulers, against the authorities, against the powers of this dark world and against the spiritual forces of evil in the heavenly realms. [13] Therefore put on the full armour of God, so that when the day of evil comes, you may be able to stand your ground, and after you have done everything, to stand. – Ephesians 6:10-13

PRAYER
Against Injustice

Father,

In Jesus' name, I thank you that Christ leveled the playing field. I thank you that in Jesus, everyone has forgiveness of sin and equal value in your family. I pray for justice to flow like a mighty river through our nation and through our world. I ask for honesty, integrity, justice and righteousness to reign from the federal government to the state and local governments, in Jesus' name. I ask that you will oppose those who oppress others, in Jesus' name, and dismantle the web of sex trafficking and slavery around the world. I pray for my brothers and sisters in Christ who are suffering in chains for your name. I ask that you will bring all the power and authority of the resurrection power of Jesus to set those prisoners free, to bring them comfort and to oppose the devil's attempt to bring despair, pain and discouragement. I ask for you to protect children of those persecuted. I pray for their food, clothing, and comfort. I ask that the church of Jesus Christ will rise up and work to protect the poor and suffering around the world. Awaken the consciences of those who have fallen asleep to the cries of the suffering, in Jesus' name. Dismantle attitudes and spirits of prejudice and racism. Start this good work in your church, Lord. May the church of Jesus Christ be known for its love. May the body of Christ be strengthened to do its good work for your glory across the globe, oh Lord.

In Jesus' name, Amen.

READING

Ephesians 6:5-9

[5] Slaves, obey your earthly masters with respect and fear, and with sincerity of heart, just as you would obey Christ. [6] Obey them not only to win their favour when their eye is on you, but as slaves of Christ, doing the will of God from your

heart. [7] Serve wholeheartedly, as if you were serving the Lord, not people, [8] because you know that the Lord will reward each one for whatever good they do, whether they are slave or free.

[9] And masters, treat your slaves in the same way. Do not threaten them, since you know that he who is both their Master and yours is in heaven, and there is no favouritism with him.

HISTORICAL RESEARCH

The city of Ephesus was a pagan Greek city. Paul wrote to a church planted in a culture running on slave labor in a way that made slavery in the pre-Civil-War South look like child's play. The church's congregation showed the beginnings of the revolutionary power of the cross, where slave and slave owner have equal value and standing in Jesus. Paul taught them that they are no longer to operate under the thinking of the world. Paul himself could not dismantle the entire Greek slave trade culture, but he did teach the men and women of Ephesus how to function in that society as believers. Just as we discussed earlier in our study, a society is changed little by little as individuals are transformed by Christ. Mark Cartwright explains in the Ancient History Encyclopedia how slavery looked in Ephesus:

"It is impossible to say with accuracy how many slaves (douloi) there were in Greek society and what proportion of the population they made up. It is unlikely, due to the costs, that every single citizen had their own slave but some citizens undoubtedly owned many slaves. Accordingly, estimates of the slave population in the Greek world range from between 15 and 40% of the total population. However, a defense speech made in a court case in Athens by Lysias, and hints from others such as Demosthenes, strongly suggest that if every citizen did not have slaves then they certainly desired them and to be a slave owner was considered a measure of social status. Slaves were not only owned by private individuals but also by the state, which used them in municipal projects such as mining or, as in the case of Athens, the police force.

The relationship between slaves and owners seems to have been much as in any other period of history with a mix of contempt, distrust, and abuse from the owners and contempt, theft, and sabotage from the enslaved. Source material is always from the viewpoint of the slave owner but there are references in literature, particularly in Greek comedy, of friendship and loyalty in at least some owner-slave relationships. Whilst the flogging of slaves is commonly referred to in Greek plays, there were also treatises written extolling the benefits of kindness and incentives in slave management."
— https://www.ancient.eu/article/483/greek-society/

Wow! Imagine what it would be like to live in a culture where owning people and treating them like property was normal. The writer says that the relationships between the slave owners and slaves were wrought with contempt, distrust, abuse, and sabotage in the society. The slave owners and slaves alike in Ephesus experienced Jesus' transformation. Lives and hearts grew with forgiveness and a new sense of trust and selflessness. For the slave, there was no more hopelessness, anger, bitterness and resentment. For the slave owner, there was no more justifiable pride, anger or feelings of superiority. Paul's teaching to slaves encouraged an attitude like Joseph's, when he was a slave in Potiphar's house, and even when he was unjustly in prison. His righteous attitude and ability to forgive brought the blessing and favor of the Lord on everything he did. Perhaps Paul was thinking of him, when he penned these words to the Ephesian slaves. As a believer in Jesus, the hope and love of Christ can shine in your heart no matter what situation you are in. In the 1800's in America, black slaves received peace and hope from their relationship with Christ, as they waited eagerly for their redemption. They had hope, even if they never experienced freedom in this world. They had hope for heaven. Many powerful spirituals were written to express the pain and hope these men and women lived in as believers while in the bondage of slavery.

Slavery is now illegal everywhere in the world. Slavery still exists illegally, but the light of Christ has changed the world person-by-person, till even nations where Christianity is not the major belief system have adopted laws that reflect the nature of Christ in the world. The very nature of the gospel brings equality to all people regardless of race, gender or social status. When we are part of the body of Christ, bought by his blood, we are all equally valuable.

The book of Philemon is a one-chapter letter to a slave owner named Philemon asking him to take back an escaped slave, who is also a believer, named Onesimus. From the letter, Onesimus used to be a "useless" slave. (see v 11) Perhaps there was a lot of drama between Onesimus and his owner Philemon? However, Jesus touched his life and at the time Paul pens the letter, he is a hard worker, helpful and willing to go back to the man he wronged to ask for forgiveness. Paul and Timothy respectfully ask Philemon to take him back as a brother, but not a slave. This gentle and respectful exhortation lays the groundwork for believers to know God's perfect will concerning this issue. Take time today to read this one-chapter book and imagine the power of Christ to transform the hearts of a slave and a slave owner.

PHILEMON

Read the book of Philemon (Don't worry! It's only 1 chapter!) and then answer the following questions.

96. In what verse does Paul ask Philemon to take Onesimus back as a brother and not a slave?

97. What is the Lord revealing to you about Paul's teaching about slavery and unity among the races in the body of Christ through the book of Philemon?

98. How does this help you understand Paul's teaching in Ephesians 6:5-9?

BRINGING IT HOME

If Christ can transform the life of a slave and bring hope and healing, Christ can overcome anything you may be struggling with in your life.

What do you expect from the Lord? He offers life and freedom! Slavery is no longer an acceptable part of our society, but we can apply this passage to situations like employment or running a business. If you run a business or are in management, how do you treat your employees or those under your authority? As an employee, how do you respond under oppressive situations or even just on-the-job situations in general? How can we foster an attitude that we are working for the Lord, instead of working for a boss or employer or investors?

EVER-INCREASING STRENGTH

MEMORY VERSE

[10] Finally, be strong in the Lord and in his mighty power. [11] Put on the full armour of God, so that you can take your stand against the devil's schemes. [12] For our struggle is not against flesh and blood, but against the rulers, against the authorities, against the powers of this dark world and against the spiritual forces of evil in the heavenly realms. [13] Therefore put on the full armour of God, so that when the day of evil comes, you may be able to stand your ground, and after you have done everything, to stand. – Ephesians 6:10-13

PRAYER
Spiritual Warfare for Beginners

Father,

In Jesus' name, I pray that you fill me with your Holy Spirit of wisdom and revelation, as I learn about spiritual warfare. The unseen world can seem confusing and scary at times. I don't want to live in fear, but in confidence in Christ. Remove fear and fill me with your love. I know that you love me. Open the eyes of my heart to see the hope I have in Christ in spiritual warfare. I remember your truth that I have a rich inheritance in the family of God. I am a child of God. I was crucified with Christ in his death and raised up in his resurrection power. I know I am seated with Christ in heavenly realms far above every rule and authority. Colossians 3:3 says that my life is hidden with Christ in God. Thank you for protecting me, Lord. Thank you that the blood of the Lamb, Jesus Christ, covers my life and my family. I declare that the devil is defeated at the cross. Lead me not into temptation, Lord, but deliver me from the evil one.

In Jesus' name, Amen.

READING

Ephesians 6:10-23

[10] Finally, **be strong in the Lord and in his mighty power**. [11] Put on the full armour of God, so that you can take your **stand** against the devil's schemes. [12] For our struggle is not against flesh and blood, but against the rulers, against the authorities, against the powers of this dark world and against the spiritual forces of evil in the heavenly realms. [13] Therefore put on the full armour of God, so that when the day of evil comes, you may be able to **stand** your ground, and after you have done everything, to **stand**. [14] **Stand** firm then, with the belt of truth buckled round your waist, with the breastplate of

righteousness in place, [15] and with your feet fitted with the readiness that comes from the gospel of peace. [16] In addition to all this, take up the shield of faith, with which you can extinguish all the flaming arrows of the evil one. [17] Take the helmet of salvation and the sword of the Spirit, which is the word of God.

[18] And pray in the Spirit on all occasions with all kinds of prayers and requests. With this in mind, be alert and always keep on praying for all the Lord's people. [19] Pray also for me, that whenever I speak, words may be given me so that I will fearlessly make known the mystery of the gospel, [20] for which I am an ambassador in chains. Pray that I may declare it fearlessly, as I should.

[21] Tychicus, the dear brother and faithful servant in the Lord, will tell you everything, so that you also may know how I am and what I am doing. [22] I am sending him to you for this very purpose, that you may know how we are, and that he may encourage you.

[23] Peace to the brothers and sisters, and love with faith from God the Father and the Lord Jesus Christ. [24] Grace to all who love our Lord Jesus Christ with an undying love.

My goal is not to write an entire book on spiritual warfare, although I must say it is really difficult to condense all the truth into two-and-a-half weeks of study. Even though some of the days may be longer, please know we are just scratching the surface as we study spiritual warfare in Ephesians. I will offer scriptures and personal testimonies from the lives of people I know who were set free and changed when the people of God learned to fight not against flesh and blood, but against the rulers, the authorities, the powers of this dark world and the spiritual forces of evil in the heavenly realms. Pray that you can learn what the Lord would have you learn in this study.

Over the years, many conversations have transpired between me and women who question the validity or the place of spiritual warfare in their lives. Some are afraid of it. It seems scary and full of the unknown. Another woman says she is a pacifist, so she doesn't think God would want her to fight. Entire books have been written on spiritual warfare and the armor of God. Today, we will start our discussion on spiritual warfare from the perspective of our very safe place in Christ Jesus as believers who have trusted in him by faith.

The spiritual reality is not supposed to be scary or vague and unknown. 2 Peter 1:3 says, "His divine power has given us everything we need for a godly life through our knowledge of him who called us by his own glory and goodness." So, through his divine power and knowing Jesus, we have everything we need for everything we will face. Ephesians 6:13 tells us we are to stand on the day of evil. This scriptural directive is clear, not foggy. If we are to stand, then God provides the equipment for us to stand. Reading Ephesians 6 in context will help us to understand how to be equipped in a way that can be easily applied to everyday life. Paul removes any confusion with his teaching on this topic. The Lord leads us and guides us, so we can be confident, strong and clear headed.

To the dear sister who is a pacifist, we will learn that our enemies are not just the devil and demons. Your greatest enemies are yourself and sin. But, when it comes to the devil, there is no mercy in heaven for the devil and his angels. We are not encouraged to give him mercy when he comes against us and our loved ones with deception. We are not to give him a pass when anger and confusion loom over conversations in our marriages. When your life is weighed down with a spirit of heaviness—Isaiah 61—do not give him any mercy. The place of pacifism needs to be in your heart, in your home and in your relationships. When the enemy comes to steal the peace, God has equipped and authorized you with the name of his Son Jesus Christ to stand firm on the day of evil. Jesus already defeated the devil on the cross. His resurrection sealed the deal. We need to stand in truth and our position in Christ. One of the fears women have vocalized to me is this: if we pray against the devil, will he suddenly become aware of us and attack us more? Here is the truth. He already is attacking you. You are a threat to his kingdom. Your witness troubles him. Your praise shakes him. Your prayers dislodge him and send him running. He must work overtime to get you to take your eyes off of Jesus and to fixate them on your own personal problems, failures, sicknesses and more. He tries to keep believers in a place of doubt and his biggest tool in the Western world is to trick people into believing that he doesn't exist. In John 10:10, Jesus said, "The thief comes to kill, steal and destroy; I have come that they may have life and have it to the full." The devil wants to destroy your future, your marriage, your children and your hope. Jesus comes to bring a future and a hope for you and for your posterity. Standing against the enemy will not incur more pressure; instead, you will relieve the pressure you are already under! Today, we will learn to stand in Christ through his power. Let's get started!

WORD SEARCH

Read through Ephesians 6 again. This time, look for frequently-occurring words and phrases. Write those in the space below. Beside each one, put a tally mark for each time it occurs. Example: STAND | | | | = 4 times

Which words jump out at you in your list above? Did you also find that the word "stand" was listed four times? Did you know that the words for "stand" in the Greek are not all the same? Three times the word means to stand firm, be established and planted. The fourth time it literally means to resist, set against, and oppose. The Greek word is anthistémi. It is found in the verse: "Therefore, put on the full armor of God, so that when the day of evil comes, you may be able to stand your ground." Stand in the armor of God, so you can resist, oppose, and set against the enemy by the power of God, in the day of evil.

The armor of God is a passage I have known since my youth. The wording is so familiar, I can read right over it without pondering it, which isn't necessarily a good thing. Let's take time to pull this important passage about spiritual warfare apart, like cutting up a steak and slowly enjoying every bite. Instead of gobbling down the meal without tasting it, take the time to savor every texture, color and flavor. Let's serve up some Greek meanings for these familiar words!

GREEK WORD STUDY

Let's also look at the phrase "be strong." In English, the meaning for "strong" is straightforward. The phrase "be strong" in our language just implies that you get yourself in the place or state of being strong. The Greek word for "be strong" is endunamoó. It means: to empower, "I fill with power," "strengthen or make strong." The root word is "dynamo" where we get our word "dynamite" or "dynamic." The "en" added at the beginning intensifies the "dynamo" by adding an impartation, "sharing power or ability" which is similar to our English word "empowered." Notice the definition I found on biblehub.com shows an impartation in the meaning.

> **HELPS™ Word-studies**
> 1743 *endynamóō* (from <u>1722</u> /en "in," which intensifies <u>1412</u> /dynamóō, "*sharing* power-ability") – properly, to impart *ability* (make able); empowered.

THE DYNAMITE THAT BRINGS ORDER FROM CHAOS

Looking at the Greek, the idea of being strong in the Lord implies we are imparted with strength by the Holy Spirit. To overcome our spiritual enemies, we must be empowered by the Spirit of the Lord. It is an ever-increasing strength. The power from the Lord continues to intensify! Just two Sundays before I wrote this section, my father preached on Ephesians 1 and the power of Christ to raise us up from the dead. We were, in fact, raised with Christ at his resurrection. The power, or strength, of Christ's resurrection is in us. The Greek root "dynamóō" is the same word we get our word "dynamite" from. Dynamite is used to blow things apart into chaos. The "endynamóō" of God is the power to bring the chaos and disorder of our lives back into order, and to give us wholeness and freedom. This power fills us when we are in the battle. The devil is trying to wound us and destroy us, but the strength of the Lord is healing us, directing us, and ordering our lives in ever-increasing strength! In spiritual warfare, we have the reservoir of the Lord's strength to continually drink from.

BE FILLED!

Paul says in Ephesians 5:18, "Do not get drunk on wine, which leads to debauchery. Instead, be filled with the Spirit." In this passage of contrasts, Paul says that instead of drinking wine to help deal with emotion or to bring joy, we should fill ourselves up with the Spirit. The Spirit of God brings believers what many people look for in the ways of the world. Wine brings a type of boldness when you drink it, because it lowers your inhibitions. The Spirit of God brings a different type of boldness when he fills you, because he replaces your fear with his presence. He roots out the problem, instead of covering it up or numbing it. To be filled is a command to believers, which infers the possibility of not being filled with the Spirit. How is this possible if all believers in Jesus have the Holy Spirit living inside of them? Romans 8:9 says, "You, however, are not in the realm of the flesh but are in the realm of the Spirit, if indeed the Spirit of God lives in you. And if anyone does not have the Spirit of Christ, they do not belong to Christ."

Since, as we learned in Week Five, our bodies are the temple of the Holy Spirit, we can look back to the original temple as an example of the difference between having the Holy Spirit and being filled with the Holy Spirit. When Solomon built the temple and dedicated it in 1 Kings 8, the Spirit of God descended on the temple and filled the temple so much that the priests could not even stand to minister. However, this filling of the entire temple only lasted for a short time. After that, his Spirit dwelt in the Holy of Holies, the inner sanctuary of the temple where only the high priest could enter on special occasions to minister in God's presence. However, we are now in the new covenant. The Lord dwells in the inner sanctuary of our spirit. But, he can fill every space there even more, as we surrender to him. This filling comes by prayer and surrender. In Christ there is a greater filling of the new temple than Solomon's temple ever experienced! In your own personal body and in the greater body of Christ, there is a never-ending supply of the Holy Spirit to bring glory to God. He is always accessible!

In Acts 1:12-14, the disciples prayed together in the upper room, waiting on the Holy Spirit. Jesus already breathed the Holy Spirit on them in John 20:22, but they were instructed to wait on the baptism of the Holy Spirit before they entered their earthly ministry. Baptism means to be completely immersed. In this case, it means complete immersion in the Spirit of God. As we learned in Ephesians 1:17, Paul taught the Ephesians, who had already received the Holy Spirit, (and even had manifested spiritual gifts like tongues and prophecy) to continually pray for the Spirit of wisdom and revelation to fill them. As we learned in Week Two of our study, our relationship with the Holy Spirit is not focused on our "arriving" at a place of being finished; it is a relationship of knowing God and drawing close to him for the pure reward of his presence.

If you feel unsure or afraid that God won't fill you, here is some assurance. When you ask, believe that the Lord will answer you. You do not need to be afraid of the Spirit of God or doubt that God desires to fill you with his ever-increasing power. In Luke 11, Jesus taught his disciples on prayer and specifically about praying for the Holy Spirit. Feel free to read the whole chapter for more insight, but I am just going to show you a little part of the passage here.

Luke 11:9-13

[9] 'So I say to you: ask and it will be given to you; seek and you will find; knock and the door will be opened to you. [10] For everyone who asks receives; the one who seeks finds; and to the one who knocks, the door will be opened.

[11] 'Which of you fathers, if your son asks for a fish, will give him a snake instead? [12] Or if he asks for an egg, will give him a scorpion? [13] If you then, though you are evil, know how to give good gifts to your children, how much more will your Father in heaven give the Holy Spirit to those who ask him!'

Jesus teaches us something simple here about prayer. The door that is knocked on gets opened. The request that is made is answered. God is a good Father. You don't need to be afraid when praying for the Holy Spirit to fill you, direct you or empower you. Do not be afraid that you will get an evil spirit. Some people get scared that asking for the Spirit of God will result in something weird. But receiving the Spirit is a basic promise of God that you can stand on. If you ask the Father in Jesus' name for the Holy Spirit, you will absolutely only get the Holy Spirit, his power, his fruit and his gifts! This is not always an emotional interaction—it can be, because God touches our emotions—but, it is always a faith interaction. We pray and ask God in faith and he answers us, the way Jesus promised he would!

In fact, you won't always feel the work of the Holy Spirit. There is not a prescribed equation that you can solve to know he hears you other than the fact that he promised he would. That is why it is called faith. We ask in faith and we receive in faith. When asking the Holy Spirit to fill us with wisdom and to lead us, we are not to doubt.

If any of you lacks wisdom, you should ask God, who gives generously to all without finding fault, and it will be given to you. But when you ask, you must believe and not doubt, because the one who doubts is like a wave of the sea, blown and tossed by the wind. That person should not expect to receive anything from the Lord. Such a person is double-minded and unstable in all they do. – James 1:5-8

Paul told Timothy,

"For this reason I remind you to fan into flame the gift of God, which is in you through the laying on of my hands. For the Spirit God gave us does not make us timid, but gives us power, love and self-discipline." – 2 Timothy 1:6-7

God is in us! The Spirit of God will not make us afraid. As we walk in him, we will see more power, love and self-discipline in our lives. The true evidence of the Spirit of God in our lives is that the fruit of our lives looks more and more like Jesus. (See Galatians 5:13-26)

Paul told the Thessalonians, "Rejoice always, pray continually, give thanks in all circumstances; for this is God's will for you in Christ Jesus. Do not quench the Spirit." – 1 Thessalonians 5:16-19

The Spirit-filled life is a praise-filled, thankful life always connected with the Father. Praise the Lord and pray continually as you go about your day. Surrender your daily worries as they come up. Seek the Lord for direction in every issue. Ask the Lord to ignite that relationship through continual faith-filled prayer and surrender, not quenching the move of the Spirit in you through negativity, thanklessness, unbelief, disobedience, and fear. Don't just rely on emotions and physical resources to solve your problems or make decisions. Emotions rise and fall. Situations change. But, when we are full of the Spirit, not emotionalism, we will find new boldness in place of timidity. We will find the power, the love and the self-discipline we need for every situation in life. So, ladies, we must remember that in order to battle in the spirit realm, we must surrender ourselves and ask to be filled with the Holy Spirit. We STAND in the armor of God, which he equips us with.

CROSS REFERENCE
Walking in the Spirit

The heart of the discerning acquires knowledge, for the ears of the wise seek it out. – Proverbs 18:15

'This is what the Lord says, he who made the earth, the Lord who formed it and established it – the Lord is his name: "Call to me and I will answer you and tell you great and unsearchable things you do not know." – Jeremiah 33:2-3

I want to establish, before we continue in our study of our spiritual battle, the utmost importance of seeking the Lord for guidance on how he wants you to engage the specific spiritual situations you face. The Christian walk is a life of intimacy with the Lord, not trying to figure things out through stressful fretting. We are complex children of God, created with a body, mind, soul and spirit. There can be many roots to the fruit in our lives. Your anger issues could be simply from bad eating and blood sugar problems, but it also could be from unforgiveness accompanied by spiritual oppression. Temporary anxiety may be simply a lack of trust in the Lord, and to overcome it you would need to confess that as sin and ask for forgiveness. Ask the Lord to fill you with faith and to open your eyes to see him in the middle of your situation. However, long-standing, crippling anxiety could also be a deep-seated stronghold rooted in abandonment from childhood, rejection or other areas of weakness. Jesus wants to bring deliverance and healing to your heart and life. This is why it is important to seek the revelation of the Holy Spirit on each situation you find yourself in. I encourage you to read 1 Corinthians 2 for revelation on the role of the Spirit of God in helping you to understand the roots of the situation you are in. But, here is one excerpt from that passage:

1 Corinthians 2:10-13 [10] these are the things God has revealed to us by his Spirit. The Spirit searches all things, even the deep things of God. [11] For who knows a person's thoughts except their own spirit within them? In the same way no one knows the thoughts of God except the Spirit of God. [12] What we have received is not the spirit of the world, but the Spirit who is from God, so that we may understand what God has freely given us. [13] This is what we speak, not in words taught us by human wisdom but in words taught by the Spirit, explaining spiritual realities with Spirit-taught words.

Being led by the Spirit of God is the most important part of your intimate walk with Christ. God knows your heart. The Spirit of God knows exactly what is going on and what you need for victory. As I said in earlier chapters, sometimes Jesus spoke healing to an ailing body, while other times he cast out a demon to bring healing. He was always in communication with the Father to hear from him. He is our example and he lives in us! It is crucial to listen to the Lord to gain peace and direction in how to pray.

In tomorrow's study, we will learn about our different enemies. The flesh is one of our enemies. When Ephesians says that our battle is not against flesh and blood, it is not ignoring the multitude of other scriptures that speak of our battle against our carnal self. This scripture specifically means that we are not to see other people as our enemies. In your conflict with a family member, do not forget that he or she is not personally the enemy or the root of the problem. Instead of fighting a person, our attack is implemented spiritually by praying for our family members for conviction of sin and the move of God in their lives. We also pray against the accusations, lies and confusions of the devil that are undermining the relationship with those family members. Finally, pray for the Holy Spirit to move in power to bring truth, light, love, peace and forgiveness.

Jesus said in Mark 8:34 that we must take up our cross and follow him. We do not live according to the flesh, because we were crucified with Christ. (Matthew 26:41, Romans 6, Romans 8:1-13, Romans 13:14, Galatians 5:13-26) Our battle with our flesh or self happens every day. We can't cast out our flesh and we can't crucify the devil. If you need to crucify your flesh, rebuking the devil will do no good. However, if you are being tempted and tormented by the devil, trying only to crucify the flesh will be equally futile. This is why we are led by the Spirit.

In my experience, many Christians live in reaction instead of revelation. Whether you believe in spiritual warfare or not may have more to do with your reaction to seeing someone use it incorrectly, or not use it at all, than it does with what the scriptures say on the issue. So, be sure that your walk with the Lord is based upon the truth of God's Word and the revelation of his Spirit, not fear, emotion and reaction.

BRINGING IT HOME

Ask Jesus if you are living in revelation through his Word and by his Spirit or if you are living in reaction and fear concerning spiritual warfare. Be open to what he has to say. Ask the Spirit of God to fill you and teach you through his Word.

In your prayer time, ask the Lord to take away any fear of the Holy Spirit.

Develop the habit of going to Jesus and praying through emotions, trials and difficulties. Don't just say, "Bless me or help me." Ask the Lord to open your mind, heart and spirit to understand the truth of your situation and to lead you in the direction you should go. Have you ever asked Jesus to teach you how to pray for the specific situation you are concerned about?

KNOWING & UNDERSTANDING YOUR ENEMY

MEMORY VERSE

[10] Finally, be strong in the Lord and in his mighty power. [11] Put on the full armour of God, so that you can take your stand against the devil's schemes. [12] For our struggle is not against flesh and blood, but against the rulers, against the authorities, against the powers of this dark world and against the spiritual forces of evil in the heavenly realms. [13] Therefore put on the full armour of God, so that when the day of evil comes, you may be able to stand your ground, and after you have done everything, to stand. – Ephesians 6:10-13

PRAYER
Spiritual Warfare: Praying for Understanding

Father,

In Jesus' name, I thank you for my salvation in Jesus. I pray that you remove my fear and open my heart to understand the deep things of God. I give you my mind and ask for supernatural understanding. I pray that any ideas and preconceived ideas that I hold which are not true will be uncovered, so I can know they are lies. Strengthen me in my inner being so that I will walk in faith in Jesus Christ. Fill my mind with your Spirit and with your revelation concerning spiritual warfare. I do not want to live in fear or ignorance. I want to stand firm in the battle. According to 2 Corinthians 10:5, I take captive all fearful, doubtful and deceptive thoughts and make them obedient to Christ Jesus. I will walk by faith and not by sight. I stand against the devil and his confusion and distraction and command him to leave in Jesus' name. Lord, I receive your truth from your Word. I am your student, Father.

In Jesus' name, Amen.

READING

Ephesians 6:10-24

[10] Finally, be strong in the Lord and in his mighty power. [11] Put on the full armour of God, so that you can take your stand against the devil's schemes. [12] For our struggle is not against flesh and blood, but against the rulers, against the authorities, against the powers of this dark world and against the spiritual forces of evil in the heavenly realms. [13] Therefore put on the full armour of God, so that when the day of evil comes, you may be able to stand your ground, and after you have done everything, to stand. [14] Stand firm then, with the belt of truth buckled round your waist, with the breastplate of righteousness

in place, [15] and with your feet fitted with the readiness that comes from the gospel of peace. [16] In addition to all this, take up the shield of faith, with which you can extinguish all the flaming arrows of the evil one. [17] Take the helmet of salvation and the sword of the Spirit, which is the word of God.

[18] And pray in the Spirit on all occasions with all kinds of prayers and requests. With this in mind, be alert and always keep on praying for all the Lord's people. [19] Pray also for me, that whenever I speak, words may be given me so that I will fearlessly make known the mystery of the gospel, [20] for which I am an ambassador in chains. Pray that I may declare it fearlessly, as I should.

[21] Tychicus, the dear brother and faithful servant in the Lord, will tell you everything, so that you also may know how I am and what I am doing. [22] I am sending him to you for this very purpose, that you may know how we are, and that he may encourage you.

[23] Peace to the brothers and sisters, and love with faith from God the Father and the Lord Jesus Christ. [24] Grace to all who love our Lord Jesus Christ with an undying love.

WHAT ARE WE FIGHTING AGAINST?

In this world, we are tempted to see actual people as our enemies. However, use your Bible Hub app to look up Ephesians 6:12 in the search bar. After you get to the verse, click on the link to look up the Greek words for each of our enemies listed in Ephesians 6:12.

NOT AGAINST	AGAINST
	(these are all different things or he wouldn't list them separately)
_____	_____
_____	_____
_____	_____

I am not sure if you are seeing a pattern in your search, but it is very clear from the Greek words Paul used that we are fighting against an organization of evil in the heavenly realms. Each of these Greek words indicate that the "power" is not an impersonal or metaphorical force, but it is organized with demonic beings in authority. As the late spiritual warfare teacher, Derek Prince, liked to say, "Evil is a person. It has a personality." The first word "ruler" denotes a preeminent ruler with headship over others. It also means "from the beginning" or a starting point. Maybe think of this as, "The buck stops here." Satan is at the top of the kingdom of darkness. Demonic powers and forces are not random little beings that roam around aimlessly. They have a preeminent ruler—the devil. Below the devil, there are other levels of arch-evil or fallen angels.

The devil is not our only enemy. Throughout scripture, we see our enemies include the world, the flesh and the devil. However, since our scripture is Ephesians 6:12, we are focusing on what is covered in this passage. We will look more deeply into our other enemies throughout the rest of our study as well.

The second word "authorities" specifically talks about power over a designated jurisdiction. These would be lower authorities, under Satan's command, but still very powerful and intelligent. A biblical example of this is from the book of Daniel Chapter 10. Daniel was fasting after seeing a troublesome vision about a great war. An angelic messenger comes to him, in answer to his prayers for understanding.

[12] Then he continued, 'Do not be afraid, Daniel. Since the first day that you set your mind to gain understanding and to humble yourself before your God, your words were heard, and I have come in response to them. [13] But the prince of the Persian kingdom resisted me twenty-one days. Then Michael, one of the chief princes, came to help me, because I was detained there with the king of Persia. [14] Now I have come to explain to you what will happen to your people in the future, for the vision concerns a time yet to come.' — Daniel 10:12-14.

Here, the veil that hides the spiritual world from the physical world is pulled back for Daniel to see the inner workings of the spirit realm. The angelic messenger tells him that he was detained for twenty-one days by an evil spiritual being with authority over the great Persian Empire. The name of the evil being is the Prince of Persia. Since a physical prince cannot detain an angelic being in battle, we know he is not a physical prince, but a spiritual prince. Also, further on in Daniel 10, which I encourage you to read, Daniel is told that when the messenger leaves to go back, there is an evil Prince of Greece coming to fight him. The only support he had against this evil spiritual leader and his organization of power was Michael, the angelic prince of the Jewish people. We know that Michael is an arch-angel of God. He is assigned by God to protect the nation of Israel. In the same way, there are also evil principalities with jurisdiction over nations and empires, as well as protective angels, like Michael. In the physical world, after the Persian Empire, the Greek Empire rose as the dominating empire of the world. These two empires were enemies in the ancient world. We see from this passage, that the rising and falling of nations is not brought about by physical leaders alone, but also by spiritual beings in high places. I need to point out that the fantastic organization of these beings is not because of Satan's great leadership, but because they were already organized in rank as angels of God before they rebelled against him at the beginning of time.

In Luke 10:18-20, Jesus says, "'I saw Satan fall like lightning from heaven. I have given you authority to trample on snakes and scorpions and to overcome all the power of the enemy; nothing will harm you. However, do not rejoice that the spirits submit to you, but rejoice that your names are written in heaven.'"

Here we have Jesus' own account of the day when Satan fell from heaven, along with his assurance that we have authority over spirits and that our focus should be on our salvation. Jesus said that the spirits must submit to us. The word for "powers of this dark" world is literally kosmokrator, which comes from kosmos or world and krateo or "to rule." Remember that Ephesians 2:1-2 says, "As for you, you were dead in your transgressions and sins, in which you used to live when you followed the ways of this world and of the ruler of the kingdom of the air, the spirit who is now at work in those who are disobedient."

Jesus teaches us that the world is one of our enemies. In John 15:19 he says, "If you belonged to the world, it would love you as its own. As it is, you do not belong to the world, but I have chosen you out of the world. That is why the world hates you."

Have you ever seen how the world persecutes believers in Jesus? If a celebrity becomes a believer or shares his or her opinion on truth, it seems like all hell literally breaks loose. It is a perfect picture of how the world itself hates Jesus. World powers like Hollywood, the media, the governments and other powerful institutions are being used by the enemy in his plan to oppress the truth with wickedness and turn more and more people away from Christ. Racial division and riots, hatred and taking sides, brother against brother—such explosive conflicts cause people to wring their hands and try to figure out which side to join. When you see this happening, don't be surprised and don't look for powerful men and women or even political parties to blame. Don't go on social media to gripe and slander people. Get on your knees and go to battle in your prayer closet. Pray with other believers. Spiritual warfare through prayer is a powerful weapon.

When you hear about a historic battle, the opposing generals are named, instead of the list of every name of every foot soldier on the field. For example, "Grant and Lee met in the battle that fateful day." In an organized and strategic battle, the two organized forces meet, but it is really a battle of the commanders. In our case, the two commanders are Jesus and Satan. Jesus has angels at his beck and call. Do you remember what he said in the Garden of Gethsemane? Matthew 26:53 records it, "Do you think I cannot call on my Father, and he will at once put at my disposal more than twelve legions of angels?"

We are also soldiers on God's battlefield! Jesus told Peter in Matthew 16:18, "And I tell you that you are Peter, and on this rock I will build my church, and the gates of Hades will not overcome it." Jesus declared to Peter that the church would not be hiding from the devil or cowering in fear, but that it would be making a frontal assault on the kingdom of the darkness and the gates of Hades would not overcome the church! Praise the Lord! What is your mindset in spiritual warfare? Is it fearful? It should not be. We are part of a battle to set the captives free and establish the kingdom of God in the hearts of men, women and children.

What about the other side? Before you belong to Christ, you are on the wrong side of the battle, even if unknowingly! Ephesians 2:2 reminds us of this. Also, we see that when Jesus cast demons out of people, they are referred to as evil spirits. These are not all the devil himself. Mark 5:1-20 gives us an account of Jesus setting free a demonized man. Mark 5:9-10 says,

> Then Jesus asked him, 'What is your name?'
>
> 'My name is Legion,' he replied, 'for we are many.' And he begged Jesus again and again not to send them out of the area. – Mark 5:9-10

We see several specifics about spiritual warfare here. One important point is that the enemy was organized into a legion. To find information on what a legion is, you can use an online Bible dictionary such as this entry from Easton's Bible Dictionary found on biblestudytools.com,

> **Legion** – a regiment of the Roman army, the number of men composing which differed at different times. It originally consisted of three thousand men, but in the time of Christ consisted of six thousand, exclusive of horsemen, who were in number a tenth of the foot-men. The word is used (Matthew 26:53; Mark 5:9) to express simply a great multitude.

Secondly, we see that the demons made the man physically harm himself. Thirdly, we see that the demons were assigned to an area and were extremely distressed at the thought of leaving the area. Fourthly, we see that Jesus had total authority and control over the situation. Remember our lessons in Week Two? Thankfully, Jesus is exalted above all other powers and authorities and we are seated with him in heavenly realms. If God is for us, who can be against us? Do not be afraid! Be strong in the Lord and in his mighty power! In fact, the words "mighty power" in the Greek imply dominion or to dominate. The kingdom of God dominates the kingdom of evil. We are filled with dominating power to bring about the defeat of Satan.

GREEK WORD STUDY

Finally, what are these spiritual forces of evil in the heavenly realms? Interestingly enough, HELPS™ Word-studies, found on biblehub.com, says that the Greek word for evil is ponēría.

> **HELPS™ Word-studies**
> **Cognate: 4189** *ponēría* (from 4192 /*pónos*, "pain, laborious trouble") – properly, *pain*-ridden evil, derived from 4192 (*pónos*) which refers to "*pain (pure and simple)*" – resulting in "toil, then drudge, i.e. '*bad*' like our . . . criminal" (*WP*, 1, 325). See 4190 (*ponēros*).

These organized spirits are beings that have authority over pain-ridden evil, toil, and drudgery. This eye-opening word study helps us to have more of a realistic understanding of who we are fighting against in the unseen spiritual battle we face every day.

This is the very reason Paul tells us to "suit up!" in the armor of God. This is why we cannot dabble in the devil's kingdom. 1 John 5:19 says, "We know that we are children of God and that the whole world is under the control of the evil one." His kingdom is a kingdom of death, destruction, chaos and pain-ridden evil. We must be in the Word of God, so we have a weapon to use against the lies and temptation, and faith to stand against the fiery darts that the devil sends our way. So, while the devil and his cohorts have a master plan to attack and destroy the children of God, God has a master plan to destroy the works of the devil and to give us life.

> The thief comes only to steal and kill and destroy; I have come that they may have life, and have it to the full. – John 10:10

> Since the children have flesh and blood, he too shared in their humanity so that by his death he might break the power of him who holds the power of death – that is, the devil – and free those who all their lives were held in slavery by their fear of death. – Hebrews 2:14-15

> The one who does what is sinful is of the devil, because the devil has been sinning from the beginning. The reason the Son of God appeared was to destroy the devil's work. – 1 John 3:8

The Lord provides us with the armor of God to protect us from the enemy. He provides us with an ever-increasing power from the Holy Spirit. He provides us with prayer and authority to overcome all the power of the evil one. Are you ready to learn about how to battle and wage war against the evil one?

SPIRITUAL FORCES OF EVIL IN THE HEAVENLY REALMS

Remember that Ephesians 6:12 says, "For our struggle is not against flesh and blood, but against the rulers, against the authorities, against the powers of this dark world and against the spiritual forces of evil in the heavenly realms."

The spiritual forces of evil in the heavenly realms can also be those personal demons—the inflictors of pain—which are assigned to specifically harass and attack individuals and families. Here is the big secret. You are not a puppet of the enemy. Tempting you is so much easier for the devil than playing "puppet master." Scripture after scripture says that his weapons against us are accusation, deception and temptation, with the bait being our own evil desire. If you have time, you can do a word search for: devil, Satan or temptation to read examples of how the enemy attacks us.

ACCUSATION

The enemy desires to heap condemnation upon us and to get you to heap condemnation on your family members and other believers. He wants us to see the worst in ourselves and other people, instead of seeing who we are, and who they are, in Christ. This battle is in our minds. For example, a woman who was sexually abused will frequently be harassed with lies about the reason this unspeakable event or series of events happened. The enemy will say that it was her fault, or that she is somehow dirty, or undeserving of true love and protection. This may not even be a straight-forward thought, but an underlying lie that frames the way she lives. She may think things like, "What's wrong with me," or "Why can't I do anything right?" or "Everything bad happens to me." These are false accusations from the enemy to depress her and to keep her from the power and freedom that Jesus Christ has for her life. This is false guilt that stands against the truth of who she is in Christ. The lies need to be taken captive in Jesus' name and spirits of shame, abuse, worthlessness, condemnation and false guilt need to be commanded to leave. Finally—and importantly—she needs to pray for the Holy Spirit to fill her and replace the lies with truth.

On the other hand, the enemy will use the same situation in the woman's life to accuse all men and tell her that all men are pigs and abusers. This will also keep the woman in emotional and spiritual chains, because she will not have a true picture of the men in her life. I call this living in reaction. This general false accusation against all men will put walls between her and her husband or other men who are not pigs and abusers. It could negatively influence her intimacy with her husband, because she may always associate sexuality with shame and dirtiness or fear and anger. It can also affect how she feels about men or women in general—depending on the source of the abuse—and cause identity confusion. The devil always spins confusing lies about our true identity. That is what he did to Jesus in the wilderness, when he tried to confuse Jesus and accuse him of not being the Son of God. The devil even kept tempting Jesus to prove something that was actually true. He was the legitimate Son of God. There was no need to prove it. In order for freedom to come, the woman needs to pray for God to deliver her from the lies and accusations that raise themselves up in her heart and mind. A woman who has been through abuse like this will need to pray to forgive the abuser, not to excuse him or her, but to put vengeance into the hands of the Lord, instead of harboring poisonous bitterness in her heart. She needs to be willing to hear from Jesus and to admit that there are things in her life that are keeping her from freedom and truth. Any spirits that gained access to oppress her, through the abuse, must be rebuked and commanded to leave in Jesus' name. "Open the eyes of my heart, Lord. Show me the lies. Lead me in the way everlasting. In Jesus' name." Jesus can heal her heart and set her free from the accuser, who lies about her identity, her value, and the character of the opposite sex. Remember, this is a process and a walk with the Savior, not a liturgical prayer. Walk with Jesus.

> Then I heard a loud voice in heaven say: 'Now have come the salvation and the power and the kingdom of our God, and the authority of his Messiah. **For the accuser of our brothers and sisters, who accuses them before our God day and night, has been hurled down.** – Revelation 12:10

> Therefore, **there is now no condemnation for those who are in Christ Jesus**, because through Christ Jesus the law of the Spirit who gives life has set you free from the law of sin and death. For what the law was powerless to do because it was weakened by the flesh, God did by sending his own Son in the likeness of sinful flesh to be a sin offering. And so he condemned sin in the flesh, in order that the righteous requirement of the law might be fully met in us, who do not live according to the flesh but according to the Spirit. – Romans 8:1-4

> For the entire law is fulfilled in keeping this one command: 'Love your neighbour as yourself.' **If you bite and devour each other, watch out or you will be destroyed by each other.** So I say, live by the Spirit, and you will not gratify the desires of the flesh. – Galatians 5:14-16

DECEPTION

The enemy wants us to follow the thinking patterns of this world and to be deceived into believing arguments and pretensions against the Lord and against others we are in relationship with. He wants you to believe that there is nothing more for you than what you already have, so you are hopeless. Once you believe the enemy's lies, you are battling God's truth in your life right alongside the devil. He will have you at war with yourself and with others. You may even believe that the truth is a lie. If you are living in fear, this will be especially true. Fear works against you to keep you from enjoying life, to keep you from being thankful, to keep you from being content. Fear convinces you that this fear is your protection and that any attempt to help you to see the lie is actually a lie that wants to disarm what is protecting you. For example, someone with an eating disorder is afraid of food and really believes that she is fat. Even if everyone else believes she is beautiful and sees that she is perhaps getting too skinny or unhealthy because of the eating disorder, she will think they are just lying to her. The philosophies of the world have taken her captive and she cannot see the truth. The truth becomes her enemy, because she thinks that if she listens to the pleas of concerned friends or family to see herself differently than she currently does, she will lose the battle and be forever doomed to be unattractive and fat. That is how fear dominates someone with a false sense of reality. The enemy lies to the person. If you believe the lie, you cannot believe truth.

> See to it that no one **takes you captive through hollow and deceptive philosophy**, which depends on human tradition and the elemental spiritual forces of this world rather than on Christ. – Colossians 2:8-9

It says in 2 Corinthians 10:5, "We demolish arguments and every pretension that sets itself up against the knowledge of God, and we take captive every thought and make it obedient to Christ." Negativity, fear and anxiety are some of the most powerful liars that raise their heads up against the knowledge of God and the victory we have in Christ. Emotions that were given to us by the Lord are suddenly used against us by our enemy Fear to get us into a place where we can't get out of bed, we can't get negative thoughts out of our heads, we can't stop eating, or we can't overcome nervous habits that are breaking down our health. I know women in these situations who have defeated the enemy by seeking the Lord for revelation and understanding of their situation, standing on the truth of the Word of God, confessing the truth of who they are in Christ, and expelling the devil from their circumstance and life! Jesus wants to speak truth to you to set you free.

TEMPTATION

> When tempted, no one should say, 'God is tempting me.' For God cannot be tempted by evil, nor does he tempt anyone; but each person is tempted when **they are dragged away by their own evil desire and enticed.** Then, after desire has conceived, it gives birth to sin; and sin, when it is full-grown, gives birth to death. – James 1:12-15

The next step to find freedom requires dying to our enemy, the flesh. This scripture in James uncovers the devil's best hidden secret. He tempts you by agreeing with you. Like the most cunning advertiser, he wants you to have everything your little heart desires; so he sells sin in beautiful, attractive ways that are personalized to fit your needs and wants. Why? Because he knows that when you get the object of your own evil desires, that sin will lead to death—death to unity, death to relationships, death to churches, death spiritually and even physical death, to name a few things. Self is, perhaps, our biggest enemy, because the temptation is not about some weird, foreign thing, but what we are familiarly hungry for.

> For everything in the world – the lust of the flesh, the lust of the eyes, and the pride of life – comes not from the Father but from the world. – 1 John 2:16

Self exalts perfection over people. Self exalts my needs above the needs of others. My schedule. My stuff. My reputation. My future. My life. For example, have you ever asked your husband or kids to help you around the house and they cheerfully do their best, but it's not exactly how you would have done it? When that happens, have you thanklessly complained and nagged? Perhaps passively 'redone' everything they did wrong? Little eyes see that, too! On a side note, when I was wrestling with this as a young mom, the Lord showed me that I needed to cheerfully come alongside my children and teach them how to do what I needed them to do in a non-critical way. We would work together to clean the room, talking about how and why we were doing specific things. In my flesh, I wanted to delegate and walk away. But, God showed me that I was putting my children in a lose-lose situation. Even teens need instruction on how to clean or cook. God showed me that my hesitation to help was more out of selfishness than anything. I wanted the free time and I didn't want to be bothered at that moment to do something like load the dishwasher with my son.

When criticism—whether direct or passive—happens, it injures the other person and demeans their offering. Think of how imperfect your offering is to God. You bring what you can and you know that it isn't always perfect, simply because you cannot be perfect the way God is perfect. Being angry with a family member because he or she doesn't do something the way you would do it is very damaging to the relationship. It attaches failure to the relationship. It keeps the person from feeling secure and loved. This is exalting self. Your ideas and desires are then exalted above the needs and hearts of other people. Fear of things not going your way can lead to the sin of manipulation and control. People need space and grace for personal growth. They need to be thanked, and they need praise for the good things they have done—even if they aren't done perfectly. During teachable moments, they need positive encouragement in areas where they can grow. How do we avoid temptation to sin in this area of getting our way? We pray. We ask forgiveness of those we have injured. We repent for the sins of selfishness, control and hurting others. If there is an area of weakness in a loved one, we pray for the Lord to work in his or her heart and to help them to grow and to overcome. Put them in the Lord's hands and ask him for teachable moments with them.

How else do our evil fleshly desires drag us away and entice us? In Matthew 4:1-11, the devil tempted Jesus with temporary pleasure when he said he would give Jesus all the kingdoms of the world and their splendor, if only he bowed down to him. This appeal was to Jesus' humanity, or his flesh. Thankfully, he was perfect in every way and did not choose the temporary; he chose the eternal. He spoke the Word of God to the devil and commanded him to leave. How many times do we compromise with the devil, taking his offering of temporary pleasure, justifying sinful behaviors that fill up the selfish hungers of our flesh?

BRINGING IT HOME

Ask God to give you hope in Christ and to protect you from the lies of the enemy, as you learn about the power of God to deliver you from the evil one.

To find more help on overcoming specific strongholds of the enemy, reference the Prayer Index in the back of the book.

PUTTING ON YOUR ARMOR
PART 1

THE HELMET OF SALVATION

MEMORY VERSE

[10] Finally, be strong in the Lord and in his mighty power. [11] Put on the full armour of God, so that you can take your stand against the devil's schemes. [12] For our struggle is not against flesh and blood, but against the rulers, against the authorities, against the powers of this dark world and against the spiritual forces of evil in the heavenly realms. [13] Therefore put on the full armour of God, so that when the day of evil comes, you may be able to stand your ground, and after you have done everything, to stand. – Ephesians 6:10-13

PRAYER
Spiritual Warfare Prayer

Father,

In Jesus' name, I praise you because you are glorious. I praise you for Jesus Christ your Son, our Sovereign Lord.

I ask that you fill me with the Spirit of wisdom and revelation that I may know you and understand this battle that I am living in. Open the eyes of my heart so that I may see you and the hope that I have in you, in Jesus' name. I need to know that I have hope in the battle, Lord. Right now, I acknowledge that my battle is not against flesh and blood. I am not battling people in this world. I am not battling against my spouse or children. I am not battling against non-believers or family members. I am battling against spiritual rulers and authorities in my life. I am battling against things seen and unseen that raise themselves up against the knowledge of Christ Jesus.

I stand against lies and darkness that come against me in Jesus' name. No weapon formed against me shall prosper, in Jesus' name. I acknowledge the power of Jesus and I praise you that I am seated with him in heavenly realms above all rule and power and authority.

I know that in Christ and his resurrection power I am victorious. So, I stand in the armor of Jesus right now. I put on the helmet of salvation. I praise you for my salvation, in Jesus' name. I thank you for your protection and that you protect my head, my life, my authority through Christ. I fix my thoughts on you. You are my hope and my salvation. I praise your holy name! In you I am safe and secure. I have a future and a hope! I take up the garment of praise and worship your name!

You are good and there is none like you. I stand against a spirit of despair and pray that you lift up all heaviness from me, in Jesus' name. I am your child and I rejoice that my name is written in heaven!

I stand firm in the truth of Christ. I buckle your belt of truth about my waist. I pray that your truth will secure my life. Defend me against the lies of Satan, in Jesus' name. I know that I am vulnerable apart from you, Lord. I ask in Jesus' name that you will reveal to me any lies that I am believing and allow me to walk in your truth.

I thank you that I am seated with you in heavenly realms.

In Jesus' name, Amen!

READING

Turn in your Bible and read Ephesians 6:10-24

LISTS
Putting on God's Armor

List the pieces of the armor of God, including the weapons. Also state their functionality.

> **TODAY'S BIBLE STUDY TOOL**
>
> **Lists.** Lists can be within one verse, a few paragraphs, or an entire chapter. It is helpful to compile your findings into a list. Examples: Days of Creation, Fruits of the Spirit, etc.

When you think of the armor of God, what do you think of? What imagery comes to your mind? At first glance, one may think of the armor of God as an invisible mystical armor that you put on through prayer. In fact, many people would suggest this practice. The armor listed in Ephesians Chapter 6 depicts the image of the type of armor a Roman solider would wear. But, let's look at the armor of God. Each piece describes the fruit of a life that is filled with the Spirit.

- Truth (another name for the Spirit is the Spirit of truth)

- Righteousness or holiness

- Readiness to share the gospel and evangelize

- Faith

- Salvation (notice this is listed separately from righteousness)

In light of what we learned in Week Ten, Day 5, that our enemy attacks us with accusations, deception and temptation, and that he uses our own evil desires and inclinations to trap us, the armor of God makes a lot more sense. A life submitted to the Lord from your head to your toes will be protected from temptation and attack, sheltered by the Most High. Psalm 91:1-2 says, "Whoever dwells in the shelter of the Most High will rest in the shadow of the Almighty. I will say of the Lord, 'He is my refuge and my fortress, my God, in whom I trust.'"

WORD STUDY
Helmet

I decided to see where else in scripture it references the armor of God. So, I did a word search for the word "helmet." Did you know that in Isaiah 59 it describes a situation where God puts on his own armor? Here is the account from verses 15b-17. This prophecy describes when God comes to deal with the sin of the world. This is none other than Jesus, clothing himself in righteousness, in order to go to war for us and to deliver us from our sins!

Isaiah 59:15b-17

The Lord looked and was displeased
    that there was no justice.
He saw that there was no one,
    he was appalled that there was no one to intervene;
so his own arm achieved salvation for him,
    and his own righteousness sustained him.
He put on righteousness as his breastplate,
    and the **helmet** of salvation on his head;
he put on the garments of vengeance
    and wrapped himself in zeal as in a cloak.

> **TODAY'S BIBLE STUDY TOOL**
>
> **Word Study.** Dig deeper into the meaning of a word by seeing what other scriptures have to say about it.

When we put on the armor of God, it isn't God's armor just for us. It is his armor! He wears it. I once heard a missionary to Mexico say, "It's God's armor. Don't let the devil know you are in it!" Jesus was kept by his righteous life. When we are in Christ and walk in him, we are also protected by his righteous life. Sin exposes us to death and destruction in more ways than one. So, how do we put on this armor? In today's study, we will start with examining the helmet of salvation.

The first five pieces of armor protect us against the lies and attacks of the enemy. Let's think on this, starting with the helmet of salvation. First of all, we have zero protection against Satan, if we are not saved by the grace of God. We have no position in the heavenly realms, apart from Christ. Salvation covers the head, spiritually speaking. The head is a symbol of authority in scripture. If your head is not protected, your whole body is in mortal danger. If your spiritual head is not saved, your whole body is headed for hell and under the dominion of the enemy. Salvation by the Lord removes the devil's ultimate authority in your life and dethrones the authority of sin and death. It's important to remember, when doing spiritual warfare, that truly, the battle is the Lord's. Salvation is a game changer.

The head also represents your thought life. The main method of attack the devil uses is to launch lies, guilt and deception at a believer. He wants to keep you in a place of negativity, despair and faithlessness. Isaiah 26:3 says, "You will keep in perfect peace those whose minds are steadfast, because they trust in you." The Christian life is a faith-filled, positive life. When your mind is fixed on Christ, or is steadfastly focused on him, it is protected. They say there are two types of people—those who see the glass half full and those who see the glass half empty. That is because there is more than one reality. There is a physical reality that is full of mortality and fallenness. There is also the spiritual reality that is full of salvation, redemption and hope. You are seated with Christ in heavenly realms. Faith connects the two realms, so we can see the power and goodness of God in the land of the living.

Where is your mind? Is your mind protected with hope or is it always fretting, worrying and entertaining negative thoughts? Praying for protection over your mind from lies, deception and faithlessness is a very important practice. Also, pray for the positive! Pray for God to renew your mind with his truth. This is not mind over matter philosophy. This is the power of God and his Word to renew your mind. It does not come from yourself. It comes from God. He commands us to put on the helmet and to renew our minds. Romans 12:2 says, "Do not conform to the pattern of this world, but be transformed by the renewing of your mind. Then you will be able to test and approve what God's will is — his good, pleasing and perfect will."

Our part of the putting on of the helmet is to choose to walk in what God has given us. We choose to focus our minds on truth. We choose to obey him, through his Spirit. We choose to pray for our minds to be filled with his Holy Spirit and with hope. We choose to confess the truth out loud and rebuke the lies of Satan in the name of Jesus. 1 Thessalonians 5:8 says, "But since we belong to the day, let us be sober, putting on faith and love as a breastplate, and the hope of salvation as a helmet." Hope protects our thoughts. When hopeless thoughts come around, do you stand your ground? Do you put on the hope of salvation as a helmet? Find hope-filled scriptures to memorize and to dwell on when you are in bed at night. When you feel heavy with despair, rebuke a spirit of despair and put on the garment of praise.

I know women who were set free from enemies of crippling fear and depression. In an attempt to find answers, it's easy to blame "your personality" or "your body chemistry." But, what if you were just raised to think in a negative way? This may be the only way you know how to live. What if there is an enemy that you cannot see that has been claiming ground in your life by manipulating your weaknesses or taking root in some sort of trauma, abandonment or abuse you lived through? Jesus' mission was to deliver you from all such bondage that sin in a fallen world brings. Isaiah 61:1-3, which is the scripture that Jesus read from in the synagogue when he initiated his public ministry, says,

Isaiah 61:1-3

The Spirit of the Sovereign Lord is on me,
    because the Lord has anointed me
    to proclaim good news to the poor.
He has sent me to bind up the broken-hearted,
    to proclaim freedom for the captives
    and release from darkness for the prisoners,
to proclaim the year of the Lord's favour
    and the day of vengeance of our God,
to comfort all who mourn,
    and provide for those who grieve in Zion –
to bestow on them a crown of beauty
    instead of ashes,
the oil of joy
    instead of mourning,
and a garment of praise
    instead of a spirit of despair.
They will be called oaks of righteousness,
    a planting of the Lord
    for the display of his splendour.

When Jesus read the first part of this prophecy, he said, "Today this scripture is fulfilled in your hearing." (Luke 4:21) Jesus' mission was to fulfill this prophecy to set the prisoners free. By reading it aloud, he was making a formal and public declaration of the truth. He was telling everyone there, as well as the devil, "The day of the Lord's favor is here! I AM the deliverer!" Verse 3 says our deliverer gives us a garment of praise instead of a spirit of despair. Do you put off the spirit of despair? Do you put on the garment of praise? Putting on praise is part of putting on the full armor of God. The helmet of salvation is the helmet of hope and we put it on with praise and worship! When he binds up our broken hearts, when he proclaims freedom over us, and when he sets us free from spiritual bondage to evil spirits of despair and depression, we are on display to show off his splendour! Our testimonies reflect his greatness. We are given beauty for ashes, the oil of joy instead of mourning and a garment of praise in place of a spirit of despair! Hallelujah!

Today, if you feel like a prisoner in a dark dungeon of depression, ask the Lord to protect your mind. Ask him what put you in that prison. Is it a spirit of despair—or heaviness—as the KJV says? If spirits of heaviness, hopelessness and despair are attacking you, rebuke them in Jesus' name. Put them off and command them to leave you. Then put on the helmet of salvation and the garment of praise. Sing aloud to the Lord. Let your mouth be full of his praises and his truth be on your lips. Fix your mind on Jesus and the hope you have in Christ. When those negative, heavy thoughts come back, rebuke the spirit of heaviness in Jesus' name and put on the garment of praise again! In this way, you will stand your ground. For more information on depression, reference the index in the back of the book.

BRINGING IT HOME

What is your focus when things get difficult in life? Are you focused on the physical reality of a person, place or thing that's difficult, or do you ask God to reveal to you what the root of the problem is? Is your armor on in every area?

Teach your children about the armor of God today. No matter how little they are or how old, we moms are very good about talking to our children about what protects them. If you would make sure they are properly buckled into their car seat, wearing their coat to school, or eating a healthy breakfast, how much more would you want them to understand the armor of God?

PUTTING ON YOUR ARMOR
PART 2

THE BELT OF TRUTH

MEMORY VERSE

[10] Finally, be strong in the Lord and in his mighty power. [11] Put on the full armour of God, so that you can take your stand against the devil's schemes. [12] For our struggle is not against flesh and blood, but against the rulers, against the authorities, against the powers of this dark world and against the spiritual forces of evil in the heavenly realms. [13] Therefore put on the full armour of God, so that when the day of evil comes, you may be able to stand your ground, and after you have done everything, to stand. – Ephesians 6:10-13

PRAYER

You may also pray the Armor of God prayer in the Prayer Index.

Father,

In Jesus' name I thank you for leading me into all truth. I pray that you continue to bring revelation to my heart, as I study your Word. I pray that you will build me up in my inner being, so that Christ may dwell in my heart through faith. Lord, teach me that flesh and blood are not my enemies. Teach me to listen to you, when I am in a conflict. Help me to walk in the truth of your Word and to speak it aloud, that I may grow in faith. In Jesus' name, I put off all negative, complaining thoughts and rejoice in your goodness and grace. I praise you for the cross and for your victory and hope!

In Jesus' name. Amen.

READING

Open your Bible and read Ephesians 6:10-24.

THE BELT OF TRUTH

Day 1 of this week taught us the importance and function of the helmet of salvation. Now, if our head is secure, what other armor is needed? The belt of truth refers to the belt worn by a Roman soldier. It is more than a functional belt to keep your pants up, especially since Roman soldiers wore skirts, not pants. This leather strap, embedded with metal decoration on leather straps hanging down from the front, would be used to hold weapons and implements, as well as for tucking in extra clothing to keep it from getting in the way. All of this symbolizes how the belt of truth holds a spiritual soldier's armor and weapons together. Truth is the trademark of the kingdom of God. Lies are the trademark of the devil's kingdom.

WORD STUDY

Our directive to put on the belt of truth from Ephesians 6:14 in the NIVUK says, "Stand firm then, with the belt of truth buckled around your waist." However, I remember when I was little hearing this verse read differently in the KJV. What's the difference? Let's look at the original language on biblehub.com.

- Select Ephesians 6:14
- Click on GRK for Greek

When you see the charting of the verse, what do you notice? The word for "waist" is not there. The transliteration from the Greek is "loins." The original Greek says to gird up your loins. Loins seems like an old-fashioned word; does it really mean waist? Hmmm. I wondered about this, so after coming to the Greek chart for the verse, I clicked on the hyperlinked concordance number for loins. HELPS™ Word-studies says this about the Greek word for loins:

> **HELPS™ Word-studies**
> **3751** *osphýs* – properly, the hip (reproductive area); used figuratively in 1 Pet 1:13 of the "reproductive" (creative) capacity of the *renewed mind* (cf. Ro 12:1-3).
>
> [3751 (*osphýs*) is "the seat of generative power (Heb 7:5,10, *Abbott-Smith*). "To smite the loins" referred to a fatal blow – "forever ending" anything that would (could) come from the slain.]

Most of the modern versions do not say loins, but this word study we've done reveals a deeper message about the purpose of belt of truth. It's more than just something to tuck your tunic into. The leather hanging down from the front of the belt protected the reproductive organs of the soldier. Truth protects your ability to produce life. If a believer is not protected with the truth, that person can be deceived by lies, and the life-giving power of the gospel is stolen. In Matthew 13, Jesus teaches the parable of the sower. In the parable, a sower is sowing his seed. The seed is the message about God's kingdom. Jesus says, "Listen then to what the parable of the sower means: when anyone hears the message about the kingdom and does not understand it, the evil one comes and snatches away what was sown in their heart. This is the seed sown along the path." – Matthew 13:18-19

He describes the devil as a bird who is able to steal the Word of God from the hard ground of the path. A hard heart is a heart that will not receive truth. Imagine the enemy as a bird reaching into a hard heart to pluck out the Word before it takes root. That is a frightening picture! But still, Jesus says this is an accurate representation. The truth of the message of the kingdom is a seed that will germinate in a fertile heart. But, life cannot be produced when the heart is hard against truth. For this reason, when I share the gospel with people, I pray for their hearts to be softened to receive the truth. We need to pray for the Holy Spirit to bring revelation to the non-believer, so that the eyes of the person's heart will be opened to see and hear the truth of salvation. I also do spiritual warfare against the devil, that he will be bound or prohibited from stealing the seed of the Word out of the person's heart.

In contemplating the nature of the enemy and how he functions when he attacks a believer to steal truth, I realized that his method is more complex than when he plucks the Word out of an unbeliever's heart. He tries to steal the truth of the Word from a believer by twisting the truth into a lie. When the truth is corrupted with twisting, it is no longer the truth. It is a lie. It no longer has the life-giving power of a seed. However, when you believe the truth and walk in the truth, it protects you and produces life in you. When your life is protected by truth, it will germinate life in those around you. You will even be able to speak the seed of truth into the life of a friend and he or she can become born again! Truly we are life bearers, in Jesus. Do not let the devil steal your life-giving truth with lies! Put on the belt of truth.

So, how do we do that? No matter how much you pray to put on the belt of truth, if you don't learn the truth, if you don't live in the truth, if you believe lies, if you speak lies, there is no chance that the belt of truth is going on you. Truth itself is the protection. Let's review from last week what the Lord said in Isaiah 59, "The Lord looked and was displeased that there was no justice. He saw that there was no one, he was appalled that there was no one to intervene." – Isaiah 59:15

The first step to putting on the belt of truth is to admit that you are open to deception. As Isaiah 59:15 implies, there is no one who is righteous. Pride comes before a fall. I make a regular practice of asking the Lord to protect me from my own deception. This goes along with what Jesus taught his disciples to pray, "and lead us not into temptation, but deliver us from the evil one." (Matthew 6:13) Take this part of the Lord's prayer very literally. It's not just a flowery request. It should be the cry of our hearts. "God, I know my flesh is easily led astray. I know I can be deceived. Please lead me not into the temptation of my own evil desires. Deliver me from the evil one!"

THE TRUE JESUS VS THE ANTICHRIST

Next, to put on the belt of truth, look to Jesus himself. If you searched for the word "truth" in your Bible app, this famous passage will be near the top of the search results. John 14:6-7 says, "Jesus answered, 'I am the way and the truth and the life. No one comes to the Father except through me. If you really know me, you will know my Father as well. From now on, you do know him and have seen him.'"

When the enemy wants to deconstruct your faith, he will take your eyes off of Jesus, or he will begin to shoot arrows of doubts towards you concerning the power and divinity of Jesus. When I was newly married, even though I had been a Christian most of my life, I began to have an overwhelming number of doubts about Jesus. This was a strange and new battle. These anti-Jesus, or antichrist thoughts were causing me to doubt the veracity of the gospel, as well as the divine nature of Christ. I prayed and prayed about it, but was afraid that if I dismissed these questions and doubts I would be missing some other truth. Did you notice that I used the phrase 'I was afraid'? Fear and doubt tag-team to deconstruct the faith of a believer. That should always be a giveaway as to the source of the thoughts. I struggled reading the New Testament—especially the gospels. I didn't give in to the thoughts, but I definitely did not fight them whole-heartedly. I let them swirl around in my head, causing confusion, fear and doubt. One day I realized that I didn't struggle with the idea of God the Father or the Holy Spirit—only Jesus. In that moment, I had a respite from the onslaught of lies. The truth broke through! How silly of me, to believe every part of the Bible, including the Holy Spirit, but struggle with doubts about Jesus! However, the struggle was real!

I spent hours on the phone with my father, over the first several years, as I battled against the intense and confusing thoughts. He shared with me that he had the same attacks from the devil when he was a new Christian in his twenties. He told me that I was being attacked by a spirit of antichrist, as described in 1 John 2:18-27—this is not THE antichrist, as in the person described as ruling during the very end of time, but the spirits that scripture tells us will go out into the world in the days between Christ's ascension and his return. The account my father unfolded to me was one of a daily battle where he slept with his Bible under his pillow, so when he woke up in the middle of the night he could read it to counter the attacks. On the golf course, he would pray with every step he took from one hole to the next, rebuking the antichrist spirit, in Jesus' name. The attacks would leave for a while, only to come back with more disparaging, doubtful thoughts about the person of Jesus. One day, he said, it left and never came back. This gave me hope and also the knowledge that I was probably in for a long battle.

CROSS REFERENCE

Let's open our Bibles and look at what 1 John 2:18-27 says about the antichrist spirit.

Jesus himself is our protection from antichrist thoughts. Jesus is the way, the truth and the life. The more I studied Jesus, the more I got into his Word, put on the belt of truth, declared who Jesus was aloud and rebuked the spirit of antichrist, the weaker and weaker those thoughts became. I knew beyond a shadow of a doubt that if God could just reveal Jesus to me, in all of his glory, no devil in hell would be able to stop what I would do for him! And guess what? God did that through his Word! I now see the truth! Jesus is the Truth! Learn about him, not what other people say about him, but read God's Word yourself. Press in for revelation yourself. Know the power of the resurrected Christ. Rebuke the antichrist spirit and speak scripture aloud about the person of Jesus Christ until your faith grows from a mustard seed into a large tree! When you do this, you will be protected from deception that comes from the lies of the world, the flesh and the devil.

OVERCOMING LIES WITH TRUTH

Now, if you are aware that you have a weakness for believing lies, or that you have a weakness in telling little white lies, or putting on a show to make yourself look good, then what does putting on the belt of truth look like? It looks like repentance. It looks like calling out to God for help. It looks like relinquishing the pride or fear in your heart that keeps you from speaking the truth. Instead of caring about what other people think, ask God to help you care about what he thinks. When you begin to call out to the Lord, you will realize the "struggle" is not against flesh and blood. Your way of dealing with problems will take on a whole new look. You will fight, through prayer, in the heavenly realms against the powers and principalities that come against you to pull you into a state of deception. You will work in the Spirit to put on truth. Putting on truth is a choice. Get into God's Word and let it fill your mind. Put on truth by listening to the Spirit. Decide to live a pure and Spirit-saturated life that is motivated by a love for God. Living like this is the "putting off" of the old self and the "putting on" of the new self. Ephesians 4:22-28 describes this type of life in Christ. In fact, it is the same Greek phrasing used in both that passage and the Ephesian 6 verses. We are to put on the belt of truth, the same way we put off our old way of life and put on our new life.

Ephesians 4:22-28

²² You were taught, with regard to your former way of life, to **put off your old self**, which is being corrupted by its deceitful desires; ²³ to be made new in the attitude of your minds; ²⁴ and to **put on the new self**, created to be like God in true righteousness and holiness.

²⁵ Therefore each of you must put off falsehood and speak truthfully to your neighbour, for we are all members of one body. ²⁶ 'In your anger do not sin': do not let the sun go down while you are still angry, ²⁷ and do not give the devil a foothold. ²⁸ Anyone who has been stealing must steal no longer, but must work, doing something useful with their own hands, that they may have something to share with those in need.

PRACTICAL APPLICATION

We do this transformative "putting off" and "putting on" by the power of the Holy Spirit and repentance in the name of Jesus. Ask the Lord some questions about yourself today. Write down what the Lord brings to your heart.

- Am I living in truth in every area of my life?

- Am I easily deceived?

- Do I know your Word, oh Lord?

- Am I living to please myself?

- Am I prepared to share the life-giving truth of the gospel or good news about Jesus with others at all times?

- Do I really trust you, Lord? Do I trust you with every part of my life?

- Do you see me as a person who believes in your ability to direct my life or am I directing my own life?

> **TODAY'S BIBLE STUDY TOOL**
>
> **Practical Application.** How can I personally apply this scripture to my life today? What changes do I need to make? What prayer should I pray? Don't forget to ask the Holy Spirit for help!

Lastly, if you or someone you love struggles with habitual lying, there may also be a stronghold of lying and deception in yourself or that person. This does not mean the devil owns him or her. The inability to control when you lie, or even know you have lied, is a sign you have given a place for the devil in your life. You have opened the front door and unintentionally invited him in. In this case, it is important to repent—or teach and pray for repentance in the life of the other person—and resist the devil, in Jesus' name.

When my children were younger, I discovered that certain ones had a propensity for lying. Whether it was hiding homework, or spinning tall tales, these kids could certainly pull the wool over my eyes, and I am not easily deceived. I came to discover that a source of temptation for one child was the desire to be liked. What starts as an innocent longing for companionship can become a full-blown stronghold, if the person with a weakness to lie falls into repetitive temptation to sin by lying.

The enemy can develop a deep-seated stronghold of deception, when the individual lying has given him or herself over to lying by giving in to this temptation and obeying the enemy. (Romans 6:16) In these cases, eventually, the lying becomes more and more elaborate and unnecessary. Psychologists call this pathological lying. The person lying may even lie for absolutely no reason at all. In my experience with it, even normal, everyday families can experience this problem in varying degrees. In this case, you have a full-blown spiritual emergency. What is the answer? Good old-fashioned repentance, confession of sin, righting wrongs, asking the Holy Spirit to change your heart and show you why you struggle with lying are in order. Oh, and don't forget to command spirits of lying and deception to leave, in Jesus' name and ask the Holy Spirit to fill you where the stronghold existed. This spiritual condition must be dealt with in children by giving consequences in love and grace. Be thoughtful and consistent with your consequences. Be careful not to exacerbate the problem by disciplining in anger—which is different than talking seriously or sternly about a problem. Children can be taught to pray and ask the Lord why they lie. God will speak to the heart of a child! A child can also learn to repent from lying and to stand against the devil, in Jesus' name.

WORD STUDY
Renounce

Ladies, for some of you, the thought of speaking out loud in spiritual warfare may seem too militant or aggressive. But, it is simply confession of the truth about where you officially stand. When you stand against a liar whom you once believed, you must renounce his lies.

> Rather, we have **renounced** secret and shameful ways; we do not use deception, nor do we distort the word of God. On the contrary, by setting forth the truth plainly we commend ourselves to everyone's conscience in the sight of God. – 2 Corinthians 4:2

The dictionary at merriam-webster.com says to renounce is to give up, refuse, or resign, usually by a formal declaration. This truth from 2 Corinthians 4:2 is transferable to any and all behaviors and beliefs which we must renounce and give up to the Lord, whether it's lust, pride, selfishness, hatred, gossip, fear or lying. This list is not exhaustive. Verbalizing your stand is part of the process of repentance and freedom from the enemy's strongholds.

When you have believed a lie and it has had authority in your mind, you need to renounce it by the power of the name of Jesus. This exalts Jesus above the lie and lets the devil know where you stand. Let's go back and review 2 Corinthians 10:5, "We demolish arguments and every pretension that sets itself up against the knowledge of God, and we take captive every thought and make it obedient to Christ."

By renouncing the lie out loud, you demolish the argument. You cut off the authority you gave it by believing it and you submit your mind to Jesus. In this way, if the enemy has power in your life, due to unconfessed sin and lies you have believed, he is cut off. You can command evil and its lies to leave in Jesus' name. Jesus gives you authority. For example: If your father always told you that you are worthless and you will never amount to anything, that lie is established in your life. Usually, along with those types of lies from a parent come spirits of rejection and failure. When you are in prayer with the Lord, you can:

- Forgive your father in the name of Jesus.

- Renounce the lie that you are worthless and a failure.

- Command failure, rejection and abandonment to leave in Jesus' name.

- Ask the Lord to replace the lies with the truth and to fill your mind and life with the Holy Spirit. Declare this truth aloud!

PRAYER TO OVERCOME LYING

Praying to break the stronghold of lying can look like this:

Father,

In Jesus' name, I have lived in lying for so long that I cannot control it anymore. I repent of my sin of lying. I know the devil is the father of lies. I do not want to speak his language. I pray that you purify my heart from all lying. I give my tongue, my heart, my desires and my intentions to you. I thank you for the forgiveness of Jesus. I rebuke spirits of lying, deception and deceit, exaggeration, hiding and sneaking, in Jesus' name. I command the devil and all deceptive, lying spirits to leave me, in Jesus' name. Fill me with the Holy Spirit and truth.

In Jesus' name, Amen.

Lying is a heart problem. It needs to be dealt with from the inside out.

Now what does putting on the belt of truth look like after dealing with this stronghold in prayer? If you have been weak in that area, you will need to give those lies back to the Lord, and renounce them, whenever they come up again. In the case of the example of lies a father spoke over a daughter, take the relationship with your father back to the Lord and pray to forgive him, every time that pain and unforgiveness and lies try to dominate you. Stand in the truth of who you are in Christ. Confess the truth aloud. Command the enemy to leave in the name of Jesus. Stand in the day of evil.

BRINGING IT HOME

- Learn and embrace the power of speaking the written Word of God out loud to combat lies.

- Focus on memorizing scripture that exalts Jesus like Colossians Chapter 1 and Ephesians 1.

- When you are full of confusing thoughts about Jesus, read portions of the New Testament out loud. Next, rebuke an antichrist spirit and antichrist thoughts and command them to leave in Jesus' name.

- Ask yourself if you justify any form of lying. Have you gotten into a habit of allowing sin in your life?

PUTTING ON YOUR ARMOR
PART 3

THE BREASTPLATE OF RIGHTEOUSNESS

MEMORY VERSE

[10] Finally, be strong in the Lord and in his mighty power. [11] Put on the full armour of God, so that you can take your stand against the devil's schemes. [12] For our struggle is not against flesh and blood, but against the rulers, against the authorities, against the powers of this dark world and against the spiritual forces of evil in the heavenly realms. [13] Therefore put on the full armour of God, so that when the day of evil comes, you may be able to stand your ground, and after you have done everything, to stand. – Ephesians 6:10-13

PRAYER

You may also pray the Armor of God prayer in the Prayer Index.

Father,

In Jesus' name I thank you for leading me into all truth. Thank you for all that I am learning about your armor and my position in Christ. I rejoice in my salvation! I thank you that Jesus, your only begotten son, loves me and died for me. All things were created through him and for him, yet he gave himself as a sacrifice for my sin. I pray that you continue to bring revelation to my heart, that I may know Christ and all the riches I have in him. I pray that you will build me up in my inner being, so that Christ may dwell in my heart through faith. Lord, teach me that flesh and blood are not my enemies. Teach me to listen to you, when I am in a conflict. Help me to walk in the truth of your Word and to speak it aloud, that I may grow in faith. In Jesus' name, I put off all negative, complaining thoughts and rejoice in your goodness and grace. I praise you for the cross and for your victory and hope! Guard my heart today, Lord. I put on righteousness, faith and love as a breastplate. I fix my eyes on you, Jesus.

In your great name, Amen.

READING

Open your Bible and read Ephesians 6:10-24.

BREASTPLATE OF RIGHTEOUSNESS

> Stand firm then, with the belt of truth buckled around your waist, with the breastplate of righteousness in place. – Ephesians 6:16

Today, let's look at what protects the heart—the breastplate of righteousness. My friends have a cabin in the mountains of Virginia, which they built as ministry venue and a place of rest for their family. Many people have benefited from their generosity and hospitality. Over the years, youth retreats, family gatherings and leadership events have transpired on the land that is backdropped with mountains and covered in prayer. On the wall of the main room of the cabin hangs a well-placed plaque with this gentle reminder: "Above all else, guard your heart, for everything you do flows from it." (Proverbs 4:23) Everyone who comes through their home-away-from-home can read this most important truth, and hopefully it will be impressed upon them for the rest of their lives. What you allow into your heart—what you love, what you fix your heart on—will direct the rest of your life. Righteousness will guard your heart.

1 Thessalonians 5:8 says, "But since we belong to the day, let us be sober, putting on faith and love as a breastplate ..." This passage defines our spiritual breastplate: faith and love. Let's look at how these two sisters of righteousness work together to protect our hearts. Our righteousness in Christ is, practically speaking, faith and love. Let's take a look at Ephesians 2:1-10 to recall how faith is our protection of righteousness. I encourage you to open your Bible to read the entirety of the passage, but I will just give you the highlights here.

> As for you, you were dead in your transgressions and sins, in which you used to live when you followed the ways of this world ... All of us also lived among them at one time ... Like the rest, we were by nature deserving of wrath. But because of his great love for us, God, who is rich in mercy, made us alive with Christ even when we were dead in transgressions ... For it is by grace you have been saved, through faith – and this is not from yourselves, it is the gift of God – not by works, so that no one can boast. For we are God's handiwork, created in Christ Jesus to do good works, which God prepared in advance for us to do. – excerpted from Ephesians 2:1-10

FAITH

Faith in the righteousness of Christ is, perhaps, one of the single most important components of spiritual warfare. Faith in Christ is the vehicle by which we arrive at the destination of God's grace. This is where we come alive—not by our own works—but through surrendering to the work of Christ. Faith is our righteousness. Romans 4:3 says, "... Abraham believed God and it was credited to him as righteousness." Do you remember what we learned about the state of our righteous works, apart from Christ, from our previous studies? "Our righteous acts are as filthy rags." (Isaiah 64:6) If our own righteous rags are all that protect our hearts, we are in grave danger. Ephesians 2 says that in our nature we were deserving of wrath. BUT, because of his great LOVE, we were brought from death to life! Jesus carried the guilt of our sin, even though he was perfect in every way.

How does this righteousness in Christ work in spiritual warfare? The weight of our heavy guilt was credited to Jesus, so that he could carry it to the cross, and his righteousness was credited to us, so we could be free from the chains of the enemy. Think of it like this; imagine your name was suddenly added as a co-owner to the bank account of the technology giant Apple. At the time of the writing of this book, Apple was just declared the first trillion-dollar company in history. Most of us have no concept of how much money that is. We wouldn't even know how to spend it! But imagine that your bank account went from being in the red, with more bills than you can pay—the type of situation where a $30 tank of gas might as well be a million-dollar tank of gas—to suddenly being a co-owner of Apple and having access to more money than anyone has ever seen in human history. This is what Jesus did for us on the cross. Except instead of temporary money to buy things that are fading away, we have eternal riches that ensure our good favor in the family of God. Our debt of sin and back-owed bills are paid. All accounts are up to date and current, and the resources available will cover any and all incoming life surprises. When you owed the debt of sin, you were poised to lose everything. The collectors could come and take away anything you owned, including your life, to pay the debt. So, by removing our debt, our guilt, and the authority of it, Christ removed the devil's authority as a collections agent to kill, steal and destroy. In doing all this, Jesus defeated the devil and his organization of power!

CROSS REFERENCE

Let's cross reference to Colossians 2 to see how Jesus' death and resurrection triumphed over our enemies!

Colossians 2:13-15

[13] When you were dead in your sins and in the uncircumcision of your flesh, God made you alive with Christ. He forgave us all our sins, [14] having cancelled the charge of our legal indebtedness, which stood against us and condemned us; he has taken it away, nailing it to the cross. [15] And having disarmed the powers and authorities, he made a public spectacle of them, triumphing over them by the cross.

When a believer goes into spiritual warfare, that person absolutely needs to have faith that every victory obtained is through the righteousness of Christ. Because Jesus is righteous, he could go to the cross and be a substitutionary sacrifice for our sins. Do you see what Colossians 2:14 says? What did Jesus cancel the charge of? Our legal indebtedness. Our debt stood against us, testifying against us and condemning us. The devil simply uses "our record of debt" to bring charges against us, to try to gain ground into our lives. Do you remember what Ephesians 2 says about our old position before Jesus? We were under the authority of the prince of the power of the air. Satan is our accuser. He always levies lies against believers, bringing up the past and twisting the truth of who we are in Christ. Jesus, however, took away every position of the enemy, every footing of accusation that he has, and nailed it to the cross. It says in verse 15 that he disarmed the powers and authorities, made a public spectacle of them and triumphed over them by the cross. It is this power and authority that we stand in, when we go into battle. We cannot stand in battle with the frequency of our church attendance, the amount of times we read the Bible a week, the amount of money we put in the offering or if we teach Sunday school. It doesn't matter if you are a good person, quite frankly. Why? Because the devil is a slick lawyer, the ultimate legalist. For every good work you try to stand on, he will have one hundred of your sins to throw up in your face. However, if you stand in the righteousness of Christ, he has nothing. Jesus has disarmed him of his accusations.

When I need to do battle against some heavy-hitting enemies, such as praying for someone who is oppressed by occult curses and attacked by demons at night, do I do this on my own righteousness? You better believe the answer is no! I speak as King David did, when he came against Goliath, and said, "You come against me with sword and spear and javelin (my own might and power), but I come against you in the name of the Lord Almighty, the God of the armies of Israel, whom you have defied." – 1 Samuel 17:45

David refused the natural armor of King Saul, and chose to oppose his opponent in the supernatural power of the Lord. In those moments, when I stand in the valley with my enemy taunting me and my God, and my flesh wavers as I fearfully remember my own weakness, I steady myself in the breastplate of righteousness and remember Jesus is the one doing the work. I refute the enemy with this declaration, "I stand in Jesus Christ, the Son of the living God, who died for me and rose again on the third day! In this power alone, the name of Jesus Christ, do I oppose you, Satan!"

Our faith in his power and his victory shields our hearts. To dig deeper into this discussion of faith, take time to read Romans 4:1-8.

LOVE
Walking in Christ's Righteousness

Faith is trusting in Christ's righteousness; love is responding to Christ's righteousness. "We love because he first loved us. Whoever claims to love God yet hates a brother or sister is a liar. For whoever does not love their brother and sister, whom they have seen, cannot love God, whom they have not seen. And he has given us this command: anyone who loves God must also love their brother and sister."

We already learned in Week Eight that when you live in unforgiveness, you expose yourself to the devil's stronghold in your life, and God cannot forgive your sins. The opposite of being exposed by unforgiveness is being protected by love and cleansed by righteousness! 1 Corinthians 13:4-7 explains in detail what love looks like in a practical way: "Love is patient, love is kind. It does not envy, it does not boast, it is not proud. It does not dishonour others, it is not self-seeking, it is not easily angered, it keeps no record of wrongs. Love does not delight in evil but rejoices with the truth. It always protects, always trusts, always hopes, always perseveres. Love never fails."

Love is practical. When you walk as Jesus walked, in practical love, your heart is shielded by Christ's righteousness, as it is manifested in you by the Holy Spirit. Everyone loves a good debate. I am familiar with all of the debates over whether our protection comes exclusively from being a Christian who stands in the finished work of Christ, or if our protection comes from walking in godliness, which, of course, is only done by the power of the Holy Spirit. God's Word teaches that it's not either/or. It is both.

GOD'S LOVING DISCIPLINE BRINGS RIGHTEOUSNESS

Faith in Christ involves repentance, which means turning from your sin. When convicted of sin by the Holy Spirit, a sinner turns from sin and embraces the forgiveness of Christ. This is the foundation of our protection in Christ's righteousness. But, Jesus doesn't stop his work there. He is constantly doing a sanctifying work in the life of a new believer, making the person more like himself, through the Holy Spirit. Honestly, because we all have unbending, hard areas in our hearts, God will discipline us all so we become aware of those areas and can yield them to the transforming work of his Spirit. But when we are unbending to the conviction of the Holy Spirit about those hard areas and don't submit to his discipline, God may bring some refining situations into our life to further discipline us and help us submit and obey him for our good and for his purposes for us. In this case, the devil would not be the root of our problems, but our own unwillingness to follow the Lord would be why God would enact further discipline. All this discipline is a sign that we are a true son or daughter and that God the Father loves us! Even in times of discipline, we are protected by the love of God because we know that his goal is our spiritual growth and a renewed relationship with him.

CROSS REFERENCE

Let's cross reference to a key passage in Hebrews that teaches us about the love of God to bring our lives into alignment with our position in Christ.

Hebrews 12:4-13

[4] In your struggle against sin, you have not yet resisted to the point of shedding your blood. [5] And have you completely forgotten this word of encouragement that addresses you as a father addresses his son? It says,

'My son, do not make light of the Lord's discipline,
and do not lose heart when he rebukes you,
[6] because the Lord disciplines the one he loves,
and he chastens everyone he accepts as his son.'

[7] Endure hardship as discipline; God is treating you as his children. For what children are not disciplined by their father? [8] If you are not disciplined – and everyone undergoes discipline – then you are not legitimate, not true sons and daughters at all. [9] Moreover, we have all had human fathers who disciplined us and we respected them for it. How much more should we submit to the Father of spirits and live! [10] They disciplined us for a little while as they thought best; but God disciplines us for our good, in order that we may share in his holiness. [11] No discipline seems pleasant at the time, but painful. Later on, however, it produces a harvest of righteousness and peace for those who have been trained by it.

[12] Therefore, strengthen your feeble arms and weak knees. [13] 'Make level paths for your feet,' so that the lame may not be disabled, but rather healed.

If you love Jesus, you will embrace his sanctifying work of discipline that makes you more like Christ, which in turn, protects you from Satan's temptations. A person who loves Jesus will resist the devil and struggle against sin, standing in the grace of God through the whole process of becoming more like Jesus—notice I said struggle against sin, not that you are ever done with the battle for your heart! I don't want to give you the defeating impression that you will ever be free from this battle till you are free from your physical life—however, if you love the world, if you love your self-life, and if you love sin more than Jesus, you may find yourself resisting Jesus and quenching the Holy Spirit's work, instead of resisting the devil and dying to self. A person in this position has already fallen into temptation and is dropping the breastplate of righteousness. This is a dangerous place! Here are some examples of how love protects us from sin.

- If a man loves with Christ's love, he will not want to steal from someone. That would be hurting them.

- If a woman loves her friend, she will not gossip about her.

- If a man loves his wife, he will not be unfaithful to her.

- If a woman loves Jesus, she will not want to trample his gift of grace underfoot, by nursing a grudge.

- If a believer loves Jesus, that believer will not choose to turn to the occult for fortune telling or power.

Love is pretty common sense and compelling.

Any of these sinful behaviors is dangerous, exposing your heart and others' hearts to spiritual attack. These behaviors open up the offender and those connected to him or her to the damaging effects of sin, and they welcome the enemy into relationships. The answer? Go back to square one.

- Confess your sin to God and repent with faith that God loves you and forgives you.
- Ask the Holy Spirit to fill you, strengthening your inner being.

1 John 1:9 says, "If we confess our sins, he is faithful and just and will forgive us our sins and purify us from all unrighteousness." The condition that John gives the church for purification from sin is that we must confess our sins. When we are purified from unrighteousness, this means we will stand in righteousness! I know too many Christians that just "try to do better next time," without confessing their sins. A believer protected by standing in the righteousness of Christ will not stand simply in his or her own ability to do better next time. Standing with the breastplate of righteousness on means living a life of confession of sin and then walking in the power of God to overcome the sin. Don't just get frustrated with yourself and hope for the best the next time. The correct way to stand is by trusting in the atonement of Christ which cleanses our sin, then choosing to walk in the Spirit. Only the atonement of Christ protects you.

LET US BE SOBER

Let's remember our secondary verse about the armor, But since we belong to the day, let us be sober, putting on faith and love as a breastplate. – 1 Thessalonians 5:8

Let us contrast the positive behavior of a person standing in Christ with an opposite behavior. What is the opposite of sober? Drunk. Drunkenness is the new "cool" sin in a culture that is obsessed with alcohol. I literally am floored by the number of believers who wink at drunkenness, as if it were an innocent little pleasure. Alcohol is making its way into every part of our lives, with the new "wine mom" culture. Some Christians who choose to socially drink by having wine with dinner or at a wedding need to prayerfully ask the Lord to help them take the necessary precautions to prevent themselves from crossing the line into the sin of drunkenness. Many do not even know when they are crossing the line.

One dear friend of mine related to me an experience of an evening she had out with friends after a very difficult week. They indulged in a couple margaritas and found themselves intoxicated. This was not at all a normal occurrence for my friend. Being sweet, dedicated believers, those involved were embarrassed and a bit shocked by the incident—the margaritas were stronger than they were used to having. When she told me about it later, I asked her if she ever confessed her sin to God and repented. A stunned look came over her face. "No, actually; now that you mention it, I didn't. I really decided not to do it again. It's not like me at all." I discussed with her that it was noble to make the decision to not get drunk again, but that God requires us to confess our sin to him for our healing and purification from all unrighteousness. Otherwise, we are not walking in relationship with him; instead, we are just being religious. She thanked me and told me she hadn't thought of it that way.

Over the past two decades of ministry, I can tell you more than one story of believers who found themselves in unalterable life situations due to a night of drinking gone awry. What about the young twenty-something man who was shocked to find himself in bed with a neighbor the morning after drinking too much? What about those who have lost loved ones due to drunk driving accidents? Many of us know of less "shocking" situations like marital fights that have broken out after a bit too much wine. This seems little compared to a death, but how many marriages have died after a habit of nightly fighting and saying things that are hard to take back after drinking too much? A righteous life is a life of sobriety, faith and love. A life of confession and repentance purifies us from unrighteousness, when we find ourselves in sin. Righteousness protects the heart.

Also, the apostle Paul challenges Christians to act in love concerning alcohol, not in a selfish attitude of, "I can do what I what, because I have freedom in Christ." You may be able to control yourself with alcohol, but you need to always be aware that your friend may not. Romans 14 goes into detail about how to make sure you are walking in love for God and other people in the area of alcohol, food and faith. I encourage you to prayerfully read over it to learn more about this topic. The truth in this passage brings us back to the concept that love protects us as a breastplate of righteousness. If we are acting in love, our lives will be protected and we will protect those around us!

BRINGING IT HOME

Spend time thanking God for the righteousness he has credited to you through Jesus. During this time, confess your position in Christ out loud. "I am redeemed by Jesus. I am saved by his sacrifice. I am no longer guilty of my sin!"

Ask God to teach you to walk in love for him and for others. Ask the Lord to convict you of any unconfessed sin and to deliver you from any strongholds of the enemy that may have resulted from your sin, in Jesus' name.

Are you walking in a life of sobriety or do you allow yourself to slip up in this area? Ask the Lord to show you the truth.

PUTTING ON YOUR ARMOR
PART 4

THE BREASTPLATE OF RIGHTEOUSNESS: PERFECTED IN LOVE

MEMORY VERSE

[10] Finally, be strong in the Lord and in his mighty power. [11] Put on the full armour of God, so that you can take your stand against the devil's schemes. [12] For our struggle is not against flesh and blood, but against the rulers, against the authorities, against the powers of this dark world and against the spiritual forces of evil in the heavenly realms. [13] Therefore put on the full armour of God, so that when the day of evil comes, you may be able to stand your ground, and after you have done everything, to stand. – Ephesians 6:10-13

PRAYER & DECLARATION OF TRUTH

Father,

In Jesus' name I pray today for greater revelation of your love, so that I can rest in you. I claim that I am bought with the blood of Jesus—redeemed by the blood of the Lamb. I am loved by God. I am highly favored, as a part of his family. Lord God, thank you for all of these truths. Thank you for who I am in Christ. You have lavished your love upon me and I do not need to live in fear. I love you, Father God! Your name is my strong tower; I run into your name and am safe, in Jesus' name. I pray that you fill me with your Spirit of wisdom and revelation to understand your love for me. I stand against all spirits of fear and confusion, panic and anxiety in the name of Jesus and command them to be silent and to leave me in Jesus' name. I will loudly declare the truth that I am seated with Christ in heavenly realms high above all authority that would try to assert itself in my life. By the righteousness of Christ and his sacrifice for me, I am free from the power of the enemy. I am strengthened by the love of Christ and I am confident and free as I stand before his throne.

In Jesus' name, Amen!

THE PROTECTION OF LOVE

Love and faith are both part of the breastplate of righteousness, because we cannot know the love of God without faith. Faith is trusting in God. We trust him, because of who he is. When you trust Jesus, your faith is living proof of the realities of the unseen world. When we go to sleep at night, we pray to a Father who commands his angels concerning us. When we need the weather to be nice for a church picnic, we know who created our weather systems and who loves us. If he doesn't have other important plans for the weather, why wouldn't he answer our prayers? When we feel like a failure and can't imagine why God would love us, we know what scripture says about Jesus' love for us; we know that his love is sacrificially alive and active. Romans 5:8 says, "But God demonstrates his own love for us in this: while we were still sinners, Christ died for us." This love is greater than any love we have experienced on earth! This is why we trust him and love him. 1 John 4:19 says "We love because he first loved us."

CROSS REFERENCE

Let's cross reference to the bigger picture of this passage to understand, in context, how the love of Christ protects us in spiritual warfare. (Are you noticing a beautiful love theme in 1 John?!)

1 John 4:16-21

[16] And so we know and rely on the love God has for us.

God is love. Whoever lives in love lives in God, and God in them. [17] This is how love is made complete among us so that we will have confidence on the day of judgment: in this world we are like Jesus. [18] There is no fear in love. But perfect love drives out fear, because fear has to do with punishment. The one who fears is not made perfect in love.

[19] We love because he first loved us. [20] Whoever claims to love God yet hates a brother or sister is a liar. For whoever does not love their brother and sister, whom they have seen, cannot love God, whom they have not seen. [21] And he has given us this command: anyone who loves God must also love their brother and sister.

ASKING QUESTIONS

99. According to verse 16, how do we have confidence on the day of judgment?

100. According to verse 18, what drives out fear?

101. According to verse 18, what does fear have to do with?

102. According to verses 19-21, why does God command us to love our brothers and sisters?

WORD STUDY
Fear

Let's dig into this passage at biblehub.com to understand what some of the implications are in the Greek language for the word "fear." HELPS™ Word-studies says this about the word for fear in 1 John 4:18:

HELPS™ WORD-STUDIES
  5401 *phóbos* (from *phebomai*, "to flee, withdraw") – *fear* (from Homer about 900 bc on) 5401(*phóbos*) meant *withdrawal, fleeing* because feeling inadequate (without sufficient *resources, Abbott-Smith*).

Withdrawal is a commonplace reaction of someone who is overwhelmed by feeling inadequate or insufficient. It is a feeling of powerlessness. Jesus' disciples reacted in fear in the garden, when he urged them to pray, so they wouldn't fall into sin. (Matthew 40:26-36) Emotional sleep is often a result of being overwhelmed by fear. Even though Jesus was right there with them, their eyes weren't open with faith to see or comprehend that God was about to secure the biggest victory in history that very weekend. So, instead of living in victory, they slept in fear. This is an example of a side effect of fear that comes from a weakness in one's nature or flesh.

Torment / Punishment

In 1 John 4:18, the NIVUK says, "fear has to do with punishment." I looked up the word "punishment" on biblehub.com and this is what HELPS™ Word-studies says,

> **HELPS™ WORD-STUDIES**
> **Cognate: 2851** kólasis (from kolaphos, "a buffeting, a blow") – properly, punishment that "fits" (matches) the one punished (R. Trench); torment from living in the dread of upcoming judgment from shirking one's duty (cf. WS at 1 Jn 4:18).
>
> **Perfected love casts out tormenting fear (2851 /kólasis)**
> 1 Jn 4:17,18: "¹⁷ By this, love is perfected [brought to its higher stages] with us, so that we may continuously have confidence in the day of judgment; because as He is, so also are we in this world. ¹⁸ There is no fear in love; but perfect love casts out fear, because fear involves punishment [2851 /kólasis, "torment"], and the one who fears is not perfected in love."

The idea of failing God or not being enough to accomplish his task for you in this life can fill you with tormenting fear of failure or rejection. Believers can also be tormented by the question of whether or not they are really saved, even though they have confessed their sin and desire to follow Christ. Another source of insecurity is if you have been abandoned, hurt or rejected by people who should have protected and loved you, like parents or church leadership. This kind of pain can subconsciously be projected onto God and create a lie that God will not love you, accept you, or stick with you through trials, even on judgment day. 1 John 3:19-23 has more wisdom about this for people who are bound up in fear. "This is how we know that we belong to the truth and how we set our hearts at rest in his presence: if our hearts condemn us, we know that God is greater than our hearts, and he knows everything. Dear friends, if our hearts do not condemn us, we have confidence before God and receive from him anything we ask, because we keep his commands and do what pleases him. And this is his command: to believe in the name of his Son, Jesus Christ, and to love one another as he commanded us."

We live in the righteousness of Christ. Satan does not have unlimited access to you. However, if you do not give lies and traumas to the Lord, they can become a stronghold in your life for fear. A stronghold, according to Strong's Concordance, is "a cliff, or lofty and inaccessible place; figuratively, a refuge — (or) defense, high fort (tower)." As a believer, an area of pain and insecurity in your life can be a fortress in you where the Lord holds you—in your weaknesses he is strong—or a fortress where the enemy holds you captive, as you surrender to your fear. It is up to you whether you raise the white flag to surrender to the Lord, and allow Jesus to take over the weak areas of your life, or raise the white flag to the enemy. If fears and weaknesses are not submitted to the Lord, these strongholds of fear in the physical realm can give the enemy a place of authority to torment you and levy attacks against you in the spiritual realm. This can overwhelm a believer who has not been perfected in love and make him or her feel defeated. Even people who are strong in their faith and walk in the knowledge of God's love walk through times of fear or torment, because—as we will learn about today—this perfecting in love is a process where love casts out fear on a daily basis. Do not fear! Whether you just have a physical or natural tendency to fear or if you are also engaged in battle with the enemy, Jesus Christ knows what is going on. He has authority and power over all of your weaknesses and gives you everything you need to overcome fear in his love. Any stronghold of fear can become a strong tower of Christ!

LOVE OVERCOMES
When Satan Exploits My Weaknesses

Having grown up living in tremendous fear, I can testify that fear is torment. Each of us has personal weaknesses; insecurity was definitely an overwhelming weakness of mine in the first three decades of my life. When you have a weakness like fear or insecurity, the enemy will try to exploit this area and attack you with harassing and tormenting spirits and lies that target those weak areas. We learned about the enemy's nature in Week Ten. The tormenter can attack you with lies that invoke fear, if you have not been perfected in love. This is, in simple terms, the enemy being a bully, because he knows you have been hurt, abandoned or rejected by someone or are even generally insecure. Let me give you a real-life example. This happens on the football field, where an opponent may know that an athlete on the other team has a bad shoulder. A dirty play can happen where the opponent intentionally targets the injured shoulder when tackling that player.

What do we do when we are targeted for attack like this in our spiritual lives? Well, an injured athlete will go to physical therapy to learn exercises to strengthen the muscles that are atrophied or weak from injury. Through PT, patients who are faithful to do their doctor-prescribed at-home exercise program can quickly regain strength and be back in the game again. While it may seem counter-intuitive, after certain types of injuries or surgeries, doctors will encourage immediate movement and prescribed exercise. While a patient's tendency may be to favor the injured body part or not to keep moving, depending on the situation, a doctor will encourage mobility for faster healing and better blood flow. In the same way, in order to overcome an attack of a spirit of fear and anxiety or fear of rejection and failure, you need to be strengthened by the love of God. Do not allow avoidance to keep you from getting the help you need. The injured part of your heart may feel terrible now, but the more you avoid spiritual rehabilitation and strengthening through Christ, the worse off you will find yourself in the long run. What does doctor Jesus order for someone who is weak with insecurity, anxiety, fear, panic, or worry? 1 John 4:18 says you need the "therapy" of love that casts out fear. We need to be perfected in love! Since some of you may be feeling uneasy and overwhelmed about the word "perfected," because you feel so inadequate in the area of anxiety, let's look into the Greek definition of what it means to be perfected. I guarantee you won't be disappointed!

WORD STUDY
Perfected

If you are still at biblehub.com with me in 1 John 4:18, click on the word "perfected." You will be able to see what I see there. There is so much more there than what I can put in this book! HELPS™ Word-studies gives us a bit more insight into the meaning.

> **HELPS™ Word-studies**
> **Cognate: 5048** *teleióō* – to consummate, reaching the *end-stage*, i.e. working through the entire process (stages) to reach the *final* phase (*conclusion*).
>
> [This root (*tel-*) means "reaching the *end* (*aim*)." It is well-illustrated with the old pirate's telescope, unfolding (extending out) one stage at a time to function at full-strength (capacity effectiveness).]

What does it mean to be perfected in love? First of all, it doesn't mean you have to be perfect in order to have relief from your fear. Instead, it implies a process of transformation by the power of knowing God's love which moves you towards a greater state of perfection. Each step with Jesus moves us towards freedom and towards our perfected heavenly state, where we will experience the ultimate consummation of God's love. Before you reach heaven, you can go from victory over fear to victory, here on earth, until you reach a state of perfected security and love in heaven. To experience this process, you need to receive more and more revelation of the love of Christ, by his Spirit through his Word. You cannot leave out either of these components. It must be by his Spirit (asking for wisdom and revelation of Christ) and through his Word. Romans 10:17 in the New King James Version says, "So then faith comes by hearing, and hearing by the word of God." The Word of God builds up our faith so we can be perfected in God's love to help us walk in his righteousness. When God reveals his love for you, and teaches you how he loves you in the middle of your fear, this revelation will continue to drive out fear.

Isn't it ironic that this passage, which John penned to increase our understanding of God's love, made me more fearful when I was younger? I always equated this passage with perfection. I could never be perfect and I was afraid of the judgment of God. I would think about my fear and how I couldn't overcome it, and I would become more fearful that I would be a big disappointment to the Lord. This is how fear works. It twists reality and creates an alternative reality. I say this from personal experience. If your weakness is fear and the enemy has you in a stronghold of fear, probably reading this day's study will ignite an underlying nervousness in you. A spirit of fear does not want to be uncovered. It wants to hold you in chains. But, it is so small and powerless in comparison to the power of the resurrection of Christ. Fear may feel like a mountain to you, and your faith may feel so tiny, but all you need is faith the size of a mustard seed and you can tell the mountain to be thrown into the sea. Fear and anxiety may make you lie awake at night, grind your teeth, be socially awkward, or make your heart suddenly skip a beat or race, but fear is nothing compared to Jesus. Focus on the cure and not the "disease" or problem. Jesus already defeated fear on the cross and he wants to set you free through a deeper knowledge of his love. Sometimes therapists will have patients rehash old fears over and over, in hopes that by confronting them they will get better. But I contend that you need to lay your fear down beside Jesus and compare it to him. Jesus will confront your fears for you, when you confess them and turn them over to him. If there is any reason to write down a list of your fears, it should be to give them up to Jesus one-by-one and renounce them in his name, not to dwell on them and think about them over and over.

WORD STUDY
Casts Out

How does perfect love cast out fear? In looking up the Greek for the phrase "casts out," I was pleasantly surprised and beyond excited! The Discovery Bible's HELPS™ Word-studies indicates that the Greek verb tense for "casts" is present indicative active form. Verb tenses in Greek are much more complex than in English. In Greek the tenses function so that they can add adverbs to verbs. There is a lot more packed into one Greek word than what we have in most English words. A verb in the present tense Greek means that the action is not just happening in the present, but it is a continuing action into the future. This means that the casting out of fear is something that not only happens in the present moment, but also in the future as this verb form focuses on the ripple effect of the casting out. It keeps on happening! In English, imagine telling your child, "John, I want you to brush your teeth in the morning." Of course, you want him to brush every morning—not just today. The present indicative active tense communicates this attitude. This tense is very unusual to see in a passage in this way, and it occurs all through Chapter 4 of 1 John. For example, when verse 20 says, "Whoever claims to love God yet hates a brother or sister is a liar. For whoever does not love their brother and sister, whom they have seen, cannot love God, whom they have not seen."

The word "hates" is also in present indicative active tense. Knowing this about what looks to us as simple present tense in English helps us to see that this verse is addressing a person who is living in unrepented anger and hatred that is continuing into the future. The phrase "cannot love God," in the Greek present indicative active tense, means that you cannot continue loving God in this state. If you say you do, yet you refuse to repent of your continuing hatred, you are a liar. Bold truth! This beautiful revelation about this kind of present tense opens up the truth that our casting out of fear continues, as we stand in the love of God. If God requires you to battle, remember that he provides the ever-increasing strength, the armor and the authority for you to be more than an overcomer! Sometimes you need to stand against fear constantly throughout your day, especially when you are facing an intense situation. This would also involve fixing your heart on the love of God throughout the days when you are full of anxiety. This continuous standing against fear is similar to the act of forgiving someone over and over in a day. Jesus said, in Matthew 18:21-22, that we must forgive "seventy times seven" when sinned against. In the same way, we need the love of God to strengthen us to cast fear out over and over and over!

So, our stand against fear is something that we do in our breastplate of righteousness. Our victory was obtained at the cross in the past. But, now we cast out fear in the very moment we are afraid, in Jesus' name. (Praying in the name of Jesus is part of standing in the authority and righteousness of Christ, not in our own!) Even though the victory was obtained on the cross, we obtain a new victory, through the cross, every time we stand against our fear in the name of Jesus. Finally, we rest in this moment in the love of Christ. And this process will keep going into the future. I think this insight into the Greek meaning of how "cast out" is a continuing process answers both extreme positions that people take on fear. One position, the "get over it" school of thought, says that an anxious person should just see the facts, calm down and react appropriately—or rather, unemotionally. The other end of the spectrum is the school of thought that says there is no victory over fear, because this fear is just part of living as an imperfect being. Some people, who haven't seen a ray of light in victory over anxiety even contend that God created them this way and victory isn't possible. It's true that, like all of us, anxious people are born into weakness and sin, but in our weaknesses Christ is strong. Both schools of thought live in reaction and not in revelation of our position in Christ. Revelation shows us there are two types of casting out of fear. The first type happens as you are rooted and established in God's love; fear is driven out without your having to deliberately cast it out, because your security is growing. The second type occurs when you resist a spirit of fear that has no right to be in you and cast it out in the name of Jesus, knowing it will be continuously cast out because of Jesus' power. Jesus is your righteousness. Stand in him!

To be perfected in love is to grow and be strengthened in your knowledge of the love of Christ. It is comfort, peace and confidence, as you mature in the security of God. As you grow in knowing Jesus, the less afraid you will be. Your body will even respond to the peace of God, as you rest in his love, stand against fear and walk in the truth. I used to have heart palpitations every time I would think about a particular set of circumstances that I had to face. At first I thought this was normal, but God led me to pray about them. I started asking him why I was having the palpitations. One morning, as soon as I woke up, the Lord spoke to me in my mind. The first word that came into my mind when I opened my eyes was, "panic." I immediately knew, by the Spirit of God, this was the answer to my prayers for insight into my situation. I rebuked a spirit of panic and commanded it to leave me, in Jesus' name. The palpitations never came back, even though I was still confronted with the same situation several times a week. There is no safer place of protection from fear than in the middle of the love of Jesus. Let's remember how our memory verse prayer from Ephesians 3 teaches us the power of knowing the love of Christ!

MEDITATE

Spend a few minutes meditating on this passage in prayer.

Ephesians 3:16-19

[16] I pray that out of his glorious riches he may strengthen you with power through his Spirit in your inner being, [17] so that Christ may dwell in your hearts through faith. And I pray that you, being rooted and established in love, [18] may have power, together with all the Lord's holy people, to grasp how wide and long and high and deep is the love of Christ, [19] and to know this love that surpasses knowledge – that you may be filled to the measure of all the fullness of God.

CONTRASTS

2 Timothy 1:7 says, "For God has not given us the spirit of fear; but of power, and of love, and of a sound mind." (NKJV) The presence of God's Spirit in your life brings power, love and a sound mind. If you are living in the opposite of this, it is not God's will and it is not the way God made you. The contrasting traits that are not from God come from our fallen, old nature and/or from the enemy. Either way, as you are perfected in love, you can overcome these traits.

After each attribute of the Spirit from 2 Timothy, write the opposite of that attribute in the blank. The attributes of the Spirit are the opposite of the attributes produced by a spirit of fear calling the shots in your life.

1. **Power or _____?**

   Instead of power, a spirit of fear makes you feel powerless, with the need to control everything. When you are listening to a spirit of fear, you will want to manipulate situations and people around you so that you can get the results you desire. Another fruit of powerlessness is a feeling of discouragement. There is no hope for the future. Despondency can set in, when you have no hope in the practical love of God to work in your life in the here and now. Timidity or a spirit of worry can overtake you. It's almost like these spirits work in gangs when they attack people. Remember that the enemy is organized. There are no rogue spirits that do not answer to a commanding officer. Discouragement can lead to depression, which also is strongly rooted in fear. Anxiety about the future and fear of failure may hang over your head like a low-grade fever. When you are filled with powerlessness, manifesting in these ways, remember that this is not from the Spirit of God. You are not powerless. Ask God for forgiveness for listening to fear and rebuke these things by their names, in the power of the righteousness of Christ. If these evil spirits are old friends of yours, you need to let them know you are serious. They may come back around to harass you, as was their daily habit before. But, don't be afraid! Kick them out in Jesus' name every time they harass you, then confidently speak the truth of God's Word and fix your mind on who Jesus is! Remember, casting out is a process.

2. **Love or _____?**

   The opposites of love are apathy, selfishness and insecurity, not hate. If you are not filled with the Holy Spirit, your Christian life may be full of apathy and complacency. Like a marriage or a friendship that is not in a terrible place, but it isn't being nurtured and thriving, apathy will cause you to take Christ for granted. You may find yourself skipping worship at church for selfish reasons. You may decide that God will understand if you aren't reading your Bible or praying. That type of apathy in your relationship with God, in the same way as when you are apathetic with others, is a slow fade that can lead you to a dangerous place. Apathy is a religious spirit that works with your self-centered weaknesses to keep the fire and power of God from lighting in your heart and to keep you from fulfilling your role in the body of Christ. Repent of apathy and complacency and stand against them, in Jesus' name! Ask God to fill you with his love. The passion of love that has burnt out doesn't just "come back out of no-where." The flame must be fanned by the activities that bring intimacy. In a marriage, doing the right thing, instead of what you feel like, is an important step towards bringing back love. Dating, going out of your way to compliment the other person (even if you don't feel like it), spending time together talking, remembering to decorate your relationship with special things like you did when you were first together will all fan love into flame. Do the same thing with your relationship with the Lord. Don't wait for a feeling to come back. Go to worship. Spend time in prayer. Read your Bible. Get back in an accountability group. Set aside time to be alone with God. Get rid of the sin and distractions that come between you and God. These actions will help fan into flame your love for the Lord.

3. **Sound Mind or** _____?

"Mental illness" is a phrase used more and more as our society moves further and further away from the Lord. More people are exposed to trauma, due to our godless society, to the disintegration of the home, and to graphic online content. Coping skills are taught to the anxiety-ridden so they can "just get by." Counselors tell patients to expect to always be in a state of dysfunction; they will always need their medicine and will live with a battle in their mind for the rest of their lives. However, God's Word says the Holy Spirit gives believers a sound mind. Other versions of the Bible say self-control, instead of sound mind, but according to HELPS™ Word-studies at biblehub.com the Greek word means: *"safe-minded, issuing in prudent 'sensible' behavior that 'fits' a situation, i.e. aptly acting out God's will by doing what He calls sound reasoning."* The Spirit of God, through the love of God can heal the mind and soul. We need faith in the love of God to know that he can do more than we can ask or imagine through his Son that he loves and through his Spirit!

PRAYER AGAINST FEAR

Father,

In Jesus' name, you see my weaknesses, my failures and my fears. Fill me with your love now. Teach me to rest in your love, as you build your character in me. Give me hope and fill me with confidence in you. I ask forgiveness for listening to fear and obeying it. Purify me from fear and doubt, in Jesus' name. I stand in the righteousness of Christ, believing that he loves me and that his death and resurrection are more than enough to destroy and cast out the fear in my life. I cast out spirits of anxiety, worry, fretting, rejection, depression, abandonment, failure, torment, despondency and fatherlessness, in Jesus' name. I am not under the power of fear and my identity is not in anxiety; I am in Christ! I have a good Father and he loves me! I am his beloved daughter, in whom he is well pleased. Thank you, God, for your Spirit. Fill me with your Spirit to bring your love, power and a sound mind.

In Jesus' name, Amen!

The breastplate of righteousness protects the heart with faith and love. Through the substitutionary work of Jesus Christ, Satan is defeated. So, we stand in the righteousness of Jesus. But, also, when we stand in the righteousness of Christ, his great love does a work in our lives that brings about confidence, freedom and sanctification. When you choose to walk in the love of Christ and not selfishness, his love protects you and those around you from the ravages of sin and Satan. Remember, every time fear comes against you, resist it in the name of Jesus!

WORD STUDY
Love

Take time today to look up the word "love" in your Bible app. Write down the scriptures that encourage you the most about God's love. Put them up in places you can see and say them out loud frequently, throughout the day. Using the same method we have used with our prayers from Ephesians, you can insert your own name into the text as you pray and confess the text out loud. I will get you started with one. I know this word study will encourage you and bless you beyond measure! Have fun basking in the love of our Good Father!

See what great love the Father has lavished on us, that we should be called children of God! And that is what we are! – 1 John 3:1

Prayer and Confession Version – See what great love the Father has lavished on me, that I should be called a child of God! And that is what I am!

BRINGING IT HOME

- Are there fears in your life that you have lived with, thinking that they are just your personality or that you will never have freedom from them? Ask the Holy Spirit to reveal the truth to you.

- Do you struggle with depression? Ask the Lord if your depression is rooted in fear.

Allow yourself grace to grow in the love of God, being perfected daily. Don't let doubt defeat you if you don't see all your fears leave overnight. It is a continual strengthening and growth process, as his love casts out your fear. If you are overwhelmed by fear and cannot get peace of mind, do not be afraid to take your stand against a spirit of fear or anxiety, in Jesus' name. If you still struggle after doing this, ask another believer to come alongside you while you cast out these enemies and to agree with you in prayer to be filled with the Spirit of wisdom and revelation to know the love of God. Stand in prayer with your prayer partner for this supernatural filling of love, using our prayer from Ephesians 3,

And I pray that you, being rooted and established in love, may have power, together with all the Lord's holy people, to grasp how wide and long and high and deep is the love of Christ, and to know this love that surpasses knowledge – that you may be filled to the measure of all the fullness of God.

Living in accountability is a powerful weapon against the enemy, and together we experience more of the fullness of God.

PUTTING ON YOUR ARMOR
PART 5

THE PREPARATION OF THE GOSPEL OF PEACE

MEMORY VERSE

¹⁰ Finally, be strong in the Lord and in his mighty power. ¹¹ Put on the full armour of God, so that you can take your stand against the devil's schemes. ¹² For our struggle is not against flesh and blood, but against the rulers, against the authorities, against the powers of this dark world and against the spiritual forces of evil in the heavenly realms. ¹³ Therefore put on the full armour of God, so that when the day of evil comes, you may be able to stand your ground, and after you have done everything, to stand. – Ephesians 6:10-13

PRAYER
& Declaration of Truth

Today, Lord Jesus, I thank you for your sacrifice and for your transformation of my life. I have a testimony, because of you. You have brought me from darkness to light by your precious blood. You are my Passover Lamb, that protects me from judgment and death. Steady me and prepare me for the battles that I must face in this life. Help me to go confidently forward, claiming the ground you have ordained me to claim in my life. Through the blood of Jesus Christ, my life and my family are delivered out of the hands of the devil. Through the blood of Jesus, I am purchased for adoption into a new family. Thank you, Father, for your goodness to me!

In Jesus' name, Amen!

READING

Ephesians 6:14-16

¹⁴ Stand firm then, with the belt of truth buckled round your waist, with the breastplate of righteousness in place, ¹⁵ and with your feet fitted with the readiness that comes from the gospel of peace. ¹⁶ In addition to all this, take up the shield of faith, with which you can extinguish all the flaming arrows of the evil one.

How many of you are into shoes? My teenage son currently owns more shoes than I thought it was possible for a boy his age to fit in a closet. Being a serious athlete, he needs the right kind of shoes for each sport he is in. He has a pair of basketball shoes for games and a pair for practice, track spikes for sprints, and now, I have recently been informed, he needs special high jump spikes. Along with these various specialty shoes, which he cannot wear off of the court, he also has a pair of regular tennis shoes for everyday use. It does not stop there. He has two different types of L.L. Bean boots, one pair of men's fashion boots and another for hiking/ wearing in the snow. To top it all off, for quick casual wear, he also has a pair of white Crocs. He is such a shoe "horse"—as my mom would say. The other day, when he had to wear a pair of ugly shoes to work, he was mortified to learn that we were going directly to the dentist after work. He asked, "Do I look messy enough that people will assume I was gardening? I don't want anyone to think I would actually choose to wear these in public." We assured him, with a chuckle, that he was sufficiently dirty and disheveled to communicate that he had just been doing yard work all morning.

While Ellis has paid for a number of these shoes with his own money, we also chipped in a significant amount, when necessary. I don't know that I want to take the time to add up how much it cost for all of those shoes. But, if you are a serious athlete, you really need to be shod with the right footwear to have optimum performance. Once, we bought him a pair of shoes for basketball, only to find out that he grew out of them too quickly to wear more than a couple of times. Moms, do you know the struggle? I still remember looking at those spanking-new, barely used shoes, and feeling like a little bit of me died inside. The cost of sports shoes is usually not a big deal, unless you know that the shoes are not getting worn!

Did you know that your spiritual footwear was purchased at a price? It was more expensive than all the shoes you ever bought. In fact, more than one person paid for them, and most believers never put them on, even though they participated in paying for their custom-fit, hope-bringing, battle-ready shoes! Curious to find out more?

Today, we are focusing on putting on our shoes for battle. Ephesians 6:15 says, "and having shod your feet with the preparation of the gospel of peace ..." So, let's start with a word study of the word "preparation." Strongs Concordance says that the Greek word for preparation is hetoimasia, which also means: foundation, firm footing; preparation, readiness. Go to your Bible app and type in the word "ready." See what verses you get! Write your findings below.

CROSS REFERENCE
Be Ready!

1 Peter 3:15-16 (NKJV) says, "But sanctify the Lord God in your hearts, and always be **ready** to give a defense to everyone who asks you a reason for the hope that is in you, with meekness and fear ..." The word "ready" in this passage is closely related to the word "preparation" in Ephesians 6:15. They have the same root word, with slightly different forms. (ready vs readiness) Both passages of scripture describe the role of a Christian to be ready to share his or her faith. Ephesians 6:15 describes the shoes as the "preparation of the gospel of peace" and 1 Peter 3:15 says, "Always be prepared to give an answer to everyone who asks you to give the reason for the hope that you have." Our feet take us wherever we go, and wherever we go, we should go with purpose, ready to bring the hope of the gospel of peace!

We are the modern day, New Covenant children of Abraham! God made a promise to the children of Israel—the descendants of Abraham—when they came out of Egypt. In Deuteronomy 11:24-25 he said, "Every place where you set your foot will be yours: Your territory will extend from the desert to Lebanon, and from the Euphrates River to the Mediterranean Sea. No one will be able to stand against you. The Lord your God, as he promised you, will put the terror and fear of you on the whole land, wherever you go."

The children of Israel came out of slavery and into the promised land. We came out of the slavery of sin and into the promised land of the Lord's favor, blessings and victory. Wherever we go, we should be dispossessing the devil's territory, by sharing the good news of the Lord and setting the captives free. Where we walk and where we live in this life is not to our own glory, for the building up of our own temporary wealth and kingdoms, but to the glory of God and to bring about the kingdom of God in the hearts of men and women.

In this way, I believe the shoes are not only a defensive part of our armor, but also an offensive part! Jesus said to Peter, in Matthew 16:18, "And I tell you that you are Peter, and on this rock I will build my church, and the gates of Hades will not overcome it." This is a picture of the church advancing and attacking the devil's kingdom. (Again, not attacking people, for our battle is not against flesh and blood, but against the unseen spiritual enemy, the devil. In this way, the people who are trapped in his kingdom can be set free, by the blood of Jesus.) Our battle shoes are for moving forward and claiming ground for the Lord. Are your feet shod with readiness to bring the gospel? Let's see what Romans says about the beauty of the feet of those who are always ready to bring good news.

Romans 10:8-15

⁸ But what does it say? 'The word is near you; it is in your mouth and in your heart,' that is, the message concerning faith that we proclaim: ⁹ if you declare with your mouth, 'Jesus is Lord,' and believe in your heart that God raised him from the dead, you will be saved. ¹⁰ For it is with your heart that you believe and are justified, and it is with your mouth that you profess your faith and are saved. ¹¹ As Scripture says, 'Anyone who believes in him will never be put to shame.' ¹² For there is no difference between Jew and Gentile – the same Lord is Lord of all and richly blesses all who call on him, ¹³ for, 'Everyone who calls on the name of the Lord will be saved.'

¹⁴ How, then, can they call on the one they have not believed in? And how can they believe in the one of whom they have not heard? And how can they hear without someone preaching to them? ¹⁵ And how can anyone preach unless they are sent? As it is written: **'How beautiful are the feet of those who bring good news!'**

BEAUTIFUL FEET

Take a moment of remembrance right now to thank God for the person who led you to Christ. Was it a stranger? A camp counselor? A friend? A father or mother? A pastor? How would your life be different, if that person had not walked in the readiness of the gospel?

Also, take time to remember the people who shared the gospel with you before your heart was soft. Remember the people who you scorned and rejected, maybe even the people who didn't say everything quite right, but they went out on a limb and tried. They were willing to be a fool for Jesus to help bring you from death to life. Say a prayer for those people!

When we are in Jesus' army, we are on his mission. His mission is to seek and to save the lost. He said to his disciples, "'The harvest is plentiful, but the workers are few. Ask the Lord of the harvest, therefore, to send out workers into his harvest field. Go! I am sending you out like lambs among wolves. Do not take a purse or bag or sandals; and do not greet anyone on the road." – Luke 10:2b-4

Jesus always prayed the will of the Father and he taught his disciples to pray for more workers to bring in the harvest. This should be a constant prayer. Our hearts should burn for what makes Jesus' heart burn. He believed in this mission so much that he gave up his glory, his luxury and his life for it. He tells the disciples not to worry about their earthly sandals. God will provide for their needs. When you are walking in the shoes of the readiness of the gospel, you will need to trust the Lord. He may ask you to do something that takes great faith, that you can't see the outcome of in your natural mind and reality. But, if he sends you, he will equip you and provide you with everything you need to bring the gospel of peace, including courage, words, opportunities, finances and encouragement.

CROSS REFERENCE
How Much Do These Shoes Cost?

Then I heard a loud voice in heaven say: 'Now have come the salvation and the power and the kingdom of our God, and the authority of his Messiah. For the accuser of our brothers and sisters, who accuses them before our God day and night, has been hurled down. **They triumphed over him by the blood of the Lamb and by the word of their testimony; they did not love their lives so much as to shrink from death.** Therefore rejoice, you heavens and you who dwell in them! But woe to the earth and the sea, because the devil has gone down to you! He is filled with fury, because he knows that his time is short.' – Revelation 12:10-12

103. In this passage, where is our enemy the devil?

104. How was he hurled down or triumphed over?

105. What did the triumphant not do?

106. Why is there a woe spoken over the earth?

TRIUMPH

To triumph in the battle against the devil, we overcome by two weapons.

Weapon #1 – The Blood of the Lamb

This statement is holy ground for the believer in Jesus. The blood of the Lamb is your protection from the attacks and accusations of the devil. Remember that we discovered that Christ's blood sacrifice for us is our breastplate of righteous, the protection over our heart. Do you know that the devil stands before God day and night listing every negative thing he can find against you? We learn this from Job 2 and other places in scripture. How does the blood of the Lamb help us to triumph over these accusations and attacks? It may seem strange, for those who don't know the background or importance of the blood of Jesus. In the Old Testament, blood is considered sacred. After he was murdered, Abel's blood cried out to God from the ground. Hebrews says this about Abel: "By faith Abel brought God a better offering than Cain did. By faith he was commended as righteous, when God spoke well of his offerings. And by faith Abel still speaks, even though he is dead." – Hebrews 11:4

Blood was the only acceptable sacrifice to atone for sin. In the Old Covenant, a perfect animal would stand in judgment in place of the sinner, and its blood would cover the sin only one time. The animal blood wouldn't remove the sin. The covered sin was hidden from God by the blood of the sacrificial animal, but it was not removed. However, Jesus became the perfect sacrifice for our sins; fully God and fully man, he lived a life of righteousness and died in our stead. His blood cleanses us from ALL sin. The blood of Jesus removes the sin. It isn't just hidden; it is gone, washed away, and removed as far as the east is from the west. It is finished. Hebrews 12 says, "You have come to God, the Judge of all, to the spirits of the righteous made perfect, to Jesus the mediator of a new covenant, and to the sprinkled blood that speaks a better word than the blood of Abel." – Hebrews 12:23-24

CROSS REFERENCE
How Is the Blood Protection?

Let's turn in our Bibles to Exodus 12 and read the story of the Passover lamb for greater insight into the power of the blood!

107. According to verse 12, why was God going to strike down the first born in Egypt?

108. According to verse 13, what was the purpose of putting the blood on the tops and sides of the doorframe?

109. According to verse 22, how did they apply the blood of the lamb for protection?

Jesus was the perfect Passover lamb. He gave his life up during the celebration of the Passover. When he served his disciples the Passover meal—the last supper—he told them that his body was soon to fulfill the prophetic picture in the Passover meal. This sacred meal was handed down from generation to generation in Jewish homes, in remembrance of God's deliverance from the slavery of Egypt, and foreshadowing God's final deliverance from the slavery of sin. "While they were eating, Jesus took bread, and when he had given thanks, he broke it and gave it to his disciples, saying, 'Take and eat; this is my body.' Then he took a cup, and when he had given thanks, he gave it to them, saying, 'Drink from it, all of you. This is my blood of the covenant, which is poured out for many for the forgiveness of sins." – Matthew 26:26-28

How do we apply the blood of the Lamb for protection and to triumph over the devil? In Exodus, the fathers used a bunch of hyssop (a plant) to transfer the blood of the lamb to the door posts. As the late Derek Prince taught, the blood of the Lamb did no good if it was left in the basin. It was applied, through the direction of God, by the fathers to the door posts, for the protection of their families and everyone in their homes. If the father had not followed through, by applying the blood, the sacrifice of the lamb would have been in vain. The hyssop in the Old Testament covenant corresponds to something in the New Covenant—our testimony!

Weapon #2 – The Word of Our Testimony

As it says in Revelation, "They triumphed over him by the blood of the Lamb and by the word of their testimony; they did not love their lives so much as to shrink from death." – Revelation 12:11

When we testify about the work of God in our lives and when we declare and confess the truth of our position in Christ, we are taking a treasured weapon—the blood of Jesus—and are applying it to our lives. You can review the power of confession in the passage from Romans 10 that we studied earlier, "If you declare with your mouth, "Jesus is Lord," and believe in your heart that God raised him from the dead, you will be saved. For it is with your heart that you believe and are justified, and it is with your mouth that you profess your faith and are saved." – Romans 10:9-10

Our justification comes by believing. When we believe, it is "just-as-if-I'd" never sinned. But, the verbal confession applies the justification for salvation. In the same way, God requires us to be participants in victory here on earth. He has done what we could not do. He fulfilled the righteous requirements of the law and he died in our place. Now, we get to play our part. We get to open our mouths and confess the truth of who we are in Christ and what Jesus did for us.

This confession is a double-edged sword. First, it is a declaration to God and the devil. Secondly, it is a confession to others about the power and love of our Savior. When we open our mouths in declaration, confessing that we are covered by the blood, we are protected! Here are some suggestions of ways to do this. Say these confessions about the work of the blood of Jesus aloud! It should bring you great freedom to do this regularly!

- Through the blood of Jesus, I am delivered from the hand of Satan!

- Through the blood of Jesus, I am cleansed from all my sin!

- Through the blood of Jesus, I am protected from the destroyer!

- Through the blood of Jesus, I am made righteous before God, and declared not guilty of my sin!

- Through the blood of Jesus, I am whole, delivered, saved and redeemed.

- Through the blood of Jesus, I have a place in the family of God.

- Through the blood of Jesus, I triumph over the devil!

> **TODAY'S BIBLE STUDY TOOL**
>
> **Practical Application.** How can I personally apply this scripture to my life today? What changes do I need to make? What prayer should I pray?
>
> Don't forget to ask the Holy Spirit for help!

- Thank you, Lord, that the blood of Jesus speaks a better word for me than the blood of Abel.

- Thank you, Lord, that through the blood, I am being sanctified, made holy and brought near to you!

Your personal testimony is dear to God's heart. No one has a story like yours. Jesus isn't the only one who paid for your testimony. You paid for it. Your sin and the actions of those who sinned against you cost you a heavy toll. I am not talking about the debt you owe to God, but I am talking about the demanding slave master of sin and what it takes out of your life. The places your feet have walked are unique. Some of you have walked through the valley of the shadow of death. Others have carried the burden of a loved one who has made damaging choices. Other women have strived to serve God in stifling surroundings where every day is a choice to forgive or grow hardened. Each story is different. We all serve the same God, in the same family, with the same inheritance awaiting us. But we each are different. Your story will reach people who will not understand my story. Your story will encourage and draw people to Christ who would be turned off by my story. We each have a role to play and a story to tell. Are you ready to share your story of redemption? Are you ready to tell the woman behind you, crying in line at the store, that God set you free and he can help her, too? Are you ready to tell your co-worker the secrets you may be embarrassed to tell, except for the fact that Jesus redeemed you from it all? Be a star shining in the blackness of the universe. Your testimony may be the North Star that leads someone home!

I have watched my sons put on new basketball shoes and take the court with a new spring in their step. Why? Because, as silly as it sounds, they subconsciously believed that those new shoes named after the next best NBA star would improve their games. Or maybe, when you put on some new cute sandals or boots, you feel a bit more confident at work the next day. How much more confident should we be with our feet shod with the preparation of the gospel of peace? Your testimony may be embarrassing, but if the darkness of your past reflects Jesus' grace and mercy even more, focus on the Savior and his amazing grace! Someone out there in darkness needs a light to dawn. That light could be you! Be ready.

BRINGING IT HOME

Put on your shoes! Take time every day to declare the works of the Lord in the two ways that we triumph over the enemy.

- Declare out loud your position in Christ, through the blood of Jesus. Use the examples in this lesson to help you. You may want to write them on sticky notes and put them up over your kitchen or bathroom sink, or in your laundry room, so that you can do warfare for your family as you do their laundry. "Through the blood of Jesus, I declare this child to be delivered from the enemy's schemes!"

- Write down your personal testimony. Look for places to share it. Ask the Lord for opportunities to share with others what Jesus has done for you. Ask him to bring people into your life who need to hear how God delivered you from your own Egypt.

- Rebuke fear of sharing the gospel, in Jesus' name. Ask God to forgive you for living in cowardice and the fear of people. Ask him to give you his heart for others.

- Pray for the Lord of the harvest to send out more workers into his harvest field.

GOD SEES A WARRIOR

Move over D.C. Comics and Marvel women! Nothing compares to a warrior woman of God, beautiful and strong in the Spirit of the Lord.

MEMORY VERSE

[10] Finally, be strong in the Lord and in his mighty power. [11] Put on the full armour of God, so that you can take your stand against the devil's schemes. [12] For our struggle is not against flesh and blood, but against the rulers, against the authorities, against the powers of this dark world and against the spiritual forces of evil in the heavenly realms. [13] Therefore put on the full armour of God, so that when the day of evil comes, you may be able to stand your ground, and after you have done everything, to stand. – Ephesians 6:10-13

PRAYER

Holy God,

I thank you for all that you are teaching me through your Word. I feel small and insignificant to do the things you are calling me to do. I sometimes even feel unsure and confused. The world is full of chaos and I need your peace. I need your direction in the middle of my mess. Fill me with your Spirit of wisdom and revelation so that I can know you better and walk in the hope of my calling in Christ Jesus. Help me to see your promise for me and what you want to do in me and through me, by your power.

In Jesus' name. Amen.

CROSS REFERENCE

For our reading today, we are going to cross reference the first part of the story of Gideon. Open your Bible and read Judges Chapters 6-7:25.

I love the story of Gideon in Judges Chapter 6. Perhaps it is the idea that God looked on a regular Joe, who was hiding in fear, and saw a warrior that appeals to me. Maybe I am drawn to the account because Gideon is so nervous and awkward with the Angel of the Lord that he reminds me of myself second guessing things the Lord tells me? God takes this anxious man and transforms him into a leader of his people in perilous times of judgment. I like this about God and I like this about Gideon. Gideon was just a simple farmer. He wasn't a soldier. He didn't have military training, to our knowledge.

Take time to write down the questions Gideon asks the angel of the Lord from your reading.

Do any of Gideon's questions ring true to you today? Have you ever felt this way or asked these questions when talking to God?

HISTORICAL BACKGROUND

During Gideon's time, (circa 1191 B.C.) the nation of Israel was under judgment from God for idol worship. Generations earlier, the children of Israel entered the land God had promised to Abraham, and they took it handily from people who were burning their children alive in sacrifices to Molech. However, a few generations later—in about the same amount of time from the American Revolution to the 1970's—the descendants of those people of God completely forgot what their parents and grandparents sacrificed when they followed God into the Promised Land. To them, it was ancient history. They turned their backs on the living God and exchanged it for the appealing idol worship in the nations around them. Most of this idol worship was sexual and involved temple prostitution, so we shouldn't be too surprised. Sex sells, right? These are the same compromises happening in the body of Christ today. The children of Israel were not walking in truth, righteousness, readiness or salvation. They were living in unrepented sin, and God sent another nation to judge them oppressively, the way their ancestors had been used by God to judge the nations before them. Yes. God judges nations, not just people.

BIRD'S-EYE VIEW
God Judges the Nations

This story shows us an example of how God deals with nations, not just with individuals. The spiritual and social environment of the Jewish culture had completely disintegrated, as people turned away from the Lord. When living in a sin-saturated society, people find it hard to believe there was a time when the majority of the people followed the Lord and whole-heartedly obeyed his commands. Younger generations mock the "prudish behavior" and "backward thinking" of their ancestors and believe that their own new ways are better. There is nothing new under the sun. We still see this today. The consequences for this sin and rebellion in Israel, which deepened with every generation, was extreme oppression in the form of confusion, loss, chaos and war in their own land. The followers of the Lord found themselves, much like today, afraid, alone, and wondering how much worse it could get.

BUG'S-EYE VIEW
Personal Battles with Sin

Here we find Gideon, hiding in a winepress, threshing his grain. Threshing grain seems like a pretty common activity for a farmer. But, Gideon was hiding in fear in the wine press to keep from being seen by the Midianites. He couldn't even perform the simplest tasks in a normal way because of the oppression and because of fear. This is what oppression from the enemy will do to you. It will make normal activity like just preparing food, cleaning or even getting out of bed feel like a battle. This is the spiritual and emotional state of the church today. The people of God are oppressed by anxiety and unable to even function in many aspects of normal life. Signs of defeat and resignation are in their hearts. Our children are falling away from the Lord, as more and more believers deal with depression. A very high percentage of people who claim to have a relationship with Jesus Christ struggle with pornography addictions—including pastors. Social media follows us everywhere on our phones and hearts respond with jealousy. Healthy spiritual and social lives seem almost non-existent in our society.

Remember that the oppression and the heated battle with the Midianites were allowed by the Lord, to remind the Israelites to whom they belonged. This oppression wasn't just wrath and anger to destroy them; it was meant to dissolve the illusion that they were living in the Promised Land because of their own strength and savvy social and business skills. The Promised Land was given to them by God. He brought them out of slavery. He led them through the desert. He was their shade by day and their pillar of fire at night. When they entered the promised land, they faced giants guarding tall walls of a great city, but the walls of Jericho fell flat when they obeyed the Lord. Now, the nation he redeemed from the bondage of slavery is lying unfaithful in the arms of a false god. The true living God wanted them to turn back to an unadulterated relationship with him.

On an aside, what is more important to you: that your children are successful and have a happy life or that they walk in truth with God? You see, when you ask yourself this question, you realize what a good father God really is. We teach our children the difference between instant and delayed gratification. We make them go to school and do their homework, even when they say it's boring. None of us, hopefully, give our children everything they ask for just to keep them happy. Especially when those things—like eating nothing but candy and hot dogs or playing in a busy highway—are unhealthy and dangerous. All of us who are honest will agree that we enact discipline to keep our children on the right path. I even pray that God will reveal sin in my children and not let them get away with things that they may be hiding. It is more important for them to learn that they belong to God and how to walk in truth than for all their natural consequences to be taken away. When we start caring more about our children enjoying this temporary life than their eternal souls, we are in danger of sending our future generations into the full-blown judgment of God. A quick example is when parents give their children birth control when they become teenagers or when they go off to college. Why would you want to give your children the impression that you condone their having sex outside of marriage? You may say, "Johnny, you know how I feel about this issue, but if you do get into a situation, make sure you use birth control." That is basically telling Johnny that he is free to have safe sex, as long as he doesn't produce a grandchild before he graduates and gets a job. This exalts the philosophies of the world—education and money are more important than purity—above God's truth and sets your child up for spiritual failure. Real life consequences are God's way of keeping us in the truth. They are also a deterrent. When we suppress the ones that God provides, other consequences will stand up in their place. The purpose of all judgment is to draw us back to our Father.

WHAT GOD SEES WHEN HE LOOKS AT ME

While God shakes the nations to get their attention and allowed Gideon to be shaken, God also will allow a shaking or two in our lives to get our attention. When you find yourself in a personal situation where stress, trauma and anxiety interrupt daily life, seek the Lord. There is a reason that he has allowed you to walk through this trial. These are opportunities for him to show himself strong in your life. He will remind you that he is your redeemer. He will show you the way out. If there is any sin, whether it is your sin or someone else's sin that is at the root of the problems you are facing, he will reveal it to you. When you turn to him for deliverance, he will change you from a person who is crippled in your everyday life to someone who is leading others out of bondage.

GLASS HALF EMPTY OR GLASS HALF FULL?

When the angel of the Lord finds Gideon, hiding in fear, he says, "The Lord is with you, mighty warrior."—insert chuckle. He definitely does not fit the ideal picture that any casting agent working on the movie *Vengeance 3* would be looking for. He's fearful and just trying to survive the Israelite 1190 B.C. apocalypse. Gideon looks at the picture and sees it without God's intervention. Even his line of questioning shows his doubt of the presence of the Lord in his life. He sees a reality from the perspective of the physical realm. The glass is half empty. Or all the way empty.

But, God sees a different picture. God sees someone he can use to lead the people to victory. God sees someone he is getting ready to fill with power. God sees the supernatural picture. Gideon does not see himself this way, and he takes some great convincing. He is still under the impression that God uses strong people to bring about his glory. This reminds me of Moses' encounter with God at the burning bush, where Moses spent the entire time arguing with the Lord telling him that he didn't know what he was talking about. The Angel of the Lord takes the time to tell Gideon that he is going to be used by God, in spite of his weaknesses and fears. God will do all the mighty wonders. Gideon just needs to trust the Word of the Lord and be a willing vessel.

HIDING IN YOUR WINEPRESS?
Come Out to Your Calling!

Do you feel insufficient? Do you wonder who will come to rescue you? Jesus already did. He did the great work of redemption and the Father adopted you into his kingdom. You have an extraordinary calling as a woman of God. God sees you as so much more than you can ever imagine. If you feel inadequate or unable to be great for the Lord, you inadvertently have taken the first step down the spiritual path of escaping the winepress and embracing your calling. God is looking for the broken, those who have come to the end of themselves and honestly found lack. This is the first step to being a vessel of the Lord: humility! In fact, in the book of James, it shows us that we have power to overcome the devil, when we walk in humility and not pride.

James 4:6-10

⁶ But he gives us more grace. That is why Scripture says:

> 'God opposes the proud
>> but shows favour to the humble.'

⁷ Submit yourselves, then, to God. Resist the devil, and he will flee from you. ⁸ Come near to God and he will come near to you. Wash your hands, you sinners, and purify your hearts, you double-minded. ⁹ Grieve, mourn and wail. Change your laughter to mourning and your joy to gloom. ¹⁰ Humble yourselves before the Lord, and he will lift you up.

When you start to awaken to the fact that you are not good enough to be something for God on your own, this is a sign you are truly hearing from the Holy Spirit. However, in that moment of truth, do not let the devil come in and twist the truth into a despair-filled lie that you will never be good enough for God and he could never use you! The devil will pounce quickly to take your eyes off of Christ. When you look around at the world and find yourself afraid, ducking for cover—lift your eyes up to the Lord! There is where your help comes from. Fix your eyes on Jesus, the perfecter of your faith! You can't be perfect, but Jesus will perfect you for God's great work! Rest in his love. Rest in his sufficiency. Rest in his redemption. Be filled with his Spirit. Then step out in faith to answer his call. When you do this very brave act, you will be the ultimate shining light. Everyone will see God's great work and give him glory. I will leave you with this beautiful scripture of encouragement.

2 Corinthians 4:7-18

⁷ **But we have this treasure in jars of clay to show that this all-surpassing power is from God and not from us.** ⁸ We are hard pressed on every side, but not crushed; perplexed, but not in despair; ⁹ persecuted, but not abandoned; struck down, but not destroyed. ¹⁰ We always carry around in our body the death of Jesus, so that the life of Jesus may also be revealed in our body. ¹¹ For we who are alive are always being given over to death for Jesus' sake, so that his life may also be revealed in our mortal body. ¹² So then, death is at work in us, but life is at work in you.

¹³ It is written: 'I believed; therefore I have spoken.' Since we have that same spirit of faith, we also believe and therefore speak, ¹⁴ because we know that the one who raised the Lord Jesus from the dead will also raise us with Jesus and present us with you to himself. ¹⁵ All this is for your benefit, so that the grace that is reaching more and more people may cause thanksgiving to overflow to the glory of God.

¹⁶ **Therefore we do not lose heart. Though outwardly we are wasting away, yet inwardly we are being renewed day by day.** ¹⁷ For our light and momentary troubles are achieving for us an eternal glory that far outweighs them all. ¹⁸ So we fix our eyes not on what is seen, but on what is unseen, since what is seen is temporary, but what is unseen is eternal.

BRINGING IT HOME

Do you look at your situations and question whether God is really with you or not? When you see a mess, God may see a message he is getting ready to speak to the world through your life.

Ask God today, "What areas of my life am I looking at through negative, faithless glasses? Give me hope to see what you want to do in my life today."

TAKING UP THE SWORD OF THE SPIRIT

Today you will discover that you have every weapon at your disposal to destroy the devil's work in your life in Jesus Christ our Lord.

MEMORY VERSE

[10] Finally, be strong in the Lord and in his mighty power. [11] Put on the full armour of God, so that you can take your stand against the devil's schemes. [12] For our struggle is not against flesh and blood, but against the rulers, against the authorities, against the powers of this dark world and against the spiritual forces of evil in the heavenly realms. [13] Therefore put on the full armour of God, so that when the day of evil comes, you may be able to stand your ground, and after you have done everything, to stand. – Ephesians 6:10-13

PRAYER

Pray the Spiritual Warfare Prayer found in the Prayer Index. We have been deep in Ephesians. During this time, I hope your faith has been strengthened. When you study the Word of God, you are built up by the promises of God. Not only are the promises of God and the truth the Lord speaks to us in his Word a sword to cut down and expose the lies of the devil, but they also supernaturally strengthen and enlarge our shield of faith. This is very important for women in a world full of fear and turmoil. We need faith to face not only our own weaknesses and situations, but also the unseen enemies that come against us, our family, our friends and the body of Christ. We need to teach our children to rely on the promises of God and to study the Word, so they can be built up in their own faith and not just go to church or believe in Jesus because we make them do it. Train up your children in the Word! Let's dig in today and see more about how God's direction and word to Gideon strengthen him and equip him to be the man he was created to be.

READING

To start today's study on spiritual warfare, read Judges 6:24-40 and create a timeline of events in the following space.

THE SWORD OF THE SPIRIT

Ephesians 6:16-18

[16] In addition to all this, take up the shield of faith with which you can extinguish all the flaming arrows of the evil one. [17] Take the helmet of salvation and the sword of the Spirit, which is the word of God. [18] And pray in the Spirit on all occasions with all kinds of prayers and requests. With this in mind, be alert and always keep on praying for all the saints.

Gideon didn't have much of the written Word of God the way we have it assembled today in the Bible. Moses had written the Torah (Genesis—Deuteronomy), but most likely, private individuals did not have a copy of it and most had not memorized it during this era. However, Gideon DOES have something just as good. He has a message from God himself. Let's use a Bible study tool to research this angel that brought the message to Gideon! There are times in the Old Testament when we see God himself appearing as an angel. Is this one of those times?

BIBLE COMMENTARY

A Bible commentary is a tool that a Bible scholar has written after much study. Remember, it is the author's opinion, but it is something to be valued, because it frequently will include cultural and language information that is not obvious in the text. You can access many Bible commentaries at biblehub.com, including the following.

> **TODAY'S BIBLE STUDY TOOL**
>
> **Bible Commentary.** A Bible Commentary is a useful tool in Bible study. There are many available by a variety of authors. Each represents its author's understanding of the biblical passage and may explain the cultural background, as well as the intention of the original language.

Gill's Exposition of the Entire Bible has this to say about Judges 6:11:

> And there came an angel of the Lord, ... This was not ... a prophet ... but an angel of God, as expressed, and not a created one, but the Angel of Jehovah's presence, the Word and Son of God, and who is expressly called Jehovah himself, Judges 6:14.

The Cambridge Bible for schools and colleges says this:

> 11. the angel of the Lord] i.e. Jehovah Himself in manifestation; see on Jdg 2:1. Closely parallel are the appearances in Jdg 13:3-23 and Genesis 18; the Angel or Messenger appears in human form, and in the end is recognized as Jehovah; also Genesis 16:7-14, Genesis 32:24-30 (cf. Hosea 12:4.), Exodus 3:2-6. Here the Angel shews (shows) himself in the guise of a 'traveller unknown,' resting under a tree, with a staff in his hand.

Sooooo ... you may be asking why this is important. It is important because we are learning how God relates to us and how his Word is a weapon in our hands to fight in the spiritual battle we are immersed in day in and day out. Gideon may not have had the Bible in hand, but the spoken message to Gideon was truly a spiritual weapon, delivered by the Spirit of God. This is why it is called the Sword of the Spirit.

WORD STUDY
Word

The Greek word for "word of God" is rhéma.

Strong's Concordance
   rhéma: a word, by impl. a matter
   Short Definition: a thing spoken

4487 *rhḗma* (from 4483 /*rhéō*, "to speak") – a *spoken* word, made "by the *living voice*" (J. Thayer). 4487 /*rhḗma* ("spoken-word") is commonly used in the NT (and in *LXX*) *for the Lord* speaking His *dynamic, living word* in a believer to inbirth *faith* ("His inwrought *persuasion*").

Ro 10:17: "So *faith* proceeds from (spiritual) hearing; moreover this hearing (is consummated) through a *rhēma-word* (4487 /*rhḗma*) *from Christ*" (Gk text)

There is power in the spoken Word of God, whether it is spoken by God, an angel, or a person. When you open your mouth to speak truth from God's Word, faith is born in the hearts of the hearers. As we see in the word study, the consummation of this faith happens through the literal spoken Word of God! Beautiful.

Scripture is literally breathed by God. It is alive and active, from his mouth to our hearts. Hebrews 4:12-13 tells us, "The word of God is alive and active. Sharper than any double-edged sword, it penetrates even to dividing soul and spirit, joints and marrow; it judges the thoughts and attitudes of the heart. Nothing in all creation is hidden from God's sight. Everything is uncovered and laid bare before the eyes of him to whom we must give account."

That sword comes straight from the mouth of Jesus, via the Spirit of God to our spiritual ears. It awakens our faith! The Word of God gets to the root of the problems in our lives and as a skilled surgeon, he uses this knife (sword) to remove what fills us with doubt and replaces that with faith. He can reveal to you what unforgiveness is plaguing your marriage or what hidden anxieties are causing your panic attacks and depression. His Word does all this and so much more!

We need to pray God's Word aloud. The spoken Word of God is powerful, alive and active. One young lady asked me, "Why do we need to pray God's Word out loud? Can't God hear my thoughts?" Yes he can hear your thoughts. It's not about him. It's about you! You need to speak and confess the Word of God out loud. When your mouth confesses it in prayer and your ears hear it, your spirit will be built up in faith. You go through every day listening to the philosophies of the world and taking in the lies that the devil communicates to you through other people. It's time to counteract those philosophies and lies with the truth of God's Word. There are so many times I have said to myself, "I shouldn't have to do that." It usually includes cleaning the kitchen for the fourth time that day. In the physical realm, I frequently and incredulously say, "I shouldn't have to tell my kids this again. I already told them to pick that up three times!" However, because the problem is right there in front of me, I can't deny the truth that, in fact, I DO need to do it again. Spiritually, people have the same experiences. A woman may say, "I shouldn't have to pray God's Word aloud or speak it aloud to combat the devil. Jesus fights the devil for me. I don't need to do anything." Well, you may FEEL that you don't have to do anything, but that doesn't mean that your feelings are true. It says in Ephesians to "take up" the sword of the Spirit. God puts his weapon in our hands for us to wield it!

As I was taking a walk with my daughter the night before we left her at college, we were discussing all the amazing things the Lord had done over the summer to bring us growth and transformation. We discussed the way his Word has come alive to both of us over the past year. A picture of a sword lying on a table came to my mind. I turned to her and said, "You know, the sword of the Spirit does nothing when it is just lying around. That is one powerful truth right there." You have to wield or use it. In order to wield it, you have to speak it. In order to speak it, you have to know it. In order to know it, you have to pick it up and read it. You will go into battle. Everyone will. Are you prepared to use your sword? A sword does no good for a warrior if it is stored neatly away in an arsenal. When I mentioned this to my daughter she said, "Mom, people have to know how to use a sword before they fight their enemies. Who wants to go into mortal combat without any training? So many people have no idea what is in God's Word or how to properly use it in battle. They need to learn!" She is so right! We like to read books about the armor of God and wear t-shirts about the armor of God, but when are we going take our offensive weapon seriously and start to learn to use it in our day to day skirmishes and battles?

Revelation 1:12-18 is a picture of our Warrior King, risen, powerfully reigning, ready to return for his bride:

Revelation 1:12-18

[12] I turned round to see the voice that was speaking to me. And when I turned I saw seven golden lampstands, [13] and among the lampstands was someone like a son of man, dressed in a robe reaching down to his feet and with a golden sash round his chest. [14] The hair on his head was white like wool, as white as snow, and his eyes were like blazing fire. [15] His feet were

like bronze glowing in a furnace, and his voice was like the sound of rushing waters. [16] In his right hand he held seven stars, and **coming out of his mouth was a sharp, double-edged sword**. His face was like the sun shining in all its brilliance.

[17] When I saw him, I fell at his feet as though dead. Then he placed his right hand on me and said: 'Do not be afraid. I am the First and the Last. [18] I am the Living One; I was dead, and now look, I am alive for ever and ever! And I hold the keys of death and Hades.

John 1:14 tells us that the Word of the Lord is Jesus himself! "The Word became flesh and made his dwelling among us. We have seen his glory, the glory of the one and only Son, who came from the Father, full of grace and truth."

And the Lord can take on flesh. He did this in Christ, but there are occasions when we seem to see what we call "Theophanies" or appearances of God in flesh in the Old Testament. When Gideon hears the Word of the Lord from the Angel of the Lord, he acts in faith, in spite of himself. Why? Because the spoken Word of the Lord birthed faith in him! Remember that one of our spiritual defensive weapons is faith. It is our shield. And now, we see how the armor of God interacts. They are separate functioning pieces, but they are SPIRITUAL, so they are fluid and interacting, interlaced and interdependent upon one another. We may initially think of Roman armor, but this armor is more advanced than any armor known to mankind. It is more advanced than any military armor. It is the armor of our Creator God.

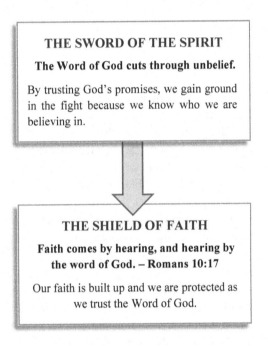

Ephesians 6:10-13

[10] Finally, be strong in the Lord and in his mighty power. [11] Put on the **full armour** of God, so that you can take your stand against the devil's schemes. [12] For our struggle is not against flesh and blood, but against the rulers, against the authorities, against the powers of this dark world and against the spiritual forces of evil in the heavenly realms. [13] Therefore put on the **full armour** of God, so that when the day of evil comes, you may be able to stand your ground, and after you have done everything, to stand.

When we put together the armor, we need ALL the armor. We need the FULL armor of God to stand against the devil's schemes. Notice how Paul lists this phrase twice in the passage? That shows he is making a point. The pieces all work together. We need the whole enchilada! Studying, memorizing and meditating on the Word of God in prayer not only is the way we take up the sword of the Spirit, but also is the way we put on the other pieces of the armor. When we are in the Word of God, it strengthens our faith, fills us with truth, prepares us to bring the gospel of peace, and clothes us with the helmet, breastplate, and belt.

When I worked as a youth leader, I remember trying to encourage the teens to memorize scripture. In the extremely affluent culture of Northern Virginia where we live, it can be difficult to even bribe teens to memorize scripture. I began to pray that the students would have a desire and hunger to learn the passages. You know, the Bible says that God's Word will not return unto him void—meaning it is never empty of life and power. I know when someone memorizes the Bible, that God can use those words later at a moment's notice, when the person least expects it.

One girl took on the challenge to memorize Colossians Chapter 1. She spent time every day memorizing it, until she could quickly say it with ease. Several months after she memorized the passage, she was being tormented by the enemy with thoughts of guilt over past sins of which she had already repented. This type of torment is a classic tool of the enemy. It is a clear example of a pretension setting itself up against the knowledge of God. When you repent and turn from sin, you are forgiven! The Bible says that God separates our sin from us as far as the east is from the west. (See Psalm 103) However, it is difficult to separate yourself from feelings of guilt. Panic attacks can come in like a flood. Sufferers experience panic attacks from the burdens they carry from the past or even from situations of abuse they have experienced. Those occurrences in a person's life can bring shame and a constant feeling that something is wrong or about to go wrong. Also, demonic spirits of panic and fear can cause physical symptoms. I'm not a doctor diagnosing this, but I am speaking from personal experience and what God showed me and the freedom he gave me.

On a particular night, the young woman's thoughts became almost palpable. It was as if guilt was standing there beside her in the bathroom as she brushed her teeth and looked at her face in the mirror. It seemed as if the thoughts were coming in from the side. This is not surprising, because Ephesians describes the devil as attacking us with fiery darts or flaming arrows. She turned and faced the side where the thoughts were coming from, and to her own surprise, she began to confidently speak Colossians 1 aloud. Instead of just saying the passage as it was written, she found herself—by the Holy Spirit, I am sure—saying "me" and "I" in place of "you." This is what she found herself praying aloud:

Colossians 1:15-22

[15] The Son is the image of the invisible God, the firstborn over all creation. [16] For in him all things were created: things in heaven and on earth, visible and invisible, whether thrones or powers or rulers or authorities; all things have been created through him and for him. [17] He is before all things, and in him all things hold together. [18] And he is the head of the body, the church; he is the beginning and the firstborn from among the dead, so that in everything he might have the supremacy. [19] For God was pleased to have all his fullness dwell in him, [20] and through him to reconcile to himself all things, whether things on earth or things in heaven, by making peace through his blood, shed on the cross.

[21] Once (I was) alienated from God and (was an enemy) in (my mind) because of (my) evil behaviour. [22] But now he has reconciled (me) by Christ's physical body through death to present (me) holy in his sight, without blemish and free from accusation.

Immediately, the guilt and the evil oppressive presence left. For the first time in her life, she used her sword and prayer to defeat a terrible, tormenting enemy. Doesn't this testimony stir excitement in you to memorize God's Word? Speak it over your own life and speak it over those you love! When you pray scripture, you know that you are praying the will of God. You are agreeing with God and agreement with God is a powerful place to be in. Are you willing to commit yourself to speaking the Word of God over your life? Through this study you are nurturing your relationship with God through his Word. Keep it up! Make it a habit.

BRINGING IT HOME

When God spoke to Gideon, it changed his paradigm. His negativity and fear about his culture was exchanged for hope. Gideon spent quite some time asking God for signs to prove that he was the one Gideon was seeing and hearing.

- Do you allow God's Word to break into places in your heart that may seem to contradict his Word?

- Do you allow the Word of God to give you hope or are you still holding onto negativity, hopelessness and discouragement?

- Do you speak the Word of God aloud or just read through it quickly to check it off your to do list?

Focus on memorizing scripture that builds your faith, and speak it out loud to encourage yourself and others around you.

TAKING UP THE SHIELD OF FAITH
A NEW HERITAGE

Trending. Women of God who are breaking free from patterns of sin and oppression in their family line. In Christ, the old identity is gone. The new is come. #newheritage

MEMORY VERSE

¹⁰ Finally, be strong in the Lord and in his mighty power. ¹¹ Put on the full armour of God, so that you can take your stand against the devil's schemes. ¹² For our struggle is not against flesh and blood, but against the rulers, against the authorities, against the powers of this dark world and against the spiritual forces of evil in the heavenly realms. ¹³ Therefore put on the full armour of God, so that when the day of evil comes, you may be able to stand your ground, and after you have done everything, to stand. – Ephesians 6:10-13

PRAYER

Pray the Spiritual Warfare Prayer found in the Prayer Index.

READING

Open your Bibles and read Judges 6:24 — 7:1-25.

- Underline all the times that God brings a new test of faith into the battle for Gideon.

- Draw a star where God gives Gideon confirmation that he is on the right path.

Yesterday, we read how the Word of the Lord—our sword—came to Gideon and cut through the fear and unbelief that kept him from seeing supernatural realities. Faith motivates us to action! He went from hiding in his winepress to cutting down an obscene altar of Baal and its Asherah pole. Did you notice he did this at night, so no one would see him? I love how the Bible doesn't hide the weaknesses, fear or humanity of the heroes of the faith. God shows us his ability to use those who are hiding and shaking in their boots to topple the very kingdom of darkness oppressing them! The power of the promises of God can cut through the thickest doubt and bring one out of a place of weakness and cowering to a place of fighting and standing.

What did Gideon do when he heard the Word of the Lord in Judges 6?

Write below the ACTION WORDS and PHRASES that describe Gideon's actions in Judges 6:24-40.

PUTTING FEET ON FAITH

As a woman, I don't just usually sit around dwelling on what I would do with a shield. But, honestly, when I contemplate the movie *Wonder Woman* that came out in 2017, I gotta say I love the scenes of Diana using her shield to give a Nazi thug a smackdown in the teeth one minute and deflecting bullets another minute. While *Wonder Woman* is a fictional story, truly, as daughters of God, we are warriors who can use our shields of faith to take out the enemy. Jesus said if we have faith as small as a mustard seed, we can move mountains! Now faith is the substance of things hoped for and the evidence of things not seen. – Hebrews 11:1 (NKJV)

You may look in the mirror and see a broken past or a hopeless heart. You may feel like a tiny speck in the universe, not much bigger than a mustard seed, but that is exactly how you are next to God, who is described in scripture as the ROCK or a mountain. You are not putting your faith in your seed-size stature, your seed-size talent, or your seed-size circumstances, you are putting your faith in the mountain, the ROCK Christ Jesus.

Psalm 121

I lift up my eyes to the mountains –
   where does my help come from?
My help comes from the Lord,
   the Maker of heaven and earth.

He will not let your foot slip –
   he who watches over you will not slumber;
indeed, he who watches over Israel
   will neither slumber nor sleep.

The Lord watches over you –
   the Lord is your shade at your right hand;
the sun will not harm you by day,
   nor the moon by night.

The Lord will keep you from all harm –
   he will watch over your life;
the Lord will watch over your coming and going
   both now and for evermore.

Your faith is promised to move mountains. Many people liken the mountain to a problem, but God is our mountain, or rock, so in a very real sense, when we trust God, he is moved by our faith! He uproots the overwhelming and insurmountable problems and throws them into the sea. Keep your eyes on him and not the hopelessness of your circumstances! Let's look today at how Gideon's faith-filled action cut off his old family identity as idol worshipers and gave him a new identity and heritage as a warrior of God. God takes people who are hiding from the enemy at one point and emboldens them to lead the charge into battle, in his name, after he transforms them! What did God ask Gideon to do that shook a nation? Gideon DEMOLISHED a demonic idol stronghold on his father's property. Before Gideon could minister deliverance to a nation, he needed to start with a little clean up at home!

CROSS REFERENCE

Open your Bible and read Isaiah 54. In this passage, the Lord spoke through the prophet Isaiah, promising a new heritage for Israel. This new heritage was prophesied to come after they experienced judgment for the sins of idolatry. (If you want to know where Isaiah fits into the biblical/historic timeline, the book of prophecy was written many generations after Gideon delivered Israel from Midian.)

In the Old Testament, Israel has a history of straying from the Lord, entering into rebellion, coming under the curse and discipline of the Lord, crying out for deliverance and then turning back to God. The cycle goes on. Generations come and go. Some generations, which we will call "the winepress generations," experience the "cycle of nations" during the time of deliverance from sin, death and oppression. The winepress is the place of crushing. The winepress is a symbol of judgment and discipline in the scriptures. The generation in the winepress knows what it means to walk in the consequences of personal sin and in the consequences of the curse of the sin of their forefathers. They also know the indebtedness they have to the Lord for his grace and mercy, when they come out on the other side of God's corrective discipline. Why does this cycle of deliverance, straying from the Lord, entering rebellion and coming into judgment happen to Israel over generations? A major reason is that people forget the Lord and what he did for their ancestors. Forgetting was Israel's weakness and it is our weakness too. The ease of forgetting where we came from is why God gave so many commands to the Israelites on how to pass on the faith to their children by giving them spiritual traditions and memorials through which they could retell the stories of their need for God and God's deliverance. The generation after the "winepress" lives in the season of blessing that comes after the crushing. They live in the season of the new wine and remembering. But the next season's grapes, the next generation, have no practical idea how that elegant wine got in the bottle. It's all just theory and stories to them. It's easy to get prideful, caught up in the blessings, but forget where the blessings came from.

We see the same thing happening to us. Your grandfather may have been saved out of alcoholism and adultery, but do you know the pain the Lord delivered him from? Do you know the struggle he went through to submit himself to Jesus Christ and the freedom he knew afterwards? How often do we actually look back and remember? God instructed Israel over and over again to set up reminders for their children of times when the Lord's hand delivered their ancestors mightily. Our forefathers and mothers who were believers are silently watching our leg of the relay race of history, a great cloud of witnesses, as described in Hebrews 12. It's easy to read the Old Testament stories and wonder how Israel could be "so stupid" for drifting away from the Lord over and over again. But keep it in perspective. It's all relative to where you are standing in history. They didn't have the big picture. For us, hindsight is 20/20. To look at the Israelites with haughty eyes and not be aware of our own personal compromises, which lead each generation further and further away from the Lord back into the winepress, is such a grievous error. We, too, have an opportunity to choose to remember our need for the Lord and serve him or to walk in forgetfulness and blindness.

However, we are the children of the promise. We are in Christ. He took our punishment and paid the price for our adoption with his own blood. He stepped into the winepress for us. He was crushed for our iniquities. Now his promise of reconciliation and healing is for us and for our children's children. To understand the reconciliation and healing we receive in Christ, we need to understand that it is God who allows the sins of the forefathers to be visited on the third and fourth generations. It is for driving us back to Christ, so we can see the true nature of rebellion. Does this mean God condones sin? Absolutely not. When we turn to Christ, we can trade a curse for a blessing. When we turn to Christ, there are many promises for our children, because our God is a Redeemer. Because of this, he promises in his new covenant, we will have a new heritage and he will not allow weapons the enemy forms against us to prevail over us.

Isaiah 54:13-17

[13] All your children will be taught by the Lord,

and great will be their peace.
[14] In righteousness you will be established:
tyranny will be far from you;
    you will have nothing to fear.
Terror will be far removed;
    it will not come near you.
[15] If anyone does attack you, it will not be my doing;
    whoever attacks you will surrender to you.

[16] 'See, it is I who created the blacksmith
    who fans the coals into flame
    and forges a weapon fit for its work.
And it is I who have created the destroyer to wreak havoc;
[17] no weapon forged against you will prevail,
    and you will refute every tongue that accuses you.
This is the heritage of the servants of the Lord,
    and this is their vindication from me,'
declares the Lord.

This promise of a new heritage of protection, which comes to those who move out from under the curse of sin and the way of life of idolatry of ancestors who did not follow the Lord, brings us back to Gideon, who was forging a new heritage for himself and his children, just by putting his FAITH in the Word of the Lord! True faith will change the entire direction of your life and your family. Since God changes you from the inside out, genuine trust in the Lord will affect how you communicate with people, as well as what you exalt in your life, and set aside as more important than anything else. A person following Jesus will want to love the things that he loves and walk in the way that he walked. These changes require sacrifice—giving up the sin that hinders and embracing the freedom in Christ that comes as the shackles of sin are shaken off at the cross. Sacrifice is not easy, and when you take up your cross and follow Jesus, it will affect others around you. Don't be surprised. Some may not like it at all. Some may feel betrayed, as you reject your old way of life. Others will breathe a breath of fresh air, as the Spirit of God working in your life brings the touch of God to your relationship with them. When you follow Christ and break away from the old, the testimony of your past life will light the way for others, as God burns up the old and rebuilds your new heritage.

For Gideon's family, the altars used for the prostitution worship of the fertility goddess Asherah needed cut down. Those idols became the fuel for the fires of worship to the living God! When we come out of fear and into faith, we can begin to act to remove the family strongholds and curses over generations. When Christ breaks down those idols in our lives, we have a testimony that does damage to the kingdom of darkness. Just as we learned in our study on the shoes of the preparation of the gospel of peace last week, we need to testify and confess the truth of our position in Christ to overcome and triumph over the evil one. Don't just try to change. Speak the truth of God's Word over your life and your family. Use the sword of the Lord to break free from family curses and to declare and triumph over Satan. When you do this, the fires of God burning in our hearts, on the ashes of the sin of our past, will light the way for many others trapped in darkness to come and find hope.

Does divorce run in your family? Occult activity? Does your family battle anxiety? What about teen pregnancy? Lying? Does your family have a history of estranged family relationships? These are examples of strongholds the enemy can have in a family. Faith in the power of God and the name of Jesus can give one small person the power to break the curse and tear down the symbols of authority that sin and the devil has held in your family for generations! The Word of God ignites faith in us to obey God. Stand in your authority! You are seated with Christ in heavenly realms, far above every other authority in your life. For example, if your family is full of a history of broken marriages, instead of agreeing with the devil and speaking his lies, you would speak the truth. A lie would say, "I am not sure if this can ever change," or "I don't even like my husband!" It may also sound like this, "Why should I even try to communicate? We are such different people. I will do my own thing and let him do his." You see, Satan the liar takes the truth and twists it into a lie. At one point you did love and like your husband. All along he had the same weaknesses he is now manifesting — the very weaknesses that you may be fixating on now. The enemy wants you to focus on his weaknesses and his failures as a spouse. The enemy wants you to think about everything that you would like to change in him, instead of celebrating everything good about him and giving him grace to change and grow — the same grace you would like extended to you, as you grow as a wife.

Breaking the curse would look like this, "God, please forgive my family for all the brokenness and divorce that has plagued us for generations. Forgive me for living in the roots of sin that will produce brokenness and separation in relationships, in Jesus' name. Do not hold this curse against my family or my children, because we are in Christ! Break it, Father, in Jesus' name. I declare that we are a redeemed generation, by the blood of the Lamb! I choose to like my husband in Jesus' name and focus on his strengths. I forgive my husband in Jesus' name! I love my husband, in Jesus' name. I am committing myself to love my husband in Jesus' name! Teach me how to love him the way he needs to be loved. Teach him how to love me. Teach us all how to walk in the new heritage you are establishing in our home, in Christ. I rebuke all spirits of divorce, separation, fear of intimacy, bitterness and brokenness and any other spirit that is present to plague my family and command them to leave, in Jesus' mighty name! Thank you, Lord Jesus, for cleansing my family and my home from this evil, in Jesus name, Amen!"

How do we go from being defeated to being an overcomer in Christ Jesus? Let's take a practical look at the timeline of Gideon's personal turning point from fear to faith. There comes a point in the time line where he puts off his fear and trusts the Lord. 1 John 5:4-5 says, "For everyone born of God overcomes the world. This is the victory that overcomes the world, even our faith. Who is it that overcomes the world? Only the one who believes that Jesus is the Son of God."

Open your Bibles and read Judges 6:24-35. After reading the following timeline. See if you can see the progression Gideon makes in his faith.

Check off each step, when you find it in the passage. Write the verse reference beside it.

____ Step 1 Gideon heard the Word of the Lord. _____

____ Step 2 Gideon discussed with the Lord what God was calling him to be and do. _____

____ Step 3 Gideon believed God. _____

____ Step 4 Gideon acted on the call of God in the face of opposition. _____

____ Step 5 Gideon was filled with the Holy Spirit and power. _____

____ Step 6 Gideon summons others to help him deliver the Israelites—his family. _____

A SPECIAL ANOINTING

Did Gideon have the Holy Spirit at this time? Well, he didn't experience the indwelling Holy Spirit the way that we do as believers. Today Christ's death, resurrection, and ascension make it possible for the Spirit of God to live in us. We have learned from earlier in our study that we are now his temple! In the Old Testament, the Spirit of God would come upon people for tasks and rest on them or anoint them for a special job. But, Gideon has a very special empowering of the Holy Spirit that we can experience today! It came about by faith, when he used part of the armor of God—the shield of faith—to help him pick up the sword of the Spirit. He obeyed what God told him to do, which was an act of faith and obedience. He tore down an ancient evil that was in his family. This act of faith was powerful! Our relationship with God is also by faith. He gives us instruction and we follow him, even if everything doesn't seem to match up in the natural physical reality. It's called obedience.

While Gideon was ACTING on his faith, the Spirit of God did something special. Can you find what it was? After this act of faith, look at Judges 6:34. Write the verse here:

Verse 34 is the first place we see Gideon receive help from the Spirit of the Lord! (Other than the word that was spoken to him.) The Hebrew wording for "came on Gideon" literally means: "God put on Gideon like a garment" or "God clothed himself with Gideon."

Can you see the power of the Word of God? It is our weapon, because it increases our faith, which is our protection! The book of James says that faith without works is dead. Gideon's faith was ACTIVE. It propelled him to action.

Abraham believed God, and it was credited to him as righteousness. – James 2:23

The proof of his belief was that he obeyed the Lord and followed him to a strange land.

Now faith is the substance of things hoped for, the evidence of things not seen. For by it the elders obtained a good testimony. – Hebrews 11:1-2 (NKJV)

Faith is more than a feeling or a thought. Faith is substance and evidence of what we cannot see. Faith moves us! Why? Because we step out of our comfort zone to follow Jesus into the unknown, even if it looks impossible. When Gideon acted on God's call, in faith, the Lord PUT GIDEON ON LIKE A GARMENT! The Lord's Spirit was already WITH Gideon, as Judges 6:12 says, "The Lord is with you, Mighty Warrior." But, now he fills Gideon. Who wants the Lord to fill them in this way today? It is all received by faith. Even if you feel empty, you can be filled. When I share the gospel with a non-believer, many times I feel nothing. I don't feel like doing it, or I just feel like it's a normal day. Why do I start sharing? Because it's what God wants me to do. I start the discussion without big feelings, or goosebumps, or "energy." I pray for God to help me, as I am having the conversation. Faith is obeying God. It's not a feeling. But, often times, after I start out in faith, the power of God will come over me part way through and I know he is giving me insight and help that are not from my natural abilities. Sometimes I feel it, sometimes I don't. But, as believers, we are called to walk by faith and not by sight.

When I shared this story about God putting on Gideon like a garment with my 9-year old Isaac, I held up a shirt. "Let's pretend that this shirt is you. It can't do anything. It just is a shell. It has a purpose and that purpose is to be worn by someone. But, you put it on." He looks at me funny, but decides to slowly follow along and put on the shirt. "Now that you have it on, go do something you can do. You can run, jump, do pull ups on the pull up bar or even take a nap and rest. When God puts you on and you are operating in his power, he is the one directing your movement and his power is what is at work in you."

It says in Acts 17:28, "For in him we live and move and have our being!" Begin to step out in faith in the battle and obey the Lord. Watch the Lord fill you with strength to do what he has called you to do! When God fills us, he clothes himself with us, as with a garment! We are filled with God's Spirit AND WE are clothed with HIS armor of righteousness!

Today, I challenge you to step out in faith to tear down the altars of your past, or even your family's past. You may not feel confident, but your faith is not in yourself; it is in Jesus. God knows your heart. He will give you direction. I challenge you to make a formal declaration today, by yourself or with your family, that you are choosing to follow the Lord. Let this prayer—this confession of your faith in the blood of Jesus and his work on the cross—be an axe to cut down the curses of generations past and turn them into the firewood for the Spirit of God to burn on in your life!

PRACTICAL APPLICATION
Prayer to Tear Down the Altars & Start a New Heritage in Christ

Father,

I thank you for Jesus! I believe he is the Son of God and the only way to heaven. I thank you that he died for my sins and rose again, giving me a new heritage in your family. I thank you that the heritage of your children is this: no weapon forged against us will prevail and we will refute every tongue that accuses us! So, by faith in the Lord Jesus, I make this good confession today.

- Today, I confess any and all sin I am holding back from you. *(Confess what the Lord brings to your heart.)*

> **TODAY'S BIBLE STUDY TOOL**
>
> **Practical Application.** How can I personally apply this scripture to my life today? What changes do I need to make? What prayer should I pray? Don't forget to ask the Holy Spirit for help!

- I forgive all who have sinned against me at any point in my life, the way that Jesus forgives me. *(Pray to forgive any specific individuals who come to mind.)*

- I thank you right now for this truth in Galatians 3:13: "Christ redeemed us from the curse of the law by becoming a curse for us, for it is written: 'Cursed is everyone who is hung on a pole.' He redeemed us in order that the blessing given to Abraham might come to the Gentiles through Christ Jesus, so that by faith we might receive the promise of the Spirit." Thank you for becoming a curse for me, Lord Jesus. I am not under the curse of my forefathers or any other curse ever spoken against me; I am in Christ Jesus! I refute and break all curses over my life and my family, in Jesus' name. *(List any the Holy Spirit brings to mind.)*

- I am standing in Christ. I belong to him and I am part of his family, in Jesus' name. I confess that my ancestors sinned against you. I ask your forgiveness. Some may have participated in the occult; some lived in deceit and sexual impurity and idolatry. I declare now that Satan has no power over me because of anything my ancestors have done. I break off all of his influence and power over me or my family due to past sin and the curse. Be gone, in Jesus' name!

Jesus, thank you that I am part of your great family, and I am a child of Abraham, a child of blessing and promise. This is all because of you! I receive the blessings of Abraham. I am a blessed daughter of the Most High God. I am loved. I am accepted. I am forgiven. I am whole. I am healed, in Jesus' name. May your Spirit and your fire ignite in me today.

In Jesus' name, Amen!

More scriptures to study on this topic:

CURSES
Genesis 3; Deuteronomy 28

GENERATIONAL SIN
Exodus 20:5; Nehemiah 1; Ezekiel 18

BLESSINGS
Genesis 26:34 – 28:9; Exodus 23:25; Deuteronomy 10:8; Proverbs 10:22; Ephesians 1:3; 1 Peter 3:9

CHRIST'S BLESSING
Jeremiah 31:29-34 (prophetic); Galatians 3; Revelation 22

BRINGING IT HOME

Are you living your life for the Lord hiding in your own "winepress" from the world? How do you think the Lord views you? God wants to call you mighty warrior and clothe himself with you!

What strongholds have been in your family for generations that you have believed will always stand tall with no hope of coming down? Ask God for faith to obey him and to act to topple the most dreaded spiritual enemies in your life. Ask the Lord to fill you with his Spirit and to help you walk in courage and in faith when he calls you to do difficult things. Teach your children of this power of God!

Also, teach your children about the children of Israel and how many of them never made their faith their own. What did this result in? Ask your children if they have made a commitment to Christ and are trusting him with their lives! Pray with them to do this.

STANDING IN YOUR AUTHORITY

MEMORY VERSE

¹⁰ Finally, be strong in the Lord and in his mighty power. ¹¹ Put on the full armour of God, so that you can take your stand against the devil's schemes. ¹² For our struggle is not against flesh and blood, but against the rulers, against the authorities, against the powers of this dark world and against the spiritual forces of evil in the heavenly realms. ¹³ Therefore put on the full armour of God, so that when the day of evil comes, you may be able to stand your ground, and after you have done everything, to stand. – Ephesians 6:10-13

PRAYER

Father God,

Today I worship you for your awesome generosity! You have seated me with Christ in heavenly realms. You looked upon me with favor and were merciful, when I turned to you in repentance. I worship you, because I am covered in the blood of Jesus that washes away my sin. Thank you for giving me authority in Christ Jesus to trample on and to overcome all the power of the enemy. Nothing can harm me. I invite your Spirit to fill me the way it filled the temple in the days of old. Teach me to stand my ground, in the authority you have given me.

In Jesus' name, Amen!

READING

Ephesians 6:16-20

¹⁶ In addition to all this, take up the shield of faith, with which you can extinguish all the flaming arrows of the evil one. ¹⁷ Take the helmet of salvation and the sword of the Spirit, which is the word of God.

¹⁸ And pray in the Spirit on all occasions with all kinds of prayers and requests. With this in mind, be alert and always keep on praying for all the Lord's people. ¹⁹ Pray also for me, that whenever I speak, words may be given me so that I will fearlessly make known the mystery of the gospel, ²⁰ for which I am an ambassador in chains. Pray that I may declare it fearlessly, as I should.

Ladies, in the middle of the battle, we are safe inside the armor of God. It protects us. It defends us. It arms us. But, armor isn't for hiding in. It is for fighting in. As women, we fight the good fight for our thought life, our emotions, our physical health, our spiritual health, our families, our churches, our communities and our friends. We've all heard the saying, "Don't mess with momma bear!" Any woman who loves her children can suddenly be transformed into an army ranger on a seek and destroy mission. If something is coming against her little ones, whether it's a sickness, a bully, or any other "problem" or "enemy" we can imagine, we are on the warpath. So, why do women get scared and timid when it comes to the idea of spiritual warfare? Honestly, I think that we've seen too many scary movies. Hollywood always loves to make the devil look big and bad and the priest or Christian trying to overcome evil look like a weak little pansy. Once I knew a teenager who told me of a personal experience where this person was physically assaulted by an evil presence. I assured this young person that I could get him help and that it didn't have to ever happen again. I basically got a "Thanks, but no thanks! I've seen how all those horror movies end." The devil has done a very successful job glorifying himself in movies. There is more than one reason that my husband and I do not allow ourselves or anyone in our house to watch witchcraft or horror movies and this is one of them. They completely glorify evil. As believers in Jesus, our spiritual reality blows the enemy away. Satan is defeated and there is nothing he can do about it, when we stand against him in the purity of the blood and the power of the name of Jesus! We can be confident in battling in the unseen reality. I have lived this reality time and time again, where I have helped people or have been a witness to others being helped to overcome evil. As believers, we should start and end our lives with what the scriptures say concerning any topic, not what we feel or what the world says about it. This topic—spiritual warfare—centers around our offensive weapon, the Sword of the Spirit, the Word of God. What does the Word teach us about battling the enemy? Let's take a look today.

THE RELUCTANT QUEEN — ESTHER
Queen Esther's Law

If you are still struggling with the idea of using your authority in Christ, or know someone who does, I hope this next story is encouraging to you. One day, as I prayed about our authority in Christ, trying to understand why we need to use our authority if the devil is already defeated, the Lord gave me a strong direction to look at "Queen Esther's law." I was blown away! I had never seen the book of Esther as a prophetic picture of spiritual warfare. I encourage you to read the book of Esther in the Old Testament to get a background on this teaching about authority. You can probably listen to it on your Bible app while getting ready in the morning or driving to pick up the kids!

I think every little girl's dream is to be a princess, and every big girl's dream is to have a princess's spending account, accompanied by a cooking and house cleaning staff. In this true story from Israel's history, Hadassah, a young orphaned Jewess, is swept into Persian King Xerxes' harem, as he searches the kingdom far and wide to find a fair virgin to be his next queen. Doesn't sound super romantic, does it? We learned about the diaspora in Weeks Four and Five. Hadassah, who is given the pagan name Esther, is a great-granddaughter of captives from the Jewish southern kingdom of Judah to Babylon. Esther's uncle Mordecai, who raised her after the death of her parents, tells her to hide her nationality and to do whatever is asked of her. Stunning Esther quickly finds favor with Xerxes and is chosen to be the next queen of Media-Persia. Here we have a young woman, without a drop of Persian blood in her veins, suddenly thrust into a position of power, authority and danger. After all, Xerxes' first queen, Vashti, was cast out of her position as queen when she refused to come to a banquet for her beauty to be displayed before all the drunken officials of the 127 provinces of the great Empire that stretched from Cush to India.

Also, positioned in the court of the king is a powerful and evil advisor to Xerxes named Haman. Haman has fixated his anger on Mordecai, Esther's uncle, who won't bow down to Haman in the city gates. Haman is so filled with rage and hatred towards Mordecai that in Esther Chapter 3 he lies to the king by twisting the truth about all the Jews—that they won't follow the customs of the empire—into a blatant lie that they are insurrectionists. He convinces the king to pass an edict that instructs the citizens of the citadel of Susa, where the king lives, and all of Media-Persia to take up arms against the Jewish people on a single day to annihilate every man, woman and child in the whole kingdom. It isn't enough that Haman take down Mordecai; he feels compelled to wipe out Mordecai's entire race. The king's name is signed to the decree, and his signet ring seals it with unchanging authority.

In the Media-Persian Empire, a law signed by the king is a law that cannot ever be repealed, even by the king. The situation of the Jews is desperate. In the spirit realm, we learned last week that during this same time period, Daniel, also living in Susa, was visited by an angelic being who told him of the Prince of Persia, an evil spirit, who stood in opposition to the people of God. We know that Haman's evil plot is of demonic origin. It's not just mere hatred for a man, but an anti-Semitic desire to destroy God's chosen people. I'm sure the devil thought he had the upper hand, when Haman convinced the king to sign the violent edict. He knew it could never be changed.

But, for such a time as this, God, who knew ahead of time what the devil was plotting, raised up Esther. Mordecai was filled with fear and grief. He and the other Jewish exiles fasted, wearing sackcloth and ashes to show their distress to God. He implored Esther to not ignore her great calling and God's purpose for putting her into the inner chambers of the king. Here's where it gets real, ladies. Everyone wants to be God's princess, and to be called a diamond or a jewel. Not very many women want to step up to answer the calling and the reason God has placed them in their position of authority in Christ. Remember that we are also seated with Christ in heavenly realms—and it is not without purpose. You have a purpose! God didn't raise up Esther just so she could have nine months of beauty treatments and queen lessons, so she could feel good about herself, and have a resilient self-esteem. God raised her up to intercede for the Jewish people, who were under the thumb of the demonic Prince of Persia, ready to be crushed. This means she had to act. She had to stand in the authority God placed her in and stand her ground.

I am struck by Esther's submissive attitude. She was the chosen queen, and in that way she was a leader or a figure head, but in every other way she was a follower. God blessed her with amazing beauty, but it was not accompanied by arrogance or excessive pride. The scriptures that describe her actions in the court, and with her uncle Mordecai, paint a picture of a woman who is willing to serve, but longing for direction so she can know what to do. She even may feel a bit of self-doubt, possibly stemming from being an orphan. But, even in her perceived weaknesses, God has a calling on her and wants her to walk in that authority.

To save her people, Esther needs to approach the king in his throne room uninvited, which is something that could incur her death. She tells Mordecai that she is unsure of her standing with the king. He hasn't called for her in 30 days. She has no rights, even as queen, to enter his presence. In Esther 4 we read:

> 'All the king's officials and the people of the royal provinces know that for any man or woman who approaches the king in the inner court without being summoned the king has but one law: that they be put to death unless the king extends the gold sceptre to them and spares their lives. But thirty days have passed since I was called to go to the king.' – Esther 4:11

Some of you may feel unsure of your standing with God, because you haven't felt his presence or heard a specific word from him in a long time. Remember that just because God is quiet, it does not mean that you have lost your position or authority in his family! You may be in the middle of a great threat or battle and feel that God is not giving you direction. Did you know that you can do what Esther does in this book of the Bible and walk into his throne room in your authority as a believer and daughter of the King?

Esther 4:12-17

[12] When Esther's words were reported to Mordecai, [13] he sent back this answer: 'Do not think that because you are in the king's house you alone of all the Jews will escape. [14] For if you remain silent at this time, relief and deliverance for the Jews will arise from another place, but you and your father's family will perish. And who knows but that you have come to your royal position for such a time as this?'

[15] Then Esther sent this reply to Mordecai: [16] 'Go, gather together all the Jews who are in Susa, and fast for me. Do not eat or drink for three days, night or day. I and my attendants will fast as you do. When this is done, I will go to the king, even though it is against the law. And if I perish, I perish.'

[17] So Mordecai went away and carried out all of Esther's instructions.

How convicting is this exchange? Mordecai tells Esther that if she walks in fear instead of walking in the authority that God has put her in, she will not be safe. Her entire family could suffer from her refusal to walk in the authority that God has called her to use. In this way, Queen Esther is a picture of the bride of Christ. We cannot be afraid or timid about spiritual warfare and standing our ground. We cannot be intimidated, even if we are shy or reserved. Each and every woman is called by God for such a time as this. You and your family can suffer when you sit in fear at the prospect of standing in your authority in warfare. You are called to stand for your corner of the world, however big or small. You are called to advocate for those who are suffering and to have hope in the face of great evil.

Let's examine why Esther would have suffered. Esther was in danger from the law that was put in effect by her own king and husband. It could not be revoked. Her only hope was to walk in her authority as queen and look for his favor and ask for mercy. As the body of Christ, we too are affected by a law that cannot be revoked—the law of sin and death. This law was also implemented by our Father God before the fall when he declared to Adam and Eve that the day they ate of the tree of the knowledge of good and evil they would surely die (Genesis 3). There are many other blessings and curses the Lord declared over the Israelites in his law. The Word of the Lord stands forever. But do not fear. Even though Jesus said, "Do not think that I have come to abolish the Law and the Prophets," he did come to bring a greater law that overshadows the former law and puts a sword in the hand of every believer to overcome and fight back against the enemy who tries to destroy us with the old law of sin and death.

When Esther came before the king, she found favor in his eyes. He extended his scepter to her and offered to give her up to half of his kingdom! Her submissive attitude and the prayers of the Jews brought her favor. On a side note, have you ever thought to pray for favor so you can carry out God's purpose for you? It's a very important prayer to pray! Esther asked Xerxes to come to a banquet she prepared for him and Haman. Here is a great picture of spiritual warfare. Not only is Esther going to the king, but she is also inviting the enemy to the confrontation! She is going to fearlessly and methodically expose him for his evil schemes. In the meantime, Haman is still plotting against Mordecai and sets up a pole to impale him on. However, the tables will soon turn. On the second day of the banquet, Esther answers Xerxes request and tells him that her life is in mortal danger, because of the law that Haman has tricked him into signing!

Xerxes, distressed and furious, storms from the room. The scriptures say that Haman throws himself at the mercy of Queen Esther, begging for his life. Now, I have to say that this is a perfect picture of the enemy when he is undone. Do not be confused if in the middle of spiritual warfare you feel like an old friend is imploring you not to sever the friendship. We see an example of this in Mark 5:10 when the Legion of demons, who had tortured a man to the point of insanity and self-harm, turns from being a big, bad, scary force into a terrified, little, begging, crying mess. They were at the mercy of Jesus. No longer could they have dominion over the man they wanted to destroy. When you are in the heat of the battle and things look utterly terrible and hopeless, remember that you are at a tipping point where the enemy will be begging you for mercy soon, as you stand in your authority in Christ and crush him underneath your feet. When I have personally been in a battle with a long time evil spiritual foe, and the Lord is uncovering his schemes and is ready to eject the evil spirit permanently from my life, I have suddenly had an awareness of a pity party or a begging that begins. I cannot describe it in any other way than a sniveling last ditch effort to keep me from standing in my authority in Christ and kicking the evil out.

What happens to Haman? His evil and destructive planning turns against him. He is impaled on the pole that he built for Mordecai. This is a pattern in the Old Testament with the enemies of God. God repeatedly sends them into confusion and turns their plots against them. I always pray this way when doing spiritual warfare. Pray that the Lord will bring confusion to the enemy and turn his plots against him! Yet, in all this victory over Haman, who is obviously defeated already, there seems to be a slight complication—at first glance. When Esther falls at Xerxes feet and begs for mercy for her people, he tells her that he cannot revoke the law. However, he gives her the authority to write a new law. He actually says,

'Because Haman attacked the Jews, I have given his estate to Esther, and they have impaled him on the pole he set up. Now write another decree in the king's name on behalf of the Jews as seems best to you, and seal it with the king's signet ring – for no document written in the king's name and sealed with his ring can be revoked.' – Esther 6:7b-8

The king gave Esther authority to override the old law with the new. What was the law that she and Mordecai wrote?

The king's edict granted the Jews in every city the right to assemble and protect themselves; to destroy, kill and annihilate the armed men of any nationality or province who might attack them and their women and children, and to plunder the property of their enemies. – Esther 8:11

The edict, which I am calling "Queen Esther's law," gave the Jews authority to rise up and fight any enemies that were trying to attack them by the authority of the first law that was still in effect. The second law overpowered the first law by putting the favor of the king and a sword into the hands of the Jewish people, but it was only stronger when the Jewish people did battle in its authority. If they didn't do the battle, they would be killed by those fighting against them in the authority of the first law.

Ladies, in Christ, the Lord has put a sword into your hand! He says, "Do as you see fit." The devil may be trying to take 'legal' ground with you. He may be pointing out all your failures or your past. He may have legal access because you have been involved with witchcraft or the occult, or even because family members have sinned this way. He may be trying to stand on the sins of your forefathers, but there is a new law, a greater law—the law of the Spirit of life! It sets us free from the law of sin and death. You have the right to fight him. You have the authority of the King of kings and it is signed and sealed with the blood of his son Jesus Christ. Not to fight this battle makes you and those you are called to protect very vulnerable to the enemy.

Remember Esther and stand. Do your part in the fight. Defend your own corner of the world. You have the right to expose the enemy before the Lord, and God has given you the right to defeat him. Romans 16:20 says, "The God of peace will soon crush Satan under your feet." The same way that Xerxes gave his signet ring to Esther to write the law, the Father has given his children authority to rebuke the devil and to resist him so he must flee!

LISTS
Tactical Training by the Master

When Jesus faced the devil in the wilderness of temptation, what did Jesus do to win that battle? **Let's find out by opening our Bibles and studying Matthew 4:1-11.** As you read the passage, look for the different tactics that Jesus uses to combat Satan. Write them on the line beside the verse in the exercise that follows.

Matthew 4:1-11

[1] Then Jesus was led by the Spirit into the wilderness to be tempted by the devil. [2] After fasting for forty days and forty nights, he was hungry. [3] The tempter came to him and said, 'If you are the Son of God, tell these stones to become bread.'

[4] Jesus answered, 'It is written: "Man shall not live on bread alone, but on every word that comes from the mouth of God."'

[5] Then the devil took him to the holy city and set him on the highest point of the temple. [6] 'If you are the Son of God,' he said, 'throw yourself down. For it is written:

> "'He will command his angels concerning you,
> 'and they will lift you up in their hands,
> so that you will not strike your foot against a stone.'"

[7] Jesus answered him, 'It is also written: "Do not put the Lord your God to the test."'

[8] Again, the devil took him to a very high mountain and showed him all the kingdoms of the world and their splendour. [9] 'All this I will give you,' he said, 'if you will bow down and worship me.'

[10] Jesus said to him, 'Away from me, Satan! For it is written: "Worship the Lord your God, and serve him only."'

[11] Then the devil left him, and angels came and attended him.

Tactic #1 vs 1

_____

Tactic #2 vs 2

_____

Tactic #3 vs 4

_____

Tactic #4 vs 7

_____

Tactic #5 vs 10

_____

What does Jesus do differently in addressing Satan in verse 10 that he does not do in verses 4 and 7?

How does Satan attack Jesus? In the forty days Jesus spent in the desert, we are only given three instances of Satan's advances against him. Read back again and look at the three tactics Satan uses against Jesus.

On the following lines, describe the type of attack Satan uses to tempt Jesus. What is that specific temptation targeting in him? What is the devil appealing to in his baiting attempts?

Tactic #1 vs 3

_____

Tactic #2 vs 5

_____

Tactic #3 vs 8

_____

In verse 3, we see that first the devil tempts Jesus in a place of extreme physical weakness. He tries to get him to turn the stones into bread and break his fast. It wouldn't be hard for Jesus to turn stone into bread. It may even seem like a helpful thing to do for himself. But, Jesus could not go against the leading of the Spirit and break his fast. That would be a sin. Even a small sin would disqualify and prevent him from being the perfect sacrifice for our sins.

How many times do you feel led into sin when you are physically weak? Do you lose your temper when you are tired and hungry? If you are resisting self-pity, there is nothing like physical exhaustion to wear down your resolve! Is it easier to compromise and gossip after you've had a little too much wine or if you feel hurt from an offense? Concerning purity, isn't it more difficult for an unmarried couple to control themselves when they are alone? These are the physically weak times when the tempter comes after you. (On a side note about the devil tempting sexually, before you are married he wants you to fall into sexual sin. Any way he can, he wants to tempt you to sin and turn from the Lord. However, after you are married, he will do his best to keep you from having intimacy with your spouse. He knows that it will make you stronger, closer and more united. So, beware and don't be deceived, he will try to get you to justify the sin and make it look okay.) He will ALWAYS use God's Word or something that seems good to tempt you to give into his suggestions. He is the father of lies.

SPEAKING WORDS IN THE AUTHORITY OF CHRIST

How did Jesus deal with the devil's lying? He SPOKE God's Word to the devil. Have you ever talked to the devil? Jesus did. He quoted scripture to the devil. The apostles did. They used God's Word and commanded the devil to leave, when they cast him out of people. They didn't argue with him. They didn't carry on a conversation with him, the way we do when we pray to our heavenly Father. They simply used God's Word to resist the devil and cast him out in Jesus' name. They used heavenly authority over the enemy's limited power.

CROSS REFERENCE
Examples from Scripture

Let's look for more examples by cross referencing other passages of scripture where the apostles or Jesus spoke to the devil to combat his lies and to extract him from a situation.

Look up the phrase "evil spirit" in your Bible app and see what comes up. I am going to look in the gospels and the book of Acts, because I know those books will give me historical accounts. She kept this up for many days. Finally, Paul became so annoyed that he turned round and said to the spirit, "In the name of Jesus Christ, I command you to come out of her!" At that moment the spirit left her. – Acts 16:18

In another passage, Acts 19:13, we see that the sons of a Jewish priest—not Messianic believers in Jesus—tried to imitate what they heard Paul say. These men were most likely part of the group that obstinately opposed the gospel in the synagogue, when Paul was reasoning with them daily. The men tried to cast spirits out of someone by saying, "In the name of Jesus" but, they added "whom Paul preaches" as they commanded the evil spirits to come out. They did not believe in Jesus themselves and they were not protected or given authority by his blood. They found themselves in a sad state. What a true blindness it is to reject Christ, even when you see miracles. This is similar to what we see the Pharisees do in the gospels.

All through the gospels, Jesus addresses Satan directly. He doesn't glorify him. He doesn't pretend he doesn't exist. He speaks directly to the enemy and tells him to leave. In Mark 8:33, when Simon Peter is trying to tell Jesus to not go to Jerusalem, Jesus speaks to Satan in his rebuke of Peter and says, *"Get thee behind me, Satan!"* (KJV)

Luke records an account of Jesus interacting with his disciples who had just come back excited from a mission "trip" where they found they were able to cast out Satan. The seventy-two returned with joy and said, "Lord, even the demons submit to us in your name. "He replied, "I saw Satan fall like lightning from heaven. I have given YOU authority to trample on snakes and scorpions and to overcome all the power of the enemy; nothing will harm you. However, do not rejoice that the spirits submit to you, but rejoice that your names are written in heaven." – Luke 10:17-20

Jesus tells his disciples—all 72 he'd sent out, not just the 12 who later became the Twelve Apostles—that he has given ALL of them authority over the enemy. This means ALL those he sends to share the gospel have this authority to trample on ALL the power of the enemy. Why does Jesus say the disciples have been given authority over snakes and scorpions? Is he encouraging them to become snake handlers? Absolutely not! From the beginning of scripture, Satan has prophetically appeared as a serpent. In fact, the first prophecy in the Bible about our hope for salvation through the Son of God is in Genesis 3:15. After Adam and Eve fall into sin, God pronounces a curse on the devil. "And I will put enmity between you and the woman, and between your offspring and hers; he will crush your head, and you will strike his heel.'" God tells the devil his end will come through a woman's seed—Mary the mother of Jesus. This is so appropriate, since the fall occurred when the devil deceived Eve. God appropriately promises that the seed of a woman will crush Satan's head. When Jesus tells these nice Jewish boys this, they would immediately know he wasn't calling them to snake handling, but that they were witnesses and participants in God's prophecy of salvation and the overthrow of the enemy's power on earth. He doesn't dispute that the demons submit to the disciples. He simply tells them not to rejoice in their authority over the enemy's power. They are to rejoice in their salvation. And so are we. Why? Jesus does the work. Our authority is only by the grace of God. Jesus wants us to keep our heads screwed on straight in the battle. Don't let your head get big so that your helmet of salvation pops off.

WHEN YOU HAVE DONE EVERYTHING—STAND!

When an unclean spirit goes out of a man, he goes through dry places, seeking rest, and finds none. Then he says, 'I will return to my house from which I came.' And when he comes, he finds it empty, swept, and put in order. Then he goes and takes with him seven other spirits more wicked than himself, and they enter and dwell there; and the last state of that man is worse than the first. So shall it also be with this wicked generation. – Matthew 12:43-45

According to Matthew 12:43-45, where does an unclean spirit go when he goes out of a man?

List the three things that the unclean spirit finds, when he returns with seven more wicked spirits.

Notice that Jesus says the inside of the man set free from a demon is in order and swept clean? But what is the problem? He is empty. It is absolutely imperative not just to rebuke the devil and command him to leave, as if it were some superstitious act or mantra. But instead, you are trading one situation for another. Be filled with the Holy Spirit. Invite the Holy Spirit into every part of your life. Do not resist his movement. Do not grieve him or quench him. When he warns you about sin, don't just enter into sin carelessly, thinking you will ask for forgiveness later. That is not a protected position in Christ. When the enemy comes knocking again, do not answer the door. Command him to leave in Jesus' name and stand your ground! Triumph over him by the Word of your testimony and the blood of the Lamb. This situation where the man is worse off at the end than he was at the beginning is not some random event the man had no control over. The problem of the retuning enemy is only successful when you refuse to invite the Holy Spirit to fill you daily (like the times he filled the Old Testament temple). When you are swept clean, but you are void of the power of God and you leave the door open for the enemy through willful and unrepented sin, your situation can end up worse off than the beginning. So, the moral of the story is resist the devil, not the Holy Spirit!

Recently, when I was experiencing a bout of extreme depression and negative thinking, I found myself feeling inadequate to even pray. I started to be aware that the depression was so severe that it was most likely related to the devil's harassment. However, he had so lied to me concerning my worth in Christ that I forgot where my authority came from. I felt utterly worthless. Technically—remember the devil is into half-truths—it is true that I am utterly worthless and wretched in sin. Apart from Christ, left alone in my weakness and sin, I am worthless, powerless and helpless. But, it says in Romans 5,

> You see, at just the right time, when we were still powerless, Christ died for the ungodly. Very rarely will anyone die for a righteous person, though for a good person someone might possibly dare to die. But God demonstrates his own love for us in this: while we were yet sinners, Christ died for us. Since we have now been justified by his blood, how much more shall we be saved from God's wrath through him! For if while we were God's enemies, we were reconciled to him through the death of his Son, how much more, having been reconciled, shall we be saved through his life! Not only is this so, but we also boast in God through our Lord Jesus Christ, through whom we have now received reconciliation. – Romans 5:6-11

BUT, I wasn't thinking about this. I wasn't thinking about the sacrifice of Jesus. I wasn't thinking about his love or his redemption or his reconciliation. I was thinking about the poor, miserable state-of-being the devil was convincing me I was in—instead of the truth that I am seated with Christ in heavenly realms.

As I pushed my little music cart through the school where I teach to the next classroom, with my hip in pain, I silently prayed, "God, help me. Help me, God."

Silence. I continued, "God, help me." Then this verse came to mind,

> I have given YOU authority to trample on snakes and scorpions. — Luke 10:19a

It came quietly. It came steadily. For the next hour, every time I started to think about my problems, this verse came. God was telling me, "I already gave you the power to crush this snake. You can do it. You are equipped. You do it."

After teaching, I found "alone" time for my pathetic little self—this is how I felt about myself at the time—and this is the gist of what I said,

> God, I thank you for Jesus. I thank you for your forgiveness over my life. I thank you for the resurrection power of Christ and that I am raised up with Christ and seated in heavenly realms. I speak right now against Satan and all evil and command it to leave in Jesus' name. Be gone to where the Lord Jesus sends you. I resist depression and worthlessness, hopelessness and pain in Jesus' name. I command you to leave me. You have no power or authority over me. I am in Christ.

The depression lifted from me gradually. It wasn't dramatic. I didn't feel any sudden change the first time I fought in this spiritual battle, but throughout the day, I kept it up. I kept standing in the power of Christ which he purchased for me on the cross.

> Therefore, put on the full armor of God, so that when the day of evil comes, you may be able to stand your ground, and after you have done everything, to stand. — Ephesians. 6:13

By the end of the day, my head was clear and I felt normal again.

BRINGING IT HOME

Never forget that any warfare we participate in is not a physical battle. It is not against flesh and blood. Remember that it is only by the blood of Jesus and by his powerful name that we can use our words to combat the devil. We don't have a lengthy conversation with him! We speak God's Word to combat the lie and we command him to leave in Jesus' name. We do not need to be afraid. Jesus is the one who has already done the work.

Teach your children to pray against Satan. I have known several families whose children were seeing apparitions when they were alone at night. Not only did the parents pray against the enemy, but they taught their children to rebuke Satan and command him to leave in Jesus' name. The harassment stopped and the children were equipped to overcome in the future. Children do not need to be taught to be afraid of the enemy, but that Jesus has already defeated the devil.

PRAYER
OUR GREAT OFFENSIVE WEAPON

MEMORY VERSE

[10] Finally, be strong in the Lord and in his mighty power. [11] Put on the full armour of God, so that you can take your stand against the devil's schemes. [12] For our struggle is not against flesh and blood, but against the rulers, against the authorities, against the powers of this dark world and against the spiritual forces of evil in the heavenly realms. [13] Therefore put on the full armour of God, so that when the day of evil comes, you may be able to stand your ground, and after you have done everything, to stand. – Ephesians 6:10-13

Since you are seated with Christ in heavenly realms, since you are a child of God, you are able to enter into the throne room of God with confidence. Prayer is not just for people like pastors and "super Christians." Every believer of the Living God has the same access, by faith, into the presence of God. Jesus paid for it with his own blood. Do not be timid about this wonderful access to our Father in heaven! Be bold, praying for his will. And don't forget! Jesus came into the world to destroy the works of the devil. So, you know that when you pray in this vein, doing spiritual warfare, you are in agreement with God's will!

PRAYER

Prayer is talking to God, but warfare prayer is so much more than just talking. We can talk to God in fear, or we can speak the truth in faith. When you pray the Word of God, you are using your weapons of righteousness to cut through the lies that rise up inside of you and give you fear or temptation. Praying God's Word is powerful! Let's see what our scriptures say about prayer. Pray the Spiritual Warfare Prayer found in the Prayer Index. Take time to allow the Holy Spirit to lead you in prayer for your family, friends or anyone else who needs special protection and "coverage" by the blood of Jesus today. Ask Jesus to make you a prayer warrior!

READING

Ephesians 6:16-20

[16] In addition to all this, take up the shield of faith, with which you can extinguish all the flaming arrows of the evil one. [17] Take the helmet of salvation and the sword of the Spirit, which is the word of God.

[18] And pray in the Spirit on all occasions with all kinds of prayers and requests. With this in mind, be alert and always keep on praying for all the Lord's people. [19] Pray also for me, that whenever I speak, words may be given me so that I will

fearlessly make known the mystery of the gospel, [20] for which I am an ambassador in chains. Pray that I may declare it fearlessly, as I should.

ASKING QUESTIONS

Write what you learn about prayer in Ephesians 6:16-20.

110. When are we to pray?

111. In what manner are we to pray?

112. What are we to pray?

113. Who are we to pray for?

114. How are we to pray for those ministering the gospel (and for yourself)?

115. Prayer is listed in the armor of God, right after the sword of the Spirit. It is a divine weapon of God with which we can demolish strongholds. How many times is the word "pray" or "prayer" mentioned in Ephesians 6:16-20? (Its frequency shows us its importance.)

Read the following passage and answer the questions.

2 Corinthians 10:4-5

[4] The weapons we fight with are not the weapons of the world. On the contrary, they have divine power to demolish strongholds. [5] We demolish arguments and every pretension that sets itself up against the knowledge of God, and we take captive every thought to make it obedient to Christ.

116. According to 2 Corinthians 10:4, what kind of power do our spiritual weapons have?

117. According to 2 Corinthians 10:5, what do our weapons do?

118. According to 2 Corinthians 10:5, what do arguments and pretensions do?

119. According to 2 Corinthians 10:5, what do we do with arguments and pretensions?

When we act and pray based on God's Word, even when the whole world is against us, we are doing warfare by STANDING our ground! This scripture in 2 Corinthians says that even our very thoughts need to come under submission to Christ. Remember what we have learned about our position in Christ from Ephesians? We are seated with Christ in heavenly realms. When the enemy comes in and tells you that you are too weak to be used by God or that your situation is too overwhelming and there is no hope, you can remind yourself AND the enemy of the truth. You are born again. You are part of God's holy and eternal family. You are redeemed. You have hope in Christ and eternal riches of God at your disposal, and a GOOD and loving Father who cares for you deeply! BUT, don't just know the truth. Speak the truth! Confess the truth. Pray the truth. This is where praying the alive and active Word of God comes in handy!

Remember that even the apostle Paul needed prayer! He asked for prayer that he could fearlessly make known the mystery of the gospel. Did he experience fear in jail? Maybe. But, he knew the answer. He knew the truth, and even in his time of imprisonment, he spent time speaking truth to those who needed encouragement. He still led the Gentile church through prayer and by writing letters from a place where he was chained in captivity. Because Paul chose to be led by God, and to walk in joy—even in his chains—today we have the encouragement of his letters in the New Testament! His example of being led by the Spirit and not giving up in the middle of trials is truly inspirational. When you are scared and feel like giving up, remember the apostle Paul and his testimony. The same Spirit of God who lived in Paul lives in you, if you are a believer and are cleansed of your sins, through Jesus Christ. Paul was an everyday person, just like you. He just chose to follow God with all his heart and to walk in the Spirit with selflessness. Remember your place in God's family. Remember who you are in Christ. Sharpen your sword, put on your armor and STAND.

Instead of letting the darkness of the world around you send you into a tailspin, light it up with prayer! Paul says to pray in the Spirit on all occasions with all kinds of prayers and requests. Take an inventory of your thought life. Is it full of worry? Are you always trying to figure out how to deal with a situation? Instead of fretting and worrying, give it to God in prayer. Your prayers are so powerful! Why? Because God is the one answering. Do you need wisdom? Ask the Spirit of God. He gives liberally, without finding fault, as it says in James 1. He won't look down on you, when you come to him asking for help.

TESTIMONY

About 13 years ago, the Lord was teaching me not to fret and worry about people I was ministering to. I didn't understand how I could care about someone and not worry about them. Every time any little thing would happen, I would need to call my father, who is also our pastor, and ask him to pray. He would give me counsel, but follow that up with the best advice that I couldn't wrap my head around.

He would say, "Briana, don't worry. Trust Jesus."

I always thought, "Of course I trust Jesus, but ..."

He knew that I really hadn't learned to trust Jesus with the situation. Anytime you blow past advice to trust God with a "Yeah, yeah, yeah ... I know," you probably aren't trusting Jesus. Well, the Lord began to teach me and I really came into freedom. One day, when walking at the park with my family, a random thought came into my mind from the left-hand side. It was in my own voice, just like all my thoughts, but it was not from me.

"I'm so worried about so and so."

It was so foreign, because I literally never thought that way anymore. I looked around, because it was so odd. I laughed out loud and turned to my husband. "Do you know what just happened? The devil just tried to plant a worry in my head. It's so hilarious, because I am not falling for it."

PRAY IN THE SPIRIT ON ALL OCCASIONS

When you pray in the Spirit, you aren't just talking to God. Let's explore this. According to the passage, Paul doesn't only instruct the leaders to pray in the Spirit. The praying in the Spirit is for all believers. When you go to prayer inviting the Holy Spirit to move through you, guide you, and fill you as you pray you are praying in the Spirit. Some people say that praying in the Spirit is exclusively praying in tongues. Someone with the gift of praying in tongues certainly can intercede with their gift in the Spirit. But, since not everyone has this gift, (see 1 Corinthians 12:28-31), praying in the Spirit can manifest or happen in other ways. The scripture says,

> In the same way, the Spirit helps us in our weakness. We do not know what we ought to pray, but the Spirit himself intercedes for us through wordless groans. And he who searches our hearts knows the mind of the Spirit, because the Spirit intercedes for God's people in accordance with the will of God. – Romans 8:26-27

This scripture is so refreshing, because it tells us that we do not have to be confident in our own praying ability to pray in the Spirit! Prayer in the Spirit is taking your burdens to the Lord as the Holy Spirit lifts them from you up to the throne of the Father. Think of times when you feel the strain of the pressures of life, or an overwhelming situation you do not have the answers for. In these times, when you go to the Lord with the burden of your heart, curled up in a fetal position on your bed, or on your knees on the floor, or driving home from work with tears filling your eyes and crying out groans that words can't express, the Holy Spirit is taking over for you in prayer! He is praying through the sounds and expression of your crying and groaning!

When I was struck with a sudden attack of appendicitis in the spring of this year, my husband drove me quickly to the emergency room. The pain was so intense, but the registration nurse in the ER still needed all my information. Those who know me can tell you that I am rarely at a loss for words. But, in that moment, when I tried to speak and could only groan, my husband jumped in and graciously became my advocate. I was relieved! Of course, my husband had all the correct information to get me registered. I was especially thankful that I did not have to do something practically impossible in my pain. In the same way, the Holy Spirit is your advocate before the Father. And guess what? God will put his burdens on you and ask you to pray for others in this way. You may find yourself praying for lost friends, the sick or the persecuted in a gut-wrenching crying. This is the Holy Spirit, putting God's heart in you. You are feeling his feelings for the lost. When you cry out with his heart's cry, he listens! I believe he wants more Christians taking time in their prayer closets, listening to his heart and praying in the Spirit—not in the flesh.

CROSS REFERENCE
Improbable Victories Through Prayer

Read Judges 7 to see the outcome of Gideon following the Lord into a desperate battle. When you are finished, answer the following questions.

120. Gideon's entire defeat over Midian was a prayerful walk with the Lord. Every step of the way he had instruction from God on what to do next. What are some things God asked Gideon to do that were surprising?

121. Why do you think God asked Gideon to reduce the number of men he took into battle? How many did he end up with?

122. What did God tell Gideon to do if he was afraid?

123. How did God confirm to Gideon that he would be with him in battle?

Praying in the Spirit is a special way of praying where we allow the Lord to lead us into battle. Prayer is so powerful that the enemy does everything he can to keep believers from true, Spirit-filled, faith-filled prayer with other believers. It's easy to stay awake to watch a late-night movie, but try praying and you'll find yourself soon drifting asleep. Prayer meetings are the least attended service of a church. They should be the service with the highest attendance. If only people knew what happens in the heavenly realms when we are united in Christ praying for the lost! All the great revivals were birthed out of heartfelt, unified, persistent prayer in believers. Prayer can change the course of the weather, save the lost and comfort the suffering. There is a new social media campaign that mocks prayer. Every time there is a tragedy, the mockers come out and say, "Don't just pray. Do something!" This mocking implies that prayer is just sending thoughts or feelings or energy in a helpless and ineffective way. Prayer, for the believer in Jesus, is entering the throne room of the Lord with confidence that he can and will intervene in the situation with his power and love. I am glad I don't just send thoughts. No one wants to get my thoughts in a tragedy, because they would mostly be negative and fearful. Are we "sending thoughts and worries" or interceding in the Spirit with groans that words cannot express?

An example of the power of Jesus to work in our lives to bring improbable victory when we pray is the first time I saw a person delivered from suicidal thoughts. Many years ago, I knew a young mom who was tormented with self-harming thoughts. She had been to "shrinks," as she put it. She was in and out of hospitals. She called me from the hospital, as a last resort. She said, "Briana, they won't let me out of here, unless I promise to go see a doctor. I told them I've been to doctors. The shrinks don't help me. But, I can't get out of here unless I promise to get help. Do you have any ideas?" I told her that I knew my father, a pastor, had counseled many people with similar situations in the past. They both agreed to meet.

I was very nervous. I had heard stories of God's healing power before, but I didn't know if this would work. I was definitely someone with little faith and very new in ministry. When the day came—17 years ago—we met in my living room. When she came in and sat down, my father asked her what was on her mind. My friend didn't mince words. She immediately recounted the traumatic event of seeing her best friend die in a terrible accident. "It's in my head. I can't get the pictures out. I see it happen over and over." After she shared what was on her heart and dad had asked many questions, he told her that he had good news for her. There was hope for her situation. Dad asked her if he could share Jesus with her. She laughed a little. "Why not? What do I have to lose?" She said it in a bit of a mocking tone. He shared the gospel with her, the simple gospel, how Jesus died for our sins and rose again and is ready to come into our lives to set us free. "Jesus can not only forgive your sin, he can heal your mind. He can go into those places no one else can go and help release that trauma." Much to my surprise, she agreed without any questions or resistance. I realized that she was at the end of her rope and she was completely open to help.

After she prayed to receive Christ, my father explained to her that we were going to pray and give her thoughts to Jesus and ask him to remove the unspeakable traumatic thoughts and to replace them with good memories of her friend. He led her in a simple prayer. "Jesus, you remember that day. You were there when it happened. You know what I saw—through tears, she described it to the Lord—Jesus, go to my mind where these memories live and cleanse my mind. Remove those thoughts, Lord. Renew my mind and fill me with your Holy Spirit. Replace those memories of the accident with all the good memories I have with my friend, in Jesus' name. Amen."

There may have been more to the prayer, but that is what I remember from the day. She looked up, relieved. Dad instructed her that when those thoughts came back, she needed to renounce them—*take captive every thought and make it obedient to Christ Jesus*—and give them to Jesus and ask for him to give her good memories to focus on. It was over. She was free and I learned a powerful lesson that day about the simplicity of the gospel.

This story is just that. It is a true story of a woman whose mind and life were touched by God. Each story is different and, as we are led by the Holy Spirit, a person can learn how Jesus can minister in the middle of his or her mess. This is not meant to diagnose or to say that saying this exact prayer will help every suicidal situation. It is faith in Christ and the work of the Holy Spirit in the individual to bring healing and hope. I share this story here as a testimony showing that surrendering our thoughts to God in prayer is a great weapon to bring freedom. It also gives an example of a time when doctors had reached a wall and Jesus opened a door.

Since you've spent so much time studying God's Word for three months, you have sharpened your sword for the time when those negative, stinkin' thoughts come calling. When you feel overwhelmed, you are not alone. When you are feeling defeated, remember the VICTOR lives inside of you! Feelings are feelings. Truth is truth. When we pray for the Holy Spirit to give us revelation through God's Word to know him better, our feelings will line up more and more with the truth of his Word.

CLOSING SCRIPTURE

Ephesians 6:16-24

[16] In addition to all this, take up the shield of faith, with which you can extinguish all the flaming arrows of the evil one. [17] Take the helmet of salvation and the sword of the Spirit, which is the word of God.

[18] And pray in the Spirit on all occasions with all kinds of prayers and requests. With this in mind, be alert and always keep on praying for all the Lord's people. [19] Pray also for me, that whenever I speak, words may be given me so that I will fearlessly make known the mystery of the gospel, [20] for which I am an ambassador in chains. Pray that I may declare it fearlessly, as I should.

[21] Tychicus, the dear brother and faithful servant in the Lord, will tell you everything, so that you also may know how I am and what I am doing. [22] I am sending him to you for this very purpose, that you may know how we are, and that he may encourage you.

[23] Peace to the brothers and sisters, and love with faith from God the Father and the Lord Jesus Christ. [24] Grace to all who love our Lord Jesus Christ with an undying love.

BRINGING IT HOME

Take time tomorrow to go back and re-read Ephesians from beginning to end. Keep praying the scriptures, even when you put down this study and move on to a new chapter in your life. The truth in Ephesians will strengthen you in the Lord and build you up in the holy faith. May the Lord bless you and strengthen you with power in your inner being to know his love so that Christ may dwell in your heart through faith!

PRAYER INDEX

Prayer cultivates our relationship with the Father. If you are praying to overcome sin, depression or even to do spiritual warfare, these prayers are not magical or "mystical silver bullets," but weapons and tools to give you confidence and to teach you how to address specific issues in the authority of Jesus' name when you do pray. For example, Jesus taught his disciples that they need to forgive seven times seventy times a day. (Matthew 18:21-22) So, praying to forgive is not a one time event, but should be a prayer that happens throughout your day, whenever the pain or begrudging thoughts come up again. Keep seeking the face of the Lord and he will reveal himself to you!

Father,

In Jesus' name, I praise you because you are glorious. I praise you for Jesus Christ your Son, our Sovereign Lord.

I ask that you fill me with the Spirit of wisdom and revelation that I may know you and understand this battle that I am living in. Open the eyes of my heart so that I may see you and the hope that I have in you, in Jesus' name. I need to know that I have hope in the battle, Lord. Right now I acknowledge that my battle is not against flesh and blood. I am not battling people in this world. I am not battling against my spouse or children. I am not battling against non-believers or family members. I am battling against spiritual rulers and authorities in my life. I am battling against things seen and unseen that raise themselves up against the knowledge of Christ Jesus.

I stand against lies and darkness that come against me in Jesus' name. No weapon formed against me shall prosper, in Jesus' name. I acknowledge the power of Jesus and I praise you that I am seated with him in heavenly realms above all rule and power and authority.

I know that in Christ and his resurrection power I am victorious. So, I stand in the armor of Jesus right now. I put on the helmet of salvation. I praise you for my salvation, in Jesus' name. I thank you for your protection and that you protect my head, my life, my authority through Christ. I rejoice that my name is written in the Lamb's Book of Life.

I stand firm in the truth of Christ. I buckle your belt of truth about my waist. I pray that your truth will secure my life. Defend me against the lies of Satan, in Jesus' name. I know that I am vulnerable apart from you, Lord. I ask in Jesus' name that you will reveal to me any lies that I am believing and allow me to walk in your truth.

Today, I thank you for the righteousness that is imputed to me in Christ Jesus. I ask for the power of the Holy Spirit to walk in that righteousness. I pray that the righteousness of Christ and the power of God to live a life of holiness will protect my heart. I put on that breastplate of righteousness. Teach me to submit to and obey your truth in the grace that God provides me, oh Lord, in Jesus' power and holy name.

I also pray, in Jesus' name, that you will ready my feet with the preparation of the gospel of peace. Everywhere I go, oh Lord, may I be ready to bring your message of good news. Do not let me lose my footing in this area. May my feet truly be the beautiful feet that bring good news to those who are lost and need to find their way. Use me, oh Lord, to bring your salvation to the lives of those who are not in your family. Bring people into my life, in special moments, who need you. Ordain for me opportunities to minister the gospel of Jesus to them.

Father, fill me with faith, in Jesus' name. I pray that your Spirit will ignite faith in me that I can fight against the devil and be protected from his diversions and lies. I take up your shield of faith, Father. Hide me in the shadow of your wing, oh Lord. Build up my inner spirit in faith. Minister faith to me and help my unbelief, in Jesus' name!

Also, I take up your Holy Word, the Sword of the Spirit, which is the Word of God. I ask that daily I will be filled with your Word. I ask that the truth of your Word will work like a mighty weapon in my hands. Teach me to fight the enemy with your Word, oh Lord. Develop in me the spiritual gifts and abilities you want me to use in this battle, in Jesus' name!

Fill me with your Spirit's power right now. None of this is possible in my flesh. I trust in your Spirit.

In Jesus' name, I pray. Amen.

OVERCOMING LYING
Week Eleven, Day 2

PRAYER AGAINST FEAR
Week Eleven, Day 4

START A NEW HERITAGE IN CHRIST
Week Twelve, Day 3

BONUS MATERIAL

STANDING IN THE PROTECTION OF THE BLOOD OF JESUS

When we open our mouths in declaration, confessing that we are covered by the blood, we are protected! Here are some suggestions of ways to do this. Say these confessions about the work of the blood of Jesus aloud! It should bring you great freedom to do this regularly!

- Through the blood of Jesus, I am delivered from the hand of Satan!
- Through the blood of Jesus, I am cleansed from all my sin!
- Through the blood of Jesus, I am protected from the destroyer!
- Through the blood of Jesus, I am made righteous before God, and declared not guilty of my sin!
- Through the blood of Jesus, I am whole, delivered, saved and redeemed.
- Through the blood of Jesus, I have a place in the family of God.
- Through the blood of Jesus, I triumph over the devil!
- Thank you, Lord, that the blood of Jesus speaks a better word for me than the blood of Abel.
- Thank you, Lord, that through the blood, I am being sanctified, made holy and brought near to you!

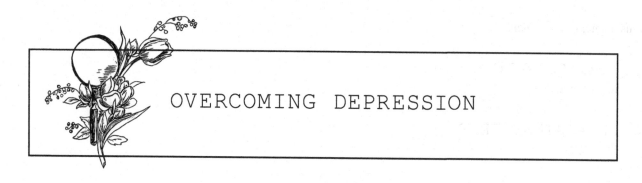

OVERCOMING DEPRESSION

Depression can come from many different sources in your life. This helpful little space in the back of the book is to provide you with a small stepping stone to overcome depression. The victory can come through Jesus, as you walk with him and allow him to work in the deepest parts of your heart. Many books have been written on depression, and I am not a licensed doctor. I am simply providing here some spiritual resources that you can use in your pursuit of freedom in Christ.

My father, Mike Dean, pastor/counselor for over 40 years and founder of Small Voice Ministries, has always taught me that depression is rooted in fear, anger or guilt. This book has already covered these three areas of weakness and/or sin and how to pray through those three issues with the help of the Holy Spirit. I include this section to focus on overcoming the spiritual roots of depression.

Fear

Fear comes in all the colors of the rainbow. It can manifest as panic, anxiety, worry, fretting, fright, and control. This is just a sampling of what you may feel when you are afraid. God made so many different personalities. Your personality may feel and experience fear in a different way than someone with a different personality. You may be a confident woman who is not afraid of the dark or spiders, but you get overwhelmed and feel like sleeping when you cannot control something that is happening in your child's life. This is a way that depression can stem from fear. A controlling fearful woman looks different than the person who is timid, nervously bites her fingers or scares easily. Both are afraid.

Do you remember the story of Martha and Mary in the Bible? What did Jesus tell Martha? In Luke 10:41-42 he says, "'Martha, Martha,' the Lord answered, 'you are worried and upset about many things, but few things are needed – or indeed only one. Mary has chosen what is better, and it will not be taken away from her.'" In this situation, Jesus tells Martha what the solution is for her feelings of being overwhelmed. Martha is an "in-control woman." She wants everything in order and if she doesn't have it the way she thinks it should be, she gets flustered and upset. Mary has chosen the best way. She chose to let go of the things that she cannot control in exchange for sitting at Jesus' feet, listening to him and enjoying her relationship with him.

If you are struggling with feeling out of control, it can lead to depression and anger. You may be afraid of the future or not ever being happy. Ask the Lord to reveal to you what your fear comes from. Pray through those issues the Lord shows you, giving them to the Lord in the name of Jesus. As we learned, coming out of fear is a consistent process of being perfected in the love of the Lord Jesus and casting out fear, whenever it comes calling. Use the Week Eleven teaching on fear to help you, if that is a weakness for you.

Anger

Anger, as you read throughout the book, can stem from many things. Allowing your anger to turn into unforgiveness can lead to bondage and depression. Individuals who have experienced a "beating down" in life, at work or in a relationship, can easily find themselves in a state of low-grade anger. Perhaps this is why we see so much road rage. Anger is allowed to run unchecked in their minds, hearts and bodies, which leads to hair-trigger reactions. Usually this can be rooted in a specific event or topic. Maybe your father cheated on your mother and you feel as if he betrayed the whole family? Maybe you grew up in an abusive home, or even experienced abuse outside of the home? Perhaps, you felt unloved by your mother growing up, but you just lived with it and stuffed it. Deep down inside you may have an anger towards her, or towards life in general, because you never received love in a way that you could relate to or feel. To deal with this anger that brings depression, you need to forgive your mother, or anyone else who has hurt you, pray for God to forgive you for walking in anger and bitterness, command a spirit of anger and unforgiveness to leave in Jesus' name and pray for God to fill you with his peace and joy through the Holy Spirit.

Anger Turned Inward

If you like to keep the peace and try to think the best of everyone, you may be a person who takes her anger about a situation, a hurt or a wrong in your life and turns the anger inward towards yourself. This would result in a type of thinking like, "What is wrong with me?!" Or you may have thoughts like, "That was stupid. Why can't I do anything right?" If you were not allowed to express emotion as a child, you had to do something with your anger; so, you may have just turned on yourself. People with eating disorders and problems with self-injury are usually living in a form of anger turned inward or self-hatred. You need to pray for God to show you if this is you. Ask for revelation and ask the Lord to show you what caused the anger. After this, forgive the person you need to forgive, or pray to forgive yourself (also known as walking in the forgiveness of Christ.) Rebuke spirits of anger-turned-inward, anger, self-abuse, anorexia, bulimia and depression in the name of Jesus. Ask the Lord to fill you with his Spirit, forgiveness, and the truth that is in Christ. This is not an exhaustive talk on this issue. It is a tool to help give you direction as you pray and walk with Jesus in this area of your life.

Guilt

Guilt is the third root of depression, because the person with guilt is weighed down with either true guilt or false condemnation that is not from God. In Christ, when we repent and turn from our sin, there is no guilt. However, if you are walking in unrepentant, willful sin like sexual sin or any other type of willful sin, you will probably feel weighed down with the depression that accompanies guilt and/or the conviction of sin. 1 John 1:9 says, "If we confess our sins, he is faithful and just and will forgive us our sins and purify us from all unrighteousness." A woman who claims to be a believer, but is living with her boyfriend can very likely experience depression from walking in unrepented, willful sin. The Spirit of God is grieved and hopefully you are, too! The answer? Do the right thing. God designed the intimacy of sex for marriage, because you become one with the person you have physical intimacy with. Turn from sin. Flee your situation. Repent. Ask God to cleanse you from the guilt and then rejoice in your freedom! Rebuke depression, unclean spirits, and guilt that may plague you, after you have repented.

Our culture is saturated with temptation. Teens that are walking in sin like sexting, or who have done shameful things in the past and stopped, can be weighed down with depression. The guilt is heavy. Certain personalities will act sad and sleepy. Other personalities will wall themselves off from parents and other people who love them. This is a state of self-protection to try to keep you from seeing the real state of his or her heart and emotions. He or she may cry every night, when no one can see, or get into dangerous behaviors to numb the pain. The answer? Again—repentance. If it is a child, friend or spouse, pray hard for them to repent! If it is you that is suffering under depression, even if you have already stopped sinning, you need to confess the sin to God and to a trusted mature believer and ask the Lord to cleanse you from all unrighteousness through your Lord and savior Jesus Christ. Jesus breaks every chain! The chains of sin are the strongest chains that hold you. But, remember that Jesus already overcame sin by his blood! Rebuke guilt and spirits of prostitution, impurity and lust and, finally, depression. Command them to leave in Jesus' name. Ask the Holy Spirit to fill you and read scripture that fills your heart and mind with the truth of how much God loves you.

Abortion

If you have had an abortion, this can bring extreme depression from the guilt of killing your baby. In Christ, there is love and redemption. Abortion is not the unpardonable sin, but it is a very serious sin. The heaviness you feel is from the great pain and loss that occurred when you believed the lies of the world and took the life of your baby. In order to gain freedom in this area, you will need to confess this sin to the Lord as murder. Ask him to forgive you and to cleanse you from all unrighteousness. Even if this happened before you were saved, you really need to deal with this situation with Jesus in prayer. Because the world celebrates the right to have an abortion, it does not equip women to deal with the fallout of grief and depression that happen afterwards. Allow yourself to grieve before the Lord over your sin and loss. After you have prayed and repented from the sin of abortion and murder, you will need to pray against the strongholds of abortion, murder and depression. Speak out loud and command them to leave. It may sound something like this:

Father,

You know what happened when I was younger. I sinned against you, against my baby, and against my own body. Please forgive me, Lord, for sinning by murdering my baby through the sin of abortion. You know why I did it. You understand the situation I was in, but it was still sin. Through the blood of Jesus, I am free from the weight and guilt of my sin. I stand purified from all unrighteousness. Jesus, you died for me and bore my sin of abortion and murder. Thank you for your cleansing. I am not under the curse of this sin, I am in Christ. I rebuke spirits of abortion, murder and depression and command them to leave me in Jesus' name and never come back.

I pray, Holy Spirit, that you will fill me right now with your power. Fill me in all the places of my life that have just been swept clean.

Amen.

False Guilt

Many times depression can come from false guilt. You can see this happen when a person has repented and doesn't "feel free." They have nagging false thoughts about sins that they have given to the Lord over and over. This is a distraction of the enemy to keep a believer from walking in true victory, confidence and power in Jesus. It also focuses the person on him or herself, instead of on the blood of Jesus. Rebuke false guilt in Jesus' name. Stand in truth!

Grief

Another way that false guilt can bring depression is when a loved one passes away. You may think through things you never got to say, or even had thoughts like, "It should have been me." This is a false guilt that can weigh you down needlessly in the middle of the grief. It is normal for people who are grieving to have the symptoms of depression. This is normal, but when you have thoughts of false guilt, rebuke them in Jesus' name. Do not dwell on things that feel true, but they simply are not true. If it helps you to feel better, pray and ask forgiveness for the things you never said, or the things you did say and didn't have time to take back. Ask the Lord to remove your false guilt in Jesus' name. You can even ask the Lord to give your loved one a message of love in heaven.

If your child has experienced loss, I want to encourage you to get him or her help from a pastor or Christian who understands the stages of grief to talk through the feelings. I have personally walked with my children through the suicide of a friend, so this topic is very near to my heart. Do not allow your child to shut off all conversations about the death, because he or she is afraid of the emotion. I am not saying to be mean, harsh or forceful, but as the parent, with strong love and encouragement, help your child understand that it is very unhealthy to bottle up feelings. Let him or her know that pain is a normal part of death and that they need to talk through their feelings to get them out, or it will cause an increasing, unbearable pain. Also, sometimes the person may just need to listen to someone explain what grief is like, so that he or she knows it is normal when the feelings come. Encouraging open communication in your family on a day to day basis, where everyone is comfortable talking about his or her feelings, without fear of being made fun of, helps when serious times come. Discussion is the vehicle to healing.

On a side note, as a parent, you are in the driver's seat. Parenting takes grit and love. Your teenager may have a grown-up body, but he or she is not grown up emotionally or spiritually. In our house, if there is an issue of any level of concern with a child, that child doesn't get to decide if he or she wants to discuss it or get help. I may give some leeway in the timetable, if they need an hour or a day to think about something. But, I let them know to prepare to talk, because God did not give my children to me for them to walk through their inner life alone. I am on their side! I am their advocate. Also, I always pray with, for and over my children and they welcome it! It is an expectation from childhood that this is the way our family functions. I have spoken with countless women who are pushed away by their children spiritually, when the children enter the teen years. Don't approach the spiritual aspect of parenting any differently than you would if your child was in a medical emergency. You are the one to take them to the doctor. You wait with them in the waiting room. You intervene. You make the decisions. They need to know that they cannot push you out. If they think they can get away with it, they will. If they know what your spiritual role is, and that it is done in love, but you aren't a push-over, they will submit to your spiritual authority. To top it off, your depressed child needs to hear you pray over him or her.

It is by praying with someone that you learn to pray. Prayer with your child is not just to help them get better. You are discipling and teaching by your example.

While depression can feel very complicated for the one who is walking in it, I encourage you to pray about the things that I listed here. This is just a starting point to encourage you to pray through the things that may be bringing you into a place of despair. Remember that in Isaiah 61 it says the Lord gives you a garment of praise for a spirit of despair. Rebuke and command despair to leave, in the name of Jesus. It clearly refers to despair as a spirit. Don't just try to get over it by stuffing it or filling up your life with things to distract you. Deal with the roots of the issue. Then, after you have pulled up the roots, deal with it as if it were truly a spirit. I will say it again, because it is very important. Command a spirit of depression and despair to leave in Jesus' name. If depression, hopelessness and anxiety run in your family, declare to the enemy that he has no right to be there, because you are not under the curse of depression that your forefathers were under; you are in Christ! Pray the prayer that Nehemiah prays in Nehemiah chapter 1 when he is praying for God to remove the judgment on the children that came through their parents. Fill your mind and heart with praise for the Lord and his redemption and love for you. Live a life of praise! King David commanded his soul to praise the Lord. Praise is not a feeling; it is a way of life for the one who loves God. Psalm 42:5 (NKJV) says,

> Why are you cast down, O my soul?
> And *why* are you disquieted within me?
> Hope in God, for I shall yet praise Him
> *For* the help of His countenance.

I also encourage you to meditate on Psalm 42 and to pray it aloud to the Lord.

Printed in the United States
By Bookmasters